CW01269643

Objectivity in Jurisprudence, Legal Interpretation and Practical Reasoning

Objectivity in Jurisprudence, Legal Interpretation and Practical Reasoning

Edited by

Gonzalo Villa-Rosas

Research Fellow, Centre for Research in Philosophy and Law, Externado University, Colombia and Hermann Kantorowicz Institute for Basic Legal Research, Faculty of Law, Kiel University, Germany

Jorge Luis Fabra-Zamora

Associate Professor, University at Buffalo School of Law, State University of New York, USA

Edward Elgar
PUBLISHING

Cheltenham, UK • Northampton, MA, USA

© The Editors and Contributors Severally 2022

Cover image: 'Philosofish' (2007), Juan Manuel Giraldo.

All rights reserved. No part of this publication may be reproduced, stored in a retrieval system or transmitted in any form or by any means, electronic, mechanical or photocopying, recording, or otherwise without the prior permission of the publisher.

Published by
Edward Elgar Publishing Limited
The Lypiatts
15 Lansdown Road
Cheltenham
Glos GL50 2JA
UK

Edward Elgar Publishing, Inc.
William Pratt House
9 Dewey Court
Northampton
Massachusetts 01060
USA

A catalogue record for this book
is available from the British Library

Library of Congress Control Number: 2022943102

This book is available electronically in the Elgaronline
Law subject collection
http://dx.doi.org/10.4337/9781803922638

MIX
Paper from
responsible sources
FSC FSC® C013604
www.fsc.org

ISBN 978 1 80392 262 1 (cased)
ISBN 978 1 80392 263 8 (eBook)

Printed and bound by CPI Group (UK) Ltd, Croydon, CR0 4YY

Contents

List of contributors		vii
1	Introduction: The meanings of 'objectivity' *Gonzalo Villa-Rosas and Jorge Luis Fabra-Zamora*	1

PART I   OBJECTIVITY AND JURISPRUDENCE

2	Objectivity of law and objectivity about law *Jaap Hage*	31
3	Is legal cognitivism a case of bullshit? *Héctor A Morales-Zúñiga*	48
4	Imputation as a supervenience in the General Theory of Norms *Monika Zalewska*	71
5	Social science and jurisprudence through Weberian and Hartian eyes: Suggesting an explanation for a puzzle *Donald Bello Hutt*	86
6	Objectivity of legal knowledge: The challenge of scepticism *Matti Ilmari Niemi*	105

PART II   OBJECTIVITY AND LEGAL INTERPRETATION

7	From Hart to Dworkin via Brandom: Indeterminacy, interpretation, and objectivity *Leonardo Marchettoni*	127
8	Can legal texts have objective meanings? *Maija Aalto-Heinilä*	145
9	Big data linguistic analysis of legal texts – objectivity debunked? *Caroline Laske*	167
10	Rethinking the legal effect of interpretive canons *Triantafyllos Gkouvas*	193

PART III OBJECTIVITY AND PRACTICAL REASONING

11 The problem of normative objectivity 216
    Jan-Reinard Sieckmann

12 Why do legal philosophers (perhaps correctly) insist on
    moral objectivity while dismissing metaethical inquiry? 233
    Thomas Bustamante

13 Moral objectivity without robust realism 253
    J. J. Moreso

14 Virtue and objectivity in legal reasoning 271
    Amalia Amaya

Index 293

Contributors

Maija Aalto-Heinilä, Senior Lecturer in Philosophy of Law, University of Eastern Finland, Finland.

Amalia Amaya, Research Professor, Institute for Philosophical Research, National Autonomous University of Mexico, Mexico. British Academy Global Professor, School of Law, University of Edinburgh, United Kingdom.

Donald Bello Hutt, Assistant Professor of Moral and Political Philosophy, University of Valladolid, Spain.

Thomas Bustamante, Associate Professor, Postgraduate Program in Law, School of Law, Federal University of Minas Gerais, Brazil.

Jorge Luis Fabra-Zamora, Associate Professor, University at Buffalo School of Law, State University of New York, United States.

Triantafyllos Gkouvas, Postdoctoral Researcher, Charles III University of Madrid, Spain.

Jaap Hage, Chair of Jurisprudence, Maastricht University, Netherlands.

Caroline Laske, Research Fellow, Institute of Legal History, Ghent, Belgium. Lecturer, University of Louvain-la-Neuve, Belgium. Heinz Heinen Fellowship, Bonn Centre for Dependency and Slavery Studies (BCDSS), University of Bonn, Germany.

Leonardo Marchettoni, Research Fellow, Jura Gentium, Centre of Philosophy of International Law and Global Politics, Department of Legal Sciences, University of Florence, Italy.

Héctor A. Morales-Zúñiga, PhD Candidate, Graz Jurisprudence, University of Graz, Austria.

Josep Joan Moreso, Professor of Legal Philosophy, Department of Law, Pompeu Fabra University, Spain.

Matti Ilmari Niemi, Professor in Property Law, School of Law, University of Eastern Finland, Finland.

Jan-Reinard Sieckmann, Professor of Legal Theory and Philosophy of Law in the Faculty of Business, Economics and Law, Friedrich-Alexander-University Erlangen-Nürnberg, Germany.

Gonzalo Villa-Rosas, Research Fellow, Centre for Research in Philosophy and Law, Externado University, Colombia. Hermann Kantorowicz Institute for Basic Legal Research, Faculty of Law, University of Kiel, Germany.

Monika Zalewska, Postdoc at Department of Theory and Philosophy of Law, University of Łódź, Poland.

1. Introduction: The meanings of 'objectivity'[1]

Gonzalo Villa-Rosas and Jorge Luis Fabra-Zamora

1. THE PROBLEM OF OBJECTIVITY

Along with other epistemic virtues such as truth and certainty, objectivity allows us to evaluate our own assertions and beliefs, as well as those of others.[2] Nevertheless, objectivity is younger than all of these concepts.[3] Its emergence as an epistemic virtue has been linked to the increasing use of technical standards in empirical methods of acquiring knowledge. More specifically, as Lorraine Daston and Peter Galison have shown, its emergence is related to the progressive shift of the scientist's role away from the Enlightenment sage archetype – according to which the sage should seek to find the truth-to-nature through the creation of pictorial representations of idealised forms of her objects of study.[4] In contrast to the Enlightenment's methods, the use of technical standards allows empirical methods to be replicated by any participant in the collective enterprise.[5] In this way, crucial epistemological claims about

---

[1] This chapter is based on sections of Gonzalo Villa-Rosas, *Objectivity as Principle: A Procedural Theory of Objectivity of the Practical Reasoning* (DPhil thesis, University of Kiel, Germany, 2022). The authors are deeply thankful to Dr. Iulia Blaj and Dr. Luca Palmieri for valuable comments on an earlier draft.

[2] Naomi Scheman, 'Epistemology Resuscitated: Objectivity as Trustworthiness' in Naomi Scheman (ed), *Shifting Ground. Knowledge and Reality, Transgression and Trustworthiness* (OUP 2011) 207.

[3] Lorraine Daston and Peter Galison, *Objectivity* (Zone Books 2008) 17.

[4] Ibid., 17–54; 115–252.

[5] Ibid., 19–27. As Scheman states, according to the democratic ideals that motivated and provided the theoretical underpinnings for the epistemology of modern science, 'all knowers are ideally interchangeable, meaning both that individually arrived-at results should be the same for all reasoners and that we can effectively function as each other's surrogate knowers. Our epistemic dependency, that is, is either eliminable or benign'. (Scheman (n 2) 227.).

the character of empirical science are increasingly based on the independence of knowledge from the knower – on the scientific claim to 'objectivity' – to the point that, as held by David B Resnik, '[o]bjectivity is science's most fundamental value because many of the other norms of science, such as honesty, openness, carefulness, empirical adequacy, testability, and precision, are justified on the grounds that they promote objectivity in research'.[6]

Although often challenged,[7] objectivity has broken the barriers of its cradle and has been conquering all realms of knowledge[8] to the extent that some practices would be other practices if the quest for objectivity should not be attributed to them. We trust judges, medical doctors, teachers, and professionals of all kinds because they take part in practices that we assume ought to be objective. For instance, imagine for a moment what history and journalism would be like without the quest for objectivity. Would these practices be what they are if we should not assume that historians and journalists ought to seek as accurate a description as possible of the facts they investigate? Rightly, Peter Novick has placed the goal of objectivity at the very heart of the professional historical enterprise as 'the rock on which the venture was constituted, its continuing raison d'être'.[9] And Charlotte Wien has argued that 'if one can speak of a paradigm within journalism, we might see that paradigm in the demand for objectivity in the dissemination of news'.[10]

---

[6] David B Resnik, *The Price of Truth. How Money Affects the Norms of Science* (OUP 2007) 51.

[7] Broadly speaking, criticisms of accounts of objectivity can be grouped into two large and related families. The first group includes those sceptical criticisms that warn about the naive character of the search for an impractical, unreal and deceitful notion that is found in the ascetic ideal of purification that endorses the negation of subjectivity by the subject itself. (For instance, on criticisms of the notion of 'historical objectivity', see Peter Novick, *That Noble Dream. The 'Objectivity Question' and the American Historical Profession* (CUP 2005 (1988)) 6.) The second group includes those criticisms that, convinced of the actual possibility of objectivity, maintain that it is not desirable. This family of critiques has been especially fruitful in feminist epistemology, feminist standpoint theory and feminist postmodernism. (For an overview see, i.a., Julian Reiss and Jan Sprenger, 'Scientific Objectivity', *The Stanford Encyclopedia of Philosophy* (Winter 2020 Edition) https://plato.stanford.edu/archives/win2020/entries/scientific-objectivity/ accessed 29 April 2021; M Janack, 'Dilemmas of Objectivity' (2002) 16 (3) *Social Epistemology* 267, 271–274.) Both families have pushed for the renewal of the concept of objectivity and without them, the contemporary offspring would not have seen the light. However, both families are, above all, pitted against a certain metaphorically resolved sense of objectivity, as we shall see below.

[8] Stephen Gaukroger, *Objectivity. A Very Short Introduction* (OUP 2012) 2.

[9] Novick (n 7) 1.

[10] Charlotte Wien, 'Defining Objectivity within Journalism. An Overview' (2005) 26, 2 *Nordicom Review* 3.

It is also true that without the quest for objectivity, neither our contemporary understanding of key legal concepts nor our current jurisprudence would be possible.[11] In fact, legal practice and jurisprudence would be other kinds of practices if we ought to assume that their participants – for instance, judges, officials, attorneys and legal scholars – should simply inform us of their own personal tastes or preferences. But at the same time, objectivity in law raises several questions, some of which are far from simple: How can jurisprudence be objective? Are there objective answers to legal questions? Can vague legal concepts be interpreted in an objective way? Is there an objective moral and an objective moral reasoning to be applied in the construction of the language of law and legal decisions? We are convinced that questions such as these are

---

[11] That is why objectivity is a major topic in jurisprudence. See, i.a., George C Christie, 'Objectivity in the Law' (1968) 78 *Yale Law Journal* 1311; Aleksander Peczenik, Lars Lindahl and Bert van Roermund (eds), *Theory of Legal Science: Proceedings of the Conference on Legal Theory and Philosophy of Science Lund, Sweden, December 11–14, 1983* (Reidel 1984); David O Brink, 'Legal Theory, Legal Interpretation, and Judicial Review' (1988) 17 *Philosophy and Public Affairs* 105; Michael S Moore, 'Moral Reality Revisited' (1992) 90 *Michigan Law Review* 2424; Jules L Coleman and Brian Leiter, 'Determinacy, Objectivity, and Authority' (1993) 142 (2) *University of Pennsylvania Law Review* 549; R Kent Greenawalt, *Law and Objectivity* (OUP 1995); Jules L Coleman, 'Truth and Objectivity in Law' (1995) 1 *Legal Theory* 33; Hilary Putnam, 'Are Moral and Legal Values Made or Discovered?' (1995) 1 *Legal Theory* 5; Ronald Dworkin, 'Objectivity and Truth: You'd Better Believe It' (1996) 25 *Philosophy and Public Affairs* 87; Brian Leiter (ed), *Objectivity in Law and Morals* (CUP 2000); Andrei Marmor, *Positive Law and Objective Values* (OUP 2001); Dennis Patterson, 'Normativity and Objectivity in Law' (2001) 43 *William and Mary Law Review* 325; Brian Leiter, 'Law and Objectivity' in Jules L Coleman and Scott J Shapiro (eds), *The Oxford Handbook of Jurisprudence & Philosophy of Law* (OUP 2002); Verónica Rodríguez-Blanco, *Meta-Ethics, Moral Objectivity and Law* (Brill Publishers 2004); Connie S Rosati, 'Some Puzzles about the Objectivity of Law' (2004) 23 *Law and Philosophy* 273; George Pavlakos, *Our Knowledge of the Law: Objectivity and Practice in Legal Theory* (Hart Publishing 2007); Verónica Rodríguez-Blanco, 'Objectivity in Law' (2010) 5 *Philosophy Compass* 240; Jaakko Husa and Mark Van Hoecke (eds), *Objectivity in Law and Legal Reasoning* (Hart Publishing 2013); Matthew H Kramer, *Objectivity and the Rule of Law* (CUP 2007); Andrés Santacoloma Santacoloma, Gonzalo Villa-Rosas and Hajime Yoshino (eds), *Truth and Objectivity in Law and Morals: Proceedings of the Special Workshop Held at the 26th World Congress of the International Association for Philosophy of Law and Social Philosophy in Belo Horizonte, 2013* (Franz Steiner Verlag 2016); André Ferreira Leite De Paula, Andrés Santacoloma Santacoloma and Gonzalo Villa-Rosas (eds), *Truth and Objectivity in Law and Morals II: Proceedings of the Second Special Workshop Held at the 27th World Congress of the International Association for Philosophy of Law and Social Philosophy in Washington, D.C., 2015* (Franz Steiner Verlag 2016).

controversial in any legal system, even though their most specific answers may vary from system to system.

The challenge posed by these questions is compounded by the very opacity of the term 'objectivity'. Like many other foundational concepts, despite its apparent obviousness and everyday use, the meaning of this term seems to escape like water through the fingers when we try to define it. What exactly do we mean when we say that a claim or belief is or ought to be 'objective'? The search for the definition of 'objectivity' becomes even more difficult when we are confronted with the fact that 'objectivity' takes on different meanings. And after we realise that 'objectivity' has many meanings, it is a short step to the taxonomies provided by various philosophical analyses of the term.

For example, Allan Megill has distinguished four senses of the term – a philosophical or absolute sense, a disciplinary sense, an interactional or dialectical sense and a procedural sense of 'objectivity'.[12] Elisabeth A Lloyd has identified four distinct meanings of 'objective' that 'are currently in broad use in contemporary philosophy' – objective as detached, objective as public, objective as existing independently and objective as really existing.[13] In turn, Heather Douglas has differentiated three distinct 'modes of objectivity' – process to the world, process to individual thought and processes to get agreement – articulated in eight distinct meanings of 'objectivity' none of which is strictly reducible to any other.[14] In the history of science, and specifically of the image, Daston and Galison have distinguished three distinct senses of the term 'objectivity' – mechanical objectivity, structural objectivity and objectivity as trained judgment.[15] Similar taxonomies appear in the domains of legal and practical philosophy. For instance, George Pavlakos identified two conceptions of objectivity – representationalism and referentialism – based on the different philosophical traditions that have tried to arrive at some understanding of the relationship between mind and environment.[16] Similarly, Matthew Kramer has categorised three dimensions of objectivity – an ontological, an epistemic and a semantic – and within them, he has identified six different species of objectivity with respect to objectivity's relationship with the law – mind-independence, determinate correctness and uniform appli-

---

[12] See Allan Megill, 'Introduction: Four Senses of Objectivity' in Allan Megill (ed), *Rethinking Objectivity* (Duke University Press 1994).

[13] See Elisabeth A Lloyd, 'Objectivity and the Double Standard of Feminist Epistemologies' (1995) 104 (39) *Synthese* 351, 353.

[14] See Heather Douglas, 'The Irreducible Complexity of Objectivity' (2004) 138 *Synthese* 453.

[15] Daston and Galison (n 3).

[16] See Pavlakos (n 11) 23.

cability; transindividual discernibility and impartiality; and truth-aptitude.[17] Finally, Mark van Hoecke has pointed out various senses commonly attributed to objectivity in law, including certainty, impartiality, generality, neutrality and reasonableness.[18]

Why does it matter that 'objectivity' has more than one meaning? One reason is that the question of whether the word 'objectivity' has one or many meanings predates that of its definition. If we do not answer this question first, we may mistakenly assume that the meaning the term 'objectivity' takes on in a certain context is applicable to other contexts in which we use the same term.[19] Now, it may happen that a word has several meanings, each of which is completely independent of the others. Nevertheless, it can also happen that a word has several meanings that have semantic connections with each other.[20] Therefore, if we intend to define 'objectivity', we must first ask ourselves why we name the many meanings of this term with the same word: Is there perhaps a hidden unity or order covered by the many meanings of the term that we fail to appreciate, and if so, how can we explain it?

The project of this volume cannot proceed without a sustained reflection on some foundational topics, which we advance in this chapter. This introduction has three parts. First, we outline a novel core-dependent account of the definition of 'objectivity' that is inspired by some Aristotelian insights. In this view, 'objectivity' is the common name under which we pack together various criteria that depend on a core instance. This conception allows us to see the fabric that illuminates the various senses of objectivity discussed in the volume. Finally, we sketch some possible lines of research that stem from the thoughts advanced in this collection.

---

[17] See Kramer (n 11) 11.
[18] See M Van Hoecke, 'Objectivity in Law and Jurisprudence' in Husa and Van Hoecke (n 11) 4–9.
[19] Michael W Pelczar, 'Focal Complexity in Aristotle and Wittgenstein' (2004) 21 (2) *History of Philosophy Quarterly* 131, 133, 139–147. As we shall see, this argument corresponds to the criticism that Axtell has raised against Nozick's approach to the 'ordinary notion' of objectivity (Guy Axtell, *Objectivity* (Polity Press 2016) 7) – see below n 69.
[20] As stated by James Pustejovsky, homonymy – also called 'contrastive ambiguity' – is a kind of ambiguity in which one lexical form has many unrelated meanings. Examples of homonymous words are terms like 'kind', 'bank' or 'orange.' In addition, polysemy 'is the relation that exists between different senses of a word that are related in some logical manner rather than arbitrarily'. (James Pustejovsky, 'Lexical Semantics: Overview', *Encyclopedia of Language and Linguistics* VIII (2006) 99; M Lynne Murphy, *Lexical Meaning* (CUP 2010) 84.) We shall argue that the various meanings of the term 'objective' or 'objectivity' are polysemous.

2. THE MEANINGS OF 'OBJECTIVITY'

Our inquiry into a definition of 'objectivity' proceeds as follows: First, we will begin by determining the normative function of the adjective 'objective'. Then, we will criticise those positions that argue that a negative sense of 'objectivity' is sufficient to define it. Third, we will explain the reasons why reductivist attempts to define 'objectivity' are untenable. Fourth, we will rule out an alternative account of the definition of 'objectivity' inspired by Wittgenstein's notion of family resemblance. Finally, in response to the defects of all these views, we shall argue for a new account of the definition of 'objectivity' premised on the Aristotelian notion of core-dependent homonymous.

2.1 Trust Us: The Normative Function of the Adjective 'Objective'

What exactly do we mean when we say 'objectivity'? To answer this question, let us maintain the course charted by Ian Hacking, who analysed the concept of objectivity by applying a strategy based on two Oxford maxims[21] to address 'fancy words conceived in philosophical sin':

> One Oxford maxim was to avoid the nouns and attend to the adjectives [...] Don't talk about truth, talk about the word 'true' and its uses. *Mutatis mutandis*, we should attend to the adjective 'objective', and not to objectivity.
> A second maxim is to think of adjectives, such as 'real' or 'rational', in terms of what is *not* real or what is *not* rational.[22]

Based on the first of these prescriptions, we can make explicit what we evaluate as 'objective'. As we have seen, 'objective' is normative in the sense that by its means, 'we evaluate our own and each other's assertions and beliefs'.[23] Clearly, utterances that are mere reports of the speaker's attitudes – such as tastes or personal preferences – are immune to any objective evaluation insofar as they report only the subjective image of the individual who holds the attitude. Thus, we can more accurately state that we use the adjective 'objective' to evaluate only those utterances by which the speaker expresses

---

[21] These maxims were introduced by Austin in John Langshaw Austin, 'Truth' in James Opie Urmson and Geoffrey J Warnock (eds), *Philosophical Papers by the Late JL Austin* (The Clarendon Press 1961) 85.

[22] Ian Hacking, 'Let's Not Talk About Objectivity' in Flavia Padovani, Alan Richardson and Jonathan Y Tsou (eds), *Objectivity in Science* (Springer 2015) 24.

[23] Scheman (n 2) 207.

her independence with respect to their content – that is, those utterances that can be true or false.[24]

Premised on the second of Hacking's prescriptions, we can understand 'objective' as opposed to 'subjective'. A very widely held picture of these terms maintains that they can be defined as opposed *sic et simpliciter* – that is, as adjectives that define each other 'like left and right or up and down'.[25] However, this picture conceals the enormous complexity of the concept of subjectivity. To see this complexity, consider for example the nineteenth-century representation of the contrast between empirical science and art reported by Daston and Galison:[26] As a result of the increasing use of technical standards in empirical science and the consequent emergence of the concept of objectivity, the creative will that ought to express itself without limits through art was progressively contrasted with scientific objectivity, which was characterised as the will of the discipline that forces the scientist to deny herself in the creation of empirical science.[27] However, is this representation of objectivity sufficiently precise? Is the will that characterises the scientist not also part of her subjectivity? Unlike a plain opposition of the terms 'objective' and 'subjective', explaining the reasons why we use the adjective 'objective' requires us to be clear about which elements of subjectivity we are opposing. Only then can we decide whether we accept the use of the adjective 'objective' and whether we trust its endorsement.[28]

In this light, let us posit that when opposed to objectivity, subjectivity is reduced to bias. This reduction implies the construction of an all-encompassing definition of bias in which all senses of different but resemble concepts can conflate. Our construction starts by accepting that, as stated by Inkeri Koskinen, we human beings are imperfect epistemic agents.[29] Based on the

---

[24] Ibid., 20; John Rogers Searle, *Speech Acts. An Essay in the Philosophy of Language* (CUP 2009 (1969)) 26–29; John Rogers Searle, *The Construction of Social Reality* (Allen Lane The Penguin Press 1995) 8.
[25] Daston and Galison (n 3) 37.
[26] Ibid
[27] Ibid., 246–250.
[28] Douglas (n 14) 470.
[29] Inkeri Koskinen, 'Defending a Risk Account of Scientific Objectivity' (2018) 71 *The British Journal for the Philosophy of Science* 1187, 1195. According to Schlosser, '[e]pistemic agency concerns the control that agents may exercise over their beliefs (and other doxastic states)'. (Markus E Schlosser, 'Agency', *The Stanford Encyclopedia of Philosophy (Winter 2019 Edition)*, https://plato.stanford.edu/archives/win2019/entries/agency/ accessed 29 April 2021. See also Patrick J Reider (ed.) *Social Epistemology and Epistemic Agency* (Rowman & Littlefield 2016); Ernest Sosa, *Judgement and Agency* (OUP 2015), ch. 9; John Broome, *Rationality Through Reasoning* (Wiley Blackwell 2013); Baron Reed, 'Fallibilism, Epistemic Possibility, and Epistemic

principle of intellectual honesty,[30] we should accept that our capacity to form true beliefs has limitations derived from our personal and cultural conditions.[31] Once we accept this, we can distinguish clear examples of those conditions that restrict our capacity to form true beliefs. These examples can be divided into influences or preferences and may include desires, emotions, ideological commitments, idiosyncrasies, inclinations, interests, misrepresentations, personal attachments, political aims, predispositions and tendencies. Nevertheless, certain concepts remain problematic, for there are undeniable differences between concepts such as assumptions, values and prejudices. For example, the idea of prejudice typically includes the notion of distortion, whereas the ideas of assumptions and values do not.[32] Similarly, while the notion of prejudice evokes the attitude we display towards the object of the preconception, the notion of bias is neutral with respect to this attitude.[33] Despite these differences, given that some accepted senses of these concepts (assumptions, values and prejudices) amount to bias qua certain kind of influences or preferences, bias can be understood as their common denominator. As a result, we can posit that when we refer to biases, we mean influences or preferences that are attributable to an epistemic agent[34] and may lead her to judgments or decisions that are erroneous or suboptimal according to a criterion of truth or correctness.[35]

Agency' (2013) 23 *Philosophical Issues* 40; Hilary Kornblith, *On Reflection* (OUP 2012) 84–107; Linda Zagzebski, *Epistemic Authority* (OUP 2012).)

[30] The principle of intellectual honesty underlies the acceptance that all human beings err. Without it, our acceptance of our limitations in the formation of true beliefs would lack support. Moreover, the principle was enunciated by Voltaire as the foundation of the principle of tolerance, as Popper has reminded us. See K Popper, 'Toleration and Intellectual Responsibility (Stolen from Xenophanes and Voltaire)' in Karl Popper (ed.), *In Search of a Better World* (Routledge 2000 (1996)), 204.

[31] Gaukroger (n 8) 33–41.

[32] Ibid., 5.

[33] See, i.a., John F Dovidio, Fabian M H Schellhaas and Adam R Pearson, 'Prejudice', *Oxford Research Encyclopedia of Psychology* https://oxfordre.com/psychology/view/10.1093/acrefore/9780190236557.001.0001/acrefore-9780190236557-e-263 accessed 4 Mar. 2021.

[34] As stated by Koskinen (n 29) 1197:
> malfunctioning equipment does not induce to talk about objectivity. But if we refuse to take the malfunction into account even after becoming aware of it, and continue using the results, questions about objectivity may arise. Or if we design software that repeats some widespread bias (e.g., facial-recognition software might have racial bias problems because of the sets of images used in the training of the algorithms), we may talk about objectivity – precisely because it is our bias that the software is repeating.

[35] This broad conception has been developed on the understanding of the subject matter reached in the purview of the empirical approach to the study of the mind. See Emily Pronin, Thomas Gilovich and Lee Ross, 'Objectivity in Eye of the Beholder:

What do we mean when we say that a statement is 'objective'? Primarily, we mean that statement is not biased. Thus, we say that the adjective 'objective' correctly describes certain statements' property of 'not being biased'. However, what criteria do we have for saying that statements lack this property? As we shall see, we use predicates such as 'mind-independent', 'impartial' or 'determinate' as equivalents of the adjective 'objective' in various epistemic contexts. These predicates correspond to criteria based on which we can say that a certain statement 'is not biased' in that context. Although correct, the definition of the adjective 'objective' as 'free of bias' tells us nothing about these criteria and is, therefore, an incomplete definition.[36] However, in its incompleteness lies its strength.[37] The explanatory strength of the notion of objectivity qua freedom from bias lies in the fact that it can serve as a starting point for the analysis of what the adjective 'objective' means because the notion of freedom from bias makes it possible to distinguish a cluster of standard cases of objectivity from that which is considered 'non-objective'.[38] As we will see below, this scope gives the notion of freedom from bias explanatory priority over any criterion of objectivity.

In everyday life, when a speaker claims that a given statement is 'objective', this is typically in response to (or in anticipation of) the challenge that the statement is biased. In other words, a speaker deploys the normative function of objectivity, by which she expresses her independence from the content of her utterances, when she responds to or anticipates the challenge that her statement is wrong or corresponds to a suboptimal outcome because of her imperfections as an epistemic agent.[39] By means of the rhetorical force of those statements that she qualifies as objective, she reinforces her independence from their content and awakens her listener's epistemic trust[40] by justifying

---

Divergent Perceptions of Bias in Self Versus Others' (2004) 111, 3 *Psychological Review* 781, 799; Rüdiger F Pohl (ed.) *Cognitive Illusions. A Handbook on Fallacies and Bias in Thinking, Judgement and Memory* (Psychology Press 2004). On preference bias, see Torsten Wilholt, 'Bias and Values in Scientific Research' (2009) 40 *Studies in History and Philosophy of Science* 92.

[36] On the problem of the incomplete definitions of predicates, see, i.a., David Barnett, 'Indeterminacy and Incomplete Definitions' (2008) 105, 4 *The Journal of Philosophy* 167, 177–180.
[37] Gaukroger (n 8) 5.
[38] Ibid., 37.
[39] Koskinen (n 29) 1197.
[40] Reconsidering Baier's influential account and building on Holton's contribution, Wilholt has enlighteningly characterised epistemic trust as a type of normatively charged reliance that we invest in our peers in common inquiry based on 'a shared sense of what the right attitude toward the aims of a collective epistemic enterprise is and on the confidence that other participants in the enterprise actually display that attitude'. (Torsten Wilholt, 'Epistemic Trust in Science' (2013) 64, 2, *The British Journal for*

those statements on the grounds of her belief that the epistemic risks arising from her own imperfections as a biased epistemic agent have been effectively averted.[41] The rational basis for this trust is premised on the fact that the authority of these statements consists of reasons that, insofar as they depend neither upon the speaker nor upon the hearer, could be accessible – at least under ideal conditions – to either of them.[42] In this vein, as expressed by Naomi Scheman, the hearer would be doxastically irresponsible to reject the statement without giving reasons that made similar claims to universal acceptability. By contrast with mere attitude reports – such as statements on matters of taste or personal preferences – objective claims, she explains, 'are always disputable, but they are not, without dispute rejectable'.[43]

To better understand this account of the normative function of objectivity, consider the various mechanisms we have used to awaken your epistemic trust as a reader of this chapter. These mechanisms aim, among other things, to anticipate any challenge from you to our belief that the arguments put forward in this chapter do not reflect objectionable influences or preferences that can be attributed to us as authors. In other words, these mechanisms are intended to prevent you from arguing that we, the authors, have smuggled our ideological commitments, inclinations or interests (for example) into the arguments of this chapter. These trust-awakening mechanisms include the documentation of the sources used as a basis for the arguments presented – which could, at least potentially, be consulted by you – and the fact that this chapter has been published by a prestigious publishing house after undergoing a blind peer review process.[44]

---

the Philosophy of Science 233, 253; cf. Koskinen, above n 29, 1188; see also Richard Holton, 'Deciding to Trust, Coming to Believe' (1994) 72 *Australasian Journal of Philosophy* 63; Annette Baier, 'Trust and Antitrust' (1986) 96 *Ethics* 231; Annette Baier, 'Trust' (1992) 13 *Tanner Lectures on Human Values* 107.).

[41] This notion of the normative function of objectivity comes from revisiting Koskinen's position, which Koskinen erroneously applied to all kinds of epistemic risk (i.e., risks that are attributed to an epistemic agent). (See Koskinen (n 29) 1188.) Evidently, finding certain kinds of errors or suboptimal outcomes does not always trigger the disclosure of the normative function of objectivity, even when those errors or suboptimal results can be attributed to an epistemic agent. This is, for instance, the case in the argument of incompetence (i.e., the lack of the ability, skill or knowledge necessary to perform an action correctly).

[42] Scheman (n 2) 227.

[43] Ibid., 208.

[44] Longino's argument for the normative criteria of objectivity, which is premised on the critical contextual empiricism she defends, has famously highlighted discursive mechanisms of this type. (See Helen E Longino, 'Values Heuristics, and the Politics of Knowledge' in Martin Carrier, Don Howard, and Janet Kourany (eds), *The Challenge of the Social and the Pressure of the Practice: Science and Values Revisited* (University

Certainly, in real conditions, only the speaker and a few peers engaged in common inquiry and situated in the same epistemic conditions as the speaker can have the same degree of access to the rationale that justifies qualifying a statement as 'objective'. Others' knowledge rests to some extent on the trust they invest in them as information providers, as well as on the reliance they place in the processes of knowledge production. This dependence is more intense the more distant the epistemic agent is from the epistemic conditions of the original issuer of the statement. In the case of non-participants in the practice, their epistemic trust is mainly based on the epistemic goals they attribute to the practice upon which they depend as epistemic agents. In fact, as suggested earlier, some practices would be other practices if the quest for objectivity should not be attributed to them. Without the quest for objectivity, empirical science would become a fanatical machination, history and journalism would turn into propaganda or sheer delusion, and the law would be nothing more than an irrational coercive mechanism. Objectivity is undoubtedly a constitutive principle[45] of all these practices.[46]

---

of Pittsburgh Press 2008) 68–86; Helen E Longino, *The Fate of Knowledge* (Princeton University Press 2002); Helen E Longino, *Science as Social Knowledge. Values and Objectivity in Scientific Inquiry* (Princeton University Press 1990).)

[45] Teleological considerations contribute to the interpretation and construction of norms in various ways. Terms such as 'principles' and 'values' generally reflect this teleological burden as normative components of ends-directed reasoning. Additionally, without some of these normative components, certain practices would not be definable in the way they are. By appealing to a well-known, long-lasting tradition regarding the classification of rules, such norms can undoubtedly be called 'constitutive'. (On the distinction between constitutive and regulative rules, see, i.a., Searle (n 24) 33–42.) Nevertheless, the term 'value' has been the subject of extensive and vivid debates about, for example, the differentiation between epistemic and contextual values. (Thomas S Kuhn, 'Objectivity, Value Judgement, and Theory Choice' in Thomas S Kuhn (ed.), *The Essential Tension: Selected Studies in the Scientific Tradition and Change* (The University of Chicago 1977) 331.) At this point and for our purposes, it is preferable to avoid any possible radiations coming from such confrontations. For this reason, the term 'principle' has been preferred in the text. (On the use of this term in theories of science, see, i.a., Resnik (n 6) 36–42.)

[46] In a more general manner, Galison has held that '[h]istory, politics, literature, documentary film, journalism – each of these and others too have had their own objectivities'. (Peter Galison, 'The Journalist, the Scientist, and Objectivity' in Flavia Padovani, Alan Richardson and Jonathan Y Tsou (eds), *Objectivity in Science* (Springer 2015) 57.)

2.2 Leaving the Task Unfinished: The Problems with the Negative Definitions of 'Objectivity'

As we have seen so far, by describing a statement as 'objective', the speaker intends to awaken her listener's epistemic trust by asserting that this statement is not biased. Based on this normative function of the term, we can posit a negative definition of 'objectivity': Objectivity is freedom from bias. As stated by Stephen Gaukroger, this conception 'may still be the most powerful general notion of objectivity that we have'.[47] Some authors, conspicuously Hacking, have also defended a negative definition of 'objectivity': '[O]bjectivity is not a virtue but the absence of various types of vice'.[48] Others, notably Koskinen, have argued for a functional account based on epistemic risk avoidance.[49]

As noted above, what often seems to be overlooked, however, is that the plain definition of 'objectivity' as freedom from bias is incomplete because it leaves out the various criteria of objectivity that are operable in different epistemic contexts. Although a thorough presentation of these issues is beyond the aims of this introduction, a few words will suffice to clarify what we refer to when we use the word 'criterion'. A criterion of objectivity amounts to the meaning that the adjective 'objective' takes on when used in a specific context. This meaning corresponds to the reason why a statement can be considered more or less free of bias in such a context. Consider, for instance, the following criteria:

First, relying on the mind-independence criterion, we can say, for example, that the more independent a description of facts is from the perspective of its issuer, and from the perspective of the community to which the issuer belongs, the more objective such a description will be. Clearly, this assessment presupposes the existence of that which is described. That is why, as Kramer has stated, the mind-independence criterion is framed within an ontological dimension of objectivity.[50] This criterion lies at the very origin of objectivity as an epistemic virtue.[51]

Second, based on the criterion of impartiality, we claim, for instance, that the greater the disinterestedness and open-mindedness[52] to the rights and interests of the participants in a practical discourse that the speaker manages to reflect in a practical statement, the more objective this practical statement will be. As mentioned elsewhere, this criterion presupposes an agreement on

---

[47] Gaukroger (n 8) 5.
[48] Hacking (n 22) 22.
[49] Koskinen (n 29).
[50] Kramer (n 11) 3–14.
[51] Daston and Galison (n 3) chs III and IV.
[52] Kramer (n 11) 53.

the procedures necessary to achieve a convergence that makes the reasons for the practical decision intelligible to the participants in the practical discourse.[53] We can therefore say that this criterion implies an epistemic dimension of objectivity.[54] In its extended sense, epistemic objectivity is 'the tendency to converge shown by subjects' beliefs about a phenomenon that they observe',[55] but in its minimal sense, epistemic objectivity requires agreement on the methods necessary to achieve such convergence.[56] This minimal sense has two main consequences: First, to the extent that observers of a phenomenon accept these methods, a statement about that phenomenon can be justified according to the rules it provides. And second, a phenomenon lacks epistemic objectivity altogether if its observers do not even agree on the possible methods for achieving intersubjective intelligibility of their beliefs about it.[57]

Third, using the determinacy criterion,[58] we assert that the more determined the meaning of a statement is, the more objective it will be. This criterion presupposes the conditions of meaning that allow evaluation of the statement's determinacy. That is why this criterion involves a semantic dimension of objectivity.[59] For a better understanding of this criterion, consider the case of disagreement over the application of a vague and comparative concept. Such disagreement cannot be resolved rationally – that is, it cannot be resolved in a way that is intelligible or justified to the participants in the discourse – given the indeterminacy of such concepts. Nevertheless, such disagreements can be resolved through the definition of standards. For instance, as Max Kölbel has shown, the disagreements arising from the application of the concepts 'longer than' and 'shorter than' can be rationally resolved through the introduction of a length standard, such as the standard *mètre* adopted by the *Comité international des poids et mesures* in Paris in 1889. Using the standard *mètre*, 'we can

---

[53] Gonzalo Villa-Rosas, 'The Two Strategies. Objectivity, Epistemic Access, and Extreme Positions' in Hajime Yoshino, Andrés Santacoloma Santacoloma and Gonzalo Villa-Rosas (eds) *Truth and Objectivity in Law and Morals. Proceedings of the Special Workshop held at the 26th World Congress of the International Association for Philosophy of Law and Social Philosophy in Belo Horizonte, 2013* (Franz Steiner Verlag 2016) 125–126.
[54] Kramer (n 11) 2–3, 53–68.
[55] Villa-Rosas (n 53) 125.
[56] Ibid.
[57] Ibid., 126.
[58] On determinacy and law, see Coleman and Leiter (n 11) 559–594. On determinacy and standards, see Theodore M Porter, *Trust in Numbers. The Pursuit of Objectivity in Science and Public Life* (Princeton University Press 1995); Theodore M Porter, 'Quantification and the Accounting Ideal in Science' (1992) 22 (4) *Social Studies of Science* 633.
[59] On the semantic dimension of objectivity, see, i.e., Kramer (n 11) 2–3, 68–82.

simply define the concept of *being 1 m long* as being neither shorter nor longer than the standard meter. This allows us to define further derived objective concepts, such as half as long or twice as long as 1 m, and so on in a way that does not reflect the mental states of the one who does it'.[60] Kölbel has elegantly called this criterion 'objectivity by design'.[61]

Mind-independence, impartiality and determinacy are examples of some meanings of 'objectivity' that are operable in different epistemic contexts in the face of which the plain definition of objectivity qua freedom of bias mutes. What we require is an account that allows us to explain the unity that lies behind the polysemy of the term 'objective' – an account that explains the relationship between the negative sense of objectivity qua freedom from bias and the various criteria that are operable in the numerous epistemic contexts in which the concept of objectivity is used.

2.3 Avoiding Polysemy: The Problems with the Reductive Definitions of Objectivity

In contrast to those who have tried to find the meaning of 'objectivity' in its negative sense, others have posited reductive conceptions of objectivity. Most notably, Bernard Williams argued as follows:

> In reflecting on the world that is there *anyway*, independent of our experience, we must concentrate not in the first instance on what our beliefs are about, but on how they represent what they are about. We can select among our beliefs and features of our world picture some that we can reasonably claim to represent the world in a way to the maximum degree independent of our perspective and its peculiarities. The resultant picture of things, if we can carry through this task, can be called the 'absolute conception' of the world.
>
> This notion of an absolute conception can serve to make effective a distinction between 'the world as it is independent of our experience' and 'the world as it seems to us'. It does this by understanding 'the world as it seems to us' as 'the world as it seems peculiarly to us'; the absolute conception will, correspondingly, be a conception of the world that might be arrived at by any investigators, even if they were very different from us.[62]

Consequently, according to Williams, the goal of science and ethics consists of explaining 'objective truth', a conception of the world that does not depend on any perspective. Similarly, Thomas Nagel famously conceived of objec-

---

[60] See Max Kölbel, 'Objectivity and Perspectival Content' (2019) *Erkenntnis* Retrieved 17 Feb. 2021, from https://doi.org/10.1007/s10670-019-00188-1.
[61] Ibid.
[62] Bernard Arthur Owen Williams, *Ethics and the Limits of Philosophy* (Routledge 2006 (1985)) 138–139.

tivity as a method of understanding that presupposes viewing the world 'from nowhere in particular' because '[a] view or form of thought is more objective than another if it relies less on the specifics of the individual's makeup and position in the world, or on the character of the particular type of creature he is'.[63] Finally, yet importantly, Robert Nozick found in the concept of 'invariance' the commonality among the different features he ascribed to objectivity:

> There are three strands to our ordinary notion of an objective fact or objective truth. First, an objective fact is accessible from different angles. [...] The second mark of an objective truth, related to the first, is that there is or can be intersubjective agreement about it. And the third feature concerns independence. [...] An objective fact is invariant under various transformations. It is this invariance that constitutes something as an objective truth, and it underlies and explains the first three features (to the extent that they hold).[64]

Moreover, this line of thought has also arisen in practical philosophy. Consider, for example, the metaphor of the 'veil of ignorance' developed by John Rawls in order to characterise the 'original position'. Contrary to John Locke, Rawls thought that our ignorance about particular facts about ourselves, others, our society and its history could serve as an epistemic mechanism to avoid biases so that, situated in a 'position of equality', we could reach an agreement about universal principles on which we could build, as moral persons, universal norms of justice.[65]

What characterises these various positions is that they argue that the diverse meanings of the term 'objectivity' are reducible to a single unified meaning.[66] The strength of this approach apparently lies in the fact that it makes it possible to avoid the polysemy of the term. But is it really possible to avoid this? Marianne Janack has rightly warned us about the open and deliberate use of metaphors in this reductionist approach. According to her, it is suspicious that, in clear contrast to the common attitude of distrust towards metaphors that is generally shown in conceptual analysis, 'philosophers and scientist writing on objectivity seem to abandon themselves to this "drive to metaphorize" with nary a blink'.[67] However, what is more concerning is that this drive leads these philosophers and scientists to replace conceptual analysis with metaphors. This replacement has at least two main consequences: First, metaphors

---

[63] Thomas Nagel, *The View from Nowhere* (OUP 1986) 5.
[64] Robert Nozick, *The Structure of the Objective World* (Cambridge Mass., Harvard University Press 2001) 75–76.
[65] John Rawls, *A Theory of Justice* (Cambridge Mass., Harvard University Press 1999 (1971)) 118–123.
[66] Axtell (n 19) 7; Douglas (n 14) 454.
[67] Janack (n 7) 274.

promote conceptual instability because they do not offer any clear criteria of objectivity that prove its operability in a concrete epistemic context.[68] Second, metaphors mask the different meanings that the term 'objectivity' adopts in different epistemic contexts. In fact, metaphors such as 'absoluteness', 'aperspectivalness' or 'invariance'[69] must be interpreted in an adaptive way to suit each epistemic context.[70] Thus, the replacement of conceptual analysis with metaphors is evidence of the reductivist positions' inability to confront what is unavoidable: the polysemy of 'objectivity'.[71]

2.4 An Inadequate Answer to the Polysemy of 'Objectivity': The Wittgensteinian Family Resemblance Approach

Other authors have recognised the complexity inherent in the term 'objectivity' by suggesting, instead, that the meaning of 'objectivity' is a 'hodgepodge'[72] of several different meanings.[73] Conspicuously, when mapping the different meanings of 'objectivity', Douglas has argued that, although there are conceptual connections between them, and these connections provide coherence to the concept of objectivity, none of these meanings is logically reducible to the others.[74] Thus, against the reductivist attempts to define 'objectivity', Douglas has argued that none of the senses of the word can serve as a surrogate for another.[75] Consequently, she has concluded that there is no single sense that captures the meaning of 'objectivity'.[76] So far, so good. Nonetheless, it seems incomplete to simply present the explication of what objectivity is

---

[68] Ibid., 275.
[69] Given the polysemy of the term 'objective', a reasonable speaker can utter a meaningful expression using this term only if she chooses a single meaning among the various possible meanings so that the chosen meaning fits the context of utterance. Thus, the existence of an 'ordinary notion' of objectivity is at least doubtful. In fact, this 'ordinary notion' inevitably privileges a certain meaning of the term over others. Consequently, the formulation of a theory of the meaning of the adjective 'objective' that starts from this 'ordinary notion' will necessarily be a biased theory. For example, Nozick's characterisation of objectivity was undoubtedly inspired primarily by his familiarity with physics, as Axtell has shown. Thus, his theory 'appears too domain-specific to serve as the basis for a univocal conception of objectivity'. (Axtell (n 19) 7.).
[70] Janack (n 7) 275.
[71] Ibid., 275, 276.
[72] See A Fine, 'The Viewpoint of No One in Particular' in W Egginton and M Sandbothe (eds), *The Pragmatic Turn in Philosophy* (Suny Press 2004) 121.
[73] Douglas (n 14) 454.
[74] Ibid., 455, 465.
[75] Ibid., 455.
[76] Ibid., 467.

as a problem of the irreducibility of the term's many meanings. Douglas's account offers no explanation of why the meaning network of 'objectivity' seems to have coherence.

Certainly, 'objectivity' is a word with many meanings, and its meanings are not accidentally tied to it. To be precise, 'objectivity' is not comparable to words like 'kind', 'bank' or 'orange', whose meanings have the same spoken or written form even though these meanings do not have any semantic connection with each other. For instance, the noun 'kind' refers to a type, and the adjective 'kind' refers to being considerate. The term 'bank' can refer to a riverbank, a raised ridge of ground or a financial institution. And the word 'orange' can be either the name of a fruit or the name of a colour. These are words with different meanings that just happen to have the same spelling and pronunciation. However, this is not the case for the word 'objectivity' because the various meanings of this word have a semantic connection (i.e., they can be associated somehow according to their meanings).[77]

A plausible way of approaching the explanation of the similarities among the various overlapping and crisscrossing meanings of 'objectivity' would be to hold that they bear a family resemblance.[78] Famously, Ludwig Wittgenstein introduced the concept of family resemblances 'in order to attack the traditional doctrine that all the entities which fall under a given term must have some set of properties or features in common, the presence of which makes it correct to subsume an entity under this term'.[79] In the famous passage §66 of his *Philosophical Investigations* (PI), Wittgenstein considered the meaning of the word 'games':

> Consider for example the proceeding that we call 'games'. I mean board-games, card-games, ball-games, Olympic games, and so on. What is common to them all? – Don't say: 'there *must* be something common, or they would not be called "games" – but *look* and *see* whether there is anything common to all. – For if you look at them you will not see something that is common to *all*, but similarities, relationships, and a whole series of them at that. To repeat: don't think, but look! […] And the result of this examination is: we see a complicated network of similarities overlapping and criss-crossing: sometimes overall similarities, sometimes similarities of detail.[80]

---

[77] On the difference between homonymy and polysemy, see above n 20.
[78] At this point, we seek to test the suggestion made by Axtell, according to which '[t]he irreducible complexity thesis tends rather to associate the concept of objectivity with what Ludwig Wittgenstein referred to as a "family resemblance" concept'. (Axtell (n 19) 8.)
[79] Hjalmar Wennerberg, 'The Concept of Family Resemblance in Wittgenstein's Later Philosophy' (1967) 33 (2) *Theoria* 107. Wittgenstein introduced the concept of family resemblances in *The Blue Book* (BB) §§17–20 and in PI §§65–71.
[80] Wittgenstein, PI §66.

Table 1.1

e	d	c	b	a
ABCD	ABCE	ABDE	ACDE	BCDE

Source: Renford Bambrough, 'Universals and Family Resemblances' (1960–1961) 61 *Proceedings of the Aristotelian Society, New Series* 207, 209.

Although a more detailed discussion of family resemblance exceeds our present purposes, we will examine the central argument that allows us to rule out the possibility that the connection between the various meanings of the word 'objectivity' falls under family resemblance. In a very enlightening interpretation, Renford Bambrough translates the informal expressions of Wittgenstein in a more formal way 'by considering a situation that is familiar to botanical taxonomists'.[81] Bambrough overlaps five different features – *ABCDE* – among different entities that are subsumed under the same concept and warns, 'it may well happen that five objects *edcba* are such that each of them has four of these properties and lacks the fifth, and that the missing feature is different in each of the five cases'. Table 1.1 above illustrates this situation.[82]

According to Bambrough's diagram in Table 1.1, if we confine our attention to any arbitrarily selected objects – say, *edcb* – we can see that they all happen to have feature *A* in common. Although the object *a* lacks the common feature *A*, it has other overlapping features with the other objects. In this way, it is clear that it is not in virtue of feature *A* that *edcba* are all objects rightly called by the same name.[83] As Bambrough explains:

> Even if the actual instances were indefinitely numerous, and they all happened to have one or more of the features in common, it would not be in virtue of the presence of the common feature or features that they would all be rightly called by the same name, since the name also applies to possible instances that lack the feature or features.[84]

Table 1.1 allows Bambrough to show the powerful Wittgensteinian view according to which 'different entities can be related to each other in a relevant way and be subsumed under the same concept without having to have a single common feature'.[85]

---

[81] Renford Bambrough, 'Universals and Family Resemblances' (1960–1961) 61 *Proceedings of the Aristotelian Society, New Series* 207, 209.
[82] Ibid., 210.
[83] Ibid.
[84] Ibid.
[85] Verónica Rodríguez-Blanco, 'Is Finnis Wrong? Understanding Normative Jurisprudence' (2007) 13 *Legal Theory* 257, 278.

Nonetheless, this cannot be said about objectivity. As we shall see, in contrast to the family resemblance cases, all criteria of objectivity are related to each other in a relevant way and fall under the same concept because they all share a core. This core is freedom from bias.

2.5 An Adequate Answer to the Polysemy of 'Objectivity': The Core-Dependent Homonymy Approach

As we have seen, the quest to make explicit what objectivity is has led us into a logjam. First, defining 'objectivity' as freedom from bias *sic et simpliciter* is incomplete, for it leaves out of the definition the multiple meanings that 'objectivity' can take on in the many epistemic contexts in which the concept is used. Second, the search for a reductive meaning of 'objectivity' has led to conceptually unstable, and therefore inconveniently metaphorical, formulations. And third, it is untenable to maintain that all meanings of the term 'objectivity' exhibit Wittgensteinian family resemblance. In the face of all these dead ends, let us ask again: How can we account for the coherence of the meanings network of 'objectivity'? As already stated, the key to answering this question lies in explaining the relationship between the negative sense of objectivity qua freedom from bias and the various criteria that are operable in different epistemic contexts.

As stated earlier, 'objectivity' is a word with many meanings, and its meanings are not accidentally linked to it – the various meanings of this word exhibit among themselves a semantic connection. Furthermore, the conundrum concerning the semantic connection among the various meanings of key philosophical concepts is an ancient problem.

In several passages, Aristotle reacts against the tendency of his predecessors to overlook the complexity of certain concepts.[86] Most often, Aristotle's target is Plato, who Aristotle claims 'systematically underestimates the complexity of fundamental philosophical concepts'.[87] In contrast to Plato, Aristotle believes we express many concepts of philosophical importance, such as 'good', 'cause', 'principle', 'nature' or 'being', in various ways.[88] Unlike other words that, despite having different meanings, have the same spelling and pronunciation by accident, the different meanings of these key philosophical terms

---

[86] See, i.a., Phys. I. 2–3, 185a20; EN I.6, 1096a11; EN I.6, 109a23–34.
[87] Christopher Shields, *Order in Multiplicity. Homonymy in the Philosophy of Aristotle* (The Clarendon Press 1999) 1.
[88] Niels Tolkiehn, *The Notions of Homonymy, Synonymy, Multivocity, and Pros Hen in Aristotle* (Universitätsbibliothek der Ludwig-Maximilians-Universität 2019) 1; Shields, above n 87, 3.

exhibit semantic connections. These connections can be explained, according to Aristotelian writings, as cases of either analogy or *pros hen* relations.[89]

Christopher Shields has reserved the term 'core-dependence homonymy' to refer to cases of this latter kind of relation.[90] According to his reconstructive work on Aristotelian sources, core-dependent homonymous terms are those that have a common name and have core and non-core instances whose relations are constrained by Aristotle's four-cause scheme.[91] The core instance has explanatory priority over the non-core instances (i.e., the core and non-core instances have an asymmetrical relation[92]) because the account of the core instance is necessarily cited in the accounts of the non-core instances, but not vice versa.[93] Finally, the non-core instances are open-ended, so new and unforeseen non-core instances can be called by the common name.[94]

In this way, objectivity criteria are core-dependent homonyms in Aristotelian terms – or, in other words, 'objectivity' is the common name under which we group various criteria that depend on a core instance. The reasons for this conclusion are as follows:

First, the semantic connection between the various criteria of objectivity and freedom from bias falls under one of the four types of cause named by the Aristotelian sources: final, efficient, material and formal cause.[95] Indeed, freedom from bias is the final cause of the various criteria of objectivity. Put another way, without the quest to formulate unbiased statements, it would

---

[89] See, i.e., ibid., 45, n 127. The names given to the phenomenon that explain *pros hen* relations are varied. For instance, this phenomenon has been referred as 'focal meaning' (Gwilym Ellis Lane Owen, 'Logic and Metaphysics in Some Earlier Works of Aristotle' in Ingemar Düring and Gwilym Ellis Lane Owen (eds), *Aristotle and Plato in the Mid-Fourth Century. Papers of the Symposium Aristotelicum held at Oxford in August 1957* (Elanders Boktryckeri Aktiebolag 1960)), 'focal connection' (Terence Henry Irwin, 'Homonymy in Aristotle' (1981) 34, 3 *The Review of Metaphysics* 523) or 'focal complexity' (Pelczar (n 19)). This chapter is largely inspired by the reconstructive work on Aristotelian sources proposed by Shields (Shields (n 87) 103–127).

[90] Ibid.

[91] Aristotelian sources do not provide any rigorous theory or a detailed list of criteria of the *pros hen* relation. This is why various reconstructive attempts have been undertaken (see, i.a., Tolkiehn (n 88) 123–174.) To address the problem of profligacy of the possible determinacy of the set of cases of *pros hen* relation – or as named by Shields, 'core-dependent homonymy cases' – Shields has reintroduced Thomas de Vio Cajetan's proposal. According to this proposal, the main criteria for the definition of the asymmetrical relation between the core case – or focal meaning – and the non-core cases falls under one of the four cause-types defined by the Aristotelian sources. (See Shields (n 87) 110–122.)

[92] See ibid., 107.

[93] See Pelczar (n 19) 136; Shields (n 87) 123.

[94] Ibid., 124–127.

[95] Ibid., 110–122.

not be possible to explain the ultimate reason that justifies the behaviours we deploy when we seek to achieve mind-independence, impartiality or determinacy. This complex final cause relation between freedom from bias and the various criteria of objectivity becomes clearer when we consider that the more independent a description of the facts from the perspective of its issuer, and from the perspective of the community to which she belongs, the greater the assurance of bias-avoidance such a description will provide. Similarly, the greater disinterestedness and open-mindedness to the rights and interests of the participants in a practical discourse that the issuer manages to reflect in a practical statement, the greater the assurance of bias-avoidance such a practical statement will provide. And finally, the more determinate the meaning of a statement, the greater assurance of bias-avoidance the statement will offer. In short, when we aim to achieve mind-independent, impartial or determined statements in the various contexts in which each of these criteria is applicable, we aim to achieve non-biased statements.

Second, this final causal relation gives freedom from bias explanatory priority over the various criteria of objectivity. This explanatory priority also implies an asymmetrical relationship between freedom from bias and the various criteria of objectivity. In effect, while freedom from bias – qua final cause of the criteria of objectivity – is part of the definition of each of these criteria, the definition of each of these criteria is not part of the definition of freedom from bias (as we have seen). Thus, while the definitions of mind-independence, impartiality and determinacy involve freedom from bias, the definition of freedom from bias, as a characteristic of the statements that we call 'objective', does not require reference to any of these criteria through which we achieve freedom from bias.

Third, and finally, given this asymmetrical relationship between freedom from bias and the various criteria of objectivity, 'objectivity' is semantically open. Freedom from bias can always be coherently connected with new and unforeseen criteria of objectivity, as the study of the history of the concept has shown us.[96]

In a nutshell, based on the principle of intellectual honesty, we should accept that our capacity to form true beliefs faces limitations derived from our personal and cultural conditions. These conditions determine influences or preferences that are attributable to us as epistemic agents and that may lead us to erroneous or suboptimal judgments or decisions. Although we should be aware of these caveats, our social life imposes on us the need to trust. When we trust, we become vulnerable to being affected by the actions of others. Because

---

[96] See Daston and Galison (n 3).

of this vulnerability, to be rational we need good reasons to trust.[97] What is objectivity, then? Objectivity is first and foremost a good reason to trust because when we describe a statement as 'objective', we assert that this statement is not biased. In other words, we use the adjective 'objective' to awaken the epistemic trust of our listener by justifying our statements in the belief that the epistemic risks arising from our imperfections as biased epistemic agents have been effectively averted.

It is this epistemic trust that certain practices seek to awaken in us as reason to depend on them when forming beliefs. This dependence would not be possible if the achievement of epistemic goals (including objectivity) should not be attributed to these practices. Since these practices would be different practices if these goals should not be attributed to them, these goals can be deemed constitutive of these practices. Making explicit the reasons why we use the adjective 'objective' has allowed us to unearth the core of this concept – that is, freedom from bias. Freedom from bias is performed through each of the criteria of objectivity – mind-independence, impartiality and determinacy – in the various contexts in which each of these criteria is applicable. Given this final causal relation, freedom from bias has explanatory priority over the various criteria of objectivity. Based on this asymmetrical relation, freedom from bias can always be coherently connected with new and unforeseen criteria of objectivity. For these reasons, the various criteria of objectivity are core-dependent homonyms.

3. THE CONTENT OF THE VOLUME

We now turn our attention to the book the reader holds in her hands. The issues concerning objectivity that emerge when agents deliberate about action are ubiquitous. Concerning knowledge of practical statements, these issues arise not only with respect to the practical statements themselves but also in relation to our intentions and our reasoning aimed at deciding what we ought to do. These different aspects can raise questions such as the following: Ought our moral knowledge be objective? How can moral knowledge become objective? Should our moral statements be objective? How can they become so? Should a moral agent form objective judgments about what she ought to do and act accordingly? How might she go about doing so? Similar questions can also be posed in relation to the law: Ought jurisprudence be objective, and how can it become so? Should legal sources be objective, and how can they become so? Should the interpretation and application of legal sources be objective,

---

[97] Onora O'Neill, *A Question of Trust: The BBC Reith Lectures* (CUP 2002) vii; Katherine Hawley, *Trust. A Very Short Introduction* (OUP 2012) Chap. 2.

and how it is possible to interpret and apply them in an objective way? These questions are reflected in the general outline of this collection.

The 13 original chapters included in this volume explore different answers to these perplexities about the multifaceted phenomenon of objectivity and its relations to multiple aspects of practical reasoning and the law. This compilation covers three broad themes. The chapters contained in the first section address a wide range of problems linked to the relationship between objectivity and jurisprudence. The second section offers an analysis of the functions of objectivity in legal interpretation. The last section deals with the function of objectivity in practical reasoning. The brief account of the meaning of 'objectivity' just given in this introduction will allow us to appreciate the common thread that makes up the underlying fabric that unites the various senses of objectivity addressed by each of the chapters that make up the present compilation.

3.1 Objectivity and Jurisprudence

The volume begins with Jaap Hage's challenge to the applicability of the distinction between the ontological and epistemic dimensions of objectivity to law. For Hage, the ontological notion of objectivity presupposes the existence of a mind-independent reality – that is, a reality independent from any belief or opinion. In turn, the epistemic notion of objectivity requires that, ideally, our knowledge about reality is a faithful representation of it. The ontological notion of objectivity corresponds to the objectivity of law, while the epistemic notion corresponds to objectivity about law. Through an exposition of the objectivity of knowledge and the nature of rules, as well as the intersubjectivity of the social brute facts and the institutional facts, Hage proposes that objectivity about law cannot sensibly be distinguished from its object – the law itself. In his view, if constructivism about law is true, law and justified knowledge of law coincide.

In Chapter 3, Héctor A Morales-Zúñiga examines the possibility of knowledge about the law through a discussion of legal cognitivism – the view that there are correct legal answers – as a putative case of 'bullshit' according to Harry G Frankfurt's provocative analysis of that notion. For Frankfurt, instances of bullshit are linguistic interactions, typical in contemporary culture, that are characterised by their lack of connection to a real concern with truth (i.e., with how things really are).[98] While the liar rejects the authority of truth, one who bullshits pays no attention to it at all.[99] Drawing on Rainer Forst's

---

[98] Harry Gordon Frankfurt, *On Bullshit* (Princeton University Press 2005) 33–34.
[99] Ibid., 61.

contributions, Morales-Zúñiga argues that the rule of law materialises a dimension of the basic right to justification, according to which every person affected by a decision is someone to whom reasons are owed. The inner morality of law and due process as components of the rule of law articulate a public space in which persons may ask for and give reasons for the application of a legal norm. In this light, the rule of law, as the institutionalisation of the right to justification, implies legal cognitivism to the extent that if legal statements did not have any cognitive content, the argumentative game would lack the drive to trigger the intersubjective sphere in which reasons are given and contested. Yet participants in this argumentative game do not provide reasons for supporting the claim that there are right answers to legal disputes, but simply take it for granted. One might therefore argue that in doing so, they do not display any real commitment to the truth and that, in consequence, they turn the whole discursive game of legal argumentation into a case of bullshit. Morales-Zúñiga, however, rejects this argument. By distinguishing the normative commitments which are implicit in speech acts of assertions and assumptions, the author proves that regarding legal cognitivism the conditions for bullshitting are not met, and consequently, that it is not a case of bullshit.

In Chapter 4, Monika Zalewska resolves several puzzles concerning the consistency of Hans Kelsen's notion of imputation, which connects conditions and consequences in the Ought-realm in a way similar to the role that causality plays in the natural sciences. In Kelsen's early work, the concept of imputation operates as an epistemological category. Just as the notion of Kantian causality indicates alethic necessity, normative imputation denotes a normative necessity that allows us to order and make cognisable the legal material granting facts a normative value. However, Kelsen's late work abandoned the Neo-Kantian paradigm, specifically the concept of relative categories *a priori*. Deprived of its epistemic function, imputation became problematic. In response, Zalewska provides a renewed understanding of Kelsen's concept of imputation based on the notion of supervenience. This interpretation not only challenges Kelsen's wrong turns in his later work but also reveals a hidden aspect of the Kelsenian understanding of law: formal equality.

In Chapter 5, Donald Bello Hutt addresses H L A Hart's puzzling reluctance to admit Max Weber's influence on his jurisprudential project. For Bello Hutt, since biographical research proves inconclusive, the solution to the quandary can be found by analysing the assumptions of these authors' theories. Hart's reticence could be based on the difference in the subject matter of the two authors' investigations. In his methodological writings Weber focused on social sciences, excluding the law as an object of study while advocating a reductive understanding of legal practices. More importantly, Bello Hutt argues that Hart could not have followed in Weber's footsteps without betraying his own descriptive enterprise.

Part I of the volume ends with Chapter 6, in which Matti Ilmari Niemi defends a 'weak' conception of the objectivity of legal knowledge based on the use of valid methods for the interpretation of legal materials. At the core of this chapter lies a distinction between a strong and a weak sense of objectivity. While mainstream legal positivists and realists advocate a strong conception of objectivity akin to the correspondence theory of truth, for Niemi, this strong understanding is not applicable to the practical domain. Consequently, Niemi outlines a weaker understanding of objectivity inspired by David Hume's ethics. According to this view, legal knowledge is knowledge of objective interpretation in which statutes and precedents play the most critical role as primary premises. As formal reasons, these sources indicate the principles of justice and the values adopted in a society as the basis of its legal system. However, statutes and precedents are not sufficient fundaments, and other types of substantive reasons must supplement them.

3.2 Objectivity and Legal Interpretation

Part II opens with a chapter written by Leonardo Marchettoni. In this chapter, Marchettoni reconstructs the Hart–Dworkin debate using tools inspired by Robert Brandom's theory of the social institution of norms. For Marchettoni, Hart's conception of the discretionary role of judges in difficult cases, which was intended to compensate for lacunae in existing laws, fails to capture the interpretive dimension of legal activity. Dworkin, who rescued the constructive role played by judges in the law, noted this deficiency of Hart's theory. According to Dworkin, the prominent role of judges in the law consists of identifying through legal interpretation the principles that make it possible to resolve difficult cases. Marchettoni argues that if we reject the idea that the best interpretation is the only one that is faithful to metaphysically independent values, we can conclude that Hart's judge is not so far away from Dworkin's judge. The difference lies in the space that divides discretion from the attempt to reconstruct the entire legal system. This space depends largely on which notion of objectivity is adopted. Thus, if we build this space on the rationale of the weak conception of objectivity defended by Brandom, thereby redefining the concept of objectivity in law, the gap between Hart's and Dworkin's theories seems to narrow.

In Chapter 8, Maija Aalto-Heinilä addresses the possibility of an objective meaning of legal texts by critically examining two types of theories concerning the objectivity of meaning. Externalists – such as Michael Moore – maintain that the world directly and causally determines the meanings of words, so these meanings are largely indifferent to the speaker's intentions, beliefs and conventions. By contrast, intentionalists – such as Stanley Fish – hold that meaning depends on the speaker's intentions because without someone's intending something by words, they are no more than still life. Aalto-Heinilä argues that both theories are connected at a deeper level: They are committed to the existence of something that underlies the ordinary forms of word use and that guarantees the objectivity of their meaning. Continuing the path once blazed by Wittgenstein, Aalto-Heinilä posits a quietist position with respect to any attempt to formulate something general and abstract – that is, any theoretical enterprise – about meaning. According to the author, our attempts to understand the meaning of the words must be restricted to solving puzzles in concrete situations as they present themselves to us in everyday life. These concrete solutions should ensure evidence of the objectivity of our practices.

In Chapter 9, Caroline Laske discusses semantic objectivity based on linguistic conventions determined by usages of most speakers of a given group. Semantic objectivity of language and meanings in a specific context can be evaluated in relation to these conventional uses. However, conventional uses of language are not necessarily free of bias because they are always the result of encoding meanings in the specific context that conditions them. Big data linguistic analysis, such as corpus linguistics, provides tools to reveal contextualised encoding of meanings, both in the context of intersubjective agreement of the use of language, as well as in that of highlighting biases. Laske's analysis focuses on two studies. The first study, by Thomas R Lee and Stephen C Mouritsen, uses corpus-based methodologies and concordances to find pragmatic uses of natural language.[100] These uses can serve as patterns for the assessment of ordinary meanings that can be applied to the context of judicial interpretation. The second study, carried out by Laske herself, aims to provide data that reveals the evolution of legal terminology to help us better understand its etymological content and conventional use.[101] For Laske, linguistic diachronic corpus analysis of legal terminology makes it possible to trace and comprehend ambiguities and vagueness whose presence distorts language use, allowing the concealment of biases and, in short, the lack of objectivity. However, she warns that, because the application of these methodologies involves making decisions regarding the selection of data and the interpretation of results, objectivity needs to be measured also in terms of the subjectivity related to these decisions.

In Part II's final chapter, Triantafyllos Gkouvas discusses the function of interpretative canons in the determination of the law's content. The argument begins with an overview of the controversies raised by the judicial application

---

[100] Thomas R Lee and Stephen C Mouritsen, 'Judging Ordinary Meaning' (2018) 127 (4) *The Yale Law Journal* 788.

[101] Caroline Laske, *Law, Language and Change. A Diachronic Semantic Analysis of Consideration in the Common Law* (Brill 2020).

of interpretative canons and describes the main distinctions made by jurists in the context of the assessment of their legal effects. Subsequently, Gkouvas explores epistemic and normative approaches to the question of whether interpretive canons have the power to modify the legal effects of ordinary laws or constitutional provisions. He argues that, despite their differences, these approaches take a similarly deflationary position on the role of canons in legal reasoning. In response to this deflationism about the role of interpretative canons, Gkouvas claims that the interaction between interpretive canons and positive law is not in itself a distinct type of metaphysical relation but supervenes, nonetheless, on some metaphysically impactful properties of the related entities. In his conclusion, Gkouvas specifies this impact in mereological terms such that the modification of the legal effect of a legal provision by a canon amounts to a re-composition of the legal content of that provision through the incorporation of the legal content of the modifying canon into the legal content of the thereby modified provision.

3.3   Objectivity and Practical Reasoning

Part III begins with Chapter 11 in which Jan-Reinard Sieckmann discusses the problem of the rational justification of objectively valid norms. For Sieckmann, this problem amounts to the conflict between the objective validity of the law (i.e., validity in the sense that every reasonable agent must accept the respective norm as valid and, hence, must apply and follow it) and individual autonomy (i.e., the capacity of individuals to self-legislate). Since autonomy requires the consent of a norm's addressees, how is it possible to provide an objective justification of norms to autonomous individuals? Sieckmann resolves this puzzle by relying on his theory of autonomous reasoning. According to this theory, autonomous agents justify normative judgments as a result of the exercise of their normative competence in the balancing of normative arguments. While normative arguments – the claims made by autonomous agents – are not objective from the semantic, ontological or epistemic points of view, statements of the validity of a norm as a normative argument are objective, since they refer to normative arguments established as valid by autonomous agents. Normative judgments that express the result of the balancing of normative arguments are objective from the semantic point of view, even if they are not objective from the ontological or epistemic point of view. According to Sieckmann, a norm's substantive definitive validity implies not only that this norm is the result of successfully completed argumentation but also that it is actually binding – that is, that its addressees must apply and follow it. This claim of bindingness (i.e., the norm's qualification as objectively valid in the sense that every reasonable agent must recognise it as valid) must therefore be justified. What can be justified against autonomous agents is, however, merely that they must accept that a norm supported by reasonable convergence of autonomous agents is claimed to be binding.

In Chapter 12, Thomas Bustamante inquires into the reasons that many contemporary legal philosophers, regardless of their theoretical disagreements about the nature of law, appear to converge in the claim to objectivity in legal and moral reasoning. This confidence in objectivity of value judgments, however, is sometimes responded with scepticism by some of the most prominent philosophers in meta-ethics, who claim that lawyers are normally not able to handle with competence philosophical arguments about the nature of morality. In response to this scepticism many lawyers and legal philosophers advocate the possibility of a methodological, instead of metaphysic, conception of objectivity for legal reasoning. In defence of the lawyers, the author argues against Archimedeanism in moral philosophy and defends that position that it makes sense, as authors like Ronald Dworkin and Joseph Raz suggest, to claim objectivity for legal reasoning, inasmuch as the legitimacy of legal judgments depends on the possibility of objective assessment of legal norms.

In Chapter 13, Josep Joan Moreso critically evaluates David Enoch's influential argument for an objectivist view of ethics and normativity.[102] For Enoch, there are normative truths that are indispensable for practical deliberation. This critical commitment leads Enoch to accept non-natural moral facts and properties as necessary components of our ontological furniture. While Moreso accepts Enoch's reasons to reject a metaethics that fails to account for the objectivity of moral practices, based on the work of Derek Parfit,[103] Moreso argues that there is still a space constituted by normative truths and normative facts that do not have ontological commitment. Moreover, at the end of the day, even though our philosophical discussions presuppose objectivity in morals, this objectivity is compatible with different metaphysical assumptions and with different metaethical theses too. According to Moreso, the objectivity of morality is not threatened at all by the fact that we continue to argue about whether its foundations are committed to Platonism or to some kind of constructivist or fictionalist approach that seeks to explain them.

In this volume's final chapter, Amalia Amaya defends the virtue approach to legal reasoning against the familiar objection that such an approach introduces subjectivity into legal decisions. In response to this challenge, Amaya argues that the mainstream consequentialist and deontological theories of legal reasoning endorse a 'methodical' conception of objectivity that consists of impersonal methods that render certain properties of subjects largely irrelevant

---

[102] Enoch's argument was primarily advanced in David Enoch, *Taking Morality Seriously. A Defense of Robust Realism* (OUP 2011).
[103] Derek Parfit, *On What Matters. Volume Two* (OUP 2011).

for evaluating legal argumentation. By contrast, a virtue approach to legal reasoning puts forward a novel 'dialectical' conception of objectivity that sees subjectivity (of the right kind) as contributing to objectivity rather than threatening it. This novel, agent-centred conception explains the epistemic status of legal judgments as a function of the subjective qualities of legal decision-makers while preserving the virtues of the methodical conception such as impartiality, the absence of bias and arbitrariness, and the sensitivity to respond appropriately to reasons. However, unlike the methodical conception, the judge of the virtue-centred picture is embodied, affectively loaded and contextually situated. Finally, to address the possible objection of relativism, Amaya argues that objective pluralism, rather than relativism, is the best explanation that allows us to understand the plurality of answers that the virtuous judge can validate as a standard of legal reasoning.

4. THE RESEARCH AGENDA

A recurrent question that arises when discussing the relationship between objectivity and action concerns the possible domain specificity of objectivity.[104] More specifically, we frequently face the question of whether there are applications to each domain of knowledge – such as that represented by morality and the law – of a general conception of objectivity or, on the contrary, whether the meaning of 'objectivity' appropriate to each domain is independent of the others. The theoretical framework set out in the first part of this introduction and the collection of chapters that the reader holds in her hands show that the relations between objectivity, morality and the law are much more complex and that the horizon of the investigative task is still far away. Every context in which knowledge of a given function in a community of practice is possible seems to demand that the meaning to which 'objectivity' refers be made explicit. This means that even within the same domain of knowledge – such as that represented by morality and the law – different senses of objectivity are possible. Consider, for example, the sense of objectivity a judge faces when evaluating a body of evidence – objectivity qua mind-independence – and the sense of objectivity a judge confronts when applying the law to a particular case – objectivity qua impartiality – or when interpreting unclear or vague legal words – objectivity qua determination. We are only at the beginning of a road whose breadth remains unexplored.

---

[104] See, i.a., Leiter (n 11) 2.

PART I

OBJECTIVITY AND JURISPRUDENCE

2. Objectivity of law and objectivity about law
Jaap Hage

1. INTRODUCTION

The notion of objectivity derives its sense from the view that there is a world that does not depend on beliefs or opinions, or on any operation of the mind, and that ideally our knowledge is a faithful reflection of parts of this world. This view supports two notions of objectivity. One notion is the objectivity of a mind-independent world; the other notion is the objectivity of a faithful representation of this world. In connection to law, the first notion concerns the objectivity of law, while the second notion concerns the objectivity about law. The objectivity about law seems to depend on the objectivity of law, because if the law itself is not objective, it is doubtful whether objectivity about law is at all possible.

This chapter investigates whether, and to what extent, the distinction between objectivity about law and objectivity of law makes sense.[1] Section 2 starts with a discussion of the objectivity of knowledge and its desirability. Section 3 continues with an introduction of the conceptual framework for this contribution. Section 4 deals with rules. Section 5 addresses objective facts and 'things' (individuals), while the sections 6–9 focus on social facts, which are for law the most interesting category. Section 10 summarises the argument and draws some conclusions.

---

[1] Much of this chapter was adapted from Jaap Hage, *Foundations and Building Blocks of Law* (Eleven 2018).

2. OBJECTIVITY OF KNOWLEDGE

Reiss and Sprenger have offered an analysis of what they call 'objectivity as faithfulness to facts'.[2][3] They distinguish three variants or aspects of this epistemic version of objectivity. Objectivity of knowledge would mean that:

> ... scientific claims are objective in so far as they faithfully describe facts about the world. The philosophical rationale underlying this conception of objectivity is the view that there are facts 'out there' in the world and that it is the task of a scientist to discover, to analyse and to systematize them. 'Objective' then becomes a success word: if a claim is objective, it successfully captures some feature of the world.

Objectivity as absence of normative commitments would boil down to the view '... that science should be *value-free*, and that scientific claims or practices are objective to the extent that they are free of moral, political and social values'.

Objectivity as freedom from personal bias, finally, means that '... science is objective to the extent that personal biases are absent from scientific reasoning, or that they can be eliminated in a social process ... scientific results should certainly not depend on researchers' personal preferences or idiosyncratic experiences.'

The picture that arises from these quotes is that scientific objectivity has to do with our (scientific) knowledge faithfully representing the facts as they really (objectively) are. Such a realistic picture would be distorted if values played a role in gathering evidence, or in accepting theories on the basis of evidence. Not only values should be barred from influencing the results of science, but also personal preferences and idiosyncratic experiences.

Implicit in this picture is the distinction between – on one hand – the facts, which as such are not tainted by distorting factors such as values, biases, or preferences and – on the other hand – our knowledge of these facts, which is threatened by becoming tainted by these factors. The strife for scientific objectivity is nothing other than the attempt to make our knowledge reflect the untainted facts as faithfully as possible.

---

[2] Julian Reiss and Jan Sprenger, 'Scientific Objectivity', *The Stanford Encyclopedia of Philosophy* (Fall 2014 Edition), Edward N Zalta (ed.),
URL = http://plato.stanford.edu/archives/fall2014/entries/scientific-objectivity/ accessed 23 June 2022.

[3] An extensive overview of different notions of objectivity that are relevant for law and jurisprudence can be found in the Introduction to this volume, footnote 11. A possible addition would be Anne Ruth Mackor, 'Legal Doctrine is a Non-normative Discipline: An Argument from Abstract Object Theory', in Sanne Taekema, Bart van Klink and Wouter de Been (eds), *Facts and Norms in Law. Interdiciplinary Reflections on Legal Method* (Edward Elgar 2016) 127–149.

Elaborating on this objectivity-metaphor, subjectivity of knowledge would then be the distortion of our knowledge by the tainting effects of personal biases, preferences, or idiosyncratic experiences.

The tainting effects of values do not necessarily stem from the person who claims to have particular knowledge (the knowing subject) and are not in that sense subjective. However, they nevertheless distort knowledge in a similar way, thereby spoiling the objectivity of the knowledge and making it subjective in the broader sense of being infected by factors that distort knowledge of the facts as they are.

An interesting addition to this view can be found in the work of Daston and Galison.[4] They describe the historical development of the notion of objectivity of knowledge in the period from the 18th to the 20th century. As an example of the beginning of this development, Daston and Galison discuss the use of scientific atlases in the 17th and the 18th century. These atlases contained pictures of parts of reality, geographical, but also botanical. They were used to train the eye of the novice and calibrate that of more experienced observers to see what is essential in nature.[5] This implied that the pictures would not depict nature in all its contingent details, but rather emphasise what is universal and ideal. A picture of, for instance, a plant or flower would focus on the essential characteristics of the kind of plant and leave out details that are peculiar to particular plants. No doubt that the producers of these atlases were to be experts in their fields, because they should be able to safeguard what is essential in their subjects and filter away the merely contingent details.

In the course of the 19th century, this approach to the knowledge of nature became more and more the object of criticism. The pictures in atlases would be subjective and not reflect nature as it really is. We should strive for a way of producing knowledge that is to a large extent mechanical, with as little human interference as possible.[6] Taking photographs, but also measurement by technological means, would be an example of this objective way of knowledge acquisition.

Remarkably, the 20th century took scientific ideals a step back from the mechanical reproduction of nature without human interference, back to more 'subjective' interpretations of mechanically created representations of nature. A good example in this connection is the interpretation of mechanically created images of galaxies.[7] This interpretation would be necessary to distin-

---

[4] Lorraine Daston and Peter Galison, *Objectivity* (Zone Books 2010).
[5] Ibid., 55–113.
[6] Ibid., 253–307.
[7] Ibid., 309–361.

guish within the images between what is the object of knowledge and what are merely redundant data.

Summarising, one might say that objective knowledge reflects the facts as they are independent of our knowledge. This knowledge is preferably produced in a purely mechanical manner, without interference of human judgement. Subjectivity spoils this objective knowledge by adding factors that either stem directly from the knowing subject (biases, preferences), or derive in some other way from factors that are outside the known facts (values). However, as the return in the 20th century to knowledgeable interpretation indicates, the move from this kind of subjective knowledge to objective knowledge also has drawbacks.

In the theory of legal decision making, we can recognise a similar tension. On one hand we have to strive for an impartial, mechanical, and therefore objective, application of the law. A computer as judge would from this perspective be ideal. On the other hand, we sometimes recognise the need for a creative, activist, and therefore subjective, interpretation and application of law. This approach seems desirable to adapt the law to new fact situations of changed societal conditions, or to make it more equitable. An experienced and well-balanced human being, with firm roots in society and political awareness, would from this perspective be ideal. Much of the literature on legal decision making, including discussions of the appropriate methods of interpretation and forms of legal reasoning, about the defeasibility of legal reasoning, about coherence, and about the roles of legal principles and fundamental rights, can be read as dealing with the balance between the objectivist and the subjectivist approach to law application and interpretation.

It must be emphasised, however, that framing discussions of legal reasoning as dealing with the tension between objective and subjective modes of acquiring knowledge about the law presupposes that there is such a thing as law that is amenable to objective and subjective ways of knowledge acquisition. In other words: objectivity, as well as subjectivity, *about* law presupposes the objectivity *of* law. This is the objectivity-metaphor again. In the following sections I will argue to what extent the law itself, as object of knowledge, is objective and to what extent the objectivity-metaphor is fruitful.

3. CONCEPTUAL BUILDING BLOCKS

To facilitate a clear and unambiguous discussion of the objectivity of law, I will introduce a conceptual framework. Unavoidably this framework makes ontological and epistemological presuppositions, and equally unavoidably these presuppositions must remain presupposed in a chapter that does not deal in the first place with ontology and epistemology in general. The same holds for the terminology that I will use. I will try to be explicit about the meanings in which I use words, but I am aware that others use the same words with somewhat different meanings, and that this may lead to confusion.

Sentences are the central elements of a natural language. They can be used to perform different kinds of speech acts, such as describing, creating, asking questions, and ordering. Notably, not all sentences are used to describe. In the order 'Open the door' there is some reference to the state of affairs that the door is open. However, in issuing this order, the person who gives it does not state that the door is open, but rather tries to induce the listener to open the door.

Propositions are the meanings of the descriptive aspect of sentences. They are language neutral. For example, the English sentence 'It is raining' and the French sentence 'Il pleut' express the same proposition. However, propositions are language-dependent in the sense that they could not exist in the absence of any language. Every proposition is expressed by a sentence in some language, although it is possible that different sentences, from the same language or from different languages, express the same proposition. It is also possible that the same sentence of the same language, used in different circumstances, expresses different propositions.[8]

Strawson rightly observed that all facts are 'the fact that ...', where the dots express a proposition, such as 'it is raining'.[9] Since propositions are language-dependent, languages are ontologically speaking prior to facts. Facts depend on what is the case, but also on languages that allow us to express what is the case.

Propositions, states of affairs and facts can be defined in terms of each other. A fact is that part of the world that is expressed by a true proposition, while a proposition expresses that some state of affairs obtains in the world. If the proposition is true, this state of affair actually obtains, and then the state of affairs is also a fact.

The world can be defined as the set of all facts.[10] Since facts are states of affairs and therefore language-dependent, the world is language-dependent too. This does not mean that with a language all the facts are given. All states of affairs are given with a language, but the world makes a selection of the states of affairs that actually obtain. For instance, given the English language, it is a state of affairs that all horses have wings. However, given the world, this state of affairs does not obtain, and it is not a fact that all horses have wings.

---

[8]   An example would be the sentence 'I am frustrated', uttered by Lillibeth and by Philip at different occasions. On one occasion it may mean that Lillibeth is frustrated; at another occasion that Philip is frustrated.

[9]   P F Strawson, 'Truth', Proceedings of the Aristotelian Society, Supplementary Volume [1950].

[10]   Ludwig Wittgenstein, *Tractatus logico-philosophicus* (Suhrkamp 1984) 1.1.

Terms are also important elements of a language. Unlike propositions, terms are not true or false, but they stand for (denote) 'things' in the world. Logicians call these 'things' which are denoted by terms, 'individuals'. Examples of individuals are President Biden, Mount Kilimanjaro, the house in which I live, the piece of music to which I am listening, the smallest prime number, or the rule that car drivers must carry a driver's license. An individual exists if there is a term in a true proposition that denotes it. The most obvious example is that Jaap exists if the proposition that Jaap exists is true. Since propositions are language-dependent, individuals are also language-dependent, in a way similar to how facts are language-dependent.

4. RULES[11]

Many facts are the result of rule-application, and if this is the case, this is crucial for their objectivity. Therefore, it is important to have some understanding of the operation of rules. All rules are constitutive in the sense that they attach new facts to already existing facts. Dynamic rules attach new facts, or modify or take away existing facts, as the consequence of an event, such as John's promise to Richard to give him €100. Fact-to-fact rules attach a fact to the presence of some other fact. An example is the rule which attaches in a timeless manner the fact that P is competent to alienate O to the fact that P owns O. For example, if Smith owns Blackacre, she is competent to transfer her property right in this real estate to Jones. Counts as-rules have the following structure: Individuals of type 1 count as individuals of type 2. These 'individuals' may be human beings, as in the rule that the parents of a minor count as the minor's legal representatives. Often, however, the 'individuals' are events. For instance, under suitable circumstances, causing a car accident counts as committing a tort, or offering money to another person counts as attempting to bribe an official. All three kinds of constitutive rules, dynamic, fact-to-fact, and counts-as rules, affect the facts in the world. A dynamic rule generates new facts, modifies existing ones, or takes already existing facts away as the result of some event. Fact-to-fact rules make that facts of particular kinds go together with other facts in a timeless fashion. Counts as-rules, finally, make that some kinds of 'things', often events, are also 'things' of another kind.

---

[11] This section was adapted from Jaap Hage, 'Separating Rules from Normativity', in Michal Araszkiewicz, Paweł Banaś, Tomasz Gizbert-Studnicki and Krzysztof Pleszka (eds), *Problems of Normativity, Rules and Rule-Following* (Springer 2015) 13–30.

Only rules that exist can attach new facts to existing facts. Rules can exist as basic social facts, or as rule-based facts. These two kinds of existence of facts in social reality are discussed in section 7.

Rules have a propositional content, and they can in some sense 'correspond' to facts. For example, the rule that criminals are liable to be punished 'corresponds' to the fact that criminals are liable to be punished, just as the descriptive sentence 'Criminals are liable to be punished' corresponds to this fact. However, in this correspondence lies also a major difference with descriptive sentences. Descriptive sentences are 'successful' in the sense of 'true', if they match the facts. They have the word-to-world direction of fit.[12] Constitutive rules are successful in the sense of 'valid', if the facts match the rule. With this match I do not mean that the rule is obeyed, but that the content of the rule is reflected in the world. For example, the rule that thieves are punishable is reflected in the world if (because of this rule) thieves are punishable. Valid rules impose themselves on the world. They have the world-to-word direction of fit, because they constrain the world in the sense that not all combinations of facts are possible. As a consequence, these rules create facts, and in this sense they are constitutive.

5. OBJECTIVITY OF FACTS AND INDIVIDUALS

Natural language does not distinguish between facts that are objective and those which include a subjective element. They are all represented by descriptive sentences which do not distinguish between more or less objective.[13] However, some facts seem to be objective in the sense that they are independent from anyone's beliefs, and not coloured by any subjective 'additions'. These objective facts would include the facts that Mount Everest is a mountain and that it is higher than the *Zugspitze*, that there are lions and other kinds of animals, and that the stretch of land that is called 'Siberia' borders on Mongolia.

Objective facts go hand in hand with objective entities. If it is an objective fact that the chair has a particular shape, then it must also be an objective fact that the chair exists. More in general, all objective facts that are facts regarding some entity such as a chair, a mountain, or a sea, presuppose that the entities they refer to exist objectively themselves. Objectivity is not only a characteristic of facts, but also of 'things'.

---

[12] J Searle, 'A Taxonomy of Illocutionary Acts', in *Expression and Meaning. Studies in the Theory of Speech Acts* (Cambridge University Press 1979) 1–29.

[13] However, there are indicators to signal that the speaker *considers* something as more or less objective. For example, by saying 'I find this picture more attractive than that one' the speaker signals that he considers his judgement to be subjective.

If objective facts are mind-independent, they are the same for everybody. Something is an objective fact or not, but it cannot be an objective fact for you but not for me.[14] This line of argument may be turned around: when we find that 'everybody' agrees about the presence of some fact, this fact is apparently the same for everybody, which may in turn be interpreted as evidence that the fact is objective. However, even then it is not certain that the fact is objective. When everybody looks at something through the same coloured glass without knowing it, the spectators may very well agree on the colour of what they are seeing. This would hardly be evidence for the objectivity of their perception.

If only for this reason, objective facts should not be defined as facts about which everybody – with a sane mind, under ideal epistemic circumstances, etc. – would agree. It may seem that the condition 'ideal epistemic circumstances' excludes the coloured glass example, and that with this condition added, it is possible to define objective facts as those about which everybody – with a sane mind, under ideal epistemic circumstances, etc. – would agree. However, it is not possible to define 'ideal epistemic circumstances' in an independent way. If everybody always uses the same coloured glass, nobody will ever notice the distortion caused by the glass and nobody would consider the objects of his perception as subjective. The same holds, more realistically, if everybody has the same cognitive apparatus which moulds our sensory input into a world that contains objects, their characteristics, and causal relations.[15]

Apart from this epistemological point that it is hard to establish whether a fact is objective, there is a conceptual issue which raises doubt on whether objective facts can even exist. This conceptual issue results from the assumption that all facts are states of affairs and that states of affairs are language dependent. Since languages are mind-dependent, states of affairs and facts are mind-dependent too. That would also hold for facts which are in all other respects objective. Therefore, the argument continues, there are no objective facts.

If objectivity is taken to mean complete mind-independency, there cannot be objective facts. However, that would mean that we lose the distinction between seemingly objective facts such as the fact that Mount Everest is a mountain and those facts which do not even seem objective, such as the fact that ice-cream tastes better than cauliflower. Facing this dilemma, one can take two directions. One is to adhere to the strict definition of objectivity and take into the

---

[14] Obviously, one person may believe a fact to be objective, and therefore the same for everybody, while somebody else believes it to be subjective, and therefore potentially different for different persons. Moral facts would be a typical example of such a disagreement (between realists and non-realists).

[15] This idea can be traced back to Kant but has found empirical support in the findings of modern cognitive science.

bargain that there are no objective facts or individuals. The other is to broaden the notion of objectivity and allow as objective those facts and individuals which are only mind-dependent because of their dependence on a language by means of which they are expressed, respectively denoted. For the present chapter I will adopt the second approach: the language-dependent nature of facts and individuals does not stand in the way of their objectivity.

6. THE INTERSUBJECTIVITY OF BASIC SOCIAL FACTS

Some facts are purely subjective, in the sense that they depend on personal tastes and preferences only. Examples would be that chocolate tastes better than cauliflower, and that paintings by Miro are more beautiful than paintings by Mondrian. For this reason, some prefer not to call these purely subjective 'facts' facts at all. Whether purely subjective 'facts' are a kind of facts is a semantic issue, and not very relevant for our present purposes.

Some other facts depend for their existence on what people think the facts are. I will call these facts 'social facts'. When we are satisfied with a very coarse categorisation, social facts may be described as facts which exist because the members of some group collectively recognise or accept them as existing. Not all kinds of facts lend themselves to existence through collective recognition. Physical facts do not, because collective recognition as such does not influence physical reality.[16] However, many kinds of non-physical facts exist through being recognised. Law abounds with examples of non-physical facts, such as people having obligations, or the possession of a particular legal status such as that of the King of the Belgians. Also, outside law there are non-physical facts, many of which exist through collective recognition. These include that somebody is the leader of an informal group, that somebody is blameworthy, or that somebody is a hero.

There are two variants on collective recognition. In the case of what I will call 'basic social facts' the facts themselves are recognised by the members of a social group, while in the case of 'rule-based facts' the facts are the result of a rule. In the case of rule-based facts, the existence of the rule is *in last instance* based on collective recognition. These rule-based facts are perhaps better known as 'institutional facts'.[17]

---

[16] This does not exclude that physical facts also count as other facts and that these other facts, which supervene on the physical facts, are social facts. For example, the fact that this piece of wood of a particular shape is also a chess piece is a social fact.

[17] Cf G E M Anscombe, *Intention* (2nd edn, Basil Blackwell 1976) and Neil MacCormick, 'Law as Institutional Fact', in N MacCormick and O Weinberger, *An Institutional Theory of Law* (Reidel 1986) 49–76.

Important aspects of collective recognition are that sufficiently numerous and/or sufficiently important members of a social group believe the fact to be present, believe that sufficiently numerous and/or sufficiently important other members also believe the fact to be present, and believe that these mutual beliefs constitute the believed fact. Social facts depend on recognition, and this recognition will necessarily exist within a group of people. The group ranges from two persons as one extreme, to everybody as the other extreme. This means that all basic social facts are facts within a group, and relative to a group.

A complicating factor is that recognition may be delegated to 'experts'. In legal theory, the classical example of such delegation of recognition is Hart's view that the rule of recognition of a legal system must be recognised by the 'officials' of the system.[18] Because recognition of basic social facts may be delegated to experts, it is not even necessary that a majority of a social group recognises the existence of a particular social fact.

Basic social facts are mind-dependent in the strong sense that their existence depends on being recognised by the members of a social group. They are therefore not objective. However, they do not depend on the recognition of individuals persons either. Whether precedents count as law depends on their recognition as such by courts and other legal decision makers, but for every individual court in the common law tradition it is a given fact that precedents count as law. For this reason, basic social facts have an intermediate status as far as their objectivity is concerned: they are neither fully subjective nor fully objective. We can use the word 'intersubjective' to denote this intermediate status.

7. RULE-BASED FACTS

If the members of a social group normally recognise the duties imposed by the leader of the group, whoever that may be, it may be said that the group has the rule that the group leader has the competence to impose duties. This rule exists through recognition and is a social rule.

It is tempting, but wrong, to follow Hart[19] in assuming that the existence of a social rule involves the existence of a critical reflective attitude with regard to behaviour covered by the rule. This characterisation of social rules is quite adequate for rules that prescribe behaviour, but less so for other kinds of rules such as competence-conferring rules. A broader, and therefore more adequate,

---

[18] H L A Hart, *The Concept of Law* (3rd edn, Oxford University Press 2012) 113–117.
[19] Ibid., 57.

characterisation of a social rule is that *a social rule exists within a group if sufficiently numerous (sufficiently important) members of the group recognise the consequences of the rule when the rule is applicable.* For a mandatory rule, this means that sufficiently numerous group members assume the presence of a duty or obligation if the rule attaches this duty or obligation to a fact situation. If the duty or obligation applies to a specific group member, this recognition typically involves that the group member in question is motivated to comply with the rule. For a competence-conferring rule, this means that sufficiently numerous group members recognise the competence of a person to whom the rule gave the competence. This recognition typically consists in the recognition of the effects of the exercise of the competence.

An issue which is in principle different from the existence of a rule is the rule's efficacy. Because not all rules are mandatory rules, a definition of the efficacy of a rule in terms of traditional compliance (doing what the rule prescribes) is not adequate. We should look for a definition that also captures the efficacy of non-mandatory rules, such as competence-conferring rules and counts-as rules. Such a definition might be that a rule is efficacious in a particular group if the consequences that the rule attaches to fact situations are recognised by sufficiently numerous and/or sufficiently important members of that group. The reader will immediately notice that this definition of the efficacy of a rule is identical to the definition of when a social rule exists. This identity is intentional: the efficacy of rules as defined here coincides with the existence of these rules as social rules.

From the definitions of what a social rule is and when such a rule exists, it follows that the facts that are generated by social rules will be broadly recognised within the group in which the rule exists. However, the existence of a social rule has more implications than the mere recognition of the facts generated by the rule. If Jack is a member of the group in which the rule exists that men should wear a hat, Jack is also required to wear a hat if he personally does not recognise the requirement. Although Jack will not be motivated to wear a hat, other group members still expect him to do so, and non-compliance may evoke admonishments, reproaches, and perhaps even informal sanctions.

These examples illustrate that social rules, like other rules, work 'automatically' in the sense that they attach their consequences to facts even where these consequences are not always recognised by everybody. However, in the case of social rules there needs to be broad recognition, because if that were lacking, the rule would no longer exist. If only Jack does not recognise the requirement to wear a hat, this does not affect his duty or the existence of the rule. However, if hardly any man would recognise the duty, neither the duty nor the social rule underlying it would exist.

This is different for rule-based rules. Sometimes the new fact that a rule attaches to a fact situation is that another rule exists. Suppose that Henriette is the leader of the social group and that, as such, she has certain competences, based on social rules which attach these competences to being the group leader. Let us assume that one of these competences is to make rules. One day Henriette announces that group members who received an inheritance must pay taxes. Starting from the moment that Henriette announces the rule, the rule exists. Moreover, the rule creates duties for the group members who received an inheritance.

It is worthwhile to take a closer look at the duties based on the rules that Henriette makes, the recognition of these duties, and the existence of the rules. Since the rule-making competence of Henriette is based on a social rule, this competence does not need to be recognised by all group members in order to exist. Let us assume that Violet received an inheritance and is for this reason a duty holder (the duty to pay inheritance tax). However, she neither recognises the competence of Henriette to make rules in general or to make this rule in particular, nor her duty to pay taxes. As the rule is a social rule, Henriette still has the competence to make rules for the group, even if Violet does not recognise the rules. The rule about inheritance tax that Henriette made exists within the group and creates consequences without Violet's recognition of the rules or her duties. Violet has therefore the duty to pay taxes, even if she does not feel obligated to do so.

Assume now that Violet is not the only one who has problems with the inheritance rule, and that most group members think that Henriette should not have made this particular rule. In other words, the rule that Henriette made is not broadly recognised. However, this rule was explicitly created and does not depend for its existence on recognition of its consequences. Therefore, the inheritance rule still exists, and the designated group members still have duties to pay taxes.

Things would be different if the group members stop recognising the rules that Henriette makes in general. That would mean that they no longer recognise the rule that gives the group leader the competence to create rules.[20] In this case the rule about inheritance taxes no longer exists as a rule-based rule. As can be seen from the example, the fact that some rule exists is an immaterial fact like many others, not principally different from – for example – the fact that a particular car is a vehicle. Like other immaterial facts, the existence of a rule can obtain as a basic social fact, or as a rule-based fact. In the former case, the existence of the rule is broadly accepted in a social group, where the acceptance of the rule consists in the acceptance of the rule's consequences if the rule is applicable. In the latter case, the existence of the rule is attached

---

[20] An alternative interpretation would be that they no longer recognise Henriette as their leader.

by some other rule to – typically – a legislative event. If the group members stop recognising the social rule that attributes the competence to legislate to the group leader, Henriette has lost this power. As a result, the rule about inheritance tax she attempted to make is not valid (does not exist) and cannot impose duties anymore. Violet has no duty to pay inheritance tax.

8. LEGAL CONSTRUCTIVISM

The account of rule-based facts that was offered in the previous section not only assumes that some facts are the result of rule application, but also that rules are self-applying in the sense that they lead to new facts even if no human being is actively involved in the creation of these new facts. Lawyers often seem to make this assumption, as the following story illustrates.

On a winter's day, the rich but somewhat eccentric spinster Eloïse Lasoeur died in her cabin on the moor at the blessed age of 87 years. Eloïse was very fond of her niece Denise Lasoeur and in her last will she bequeathed all her worldly goods to her niece. Denise, however, was not even aware of the existence of Eloïse. Moreover, no family member of Eloïse even knew whether Eloïse was still alive and where she might live. The inhabitants of the little village where Eloïse did her occasional shopping had not seen Eloïse for quite a while, but that was not unusual. Under these circumstances it was not surprising that Eloïse's death was only discovered several months after it occurred.

It seems obvious that, during the period after Eloïse died and before her death was discovered, the estate belonged to Eloïse's niece Denise. This is the case, even though neither Denise, nor anybody else in the world, was aware of Eloïse's death and the subsequent transition of Eloïse's estate. The rules of inheritance operate even if nobody is aware of their operation, and through these rules Denise became the owner of Eloïse's belongings at the moment that Eloïse died.[21]

That Denise had become the owner at the moment that Eloïse passed away is also the outcome of a good legal argument. This argument has as its premises the rules of inheritance law and the fact that Eloïse died while having bequeathed everything to Denise. For the purpose of the present discussion, it is crucial that this argument apparently reconstructs what happened independently, through the application of inheritance law. Denise became owner of Eloïse's belongings as a result of the facts of the case and the valid legal rules, and the argument is merely a means to obtain knowledge of what was independently the case.

---

[21] I assume here a legal system that does not require acceptance as a pre-condition for inheritance.

In 2010 the Dutch politician Geert Wilders was prosecuted for hate speech against Muslims. The fundamental question at stake was whether some members of society, and in particular politicians, should be allowed to express their opinion about other members of this society or their religion, even if they do so in a manner that may be considered as insulting and may very well evoke hatred. This question has no easy answer, and the case might well be considered to be a hard one, without obvious solution. In this case it is less likely that the legal outcome was already there, only to be discovered by means of an argument that reconstructs the operation of legal rules. It seems that the outcome may go anywhere and depends strongly on the arguments that are actually adduced in the legal debate. It looks as if the legal consequences of the case are *constructed* by means of the arguments, and not merely reconstructed. The legal consequences of the case would then be what the best legal argument says they are.

Amongst others through the influence of Dworkin, who proposed a theory of law according to which legal judgments are the result of constructive interpretation,[22] constructivist theories of the law have become quite popular. In Dworkin's constructivist theory of law, two aspects of constructivism can be distinguished. First, Dworkin offers an account of how to arrive at legal judgments. This is through constructing a theory of law which must on the one hand fit with existing legal materials such as case law and legislation and which must on the other hand be substantively right.[23] Second, Dworkin considers the judgments thus arrived at as law, *for the reason that they are part of such a constructed theory*. Legal reasoning is in the view of Dworkin not a way to arrive at legal judgments which were true for some other reason such as correspondence with some kind of legal reality. It is precisely the other way around: legal judgments are true because they are the outcome of a correct construction. Dworkin states it as follows: 'According to law as integrity, propositions of law are true if they figure in or follow from the principles of justice, fairness, and procedural due process that provide the best constructive interpretation of the community's legal practice.'[24]

9. A COMPLICATION

If this constructivist theory of law is correct, if only for hard cases, this has profound implications for the ontological objectivity of legal facts. Intersubjective facts depend on minds, and that is why they are not objective. Yet, for each

---

[22] Ronald Dworkin, *Law's Empire* (Fontana 1986).
[23] Ibid., Chapter 7.
[24] Ibid., 225.

individual person they are as 'real' as objective facts, and that is why they are not purely subjective. However, if legal facts are the result of construction, there is still a complication which sets off intersubjective facts from facts that are really objective.

In the process of constructing legal facts, the existence of social facts can always be claimed by adducing reasons why they *should* exist. For example, if most people believe that a skateboard is a toy, and therefore not a vehicle, it is a basic social fact that skateboards are not vehicles. However, it is still possible to argue that the acceptance of skateboards as toys is not decisive, that – for some reason – skateboards should also be regarded as vehicles, and that 'everybody' who believes differently is wrong. Such an argument is not only an argument why the existing social practice should be changed, although it is that too. The argument should also be interpreted as an argument why this particular skateboard already *is* a vehicle, even though most people do not 'see' it.[25] It depends on the successfulness of such an argument whether this concrete skateboard will be treated as a vehicle. In this connection it is crucially important that the rebuttal 'Everybody agrees that skateboards are not vehicles' is not a decisive argument in the discussion, even though it is an important argument.

A similar argument can be given why some seeming social facts actually do not exist. For instance, it is possible that a painting was donated to a museum and that 'everybody' believes that the museum owns the painting. However, if it turns out that the painting was looted 80 years ago during wartime and that the surviving family members want 'their' painting back, it may well be the case that the family and not the museum owns the painting. Of course, this requires a good argument to that effect.

This constructivism with regard to social facts has profound implications for the objectivity of the judgements that this particular skateboard is also a vehicle, or that the painting belongs to the family. The successfulness of an argument depends on the effectiveness of the argument in convincing an audience, which is *in the end* a purely subjective matter.[26] Because the judge-

---

[25] Although this is not an issue that I want to pursue here, I want to point out that disputation of the existence of social facts on the ground that they should not exist illustrates the dependence of what is on what should be. I discussed this phenomenon in Jaap C Hage, *Reasoning with Rules* (Kluwer 1997) 126–128 under the heading 'deontic collapse', and also in several papers on 'constructivist facts', including Jaap Hage, 'Are the Cognitive Sciences Relevant for Law?', in B Brożek, J Hage and N A Vincent (eds), *Law and Mind. A Survey of Law and the Cognitive Sciences* (Cambridge University Press 2021) 17–49, and other papers that are presently (November 2021) still draft versions.

[26] The clause 'in the end' is very important here, because a psychologically convincing argument can be attacked for not satisfying standards of rationality. These

ment that a skateboard is a vehicle is intersubjective, the outcome of a dispute on the question whether a skateboard is a vehicle will usually be conforming to the general opinion. However, for the fundamental question of whether social facts that need to be constructed are objective, intersubjective, or purely subjective it does not matter which outcome of legal arguments is most likely. Somehow, social facts which need to be constructed seem to be more subjective than social facts for which the views of the majority are determinative.

10. CONCLUSIONS

The notion of objectivity, as contrasted to subjectivity, became prominent during the 19th century. Objective knowledge was opposed to subjective 'knowledge', and the characteristic that distinguished objective from subjective knowledge was that objective knowledge is an untainted, preferably mechanically produced representation of the facts. The attraction of this kind of objective knowledge rests on the assumption that there are facts which are themselves not tainted in the way subjective knowledge is.

The law – or to be more precise: the positive law – is a part of social reality. The facts in social reality can coarsely be divided into basic social facts and rule-based, or institutional, facts. Basic social facts exist because they are broadly recognised as existing. Rule-based facts are attached by existing rules to other facts. Rules exist in social reality either as a matter of social fact, or as rule-based fact. The definition of rule-based facts in terms of rules that may in turn exist as rule-based facts themselves threatens to lead to an infinite regress. This regress is avoided by the assumption, as it was made by Hart, that in the end all rule-based facts are based on social facts.[27]

Basic social facts are not purely subjective, but neither are they objective. They depend for their existence on recognition, and therefore on minds. However, for each individual person, they are outside their sphere of influence, just like objective facts would be. For many a legal discussion, it is this characteristic of being outside the sphere of subjective influence that matters for the 'objectivity' of law. In this, limited, sense, positive law may be said to be objective. In a deeper sense, however, positive law is not objective, but merely 'intersubjective'.

Even the limited sense in which positive law appears to be objective is amenable to criticism. This has to do with the phenomenon that legal judg-

---

standards and the judgements based upon them are intersubjective, and amenable to the same kind of constructivist criticism, and so on... In Hage (n 25), I argue why this possibility for constructivist criticism does not lead to an infinite regress.

[27] Hart (n 18) 100–110.

ments, certainly in hard cases, are constructivist. These judgments do not reflect independently existing facts, but they create, in a manner of speaking, these facts. Legal judgments are justified because they are the conclusions from good, if not the best possible, legal arguments, and they are true because they correspond to the legal facts. However, the facts are not independent from these judgments; they exist because the judgments that truly describe them are justified. Stated in technical jargon: in the case of constructivist judgments, epistemology precedes ontology. Judgments are not justified because they certainly, or most likely, reflect independently existing facts. They are justified because they are the conclusions of good arguments, and if they are justified, they are also true because they create the facts that they describe. This is step number one.

The second step leading to the criticism of law's objectivity is that the best possible arguments about what the law is do not only refer to the law as it exists in social reality, but also to what the law should, or should not, be. What the law is, depends – not exclusively, but nevertheless to some extent – on what the law should be.

Step number three is to point out that what the law should be is *in the end* a matter of which arguments are convincing. Convincingness is in this connection a psychological, not a logical, issue. Moreover, because it is a psychological issue, it is purely subjective.

If this three-step argument is correct, the law in a concrete case is, *in the end*, not objective, not even intersubjective, but purely subjective. This seems a dramatic conclusion. Not only our knowledge of law may be tainted by subjective factors; but the very object of this knowledge also is subjective. If the law itself is subjective, worrying about the possible subjectivity of knowledge about law seems a futile enterprise. It is even doubtful whether knowledge about law can sensibly be distinguished from its object, the law itself, because if constructivism is true, the law and justified knowledge thereof coincide.

This conclusion is in my opinion true, but not as dramatic as it may seem at first sight. Positive law is a social phenomenon, and social phenomena can only exist if the members of a social group, such as a legal community, tend to agree on what the facts are. Therefore, even if legal judgments and facts are in the end subjective, they can in general easily be predicted. The subjectivity of law goes hand in hand with the predictability of law, at least in most cases. Had this been different, positive law could not have existed as a social phenomenon. Law is distinguishable from morality, amongst others because it is to a large extent – legal positivists would even say: completely – positive law. The existence of law as a separate phenomenon next to morality presupposes a central role for positive law. Therefore, law must in general be predictable, because otherwise it would not have existed. This means that even if law is in the end subjective, there can still be legal certainty.

3. Is legal cognitivism a case of bullshit?[1]

Héctor A Morales-Zúñiga

1. INTRODUCTION

'One of the most salient features of our culture is that there is so much bullshit', Harry G Frankfurt stated in his provocative and creative essay *On Bullshit*.[2] Had we not known that this sentence was written more than 30 years ago,[3] we might have thought it attempted to depict the culture of current societies. The rise of populism, the distortion of communication through the use of social media, and other related phenomena have boosted the quantity of bullshit that circulates, or at any rate, they have made it strikingly more visible.

Frankfurt has advanced a particular understanding of bullshit in accordance with which it consists of a misrepresentation of the discursive enterprise a speaker is engaged in. While it might seem a speaker is concerned with describing the world, what she is doing is something different. In this way, the speaker would be indifferent to truth.[4]

Curiously, current legal practices give the impression of being based upon a peculiar form of bullshit. For if we reconstruct the attitudes and actions of participants of a legal system, it is reasonable to maintain that they rely on

---

[1] I am grateful to Flora Ben-Azul and Johanna Heinemann for their insightful remarks on this chapter and to Flora Mandiola for her advice on matters of English style. I would like to also thank for their helpful comments the participants at the *13th Central and Eastern European Network of Jurisprudence Conference* 2018 at the University of Zagreb and at the *Seminar on Legal Theory – Katedra Teorii Prawa* 2019 at the Jagiellonian University at which I presented previous versions of this chapter.

[2] Harry G Frankfurt, *On Bullshit* (Princeton University Press 2005) 1.

[3] *On Bullshit* was originally published in the *The Raritan Review* in 1986 and was then included in Frankfurt's collection of essays *The Importance of What We Care About* in 1988. Finally, *On Bullshit* achieved bestseller status when Princeton University Press published it in the format of a small book in 2005. Hereafter, I will refer to this latter edition.

[4] Ibid., 33–34.

some idea of *objectivity*. That is to say, that when those participants state what the solution to a legal dispute is, they are not merely communicating their personal preferences regarding the resolution, but rather are seeking to provide objective answers to them.[5] In doing so, we could say, they act *as if* there were right answers to legal cases. I will label this thesis 'legal cognitivism'.

However, as many discussions about it suggest, legal cognitivism is highly dubious. Legal systems may have gaps, some rules are indeterminate or may collide with other rules or principles, and so on. Then, sustaining that a legal conflict can be decided by adopting a right answer seems to be nonsense. But still participants in a legal system act as if that were the case. It seems that, as participants, we are in fact not concerned with the truth-value of this position, but nevertheless – for whatever reason – we take it for granted.

If this account is sensible, one must say that legal cognitivism is a case of bullshit. This chapter is devoted to examining the plausibility of such an odd thesis.

To start with (2.), I shall address the very concept of bullshit. After that (3.), I shall delineate a particular conception of legal cognitivism which relies on the idea of the rule of law. Then (4.), I shall tackle the question that titles this paper. In the final section (5.), I shall offer a summary of the argument.

2. ON BULLSHIT

In the aforementioned essay, Frankfurt noted that the topic of bullshit had not attracted substantive research, so that consequently there was no theory which dealt with the concept of bullshit.[6] Nowadays, by contrast, such a theory has been elaborated and Frankfurt may well be deemed as its founder.[7] Yet, there are still some open questions regarding its proper conceptualisation. This section aims to tackle some of them.

First (2.1), I shall introduce Frankfurt's conception of bullshit. Secondly (2.2), some clarifications will be presented. Thirdly (2.3), I shall defend a par-

---

[5] See the introduction to this book by Gonzalo Villa-Rosas and Jorge Luis Fabra-Zamora.

[6] Frankfurt, *On Bullshit* (n 2) 1.

[7] See David A Borman, 'Bullshit, Social Integration, and Political Legitimation: Habermasian Reflections' (2011) 50 *Dialogue* 117; Thomas L. Carson, *Lying and Deception: Theory and Practice* (OUP 2010) 58–63; Don Fallis and Andreas Stokke, 'Bullshitting, Lying, and Indifference toward Truth' (2017) 4 *Ergo* 277; Cheryl Misak, 'Pragmatism on Solidarity, Bullshit, and other Deformities of Truth' (2008) 32 *Midwest Studies in Philosophy* 111; Erik J Olsson, 'Knowledge, Truth, and Bullshit: Reflections on Frankfurt' in Peter A French (ed), *Midwest Studies in Philosophy: Volume XXXII– Truth and its Deformities* (John Wiley & Sons 2008).

ticular version of Frankfurt's model. Lastly, (2.4) on this new version, I shall distinguish different types of intentions and analyse their moral value.

2.1 Frankfurt's Indifference-to-truth Model

Bullshit is a misrepresentation. By bullshitting, a speaker tries to get away with what she says.[8] There are, however, multiple forms of misrepresentation. Lying, for instance, is a different way of getting away with what one says. Then, if we aim to get a better grip of bullshit, some specifications need to be introduced.

A promising route is to examine the object of the misrepresentation, i.e., what is being misrepresented when someone is bullshitting. Frankfurt provides the following example: 'P is undergoing a painful condition and tells W that she feels "like a dog that has been run over." W bitterly replies: "You don't know what a dog that has been run over feels like."'[9]

A first reading of W's complaint suggests that W thinks P is *lying*, that is to say, he thinks she does not feel 'like a dog that has been run over'. However, W does not aim to criticise this alternative. He does not think that P is misrepresenting her painful condition; rather, his concern is prior to the scrutiny of P's actual feelings.[10]

A second reading consists in arguing that W complains because P's statement is *nonsense*. Talking about something without having *knowledge* about it, it might be said, constitutes an instance of nonsense. Accordingly, P would be misrepresenting the knowledge she has insomuch as she does not know how a run-over dog feels.

For our purposes, it is interesting identifying the reasons for a person to speak about something she does not know. At least two possibilities are available. On the one hand, P could be *unaware* of what she is saying. Frankfurt rejects this alternative. In his view, P really understands her statement, even if only at a minimum level of understanding that the dog's feeling is a bad feeling.[11] On the other hand, P could be *not concerned with the truth-value* of what she is saying.[12] This is expressed by the degree of specificity of P's statement – i.e., she feels like a run-over dog. 'Her statement', as Frankfurt points out,

---

[8] Frankfurt, *On Bullshit* (n 2) 56.
[9] The example corresponds to an anecdote of Ludwig Wittgenstein recalled by Fania Pascal: ibid., 24.
[10] Ibid., 27–28.
[11] Ibid., 28–29.
[12] Ibid., 30.

'is not germane to the enterprise of describing reality.'[13] Put differently: P is misrepresenting the type of enterprise she is committed to.

Frankfurt believes the latter is the type of misrepresentation that defines bullshit. Consequently, coming back to the example, what disturbs W is that P was bullshitting.

In brief, in accord with Frankfurt's account, bullshit is a misrepresentation of the enterprise of describing reality. A speaker's indifference to truth proves this misrepresentation. I shall label this view the 'indifference-to-truth model' of bullshit. This model will be the starting point of our analysis. However, as previously announced, the next subsections will slightly deviate from it.

2.2   Bullshit and Beliefs

Let me begin with a brief clarification. The indifference-to-truth model of bullshit is activity-centred,[14] that is to say, it alludes to specific mental states of a speaker. This model must be distinguished from an output-centred model,[15] which zeros in on the characteristics of a statement, such as its unclarity or rubbishness.[16] Many times, the term bullshit is employed in this sense, as when a speaker stresses the bad quality of an argument: 'your argument is bullshit.' Here, nonetheless, I restrain myself to examine the former.

What are the specific properties of the indifference-to-truth model *qua* activity-centred model? Focusing on the metal states of a speaker may contribute to discern these properties.

Consider the assertion of p. One of the mental states of a speaker x regarding p might be a *belief*. In particular, x may believe that p is either true or false. If we take for granted that the truth-value of p is belief-independent, we can differentiate the following situations:[17]

---

[13] Ibid.
[14] Harry G Frankfurt, 'Reply to G. A. Cohen' in Sarah Buss and Lee Overton (eds), *The Contours of Agency: Essays on Themes from Harry Frankfurt* (MIT Press 2002) 340. See also G A Reisch, 'The Pragmatics of Bullshit, Intelligently Designed' in G L Hardcastle and G A Reisch (eds), *Bullshit and Philosophy* (Open Court 2006) 42 (defending that the distinctive mark of bullshit is 'essentially pragmatic').
[15] Frankfurt, 'Reply to G. A. Cohen' (n 14) 340. Waal labels these models the 'intentionalist school' and the 'structuralist school', respectively: Cornelis de Waal, 'The Importance of Being Earnest: A Pragmatic Approach to Bullshitting' in G L Hardcastle and G A Reisch (eds), *Bullshit and Philosophy* (Open Court 2006) 100.
[16] See G A Cohen, 'Deeper into Bullshit' in Sarah Buss and Lee Overton (eds), *The Contours of Agency: Essays on Themes from Harry Frankfurt* (MIT Press 2002) 331–335.
[17] For the sake of simplicity, I present the possibilities in a binary form, but they might also be presented as 'believing that p is true' and 'believing that p is not true', where the latter does not entail 'believing that p is false'.

S_1: x believes that p is true, and p is true.
S_2: x believes that p is true, but p is false.
S_3: x believes that p is false, but p is true.
S_4: x believes that p is false, and p is false.[18]

Once Frankfurt's conception of bullshit is taken into consideration, these possibilities are to be expanded. For a speaker can also be *indifferent* regarding the truth-value of p. Consequently, our universe of possibilities must include as well:

S_5: x believes neither that p is true nor false, and p is true.
S_6: x believes neither that p is true nor false, and p is false.

Adapting Frankfurt's nomenclature, we may say that whereas S_1–S_4 represent cases of *deference*-to-truth, so to speak, S_5–S_6 represent cases of indifference-to-truth.[19] For the sake of a label, let me term this account the 'belief-based account' of the indifference-to-truth model.

At first sight, this reconstruction seems faithful to Frankfurt's approach. He suggests, for example, that 'the essence of bullshit is not that it is *false* but that it is *phony*'.[20] As Frankfurt argues, 'although [bullshit] is produced without concern with the truth, it need not be false'.[21] Thus, one might conclude, the membership criterion for the bullshitters' club is not placed in the column of the truth-values of statements, but in that of the bullshitter's beliefs.

Furthermore, in describing the commonalities between bullshitting and the kind of linguistic acts found in a 'bull session' – a context where people talk about personal and emotion-laden aspects of life, testing how they feel and how others react to what they tentatively say – Frankfurt states that both refer to linguistic interactions where participants are not committed to expressing 'what they really *believe* or how they really feel'.[22]

---

[18] It is noteworthy that, according to standard speech act theory, S_3 and S_4 are 'linguistically unacceptable' from a *first-person* perspective. A competent speaker cannot say 'I state that p, but I do not believe that p': John R Searle, 'A Classification of Illocutionary Acts' (1976) 5 *Language in Society* 1, 4. This remark does not affect the example, since we are adopting a *third-person* perspective.

[19] See Waal (n 15) 107–8 (discarding creationism as a case of bullshit because its subscribers 'genuinely believe that the theory of evolution is wrong.' '[T]he creationist', he pinpoints, 'cares about how things really are.').

[20] Frankfurt, *On Bullshit* (n 2) 47.

[21] Ibid., 47–48.

[22] Ibid., 36 (emphasis added). For the case of a bull session, Frankfurt states that each participant relies on 'a general recognition that what he expresses or says is not to be understood as being what he ... *believes* unequivocally to be true.' Ibid., 37 (emphasis added). Admittedly, expressing something different from what one really believes is

In my opinion, this account displays three deficiencies. To begin with, from saying that bullshit is unrelated to the truth-values of a statement does not follow that it is defined by the speaker's beliefs. Granted, this is not a conclusive objection, for it just contends that bullshit *may* be based upon the speaker's beliefs, but not necessarily though.

Secondly, some passages of Frankfurt's work give the impression that he is arguing against this account. For example, he contends that '[w]hat bullshit essentially misrepresents is neither the state of affairs to which it refers *nor the beliefs of the speaker concerning that state of affairs*'.[23] Similarly, he suggests that '[t]he bullshitter may not deceive us, or even intend to do so, either about the facts or *about what he takes the facts to be*'.[24] In this sense, a bullshitter would not be defined by telling or not telling the truth – i.e., believing that what she asserts is either true or false – but rather by a certain attitude or mental state.

Thirdly, according to the belief-based account, the core of bullshit is the lack of the speaker's beliefs as to the truth-value of a proposition that has been asserted (S_5–S_6). If bullshit as 'not caring about truth' consists of not believing that p is either true or false, then there would be an incompatibility between bullshitting and expressing deference to truth.[25] But what if one could bullshit despite believing that p is true or false? What if being truthful (S_1–S_2) or untruthful (S_3–S_4) were not a hurdle for classifying an act as bullshit?

Consider the following case. The President of the Republic U has just received an economic report that says that, in the last quarter, U's gross domestic product (GDP) was higher than U's unemployment rate for the first time in over ten years. He believes that this has happened a lot of times before. However, in order to stand out the indicator and increase his popularity, he tells the community that U's GDP in the last quarter was higher than U's unemployment rate for the first time in over a century. As a consequence, the President of the Republic U is deferent to truth: he believes his statement is false (S_3 or S_4). Should this example be discarded as a case of bullshit, and instead, be qualified as a simple lie? In my opinion, the answer is no. We would neglect some fundamental situations which are ordinarily understood as cases of bullshit by proceeding in that way. This is a clear deficiency. As I see it, in an important sense, the President of the Republic U is still being *indifferent* to truth. Yet, a paradox presents itself to us: How is it possible that

---

not equivalent to being indifferent-to-truth, yet what is relevant here is how Frankfurt focuses on the speaker's beliefs.

[23] Ibid., 53 (emphasis added).
[24] Ibid., 54 (emphasis added).
[25] Cf. Reisch (n 14) 37 (stating that a bullshitter is 'deeply concerned with other truths').

a speaker can be at the same time deferent and indifferent to truth? Let me tackle this question in the next subsection.

2.3 Bullshit, Intentions, and Discourse

The 'paradox of the belief-based account', as we might call it, can be solved either by rejection or redefinition. The former solution suggests that there is no such a thing as a paradox, for the President of the Republic U is *not* being indifferent to truth. This option leads us to retain support for the belief-based account. The cost, however, is too high. As just pinpointed, cases routinely labelled as bullshit would be left outside.

The latter solution, by contrast, states that the paradox can be dissolved by switching the focus of attention from the speaker's beliefs to the speaker's *intentions*. Accordingly, it can be said that the President does not *intend* to ground the truth of his assertions. The President is not really concerned about providing an accurate depiction of U's economy; but rather, about serving other goals – e.g., increasing his popularity. Due to this, the President is being indifferent to truth from the perspective of his intentions and deferent to it from the perspective of his beliefs.

From this perspective, bullshit is a linguistic interaction in which a speaker is detached from the commitment to discursively redeem the validity claims that she raises in the context of a particular inquiry.[26] This means that a bullshitter does not intend to bear the responsibility of giving reasons for her claims, and by that closing the doors for a rational debate.[27] As Frankfurt points out, the fault of a person who is bullshitting 'is not that she fails to get

---

[26] For the concept of validity claims, see Jürgen Habermas, *The Theory of Communicative Action: Reason and the Rationalization of Society*, vol 1 (Polity Press 1984) 8–42; Jürgen Habermas, 'What is Universal Pragmatics?' in J Habermas, *On the Pragmatics of Communication* (Maeve Cooke ed, Polity Press 1999). For the concept of inquiry, see Fallis and Stokke (n 7).

[27] See Jürgen Habermas, *Philosophical Introductions: Five Approaches to Communicative Reason* (Polity Press 2018) 88 (suggesting that participants' reflexive attitude towards problematic validity claims is part of communicative rationality). See also Borman (n 7) 132 (arguing that 'a lie can be critically challenged, and the liar pressed for reasons; but bullshit systematically frustrates the transition to discourse, and so its deflection away from the game of argumentation in which truth could be pursued, is far more fundamental'). However, Borman seems to subscribe a belief-based account insofar as he identifies bullshit with a violation of the validity claim of sincerity: 'It is clearly the validity claim of sincerity that is being violated where bullshit is produced; that is, the "indifference" toward the truth by which Frankfurt identifies the bullshitter represents a lack of sincerity, or of sincere supporting conviction, for the truth of his or her claim.' Ibid., 124.

things right, but that she is not even trying'.²⁸ A bullshitter, in spite of being objectively engaged in a space of reasons, is subjectively detached from it.²⁹ Admittedly, a bullshitter may offer reasons for her claims, but such reasons would be orientated by an end different from redeeming the validity claims raised in the concrete inquiry.

By a similar token, Cornelis de Waal – building upon Peirce's ideas – has drawn a contrast between bullshit and *genuine inquiry*, where the latter refers to 'any inquiry that is fuelled by the desire to find true answers to the questions one is asking or involved (perhaps indirectly) in asking'.³⁰ The lack of such a desire would be what allows us to single out cases of bullshit. Therefore, the distinctive feature of bullshitting, Waal thinks, consists in a 'difference of intention'³¹ – i.e., the lack of intention to find true answers. Although similar to the account here advanced, Waal's approach does not stress enough the *normative* dimension of discursive practices. Bullshit is to be understood as a detachment from the normative commitments implied by being involved in an open forum of justification.³²

In brief, being indifferent to how things really are, is neither determined by the truth-value of p nor by the speaker's beliefs regarding the truth of p, that is to say, a speaker can bullshit regardless of whether p is true or false and also regardless of her believing that p is true or false.³³ I shall label this alternative view the 'intention-based account' of the indifference-to-truth model of bullshit.

2.4   Types of Intentions and Morality

As elaborated hitherto, this account is only a fragment of a full portrayal of the concept of bullshit. Bullshit has been understood as composed of a mere *negative* intention: the intention to not discursively redeem a validity claim in

---

[28]   Frankfurt, On Bullshit (n 2) 32.
[29]   See ibid., 55.
[30]   Waal (n 15) 104. Similarly, but relying on Robert Stalnaker, see Fallis and Stokke (n 7).
[31]   Waal (n 15) 99.
[32]   In the discussion about the defining components of *lying*, some authors have argued that there must be a 'warranty of truth' which is intention-independent. This approach is quite similar to the idea of 'commitments.' Cf. Carson (n 7) 25–29. For the relation between this conception of lying and bullshitting, see ibid., 58–63. See also section 4 of this chapter.
[33]   See ibid., 62; Fallis and Stokke (n 7) 281–284. This could give rise to an internal distinction among sincere, insincere, and neutral – so to speak – bullshitters. See Reisch (n 14) 44 (arguing that '[u]nlike the liar, who deliberately obscures what he takes to be true, bullshitters may often be honest and sincere').

the context of a specific inquiry. A complete conceptualisation, in my view, requires emphasising some *positive* intentions as well.

Different positive intentions can be at stake when a speaker bullshits. A speaker may, for example, have the intention to cause others to believe that she is engaged in a discursive practice, that is to say that she is *subjectively* committed to the social rules that govern the exchange of arguments.[34] Let me call it 'deceptive intention.' As argued by Frankfurt:

> The bullshitter may not deceive us, or even intend to do so, either about the facts or about what he takes the facts to be. What he does necessarily attempt to deceive us about is his enterprise. His only indispensably distinctive characteristic is that in a certain way he misrepresents what he is up to.[35]

Although it can be discussed whether this intention to deceive is a necessary condition of bullshit, here I will leave this question open. Cases in which a speaker does not have a deceptive intention will still be deemed as instances of bullshit.[36]

Another positive intention relates to the attainment of certain aims by means of bullshitting. We can ask: What does a bullshitter intend by not intending to discursively redeem a validity claim? Let us again resort to one of Frankfurt's quotation:

> The fact about himself that the bullshitter hides ... is that the truth-values of his statements are not of central interest to him; what we are not to understand is that his intention is neither to report the truth nor to conceal it. This does not mean that his speech is *anarchically impulsive*, but that the *motive* guiding and controlling it is unconcerned with how the things about which he speaks truly are.[37]

---

[34] See Reisch (n 14) 38 (arguing that 'bullshitters *conceal* not some indifference to truth but instead a commitment to other truths' – emphasis added); Frankfurt, On Bullshit (n 2) 37–38 (suggesting that the difference between bullshit and the statements made in a bull session is that in the former there is a 'pretense' as to there being a connection between what people say and what they believe); Waal (n 15) 100 (pointing out that '[o]ften, but not always, the bullshitter tries to *hide* his indifference to truth' – emphasis added).

[35] Frankfurt, On Bullshit (n 2) 54.

[36] For a similar discussion regarding the definition of lying, see James E Mahon, 'The Definition of Lying and Deception' in Edward N. Zalta (ed), *The Stanford Encyclopedia of Philosophy* (Winter 2016 Edition) section 2.

[37] Frankfurt, On Bullshit (n 2) 55 (emphasis added).

Frankfurt draws attention to the fact that while bullshitting, a speaker is not drifting away but rather is being controlled by certain 'motives' or 'purposes'.[38] So, a bullshitter holds what might be termed 'aim-intentions'.[39]

It is worth noting that since there is a multiplicity of purposes, there is also a multiplicity of moral judgments about them. Thereby, we may distinguish between 'benign' and 'malign' purposes, and thus between 'benign bullshit' and 'malign bullshit'.[40] Consider the case of the President of the Republic U. If he was bullshitting to hide from the citizens other critical political issues and, in that way, strengthen his status, he would be debilitating the possibility for the citizens to make authorities accountable for their public decisions. President's bullshitting, we might agree, is malign.

Let me summarise the findings of this section. Harry Frankfurt's indifference-to-truth model of bullshit as an activity-centred model is plausible, but it demands some clarifications. Instead of a belief-based account of it, an intention-based account has been defended here. This account features negative and positive intentions of the speaker. In regard with the negative intention, it refers to the absence of the speaker's intention to fulfil the commitments undertaken in an argumentative interaction. In regard to the positive intentions, we may differentiate 'deceptive intentions' from 'aim-intentions'. The latter intentions, in turn, can be morally benign or malign.

As a result, bullshit can be defined as: 'A linguistic interaction in which a speaker is detached from the commitment to discursively redeem the validity claims that she raises in the context of a particular inquiry pursuing to attain certain aims.'

In the next section, I shall offer a conception of legal cognitivism that will allow us to evaluate whether or not it is a case of bullshit.

---

[38] See ibid., 56 (indicating that a bullshitter 'does not care whether the things he says describe reality correctly. He just picks them out ... to suit his *purpose.*' – emphasis added). Cf. Waal (n 15) 109, arguing that a bullshitter might not have further intentions:

> [a bullshitter] doesn't care about the truth or the correctness of his statements, either because of a total indifference to how things really are, or because of the belief that whatever he says makes no difference at all, his voice being only one in a sea of others, many of which more powerful, and all clamoring for attention.

[39] Cf. Cohen (n 16) 325–331 (distinguishing between 'tactics' and 'goals').

[40] Cf. Waal (n 15) 110–11 (expressing his scepticism as to the possibility of 'productive' bullshit: 'Bullshitting lacks the openness of mind and the ability to adapt in face of new insights that are essential for anything to be taken seriously or as worth pursuing').

3. ON LEGAL COGNITIVISM

The question whether there are right answers in the legal domain has received significant attention in recent decades. It has been claimed, for example, that legal disagreements are to be solved in accordance with a right answer.[41] In that, the legal statements by means of which such solutions are conveyed – e.g., 'x must pay €100 to y', 'the legal provision p means q' – have truth-value and, as a result, cognitive content. Legal cognitivism, as we labelled it, has been severely criticised. Questions of law, it is sustained, do not have right answers. Accordingly, legal statements have neither truth-value nor cognitive content. Deciding a legal case, some argue, is a matter of a mere subjective choice.[42] I shall label this position 'legal scepticism'.[43] It is far from the scope of this chapter discussing the many theories about legal cognitivism and legal scepticism. Instead, I shall give account of a particular version of the former which is morally anchored to the idea of rule of law. Thus, first (3.1), I shall provide a conception of the rule of law as part of the institutionalisation of a moral right to justification to then (3.2) put it together with a version of legal cognitivism.

3.1 Rule of Law, Fair Trial and Justifying Beings

The rule of law is one of the most crucial features of modern democracies. However, the concrete content of the concept is highly controversial.[44] Two types of conceptions can be distinguished: formal and substantive.[45] As

---

[41] For the *locus classicus* of this view, see Ronald Dworkin, 'No Right Answer?' in P M S Hacker and Joseph Raz (eds), *Law, Morality and Society: Essays in Honour of H.L.A. Hart* (Clarendon Press 1977); Ronald Dworkin, 'Pragmatism, Right Answers, and True Banality' in Michael E Brint and William Weaver (eds), *Pragmatism in Law and Society* (Westview Press 1991); Ronald Dworkin, 'Objectivity and Truth: You'd Better Believe It' (1996) 25 *Philosophy and Public Affairs* 87. For an understanding of Dworkin's thesis as 'weak objectivism', see in this book Chapter 7 by Leonardo Marchettoni.

[42] On the distinction between subjectivy, objectivity and intersubjectivity on the legal sphere, see in this book Chapter 2 by Jaap Hage.

[43] For some approaches on legal scepticism, see Pierluigi Chiassoni, 'Legal Interpretation without Truth' (2016) 29 *Revus* 93; Pierluigi Chiassoni, 'The Pragmatics of Scepticism' in Francesca Poggi and Alessandro Capone (eds), *Pragmatics and Law: Practical and Theoretical Perspectives* (Springer 2017); Riccardo Guastini, 'Rule-Scepticism Restated' in Leslie Green and Brian Leiter (eds), *Oxford Studies in Philosophy of Law*, vol 1 (OUP 2011) 153ff.

[44] Brian Z Tamanaha, *On the Rule of Law* (CUP 2004) 4.

[45] See Paul Craig, 'Formal and Substantive Conceptions of the Rule of Law' [1997] *PL* 467. Moreover, it is possible to trace sub-distinctions resting on different degrees

Tamanaha summarises, 'formal theories focus on the proper sources and form of legality, while substantive theories also include requirements about the content of the law (usually that it must comport with justice or moral principle)'.⁴⁶ Here I shall adopt a version of the former.

A formal conception of the rule of law, as I understand it, is composed of two elements: formal legality and a fair trial. Formal legality refers to the canonical desiderata elaborated by Lon Fuller in his *The Morality of Law*, according to which law has to be general, publicly promulgated, clear, non-retroactive, consistent, possible to comply with, constant, and there must be congruence between official action and declared rule.⁴⁷ In turn, the idea of a fair trial alludes to some procedural requirements in the application of law, such as impartiality, the right to be heard, and the duty to provide reasons.⁴⁸ For our purposes, I concentrate exclusively on the second aspect of this conception of the rule of law.

In my opinion, a fair trial can be reconstructed as the institutionalisation of the basic normative standing of human beings *qua* justifying beings.⁴⁹ This standing, as Rainer Forst has convincingly maintained, receives expression by dint of a moral right to justification borne by all human beings. Let me briefly elaborate this theoretical background.

Human beings, Forst argues, are equipped with the capacity to orientate themselves in the world by following reasons. Our beliefs and actions can be justified by means of the exercise of practical reason, thus human beings are 'justifying' or 'reason-giving' beings.⁵⁰ We take part in argumentative games which are rule-governed, i.e., in practices that are informed by internal criteria

---

of 'thickness', see Tamanaha (n 44) 91. For an approach that avoids the problematic distinction between formal and substantive rule of law, see Héctor A. Morales-Zúñiga, 'On the Moral Foundations of a Fair Trial' in André Ferreira Leite de Paula and Andrés Santacoloma Santacoloma (eds), *Law and Morals* (Franz Steiner Verlag 2019).

⁴⁶ Tamanaha (n 44) 92.
⁴⁷ Lon Fuller, *The Morality of Law* (Yale University Press 1969) 46–91.
⁴⁸ See Tamanaha (n 44) 93–99. For the procedural dimension of the rule of law, see Jeremy Waldron, 'The Rule of Law and the Importance of Procedure' in James E Fleming (ed), *Nomos 50: Getting to the Rule of Law* (New York University Press 2011).
⁴⁹ See Morales-Zúñiga (n 45).
⁵⁰ Rainer Forst, 'Introduction: The Foundation of Justice' in R Forst, *The Right to Justification: Elements of a Constructivist Theory of Justice* (Columbia University Press 2011) 1; Rainer Forst, 'Practical Reason and Justifying Reasons: On the Foundations of Morality' in R Forst, *The Right to Justification: Elements of a Constructivist Theory of Justice* (Columbia University Press 2011) 13; Rainer Forst, 'Critique of Justifying Reason: Explaining Practical Normativity' in R Forst, *Normativity and Power: Analyzing Social Orders of Justification* (OUP 2017) 21–22.

according to which the validity claims that are raised have to be discursively redeemed.⁵¹

In Forst's view, additionally, human beings understand that by the mere fact of being such beings, they owe other human beings to provide reasons for their actions. Reciprocally, they expect to be recognised as bearing the same normative status.⁵² This basic standing is expressed as a basic moral right to justification: 'The right to justification is … the right of all rights, because it determines the ground, the form and hence the content of all further rights arguments, whether in the moral or the legal realm.'⁵³

Our social practices of argumentation, then, are anchored in this basic individual claim by virtue of which human beings can ask for reasons that justify the norms – actions, institutions, decisions – that affect them in a morally significant way.⁵⁴

For our purposes, it is significant to stress as well that the right to justification is the core of human dignity.⁵⁵ As Forst puts it:

> Recognizing [human] dignity means seeing persons as beings who are endowed with a *right to justification* of all actions or norms that affect them in morally relevant ways – and acknowledging that every moral person has a duty to provide such justification.⁵⁶

Human dignity thus implies respecting the normative standing that every human being has *qua* human being in the arena of the rule-governed exchange of reasons. In negative terms, one could sustain that human dignity is violated whenever the condition of being reason-giving creatures is denied. If human

---

⁵¹ Rainer Forst, 'Moral Autonomy and the Autonomy of Morality' in R Forst, *The Right to Justification: Elements of a Constructivist Theory of Justice* (Columbia University Press 2011) 49; Forst, 'Critique of Justifying Reason' (n 50) 25.

⁵² See Forst, 'Moral Autonomy' (n 51) 54–55.

⁵³ Rainer Forst, 'The Justification of Basic Rights: A Discourse-Theoretical Approach' (2016) 45(3) *Netherlands Journal of Legal Philosophy* 7, 14.

⁵⁴ For the distinction of three dimensions of this right, see Morales-Zúñiga (n 45) 165–166.

⁵⁵ See Rainer Forst, 'The Basic Right to Justification: Toward a Constructivist Conception of Human Rights' in R Forst, *The Right to Justification: Elements of a Constructivist Theory of Justice* (Columbia University Press 2011); Rainer Forst, 'The Grounds of Critique: On the Concept of Human Dignity in Social Orders of Justification' in R Forst, *Justification and Critique: Towards a Critical Theory of Politics* (Polity Press 2014); Rainer Forst, 'The Justification of Human Rights and the Basic Right to Justification: A Reflexive Approach' in R Forst, *Justification and Critique: Towards a Critical Theory of Politics* (Polity Press 2014); Forst, 'The Justification of Basic Rights' (n 53).

⁵⁶ Forst, 'The Grounds of Critique' (n 55) 96.

dignity is affected, political power has been employed arbitrarily.[57] Therefore, a decision is arbitrary whenever no valid reasons are offered to support it and, when a decision is arbitrary, the basic right to justification is infringed upon as is the principle of human dignity.

This succinct portrayal of Forst's theory enables us to defend the following thesis: a fair trial is an aspect of the institutionalisation of the moral right to justification. In fact, the idea of a fair trial attempts to forge a legal system in which legal disagreements are settled by respecting the dignity of the members of a political community. The avoidance of arbitrariness and the respect of the right to justification are the aims of the procedural requirements shaped by this component of the rule of law.[58]

With this conception of one of the elements of the rule of law – a fair trial – we can now move towards legal cognitivism.

3.2 The Moral Grounds of Legal Cognitivism

In a somewhat puzzling passage, Ulfrid Neumann contends that the debate about truth in the legal domain does not aim to identify a *true* theory of truth, but rather the most 'adequate' theory.[59] What does 'adequate' mean here? The kind of response to the question of the right answer – i.e., a specific theory of truth – that I endorse in this chapter relies on a moral reading of 'adequate'. Legal cognitivism, I believe, is the most adequate theory of truth due to its moral credentials.[60] I am aware of the perplexity caused by this position, and I will therefore in the following briefly address some of the most common misunderstandings associated with it.

Why is cognitivism the best form of addressing the problem of right answers in the legal arena? In my opinion, the rule of law understood as the institutionalisation of the right to justification implies legal cognitivism. As mentioned above, a fair trial gives form to an argumentative practice in which our equal standing as justifying beings is honoured. When legal decisions are taken, valid reasons must be provided. Therein lies the institutional device to

---

[57] Rainer Forst, 'A Kantian Republican Conception of Justice as Non-Domination' in Andreas Niederberger and Philipp Schink (ed), *Republican Democracy: Liberty, Law and Politics* (Edinburgh University Press 2015) 155.

[58] It might be argued that this account of a fair trial endorses a substantive conception of the rule of law. Although the distinction between formal and substantive is rather problematic, it is still possible to argue that formal rule of law have *moral grounds* and, in concrete, that the idea of a fair trial rests on the moral value of human dignity.

[59] Ulfrid Neumann, *Wahrheit im Recht: Zu Problematik und Legitimität einer fragwürdigen Denkform* (Nomos Verlagsgesellschaft 2004) 13–14.

[60] See in this book Chapter 12 by Thomas Bustamante and Chapter 13 Joseph Moreso, drawing a connection between legitimacy and moral objectivity.

neutralise arbitrariness. All this, however, requires a presupposition. An order of justification, as imagined here, is possible only if *we assume that there are right answers*. If, however, one does not assume that legal statements have cognitive content, the argumentative game lacks the drive to trigger the intersubjective sphere in which reasons are given and contested.[61] Let me call this 'pragmatic legal cognitivism'.

Pragmatic legal cognitivism is morally grounded because it makes explicit an assumption that is needed to articulate a legal system that protects the right to justification and human dignity.[62] Giving and asking for reasons as well as reacting to decisions that have not been properly justified would not make sense without assuming that it is possible to draw a line between right and wrong answers. Legal cognitivism, then, is a constitutive part of an order of justification construed in light of the equal normative standing of human beings.[63]

---

[61] Cf. Aulis Aarnio, 'La Tesis de la Única Respuesta Correcta y el Principio Regulativo del Razonamiento Jurídico' (1990) 8 *Doxa: Cuadernos De Filosofía Del Derecho* 23, 38 (arguing that assuming a right answer does not help us to improve society). See also Aulis Aarnio, *Essays on the Doctrinal Study of Law* (Springer 2011) 173–175 (arguing that a regulative principle of 'maximal rational acceptability' protects the Rule-of-Law State in a better way than the useless assumption of 'one right answer'). However, even under this deflationary cognitivism, so to speak, Aarnio, ibid., 175, maintains that;

> [t]he whole concept of democracy, and sound social life too, presupposes the means to evaluate interpretative standpoints concerning the legal order in a critical sense. Hence the concepts of legal certainty, rational acceptability and justification belong closely together. They also build up a totality in which justification is a necessary tool with which to realise the other elements of the whole totality. This is why one part of the whole cannot be removed without breaking the whole.

[62] See also Dworkin's defence of cognitivism:

> We want to live decent, worthwhile lives, lives we can look back on with pride not shame. We want our communities to be fair and good and our laws to be wise and just. These are enormously difficult goals, in part because the issues at stake are complex and puzzling. *When we are told that whatever convictions we do struggle to reach cannot in any case be true or false*, or objective, or part of what we know, or that they are just moves in a game of language, or just steam from the turbines of our emotions, or just experimental projects we should try for size, to see how we get on, or just invitations to thoughts that we might find diverting or amusing or less boring than the ways we used to think, *we must reply that these denigrating suggestions are all false, just bad philosophy*.

Dworkin, 'Objectivity and Truth' (n 41) 139 (emphases added).

[63] Cf. Aarnio's description of weak cognitivism:

> It is true that the judge or scholar could consider it important to have the right answer as a guideline, although we as human beings perhaps do not succeed in finding the right answer. Still, we assume that it is 'there'. Otherwise ... all legal decision-making ... would become blind and arbitrary.

Interestingly, pragmatic legal cognitivism reminds us of William James' ideas. In his iconic essay, *The Will to Believe*, he wrote:

> Our belief in truth itself, for instance, that there is a truth, and that our minds and it are made for each other, – what is it but a passionate affirmation of desire, in which our social system backs us up? We want to have a truth; we want to believe that our experiments and studies and discussions must put us in a continually better and better position towards it; and on this line we agree to fight out our thinking lives. But if a pyrrhonistic sceptic asks us how we know all this, can our logic find a reply? No! certainly it cannot. It is just one volition against another, – we willing to go in for life upon a trust or assumption which he, for his part, does not care to make.[64]

James reads the cognitivist assumption as a psychological disposition. People *want* to believe that there are right answers. The same could be said by resorting to other expressions, such as 'we hope', 'we desire', 'we will', and so on.[65] By contrast, pragmatic legal cognitivism attempts to avoid this psychological reading, by understanding that the assumption of right answers is a pragmatic consideration that emerges when we reconstruct a legal communicative scenario that is morally grounded.[66]

Someone may object to that by saying that this account shares defects with other cognitivist theses. All of them, the criticism might go, state that there is an *external world* of right answers that needs to be discovered. Pragmatic legal cognitivism, however, does not defend what is typically known as the 'ontological thesis'.[67] It does not claim that 'there are' right answers, but that the existence of right answers is pragmatically assumed. This point has been clearly expressed by Robert Alexy:

> As a regulative idea, the concept of correctness does not presuppose that there always already exists a right or correct answer to each practical question, which only *has to be found*. The only correct answer rather acquires the character of *a goal to be strived for*. The participants in a practical discourse have to claim that their answers are the only correct ones independently of whether there is one single correct answer, if their statements and justifications are supposed to make sense.[68]

Aarnio, *Essays* (n 61) 166.

[64] William James, 'The Will to Believe' in H S Thayer (ed), *Pragmatism: The Classic Writings* (Hackett Publishing Company 1982) 192.

[65] See, for instance, Waal (n 15) 107 (suggesting that '[w]hen engaging in inquiry we should always proceed upon the *hope* that there is a true answer to the questions we ask and act from a *desire* to find that answer' – emphases added).

[66] For the idea of a rational reconstruction and pragmatic investigation, see Habermas, 'What is Universal Pragmatics?' (n 26) 28–46.

[67] Cfr. in this book with Jaap Hage's Chapter 2.

[68] Robert Alexy, 'Problems of Discourse Theory' (1988) 20 *Crítica* 43, 58–59 (emphases added).

A different objection may come from those who see in pragmatic legal cognitivism a case of *normative fallacy*.[69] A normative fallacy consists in the derivation of a factual assertion from a normative statement.[70] Pragmatic legal cognitivism would state that since there are moral reasons to there being right answers, there are right answers. This reading must be discarded. As already mentioned, pragmatic legal cognitivism does not *assert* that there are right answers but *assumes* it. In virtue of this, I have preferred to argue that pragmatic legal cognitivism is morally *grounded* because it constitutes an assumption of the rule of law and, further, that there are moral reasons to favour a rule of law-based legal system.

Finally, it can be sustained, that some legal disagreements have more than one right answer.[71] Here I need not commit myself to arguing in favour of a strong interpretation of cognitivism. It suffices to sustain that pragmatic legal cognitivism maintains that *at the very least* there is one right answer. Hence, it can be said, moral agents interchange reasons regarding the correct way of solving a practical problem *as if* there was at the very least one right answer.

Although this has been a fragmentary presentation of pragmatic legal cognitivism, it suffices for our central purposes.

Now we can address the main question of this chapter: Is pragmatic legal cognitivism a case of bullshit?

4. ON BULLSHIT AND PRAGMATIC LEGAL COGNITIVISM

Pragmatic legal cognitivism is a case of bullshit, or so one might argue. I shall call this 'the claim'.

Let me begin with the representation of pragmatic legal cognitivism by means of the following sentence:

(q) there are right answers to legal questions.

This sentence is the key to pragmatic legal cognitivism. Nevertheless, it does not suffice for its complete representation, for the propositional content of this sentence may have different illocutionary forces. Consider these two possibilities:

(i)   we assert that q.

---

[69] I thank Giovanni Tuzet for drawing my attention to this point.
[70] T D Campbell, 'The Normative Fallacy' (1970) 20 *The Philosophical Quarterly* 368.
[71] See, for instance, Peczenik's two interpretations of Dworkin's right answer thesis: Aleksander Peczenik, *On Law and Reason* (Springer 2008) 250.

(ii) we assume that q.

The illocutionary force that defines the core statement of pragmatic legal cognitivism is (ii) because pragmatic legal cognitivism *assumes* that there are right answers to legal questions.[72]

In these terms, pragmatic legal cognitivism could be criticised for being an example of bullshit. Precisely, since a speaker who advocates pragmatic legal cognitivism does not intend to provide reasons to support that q is true, then she is detached from the commitment to discursively redeeming the claim to truth that she raises. Actually, this is the very point of *assuming* the existence of right answers – the argument might continue. A defender of pragmatic legal cognitivism does not subjectively engage in a rational discourse, then, she is bullshitting.

Some might resist the claim and defend pragmatic legal cognitivism from being qualified as a case of bullshit. First, one could draw attention to the *aims* of pragmatic legal cognitivism. As seen earlier,[73] while bullshitting a speaker pursues certain aims. What is the aim pursued by assuming that there are right answers to legal questions? We have already provided an answer: the assumption of there being right answers in the legal arena is a conceptual device that allows us to ground a sphere – the rule of law – where all legal decisions be based upon an argumentative practice that respects the equal normative standing of human beings *qua* justifying beings. In this fashion, the moral right to justification and human dignity are guaranteed. We may easily agree on the moral relevance of this aim-intention, so someone could hesitate and reasonably ask: How is it possible that a theoretical stance that pursues such a laudable goal be deemed a case of bullshit? This doubt is reasonable, because we usually think of bullshit as a negatively laden-concept. Above, however, we argued that it is not so in all thinkable situations, as two types of bullshit can be distinguished: benign and malign.[74] The demarcating criterion is precisely the aim pursued by a speaker. Thus, despite acknowledging that pragmatic legal cognitivism seeks to achieve a benign aim, it still is a case of bullshit – albeit benign.

---

[72] See section 3.2.
[73] See section 2.4.
[74] Ibid.

Interestingly, Harry Frankfurt has maintained that 'bullshit is a greater enemy of the truth than lies are.'[75] He explains the wrongness of lying as follows:

> Lies are designed to damage our grasp of reality ... What we accept as real is a world that others cannot see, touch, or experience in any direct way ... the victim of the lie is, in the degree of his deprivation of truth, shut off from the world of common experience and isolated in an illusory realm to which there is no path that others might find or follow.[76]

If we continue the narrative so far elaborated, it is possible to maintain that pragmatic legal cognitivism – as a case of bullshit – contributes to solve the dark side of lies. For, by assuming that legal questions have right answers, a world of common experience is disclosed; a world in which we act as justifying beings respecting the basic moral standing of all human beings. In other terms, the specific sort of benign bullshit in question operates as a form of retrieving what is lost when we lie. Therefore, this type of bullshitting would be better than lying. Be that as it may, pragmatic legal cognitivism would still be an example of bullshit.

Secondly, an alternative objection to the claim might focus on the *public character* of the assumption of right answers. Those who argue in favour of pragmatic legal cognitivism intend to shape a public normative order of justification, thus they do not intend to *deceive* others about the type of enterprise they are engaged in. Saying so would mean that the institutionalisation of our moral standing as discursive creatures relies on a masquerade, in which we *pretend* to discursively redeem validity claims when, in fact, we are not. Of course, this constitutes a sound counterattack. Nevertheless, at least as has been examined here, this argument does not work. For we have established in a stipulative manner that holding a deceptive intention is not a defining element of bullshit.[77] Therefore, despite being potentially true that pragmatic legal cognitivism does not contain an intention to deceive others as to the lack of intention to fulfil the commitments undertaken, we can still consider it an instance of bullshit.

As a result, the claim retains its plausibility. Neither the aims nor the public character of the aforementioned assumption is strong enough to refute the claim.

---

[75] Frankfurt, *On Bullshit* (n 2) 61.
[76] Harry G Frankfurt, *On Truth* (Alfred A. Knopf 2006) 76–79.
[77] See section 2.4.

In what follows, I shall try a different strategy. This strategy challenges the claim by stepping back into the analysis of the structure of bullshit and centres on the distinction between 'asserting' and 'assuming'.

What do we do when we *assert* something? One of the things a speaker does when asserting a propositional content is taking justificatory responsibility for what is being asserted.[78] That is to say, the speaker commits herself to vindicating that she is entitled to make the assertion.[79] In Habermas's terms, a speaker who asserts a proposition undertakes the commitment of discursively redeeming her validity claim – claim to truth – in accord with its specific criteria of redemption.[80] Thereby, a communicative practice of 'reciprocal accountability' is articulated.[81] These commitments are socially grounded, so they are undertaken whether the speakers are aware of them or not.[82] In that, discursive commitments are not part of the 'natural furniture of the world',[83] on the one hand, and they are not subjectively created, on the other hand; rather, they are deontic statuses articulated intersubjectively in a social practice of communication in which individuals attribute and recognise such statuses.[84] In consequence, by asserting q – i.e., that there are right answers to legal questions – one is committed to giving reasons that justify an entitlement to claim so.[85]

By contrast, what do we do when we *assume* something? Unlike the case of a speech act of assertion, an assumption does not imply providing reasons to justify what is assumed. A speaker who assumes a propositional content does not engage in a social practice in which its participants keep tabs whether she is fulfilling her discursive commitments. In fact, quite the reverse is true. As

---

[78] Robert B Brandom, 'Asserting' (1983) 17 Noûs 637, 641; Robert B Brandom, *Making it Explicit: Reasoning, Representing, and Discursive Commitment* (Harvard University Press 1994) 171, 173.

[79] Although, this responsibility, as Brandom suggests, arises only when the initial assertion has been challenged; before that happens, it is treated as warranted, Brandom, 'Asserting' (n 78) 642. See also, with a slightly different vocabulary, Brandom, *Making it Explicit* (n 78) 178. On the connection between normative objectivity and discursive justification, see in this book Chapter 11 by Jan-Reinard Sieckmann.

[80] For a contrast of Brandom's normative pragmatics and Habermas's universal or formal pragmatics, see Anna Michalska, 'What Brandom Won't Make Explicit: On Habermas's Critique of Brandom' (2018) 44 *Philosophy & Social Criticism* 41.

[81] Jürgen Habermas, 'Robert Brandom, *Making it Explicit*' in J Habermas, *Time of Transitions* (Polity Press 2006) 143.

[82] Ibid., 144.

[83] Brandom, *Making it Explicit* (n 78) 161.

[84] Ibid., 162–63.

[85] On the debate about the intention-based, commitment-based, and mixed accounts of assertions, see Peter Pagin, 'Assertion' in Edward N Zalta (ed), *The Stanford Encyclopedia of Philosophy* (Winter 2016 Edition) section 3.

has been maintained by Ruth Manor: 'When a speaker assumes a proposition he explicitly avoids expressing a commitment to its truth and he does not put it in question (he does not cause the question of its truth to rise).'[86]

Admittedly, as just suggested, the emergence of commitments is independent from the subjective conviction of a speaker – as Manor seems to suggest ('he avoids expressing a commitment'). Rather, when a speaker *assumes* a proposition, the commitments related to an assertion do not come up and it is so because that is the sense of an assumption in accordance with the communal and normative practice of linguistic interactions. Making an assumption does not bring about the attitudes of others whereby a commitment is attributed to a speaker, she will not be *treated as* committed to the truth of her statement.[87]

In the context of a sentence that has been assumed, triggering a public contestation as for its truth-value does not make sense, although, the pertinence or correctness of assuming something could be put in question. As Manor suggests, assumptions are 'always made for some purpose',[88] then in light of a such a purpose, the pertinence or correction of an assumption could be criticised. Or, if in a discussion someone say 'for the sake of the argument, let's assume that p is true', the interlocutor could question that assumption sustaining that is out of place because it is precisely the issue that is being discussed then it cannot be assumed.[89] In other words, engaging in the game of assumptions could be criticised in the context of a broader argumentative exchange.

There are different types of assumptions. Let me call attention to a simple distinction. Some assumptions operate as *rules of thumb*, i.e., the truth-value of a propositional content is taken for granted until something different is proven.[90] In this case, there is a potential opening to a discursive stage in which the content of the assumption might be contested and, consequently, the justificatory responsibility appears. This stage is just postponed, so we may call these assumptions 'provisory assumptions'.[91] By contrast, other assumptions cannot be modified for further considerations. Then, they can be termed

---

[86] Ruth Manor, 'Pragmatics and the Logic of Questions and Assertions' (1982) 29 *Philosophica* 45, 66.

[87] On the emergence of discursive commitments, see Brandom, *Making it Explicit* (n 78) 162–63.

[88] Manor (n 86) 66.

[89] I thank Tomasz Gizbert-Studnicki for pointing this out to me.

[90] See Manor (n 86) 66 (arguing that '[w]hen a speaker assumes a proposition ... he expresses the fact that he accepts the proposition as true (possibly, *only on a temporary basis*)' – emphasis added).

[91] As can be noted, provisory assumptions seem to be close to the idea of an assertion since both understand the justificatory responsibility as having a *conditional* character.

'definitive assumptions'. Framed this way, we can provide a clearer picture of our problem: by assuming that there are right answers to legal questions, one is not committed to giving reasons that justify the truth of such a propositional content and it is so in a *definitive* fashion, because the assumption is a constitutive part of a legal system anchored in the respect of human dignity.

As a consequence, pragmatic legal cognitivism cannot be considered an example of bullshit. Bullshitting entails a detachment from a social commitment that does not exist in this scenario. Since pragmatic legal cognitivism is defined by an assumption, there are no commitments that normatively force a speaker to enter into the game of the give-and-take of reasons. The truth-value of q is not in question. An advocate of pragmatic legal cognitivism cannot bullshit because she takes part in a type of linguistic interaction in which the conditions for bullshitting are not met.

In brief, this new attempt to challenge the claim has succeed. Pragmatic legal cognitivism is not a case of bullshit.

5. CONCLUSION

This chapter has examined whether legal cognitivism is a case of bullshit. To begin with, the indifference-to-truth model of bullshit was described. Focusing on an activity-centred reading, two versions of this model were analysed: the belief- and the intention-based accounts. It was argued that the latter must be preferred. Bullshit is better defined by the intentions of a speaker. Moreover, we distinguished between negative and positive intentions, arriving at the following concept of bullshit: 'A linguistic interaction in which a speaker is detached from the commitment to discursively redeem the validity claims that she raises in the context of a particular inquiry pursuing to attain certain aims.'

Then, the chapter advocated for a morally grounded conception of legal cognitivism that we called 'pragmatic legal cognitivism'. Drawing on Forst's theory, I sustained that one of the components of the rule of law, the idea of a fair trial, can be understood as the institutionalisation of a basic moral right to justification. In virtue of this, arbitrary forms of settling legal disagreements are neutralised, the equal normative standing of human beings *qua* discursive creatures is respected, and the value of human dignity is honoured. This construction led us to sustain that it is pragmatically required to assume that there are right answers to legal disputes.

The final section dealt with the question that entitles this chapter: Is legal cognitivism a case of bullshit? Several possibilities were explored. In the end, we reached the conclusion that pragmatic legal cognitivism cannot be considered a case of bullshit. For assuming that there are right answers does not trigger the emergence of a commitment to take responsibility for the truth of what is assumed. Then, there is no commitment from which a speaker can be detached.

Let me close with a genealogical remark. In the early phases of this chapter, the intuition that drove its development was exactly the opposite: pragmatic legal cognitivism would be a case of bullshit. However, at a later stage, after having thought more deeply about the question and after having clarified some conceptual problems, I came to the conclusion I have defended in this final version. To be honest, I was of course tempted to keep the initial intuition. After all, stating that legal cognitivism is bullshit is without any doubt catchier. The problem, of course, is apparent: had I succumbed to this temptation, I would have transformed this chapter into a paradigmatic case of bullshit. It would have been a chapter written not with the intention of providing reasons for grounding certain claims, but rather would have resulted in a mere discursive farce, aimed at reaching a catchy conclusion. Instead of this, I opted for elaborating an argument that, although it may be less catchy, can genuinely claim to take part in the social practice of giving and asking for reasons.

4. Imputation as a supervenience in the General Theory of Norms[1]

Monika Zalewska

1. INTRODUCTION

The objectivity of jurisprudence has much in common with scientific objectivity, defined in general terms by Jaap Hage in Chapter 2. One of the main inquiries in the field of scientific objectivity concerns the construction of a concept of law which would be universal for any culture or time. This intention is explicitly expressed in Hans Kelsen's Normativism, and classified by Matti Ilmari Niemi in Chapter 6 as strong cognitive objectivity. Kelsen devoted his entire career to developing this project into a scientifically-objective legal science. Although his views on several elements of his theory changed during the course of its design, the general idea remained the same. His goal was to define the conditions for a theory of law which would reveal law as it is; that is to say, not law as it ought to be, nor law as interpreted from anything other than a strictly legal perspective. By doing so, Kelsen believed that his theory was able to describe any possible legal system, regardless of its cultural or social background. As such, the theory aspired to be scientifically objective. In its best-known version, the Pure Theory of Law, it develops the notion of scientific objectivity in a neo-Kantian framework in which legal science is made possible by the use of relative categories *a priori*, such as the basic norm or imputation. This view, however, is rejected in the *General Theory of Norms*, Kelsen's last book, in favour of a more analytical approach. As such, the question arises of whether the notion of scientific objectivity can be sustained in Kelsen's project, and most importantly, whether it can still be ensured by imputation.

Another question regarding objectivity in Kelsen's theory stems from the objective status of law, which Kelsen associates with the legal norm (norm as an objective meaning). Being objective, means that a norm is valid and legally

---

[1] This research has been financed by National Science Center, Poland in the framework of the research project no. 2021/41/BHS5/01174.

binding on everyone. Also, the addressees of the norms expect that they will be treated equally, that is, that under the same circumstances the same sanction will be imposed irrespective of the recipient. However, questions exist regarding what the kind of mechanism that underlies objectivity understood in this way. Why are legal norms binding in a way that, in an ideal situation, under the same circumstances the same consequences under the same circumstances should obtain? These inquiries potentially might cast light on the nature and solve the problem of imputation in Kelsen's last phase, at least to some extent.

The concept of imputation changed over time, and, with this change, so did its potential to ensure objectivity. This is particularly apparent in the final phase of Kelsen's work, signified by the book *General Theory of Norms*[2] (GTN). During this period, the description of imputation becomes vague in terms of its construction and the function it serves; however, while this can be perceived as an obstacle to establish objectivity, it can also represent an opportunity. The 'open texture' of Kelsen's last book leaves space for a more dynamic interpretation. I will use this opportunity to introduce the notion of supervenience as a bridge between norms and facts, and propose how taking the legal norm as objective meaning can foster the construction of a formal equality rule.

Hence, the aim of this chapter is to discuss the extent to which imputation is able to ensure objectivity. I will argue that imputation in GTN, as a relation of supervenience, can still form a relevant part of Kelsen's objectivity programme. The second section of the chapter discusses the problems of imputation in the GTN, by contrasting it with the neo-Kantian understanding. The third briefly explains the concept of supervenience, so that the possibility of imputation, as a relation of supervenience, can be discussed more fully in the fourth section. Finally, the fifth section will consider some consequences stemming from such an interpretation of imputation, especially the emergence of an equality rule from objectivity understood in terms of the norm as objective meaning.[3]

---

[2] Hans Kelsen, *General Theory of Norms* (Michael Hartney (trs), Clarendon Press, 1991).
[3] I would like to thank Carsten Heidemann for his valuable feedback and editing remarks.

2. PROBLEMS WITH IMPUTATION IN THE GENERAL THEORY OF NORMS

In the neo-Kantian phase, the concept of peripheral imputation was vital for Kelsen's Pure Theory of Law.[4] Imputation was theorised as a normative link distinguishing normative propositions from causal ones, and thus allowing legal norms to be cognised.[5] Hence, in the classical phase, Kelsen regarded imputation as an epistemological issue. The neo-Kantian paradigm justified such an understanding of imputation, assigning it the function of a relative category *a priori*. Just like in Kant's Critique of Pure Reason, where causality, as an *a priori* category, allowed empirical material to be ordered and cognised as phenomena, imputation puts alogical legal material into an order to be recognised as legal norms.[6] This mechanism assumes that causality and imputation are both links, albeit of different characters, between two types of fact, namely condition and consequence. While causality indicated a natural necessity, imputation serves as the Ought-connection between condition and consequence; as such, it can be regarded as normative necessity.

For instance:

Causality: If anyone heats water long enough, it must boil.

Imputation: If anyone steals, he ought to be punished.

Such a distinction seems to be a simple one, and yet it is also sophisticated. Two facts on the same level are bound by a link which determines whether they belong to the realm of Is or Ought. Hence, while the natural scientist uses causality to interpret observed phenomena, the lawyer uses imputation to consider two facts. With the neo-Kantian approach, this solution seems to provide a satisfactory explanation of the cognition of a norm, thus granting it objectivity.

A problem arises in the final phase of Kelsen's study. In GTN, Kelsen rejects the neo-Kantian paradigm, but he still maintains the concept of peripheral imputation. Therefore, the question arises: What is peripheral imputation, and what is its function in this final phase?

---

[4] Besides peripheral imputation, there is also central imputation which concerns the vertical aspect of law. This second type of imputation is not the subject of inquiry of this chapter.

[5] Hans Kelsen, *Pure Theory of Law* (Max Knight (trs), The Lawbook Exchange 1967) 89–91.

[6] Stanley L Paulson, 'The Neo-Kantian Dimension of Kelsen's Pure Theory of Law' (1992) 12 *Oxford Legal Studies* 323–24.

As stated before, imputation in GTN is defined as a link between two states of affairs, namely condition and consequence. In the Pure Theory of Law, according to the neo-Kantian paradigm, these states of affairs can be identified as two facts, and the normative link of imputation allows cognition of these facts to be associated with law. Since such an interpretation involving 'facts' in norms appears suspicious from the point of view of the separation between Is and Ought, a modally-indifferent substrate becomes either factual or normative depending on whether causality or imputation is involved. Kelsen defines it as follows:

> 'Is' and 'Ought' are two essentially different *modes*, two different forms, which can have two specific contents. In the statements that something is and that something ought to be, two different components must be distinguished: *that* something is and *that which* is, *that* something ought to be, and that *which* ought to be. That *which* is and *that which* ought to be, the content of the Is and the content of the Ought is a *modally indifferent substrate*.[7]

Unfortunately, the neo-Kantian interpretation of imputation is not possible in GTN, and Kelsen does not describe it in ATN as a relative category *a priori*. Hence, in order to function as a normative interpretation of a modal indifferent substrate, imputation requires more than just a neo-Kantian justification. This need raises the questions of the nature of imputation in GTN, and the kind of elements it links. It is therefore important to recall the core of the Pure Theory of Law, which attempts to describe the law in the most objective way possible. In the first words of his masterpiece, Kelsen writes:

> The Pure Theory of Law is a theory of positive law. It is a theory of positive law in general, not of a specific legal order. It is a general theory of law, not an interpretation of specific national or international legal norms (…) As a theory, its exclusive purpose is to know and to describe its object. The theory attempts to answer the question what and how the law *is*, not how it ought to be. It is a science of law (jurisprudence) not legal politics.[8]

Since law does not consist of empirical objects, which can be perceived by the senses, there must be another means of its cognition. It seems that the simplest answer which Kelsen provides for the question, 'what is law' is the answer 'law is what lawyers perceive as law', or in other words, Kelsen reconstructs how lawyers think. One could ask why the perception of lawyers should be important and not that of society as a whole. It seems that Kelsen's scientifically-oriented ('*Rechtslehre*') approach addressed a narrower per-

---

[7] Kelsen (n 2) 60.
[8] Kelsen (n 5) 1.

spective, that of professionals, or rather, people with the highest awareness of the complex phenomenon of law. Kelsen seems to claim that if there is any objectivity in the concept of law, this objectivity can only exist in the sphere of legal science (*Rechtslehre*), where there is agreement among lawyers about fundamental features of law. Laypeople typically lack the specific knowledge needed to grasp this phenomenon correctly and profoundly, even though they experience law each day. Similarly, although everyone knows what a tree is, only a biologist can explain the complex processes ruling its lifespan in a scientific way. Hence, in order to understand the phenomenon of law, it is necessary to reconstruct the thinking process of the lawyers.

While such an explanation was provided by the neo-Kantian paradigm in the Pure Theory of Law, this paradigm is absent in GTN, and the only potentially objective reconstruction of law is the one derived directly from the question, 'how do lawyers think?' Therefore, imputation should also provide an answer to this question, and it should play an important function as an indicator of modality. However, when deprived of its neo-Kantian background, this interpretation is accompanied by certain problems. The first one concerns the influence of imputation on this normative link, insofar that it is not clear how the link comes about. For example, we can change 'imputation' to 'X' and say that we perceive two states of affairs as normative because X makes this transformation possible. It would be reasonable to ask how X could do this, and in such cases, a possible answer would be 'X uses a', 'X works on behalf of a', or 'X works by virtue of a'.[9]

This example highlights two problems associated with this kind of interpretation of imputation in GTN. First, without its neo-Kantian background, imputation is an empty category. Since the concept of imputation does not identify the enabling condition 'a', a more complete explanation could be

---

[9] The latter formulation might suggest grounding as a possible link between legal condition and legal consequence. This possibility requires an extended discussion, however. In our initial, unpublished research with Carsten Heidemann (C Heidemann, M Zalewska, Grounding in Hans Kelsen's Neo-Kantian Theory of Law, presented during *International Seminar on Hans Kelsen 2021* organised by Institute of Legal Research of the National Autonomous University of Mexico) we argue that in the neo-Kantian paradigm, imputation cannot be considered as grounding since the factivity condition is unfulfilled: condition and consequence have a hypothetical character. On the other hand, in GTN, even if condition and consequence are treated as facts, their relationship is asynchronous; this is also not in line with a definition of grounding. However, more research on this matter is required. An argument that imputation could possibly play a vital role for grounding relation between law and facts is given in: George Pavlakos, 'A Non-Naturalist Account of Law's Place in Reality' in Bartosz Brożek, Jaap Hage and Nicole Vincent (eds), *Law and Mind: A Survey of Law and the Cognitive Sciences* (Cambridge University Press 2021) 473–89.

offered, for example, by identifying 'X' as a fairy and 'a' as magic; this would be a blatantly false theory but at least a more complete one. Furthermore, while imputation was regarded as a relative category *a priori* in the neo-Kantian paradigm, all we know about imputation outside this framework is that it is 'something' which directs our thoughts into the normative sphere. Deprived of its neo-Kantian attribute, imputation seems to be superfluous, since a similar but primary function is assigned to the basic norm. In the case of the theory of the basic norm, 'as if' is introduced as Vaihinger's theory of fictions in this last phase of Kelsen's writings. Namely, Kelsen claims that the basic norm is rather a fiction than hypothesis.

Hence, in GTN, imputation lost most of the functions of norm cognition typical of the neo-Kantian version of imputation. Although imputation could explain the mechanism behind the cognition of norms, this is not elaborated. Kelsen just states that this is what imputation does, without explaining why. Therefore, the mechanism for distinguishing the normative from the causal domain by imputation has yet to be explained, which is not possible in the epistemological sphere. In this sphere, imputation exists rather as a consequence of employing the basic norm. Therefore, if imputation is of little use in the cognition of norms, then one could ask which function it has. My claim is that imputation, when interpreted as supervenience, explains how lawyers think, and reveals some of the hidden elements of the general concept of law common among lawyers, such as formal equality, which ensures some type of objectivity inherent to law.

Hence, this chapter argues for the existence of a fruitful interpretation of the concept of imputation which solves the two problems presented above. However, the interpretation offered in the following paragraphs requires a new element to be added to Kelsen's theory, namely supervenience and justifies its introduction, considering its absence from the original version.

3. THE RELATION OF SUPERVENIENCE

Although Kelsen perceived the separation of Is and Ought to be a basic epistemological assumption, it seems to be radical only on this level. In order to *cognise* law 'as it is', one needs to separate it from other 'alien' phenomena, particularly facts. For this reason, Kelsen dubbed his theory of law 'pure'. However, in reality, links exist between law and facts, and Kelsen does not deny it, mentioning 'bridging principles', for instance.[10] I will dub this level 'ontological', following Jerzy Wróblewski's distinction between epistemo-

---

[10] E.g., 'ought implies can', or competence norms.

logical, ontological and logical levels of the Is-Ought separation.[11] Hence, since some dependency-relations exist between law and facts, it is important to determine the relationship between Is and Ought on the ontological level.

A similar question is discussed by legal positivists.[12] In their case, the link between law and fact is strong, and they consider three possible candidates which could define the relationship between law and facts: reduction, supervenience, and grounding. Of these, supervenience is frequently rejected as being too weak for defining the strong relationship between law and fact. But in Kelsen's case, this disadvantage can be regarded as a benefit, because it allows for the logical separation of Is and Ought while yet being able to account for the relationship between them.

Supervenience is a relationship believed to exist in the fields of ontology and metaphysics. One of the first attempts of grasping this relationship was made by R M Hare, who provided the following example:

> First let us take that characteristic of 'good' which has been called its supervenience. Suppose that we say 'St. Francis was a good man.' It is logically impossible to say thus and to maintain at the same time that there might have been another man placed exactly in the same circumstances as St. Francis and who behaved in exactly the same way but who differed from St. Francis in this respect only that he was not a good man.[13]

The other well-known example is the relationship between a piece of art and a forgery. Provided that all physical features of the forgery are exactly the same as the physical features of the piece of art, it can be said that the distribution of colours and shapes of the piece of art supervene on the microscopic features of the piece of art. The same microscopic features of the piece of art guarantee that the distribution of shades and colours will be alike in both cases.[14] Finally,

---

[11] Jerzy Wróblewski, *Krytyka Normatywistycznej Teorii Prawa i Państwa Hansa Kelsena* (Państwowe Wydawnictwo Naukowe 1955).

[12] Tomasz Gizbert-Studnicki, 'The Social Sources Thesis. Metaphysics and Metaphilosophy' in Pawel Banaś, Adam Dyrda and Tomasz Gizbert-Studnicki (eds), *Metaphilosophy of Law* (Hart 2016) 121–46.

[13] Richard Hare, *The Language of Morals* (Oxford University Press 1991) 145.

[14] Brian McLaughlin and Karen Bennett, 'Supervenience', in Edward N Zalta (ed), *The Stanford Encyclopedia of Philosophy*, (Spring 2018 Metaphysics Research Lab, Stanford University, 2018), https://plato.stanford.edu/archives/spr2018/entries/supervenience/ accessed 21 June 2022.

the problem of supervenience was elaborated by Jaegwon Kim,[15] who defined supervenience based on the following formulae:

> There is no difference in A without a difference in B

and

> A weakly supervenes on B if, and only if, necessarily for any x and y if x and y share all properties in B then x and y share all properties in A – that is, indiscernibility with respect to B entails indiscernibility with respect to A.

Based on this definition of supervenience and the examples provided, it can be observed that the qualities in set A (e.g., being a good man) are qualities of a higher level than those in B (e.g., being brave, kind, etc.). In Kelsen's case, there are also potentially two levels: the more basic Is-level (B), and the higher or more complex Ought-level (A). Such a framework is in accordance with the ontological dimension, in which some form of dependency exists between Is and Ought. The distinction between the epistemological and the ontological level could also refer to imputation: while on the epistemological level, imputation links two states of affairs of a hypothetical nature, on the ontological level, it links the fact of breaking a law with a consequence, on the normative level of Ought.

The introduction of supervenience to the theory rests on two assumptions: First, its introduction does not contradict the basic principles of Kelsen's theory; secondly, it does not deprive the theory of its coherence. Furthermore, if it does lose some coherence at some point, this reduction should be compensated by a gain in coherence at another point of the theory instead. Although it will be determined later whether imputation as supervenience is coherent with Kelsen's GTN, it can be stated at this initial point that the introduction of supervenience is believed to grant greater coherence to the theory of imputation.

Furthermore, it is important to bear in mind that Kelsen left his last book unfinished, and as such, it is not unreasonable to assume that there may be room for new elements to be added. There is no certainty how GTN would look if Kelsen himself had completed it, and as such, his final text is more open to a dynamic interpretation than his older books. This is not the first attempt at a dynamic interpretation of Kelsen. Bulygin and Alchourrón,[16] for example,

---

[15] Jaegwon Kim, *Supervenience and Mind: Selected Philosophical Essays* (Cambridge University Press 1993) 58.

[16] Carlos E Alchourrón and Eugenio Bulygin, 'The Expressive Conception of Norms', in Stanley L Paulson (ed), *Normativity and Norms* (Oxford University Press 1998) 383–410.

present an expressive conception of norms which coherently explains the rejection of a logic of norms in GTN. The addition of such a new element brings added value to the theory, because it can better explain the idea of law than the original theory. Hence, rather than speculating on Kelsen's intentions, the next steps of this chapter will provide an interpretation of his theory which enriches the understanding of law.

The following section will test the hypothesis that, when properly interpreted, the concept of imputation is itself an example of supervenience. This part will also elaborate the difficulties with imputation described in Section 2, and indicate the elements which imputation should bind. Neither is this an exclusive interpretation of imputation, nor is it a reconstruction of what Kelsen meant. It is important to note that this interpretation requires the introduction of a different concept of imputation to that prevailing in GTN, i.e., the link in a hypothetical judgement. This new concept relates a fact and a normative element, thus constituting a weak link between them; however, this link is weak enough to maintain the integrity of Kelsen's claim about the Is-Ought separation on the epistemological level. In the following sections it will be demonstrated that the proposed solution can be more serviceable in confronting the mentioned problems than the standard approach. As such, the understanding of imputation offered in the present chapter is a reaction to the doubts presented above, and it serves as a possible solution to them; it also potentially brings added value to Kelsen's theory without contradicting Kelsen's main intention.

4. IMPUTATION IN GTN AS A SUPERVENIENCE RELATION

Hence, in this section, imputation is to be interpreted as supervenience. This requires imputation to be analysed in the ontological sphere rather than the epistemological one. Before this solution can be applied, one issue should be solved. As epistemological analyses attempt to describe the process of thinking, while ontological ones focus on the structure of law, it could be questioned whether imputation exists on the ontological level at all. In the neo-Kantian phase, imputation was regarded as having a mostly epistemological dimension, merged with the ontological one; this was based on the conviction that the method of cognition constitutes its object. However, I propose that in GTN, the presence of imputation on the epistemological level can be understood only as a reflection of its existence on the ontological level, and that the key element allowing the recognition of the normative aspect is that the basic norm is fictional. Furthermore, the presence of a basic norm implies that the normative link exists on the epistemological level, connecting two modal indifferent substrates. Yet, on this level, imputation does not much further knowledge.

Without a sound ontological background, it would be difficult to justify the occurrence of imputation on the epistemological level. As the same normative mechanism links two elements, *viz.* condition and consequence, on the ontological level, it should be possible to explain the ratio and the function of imputation by ontological analysis. As imputation originally links two modally indifferent states of affairs on the epistemological level, thus granting them normative meaning, inquiries about the structure of imputation are valid on the ontological level. More precisely, these inquiries address the question of how to determine which two elements defined as condition and consequence are linked.

The set of conditions is limited to a group of elements starting from the fact of breaking the law (X stole a car), involving legal procedures for the first time (the moment of admitting the legal dimension of the case), or filing the act of prosecution to the court (the moment when the imputation must occur in the future). It seems uncontroversial to choose the first factual moment as a condition, i.e., X stealing a car, as this event initiates the entire procedure and the involvement of the law.

The introduction of an ontological level of analysis makes sense if imputation adds some knowledge of law to Kelsen's theory. In order to identify the proper element from the set of consequences, one must ask what precedes the fact of putting X in prison? I argue elsewhere that the element in question is empowerment,[17] understood by Kelsen as 'conferring on an individual the power to posit and apply the norms'.[18] Empowerment is the key ingredient in creating the objective meaning of a norm, thus turning it into a legal norm:[19] this can only be done by an empowered individual.[20] Additionally, this function of empowerment makes it possible to distinguish the legal norm from an order issued by a gunman in a bank. Kelsen notes that without empowerment, most acts of coercion would be regarded as crimes.[21] As Kelsen notes in GTN, in the case of empowerment being used to apply the law, the act of empowerment has the character of a command. The judge is obliged to impose a general norm on a particular case.[22] The act of putting X in prison is a consequence of the normative sphere in motion, as is the empowerment of court to impose

---

[17] Monika Zalewska, 'Objectivity and Hans Kelsen's Concept of Imputation', in Andre F Leite de Paula, Andres Santacoloma Santacoloma and Gonzalo Villa-Rosas (eds), *Truth and Objectivity in law and Morals II* (2016) 151 *ARSP/B* 147–64.
[18] Kelsen (n 2) 102.
[19] Stanley L Paulson, 'An Empowerment Theory of Legal Norms' (1988) 1 *Ratio Juris* 18.
[20] Kelsen (n 2) 102.
[21] Ibid.
[22] Ibid., 103.

a sanction on X. Hence, in this interpretation, imputation would not link the condition, understood as the fact of breaking a law, with a consequence, understood as a consequence foreseen by law for X; instead, the condition would rather be linked with the empowerment of the organ to impose the sanction. Hence, the formula would be as follows:

X stole a car, therefore the competent organ ought to impose a sanction on X

This interpretation is coherent with Kelsen's explanation of primary and secondary norms,[23] where the secondary norm states that, for example, 'One shall not steal', while the primary norm states that if one steals then one ought to be punished. In traditional positivistic doctrine and in morality, the order was reversed. The primary norm was that 'one shall not steal', and consequently, the secondary norm referred to the obligation of punishing the offender. This solution, though, had no power to distinguish a legal order from a moral one, because primary moral norms and primary legal norms would share the same structure. With the order reversed by Kelsen, and with the primary norm now containing the empowerment of the organ to impose a sanction, however, it is possible to distinguish the legal order from the moral order. This is due to the quality of the moral order, which does not have an institutional component.[24] In this construction, it is important that the accent is not placed on sanction but on the organ empowered to impose the sanction; if this were not the case, the reversed order alone could not be used to distinguish law from morality due to the fact that sanctions can also occur in a moral order. Only the institutionalisation of the sanction can make the difference, and the institutional character of a sanction depends on the empowerment of the organ. To conclude, the consequence, linked by imputation, to the condition is the empowerment of the organ to impose the sanction. Having identified condition and consequence, it can be seen that imputation links the factual realm (X stole a car) with the normative realm (the organ is empowered to impose the sanction).

Having identified the two elements linked by imputation, we can now move to the central issue concerning the nature of imputation. Are there any rules governing imputation, or, to put it in other words, what kind of thought process is used while thinking about the connection between condition and consequence in law? Supervenience can potentially be employed to bind elements of orders from different levels. The advantage of this relationship is that it is sufficiently weak as not to impair the separation of Is and Ought. As was noted before, the definition of supervenience runs as follows: There is no difference in A without any difference in B, where A is a set of features of

---

[23] Zalewska (n 17).
[24] Kelsen (n 2) 142–43.

a higher level and B is a set of features of a more basic level. Hence, A is a set of consequences (empowerment to impose a sanction S), while B will be a set of conditions (the fact of breaking a law).

It follows that, from the rule 'There is no difference in A without a difference in B', two formulas can be derived:

If the properties in A are different, the properties in B are different.

If the properties in B are the same, the properties in A are the same.

This general formula can be transformed into two imputation rules:

If the consequences (A) are different, the conditions (B) are different.

If the conditions (B) are the same, the consequences (A) are the same.

Hence, if the consequences (imposition of different sanctions) differ between two cases, then the conditions (the circumstances of breaking the law) are also different, and if the conditions (circumstance of breaking the law) are the same, the consequences (imposition of the sanction) are also the same. These two rules of imputation bring added value to Kelsen's theory, namely the rule of equality.

One could object that, in reality, different judges issue different rulings in similar cases. However, Kelsen's theory is of a general character and describes the norms on a general level. Hence, it partly describes idealised situations which can be grasped in the concept of Weberian ideal type broadly discussed by Donald Bello Hutt in Chapter 5. Such an approach is valuable, because by describing the general concept of law it is possible to identify anomalies, especially malfunctioning legal systems. One could object that this introduces a normative element to Kelsen's theory,[25] depriving it of its theoretical character; but then many theories from the empirical sciences could also be regarded as normative. For example, a general concept of a human being can be presented based on the enthymematic assumption that a human being is in full health when all organs are working properly. From a scientific perspective, it would be problematic to formulate a general theory of X focusing on anomalies of X, for example, by holding that a human being has lungs where cancer might occur. A general theory allows the constitutive form, the ideal type, to be distinguished from the anomaly, and as such it is a part of knowledge.

However, to define an anomaly, it is necessary to first define constitutive general form, understood as an ideal type; this is valid for both empirical theories and for social theories. Hence, imputation does not explain how law

---

[25] I would like to thank Clemens Jabloner for directing my attention to this problem.

functions in practice, but rather its general idea, i.e., what lawyers consider law to be. Hence, by interpreting imputation as a supervenience relation, it is possible to derive the equality rule. The following section will discuss the possibility of introducing the category of equality to GTN by interpreting imputation as supervenience. Furthermore, it will address the question of whether the objectivity of legal science can be rescued, should imputation lose its epistemic function.

5. THE EQUALITY RULE IN THE GENERAL THEORY OF NORMS?

It has yet to be examined whether, and how, imputation can contribute to objectivity in Kelsen's Pure Theory. It seems that imputation contributed to scientific objectivity in the neo-Kantian phase in a similar way as Kantian's categories *a priori* contributed to objective cognition. However, when the neo-Kantian paradigm was rejected by Kelsen, this function of imputation became doubtful. My claim is that, despite this doubt, imputation still ensures objectivity, but it does so in a different way than in the neo-Kantian period; in addition, such objectivity is associated with the concept of formal equality, which can be derived from the notion of supervenience.

At first glance, the concept of equality as a component of the Pure Theory of Law might not accord with Kelsen's intention to create a 'pure' theory of law, which is separate from morality and of formal character. In a sense, equality resembles an ethical postulate referring to the content of law, and as such, the equality principle seems to breach two fundamental assumptions of Kelsen's theory. Namely, it impairs the separation of law and morality and voids the formal character of the theory. However, there are two arguments which are able to provide a justification for assuming the principle of equality in law, even in the framework of the pure theory of law. The first refers to the distinction between *a priori* and *a posteriori*, while the second refers to the idea of law.

The distinction between *a priori* and *a posteriori* concerns the problem of the origin of the equality principle as part of law. Namely, if the equality principle is formulated *a priori* as a fundamental aspect of law, then it would be correct to say that it could impair the purity of Kelsen's theory. In such a case, equality would be perceived as a pre-existing value on which the concept of law is built. However, if equality were to be inferred *a posteriori* from supervenience, i.e., inferred from the analysis of the categories characteristic for Kelsen's theory of norms, it would arise as a consequence of the theory, rather than its underpinning. In the latter case, the concept of law is not derived from the equality principle, but rather the equality principle is derived from the concept of law.

The second argument recalls the idea of law and concerns the question of how lawyers think about law as a general concept. Do they include the equality rule in this concept, or does perhaps the equality rule bring greater benefits than morality? First, equality does not bring any guarantee that an identical, if indeed any, punishment will result from the same deeds; this hence, sustains the formal character of Kelsen's theory. Secondly, contrary to morality, law brings some predictability, i.e., it shows what can be expected if certain rules are broken. Namely, in an ideal situation, there should be absolute certainty about the sanction (and the degree of its severity) for breaking the law. This thought is embodied in the concept of imputation as supervenience, which implies the equality rule; hence, it can be argued that in the general concept of law, the equality rule is indeed implemented.

Finally, it is worth comparing such a concept of equality with Kelsen's view. Kelsen claimed that rules regarded as equality should not be understood as such. For Kelsen, the existence of an 'equality rule' means that legal organs should not introduce their own differentiations in cases which are not foreseen by law. For instance, if a law treats men and women in an equal way, judges should not differentiate between them. Instead of equality, Kelsen postulates that it is more gainful to discuss the idea of *conformity* with a law.[26]

Such an understanding of equality is weaker than that offered in the context of supervenience. The general legal norms are vague and do not include all circumstances. Therefore, even though two different cases may share several features, two judicial decisions deriving from them may differ; this would be in line with the general character of the legal norm, which does not consider all circumstances. Hence, a line can be drawn between the category of conformity with the law and the equality rule, which not only demands conformity with the law, but also that the same ruling is elicited by the same circumstances, regardless of whether the ruling is just or right. Thus, the equality rule inferred from supervenience is of a stronger character; however, since it neither introduces normative or substantial elements nor moral ones, as was argued above, it remains coherent with Kelsen's theory and can be regarded as offering added value to Kelsen's understanding of law. The incorporation of the equality rule suggests that perhaps the core of the formal idea of law, separated from morality, contains the principle of equality.

Equality could be regarded as part of the DNA of law, and if understood as deriving from supervenience, it would grant law objectivity in its application. Such an understanding would ensure that everyone in the same circumstances will be confronted with the same consequences. This, in turn, would mean that the law is binding to everyone, and hence valid, and that a legal norm is a norm

---

[26] Hans Kelsen, *Was ist Gerechtigkeit?* (Reclam, 2016) 40.

with an objective meaning. Such objective meaning can in turn only be recognised by anyone, who takes part in the game of law, because the basic norm, despite its fictional character,[27] ensures that the legal system is valid, and hence exists as law. This way, imputation finds its justified place in the objectivity program of legal science, i.e., on the ontological level. Scientific objectivity (cognitive objectivity) associated with the epistemological level is, in this framework, ensured by the basic norm. By the same interpretation, imputation on the epistemological level is substantially weakened and is dependent on the basic norm.

6. CONCLUDING REMARKS

The aim of this chapter was to provide an understanding of the concept of imputation in Kelsen's last book, *General Theory of Norms*. It does not provide a historical reconstruction of Kelsen's thought, but rather a dynamic interpretation of his theory which is potentially able to provide a better comprehension of imputation in GTN. This book almost completely rejected the neo-Kantian paradigm, leaving imputation, its component role, as an empty category. The reinterpretation of imputation as supervenience not only solves this problem, revealing the basic rules of how lawyers think, but also brings added value by exhibiting a hidden quality of law: its formal equality. Formal equality is coherent with Kelsen's theory because it is inferred *a posteriori* from existing elements in law, but with the addition of supervenience. The analysis of imputation as supervenience can potentially introduce a new dimension to the broadly-understood positivistic vision of law, one in which the conception of equality finds its place and ensures the objectivity of the addressees of the norm. The cognitive objectivity is ensured by basic norm.

---

[27] If interpreted in the same terms as fictions in science, the basic norm still contributes to the legal science project in the same manner as Maxwell's ether contributed to the development of electrodynamics. See, e.g., Paul Teller, 'Fictions, Fictionalization, and Truth in Science', in Mauricio Suárez (ed) *Fictions in Science: Philosophical Essays on Modeling and Idealization* (Routledge 2008) 243–55.

5. Social science and jurisprudence through Weberian and Hartian eyes: Suggesting an explanation for a puzzle[1]

Donald Bello Hutt

1. INTRODUCTION

Can there be an objective, i.e., value-free knowledge of law or legal phenomena? Anglo-Saxon legal positivists argue in the affirmative. They are committed to the mantra that knowledge of law is one thing, its moral correctness is another.[2]

And yet, objectivity is a category that is not of the exclusive domain of legal positivism. Hart must have had this in mind when he invited lawyers, first, to read *The Concept of Law* as an 'essay in analytical jurisprudence' and then (to other readers, perhaps?) as 'an essay in descriptive sociology',[3] as well.

It is obvious, I think, that one should not take Hart's invitation as giving up on the specificity and distinctiveness of jurisprudence as an intellectual endeavour. What is less obvious, and what Hart was ultimately not explicit about, is the extent to which social science might be auxiliary in the quest for the objective knowledge of law and legal phenomena. More concretely, Hart

---

[1] I have benefited greatly from comments by two good friends at the Tarello Institute for Legal Philosophy. I thank Natalia Scavuzzo for her time and her criticisms of an earlier version of this manuscript. I also thank Guillaume Robertson for his time, comments and very helpful suggestions. The usual disclaimer applies: all errors in this chapter are mine only.

[2] There is no need to provide here a comprehensive list of all the scholars accepting that this thesis is a shared element in the definition of legal positivism. See, for example, John Austin, *The Province of Jurisprudence Determined* (first published 1832, Cambridge University Press 1995) 157; John Gardner, *Law as a Leap of Faith* (Oxford University Press 2012) 20; Matthew Kramer, *Where Law and Morality Meet* (Oxford University Press 2004) 13, 223.

[3] H L A Hart, *The Concept of Law* (first published 1961, Clarendon Press 2012) vi.

was not explicit about the degree to which, if at all, Max Weber's methodological writings served his theoretical purposes. Some important Hartian categories, however, smack of Weberian insights. My contribution to this volume revolves around this problem.

Hence, I here contrast Hart's ruminations on the fact-value distinction and on the concomitant participant/observer-internal/external-point-of-view divides (which are central to the concern of legal positivism with objectivity) with Max Weber's take on the notion of objectivity in social sciences. Hart was reluctant to admit any influence of the German sociologist in his elaboration of these categories, but, things are more complex than what largely bibliographical remarks made by some commentators suggest (section 2). After positioning this problem in the map of the secondary literature, I shall take my cue from Brian Leiter's critique of Finnis' claim that the knowledge of legal phenomena requires the use of practical reason, and that this take was first advanced by Weber. Leiter's critique is important, but there are Weberian insights which could be of more value for positivists than what Leiter's discussion allow (section 3).

The suggested explanation to which my title alludes is the following: Hart's reluctance to admit Weber as a relevant influence, is (or could be) explained due to an important difference in the ways in which both authors sought to maintain the distinctiveness of their disciplines, and on how they understood the nature or features of participants and their role in examining the object under scrutiny. Although Weber's social scientist participates in the selection and conceptual framing of the scientific object according to her values and/or culture, she takes a larger distance with regard to it than some prominent Hartian participants, i.e., officials, do in the determination of what counts or not as law or legal. In a nutshell, although both authors would agree that no knowledge is 'presuppositionless', Weberian social scientists do not 'bring about' their object in the same way that Hartian officials identify and create law (section 4).

This leads to a conclusion that is dependent upon an exegetical reading of *The Concept of Law*: Hart's hypothetical acceptance of a Weberian influence would have been to an important extent incompatible with his methodological commitment to descriptivism (section 5).

2. THE QUANDARY: HART'S RELUCTANCE

The question whether it is possible to have an objective grasp of legal phenomena that is independent of normative desiderata hinges on the reliance on the prior and fundamental philosophical distinction between facts and values.

The divide is well-known, at least since Hume's bewilderment at the sudden change in the ways some authors argued in his days, moving from the 'ordinary way of reasoning, ... [was, and was not]'⁴ to the use of deontic propositions without additional intermediate premises linking both domains. Moreover, legal positivists claim to be continuing the tradition inaugurated by Bentham, to whom the distinction between the characters of the *Censor* and the *Expositor* was central to legal studies. Accordingly:

> [t]o the province of the *Expositor* it belongs to explain to us what, as he supposes, the *Law is*: to that of the *Censor*, to observe to us what he thinks it *ought to be*. The former, therefore, is principally occupied in stating, or in enquiring after *facts* ... To the *Expositor* it belongs to shew what the Legislator and his underworkman the *Judge* have done already: to the *Censor* it belongs to suggest what the *Legislator* ought to do *in future*.⁵

Both spheres are not to be conflated. Bentham reminds us in one of the many footnotes in the *Fragments,* that:

> the question of *Law* has often been spoken of as opposed to that of *fact*: but this distinction is an accidental one. That a Law commanding or prohibiting such a sort of action, has been established, is as much a *fact*, as that an *individual* action of that sort has been committed.⁶

As is well known, Hart took this distinction seriously as well,⁷ and in a moment, I shall present some of his views on the matter. But, before I proceed, I want to concentrate on a different, prominent and influential account in the social sciences that also relies strongly on the facts/value divide, and which has been nonetheless largely neglected by, at least, and as far as my knowledge goes, Anglo-Saxon legal positivists and others generally following that tradition. That is, Max Weber's.

Weber's take on objectivity and on the facts/values divide was most systematically expounded in a 1904 partly co-authored essay introducing the editorial policies of the new editorial board of the *Archiv fur Sozialwissenschaft und Social politik*. Before Weber took over as its chief editor, the *Archiv* was known as the *Journal of Social Legislation and Statistics* and was dedicated to elaborating value-laden analyses of social legislation enacted by the German parliament, with a view to improving the German political system. Weber saw

---

⁴ David Hume, *A Treatise of Human Nature* (first published 1896, Oxford 2018).
⁵ Jeremy Bentham, *A Fragment on Government* (first published 1756, Cambridge 1988) 7–8.
⁶ Ibid. Also, in his *Introduction to the Principles of Morals and Legislation* (first published 1789, Dover 2007) 323.
⁷ See, e.g., H L A Hart, 'Introduction' in *Essays on Bentham* (OUP 1982); 'The Demystification of Law' in *Essays on Bentham* (OUP 1982); 'Positivism, Law, and Morals' in *Essays in Jurisprudence and Philosophy* (OUP 1983) 50–51.

this as problematic and sought to take the journal in the direction of clearly distinguishing 'social policy' as a distinctive scientific endeavour from evaluative and normative assessments of proposals of social reforms. The conflation between "existential knowledge', i.e., knowledge of what 'is', and 'normative knowledge,' i.e., knowledge of what 'should be',[8] was to be avoided.

Weber also developed the point elsewhere and in different contexts. Consider, for example the following quote:

> But in no case, however, should the unresolvable question – unresolvable because it is ultimately a question of evaluation – as to whether one may, must, or should champion certain practical values in teaching, be confused with the purely logical discussion of the relationship of value-judgments to empirical disciplines such as sociology or economics. Any confusion on this point will impede the thoroughness of the discussion of the actual logical problem. Its solution will, however, not give any directives for answering the other question beyond two purely logical requirements, namely: clarity and explicit separation of the different types of problems.[9]

Similarities are undeniable. And yet, Weber's influence on Hart has not been properly theorised. It has only been mentioned in some important works, albeit largely in biographical terms. MacCormick briefly avers that when he met Hart at Oxford, the latter was enthusiastic about Weber's work, but that his knowledge of the German sociologist had been hitherto indirect. MacCormick's only theoretical comment is that:

> [w]hen Hart ascribes to sociologists the job of *external* description of legal orders, he is presumably referring to Weber's view that the sociologist is not directly concerned with a normative interpretation of the law, but with the probability that people in society will respond in certain ways to *their own* normative interpretation of the law.[10]

Lacey briefly discusses Weber's possible influence on Hart. However, after a fleeting discussion of the criticisms to which *The Concept of Law* was subjected by social scientists, he recognises that Hart's caveat that his was fundamentally a philosophical reflection and not a sociological project proper 'was clear, if unlikely to satisfy the critics'.[11] Notwithstanding, Lacey is adamant that there is an interesting question about the influence of sociology on Hart's

---

[8] Max Weber, "Objectivity" in Social Science and Social Policy' in *The Methodology of the Social Sciences* (first published in 1904, The Free Press 1949) 51.

[9] Max Weber, 'The Meaning of "Ethical Neutrality" in *The Methodology of the Social Sciences* (first published in 1917, The Free Press 1949) 8-9.

[10] Neil MacCormick, *H.L.A. Hart* (Stanford 2008) 43. Emphasis in the original.

[11] Nicola Lacey, *A Life of H.L.A. Hart: The Nightmare and the Noble Dream* (OUP 2006) 230.

work. In this context, he narrates the anecdote that when Finnis had consulted Hart's copy of *Max Weber on Law in Economy and Society*, he found it to be heavily marked and side-noted. Finnis asked Hart on two different occasions about the influence Weber may have had on his work. Hart replied that it had none, and that his idea of the 'internal aspect of rules' derived from Winch's *The Idea of a Social Science* instead.[12] Yet, Lacey points out that notwithstanding Hart's denial, his annotations 'strongly suggest that there was a Weberian undertowing in *The Concept of Law*'.[13] Lacey arrives at this conclusion from Hart's markings and annotations to Weber's discussion on the validity and legitimacy of an order, as derived from its subjects' orientation towards the order's maxims in ways that they regard as obligatory or exemplary.

As helpful as it is for my purposes here, Lacey's discussion does not shed enough light on the extent to which Weber's theses could have for understanding Hart in a philosophically relevant or interesting way. Hart's reluctance to recognise Weber as an influence remains intriguing.

Now consider John Finnis:

> [T]he evaluations of the theorist himself are an indispensable and decisive component in the selection or formation of any concepts for use in description of such aspects of human affairs as law or legal order. For the theorist cannot identify the central case of that practical viewpoint [the internal point of view] which he uses to identify the central case of his subject-matter, unless he decides what the requirements of practical reasonableness really are, in relation to this whole aspect of human affairs and concerns. In relation to law, the most important thing for the theorist to know and describe are the things which, in the judgment of the theorist, make it important from a *practical* viewpoint to have law.[14]

Finnis affirms to have arrived at this insight through Max Weber, and this partly means to him that descriptive jurisprudence is, 'inevitably subject to every theorist's conceptions and prejudices about what is good and practically reasonable ... if [it is] to be more than a vast rubbish heap of miscellaneous facts described in a multitude of incommensurable terminologies'.[15]

This is more theoretically substantive and helpful for my purposes. However, Finnis' remarks in the quote above have been harshly criticised by Leiter. I will dedicate some space here to reproducing the critique for it paves my way out of this literature review and into the upcoming sections.

---

[12] Peter Winch, *The Idea of a Social Science* (Routledge & Kegan Paul 1958).
[13] Lacey (n 11), 230.
[14] John Finnis, *Natural Law and Natural Rights* (first published 1980, OUP 2007) 17.
[15] Ibid.

Leiter rebuffs Finnis (and by extension, Perry,[16] Postema,[17] and Stavropoulos in an unpublished manuscript) for incurring in a non-sequitur in the transcribed passage above, which occurs in the slide from what he refers to as the 'Banal Truth' that 'evaluations ... are an indispensable and decisive component in the selection or formation of any concepts for use in description of such aspects of human affairs as law or legal order' to the claim that the evaluation in question involves deciding 'what the requirements of practical reasonableness really are'.[18] In Leiter's view, the 'banal truth' is insufficient to ground Finnis' claim that the 'presuppositions of the descriptive enterprise require judgments about [practical reasonableness and] that the viewpoint from which "importance" and "significance" are assessed is the "practical viewpoint".[19]

To prove his point, Leiter invites us to distinguish between *epistemic values* and *moral values,* the first of which he sees as necessary and sufficient for the demarcation of 'legal phenomena for purposes of jurisprudential enquiry'.[20] By contrast, Leiter tells us, moral values play no role in such endeavour.

This distinction is useful. Yet it is problematic in two ways: first, the 'banal truth' seems in fact too banal. The content he ascribes to it does not exhaust what Weber meant to communicate in his discussion of the separation of facts and values. Second, in order to apply his distinction between moral and epistemic values, Leiter asks us to consider an analogy which I think falls short of disproving Finnis' insight on this point. Note that I am not saying Finnis is right. Rather I want to convey that Leiter's critique falls short of disproving Finnis, and that this has consequences for whether it is possible to read Hart through Weberian lenses.

Consider, first, Leiter's brief footnote on Finnis' use of Weberian insights about the idea that the theorists' evaluations are indispensable in the selection and understanding of any concept such as law and legal orders. This, in Finnis' view, corresponds to Weber's notion of *ideal-types*.[21] Yet, Leiter avers, '[this invocation] may be misplaced'. Based on the insights by two commentators, Leiter affirms in his footnote that there is nothing normative or evaluative

---

[16] Stephen Perry, 'Interpretation and Methodology in Legal Theory' in Andrei Marmor (ed.) *Law and Interpretation* (OUP 1995).
[17] Gerald Postema, 'Jurisprudence as Practical Philosophy' (1998) 4 *Legal Theory* 329.
[18] Brian Leiter, *Naturalizing Jurisprudence: Essays on American Legal Realism and Naturalism in Legal Philosophy* (OUP 2007) 167.
[19] Ibid., 168.
[20] Ibid.
[21] Finnis (n 14), 9.

about the word 'ideal' in the term 'ideal-types'. Ideal-types, as defined by him are

> models, that abstract from certain particulars, and focus on theoretically illuminating features of varied situations; they are, as Weber puts it, 'a technical aid which facilitates a more lucid arrangement and terminology' and allows us 'to determine the degree of approximation of the historical phenomenon to the theoretically constructed type'.[22]

This is indeed banally true.[23] But Weber's methodological writings do not necessarily lead to the conclusion Leiter draws. It is one thing to say, as Weber certainly did say, that there can be no scientific knowledge of values, that no rational validity can be predicated of ideals, and that empirical sciences of the kind he was concerned with 'cannot tell anybody what [a person] *should* do'.[24] It is a quite different thing to say that values have no role in the process of determining and constructing the object of investigation in the cultural sciences. Weber clearly thought they did:

> knowledge of cultural events is inconceivable except on a basis of the *significance* which the concrete constellations of reality have for *us* in certain individual concrete situations... 'Culture' is a finite segment of the meaningless infinity of the world process, a segment on which human beings confer *meaning and significance*.[25]

Hence, Weber does not exclude values from the process of identification and study of a certain subject. He is rather saying that cultural objects or, more generally, objects worthy of scientific study are not worthy because they hold some intrinsic value, but because they are seen as valuable by the researcher:

> The transcendental presupposition of every *cultural science* lies not in our finding a certain culture or any 'culture' in general to be *valuable* but rather in the fact that we are *cultural beings,* endowed with the capacity and the will to take a deliberate attitude towards the world and to lend it *significance* ... Whatever the content of this attitude – these phenomena have cultural significance for us and on this significance alone rests its scientific interest.[26]

Weber was not concerned with the grouping and the knowledge of scattered data. Neither did he think that sciences were purely concerned with the system-

---

[22] Leiter (n 18), 167. Reference omitted.
[23] Leiter's definition is also partly circular, as it includes the notion of ideal-type in the description of what the concept allows us to do.
[24] Weber (n 9), 54.
[25] Ibid., 80–81. Emphasis in the original.
[26] Ibid.

atisation of information. Moreover, his notion of *ideal-type* is more than mere technical aids facilitating arrangement and terminology for the determination of the 'degree of approximation of the historical phenomenon to the theoretically constructed type'. They are that too, but they are *not just* that. Ideal-types are evaluative ideals, not in the sense that cultural significance should be attributed only to valuable phenomena. Rather, such phenomena are cultural:

> *only* because and *only* insofar as their existence and the form which they historically assume touch directly or indirectly on our cultural *interest*s and arouse our striving for knowledge concerning problems brought into focus by the evaluative ideas which give *significance* to the fragment of reality analysed by those concepts.[27]

Leiter is aware of this: 'The question, then, is whether the judgments of "significance" and "importance" that Finnis rightly insists are indispensable in theory-construction must make reference to moral values in addition to epistemic values?'[28] His answer is, however, too quick and the means by which the answer is provided shaky. It is too quick because his definition of epistemic values is question-begging. Epistemic values, we are told, 'specify (what we hope are) the truth-conducive desiderata we aspire to in theory construction and theory choice'.[29] He then gives examples of these values: 'evidentiary adequacy ("saving the phenomena"), simplicity, minimum mutilation of well-established theoretical frameworks and methods (methodological conservatism), explanatory consilience, and so forth'.[30] But, in contrasting this set with *moral* values, and in asserting that jurisprudence is concerned with the former and not the latter, he begs the question of whether moral values or practical reason more generally play any role in the determination of what counts as an epistemic value in the first place.

Leiter's use of an analogy to prove his point is also not very helpful. He asks us to imagine a dialogue where two participants seek to provide the concept of 'city'. One of the participants ('the Natural City Theorist' [NCT]) considers that the answer to the question hinges on requirements of practical reason, that non-conforming uses of 'city' should be determined from a practical viewpoint, that value-judgments about the importance and interest of the concept shape the enquiry, and that moral and political norms thus delineate the subject-matter. Her counterpart (the 'Descriptivist'), instead, considers that

---

[27] Ibid. Emphasis in the original. In the same vein, see Weber's critique of Meyer in 'Critical Studies in the Logic of the Cultural Sciences: A Critique of Eduard Meyer's Methodological Views' in *The Methodology of the Social Sciences* (first published in 1917, The Free Press 1949).
[28] Leiter (n 18), 168.
[29] Ibid.
[30] Ibid.

we do not need to have recourse to practical reason in order to determine what the paradigmatic uses of 'city' are. Rather, she wants to understand what is it that those places we call 'cities' have in common as a matter of fact. Moreover, she considers that an appeal to statistical usage suffices for settling the quibble about terminology, and that although the 'Banal Truth' cannot be dismissed, the demarcation of the object is still a matter of application of epistemic values.[31]

Leiter's analogy is insufficient for two reasons. First, because his discussion is framed in terms of the moral/epistemic values divide that I already indicated was problematic a couple of paragraphs back. Second, and more important for my purposes, because there is something in the nature of the object 'city' and about the features of the participants in the analogy that makes it unfit for solving the question of the degree to which, if at all, facts and value intersect in social sciences and in law so that we can speak of them objectively. Further reflection on the categories of object and participants will thus illuminate the differences between Hart and Weber which could have perhaps led the former to distance himself from the insights of the latter. I now undertake that effort.

3. WEBER ON SOCIAL SCIENCE AND LAW

I have hitherto discussed the claim that Hart and Weber shared a reliance on the distinction between facts and values, and that Hart's reluctance to recognise Weber's influence has not been adequately theorised by Anglo-Saxon jurisprudents. In this section I want to suggest a possible theoretical reason for the reluctance, which is related to a certain difference in kind between the social sciences (or cultural sciences, as he called them) Weber was interested in and law as the phenomenon in which Hart was, in turn, interested.

Neither Weber nor Hart was clear about the boundaries between these disciplines. Hart, as I already mentioned above, said that *The Concept of Law* could be read as an essay in descriptive sociology, an insight which obscures the matter more than it sheds light on it. Weber was not different in this regard. In the writings I here consider, he only mentions law in some scattered remarks, all of which express a contrast between his understanding of the social sciences as more than purely formal and explanatory disciplines and a rather formal treatment of legal phenomena. Consider, for instance the following remarks:

> There is not absolutely 'objective' scientific analysis of culture ... or of social phenomena independent of special and 'one-sided' viewpoints according to which – expressly or tacitly, consciously or unconsciously – they are selected, analysed and organised for expository purposes. The reasons for this lie in the character of the

---

[31] Ibid.

cognitive goal of all research in social science which seeks to transcend the purely *formal* treatment of the legal or conventional norms regulating social life.[32]

Moreover, consider the claim that 'the universe of legal norms is naturally clearly definable and is valid (in the legal sense!) for historical reality. But social science in our sense is concerned with practical significance'.[33]

This is where the Weber and Hart start parting ways. These fragments suggest that the conception of law Weber was considering in the quotation above was a formalistic one. That is, one in which the universe of legal norms is determined by their formal validity and existence, i.e., adequacy of prescriptive statements to formal and procedural standards dictated by other higher sources. In this sense, the universe of legality is clearly definable and valid for historical reality. This is further confirmed by Weber's discussion on the influence (or lack thereof) that this formal conception of law could have in the rejection of a materialistic conception of history. Weber criticised those who, like Stammler, thought that since economic life is regulated through law then it followed that economic development 'must take the form of striving for the creation of new *legal* forms'.[34] He rejected such correspondence by dissecting cultural significance from 'the formal identity of prevailing legal norms'.[35] In a nutshell, Weber criticises attempts to apply a formal conception of law to an analysis of cultural phenomena. Rather, cultural phenomena change the meaning and applicability of legal norms. And they could do so even to the point where the existence of such norms become practically meaningless in the face of radical social change:

> The statistical frequency of certain legally regulated relationships might be changed fundamentally, and in many cases, even disappear entirely; a great number of legal norms might become *practically* meaningless and their whole cultural significance changed beyond identification.[36]

Weber elsewhere developed the idea that there was at least one sense (the sense in which he uses the term in the essay I am here commenting on) in which law could be said to exist, which entailed that the knowledge of law was presupposed and thus prior to any application of the object/participant divide. In this

---

[32] Weber (n 9), 72.
[33] Ibid., 94.
[34] Ibid., 83. Emphasis in the original.
[35] Ibid.
[36] Ibid.

sense, law and legal rules serve the ends of scientific knowledge as a *means*, not as an object of this knowledge.[37]

> [T]he empirical legal order is a 'presupposition' of the empirical process: the 'maxims' employed by judges who decide the case and the 'means' employed by the parties to the dispute ... the legal order is also constitutive for the definition of the 'historical entity'.[38]

Hence, in these methodological writings, Weber limited his analysis to one among sundry potential uses of norms as means for obtaining knowledge, namely norms as objects whose existence is not dependent upon the perspective of any subject. The universe of legal phenomena is brought about, in this limited understanding, through the compliance with the formal and procedural conditions the legal system itself contemplates for its autopoiesis. Law is, then, sidestepped in Weber's methodological essays as a problem to which his discussion on the possibility of an objective knowledge of cultural phenomena is directly applicable. From this it follows an important consequence for my discussion: the exclusion of law from the universe of Weberian social cultural phenomena, entails that the knowledge of the former is not thought of as subjected to the same methodological requirements as the latter. Their existence does not hinge, under this specific viewpoint, on a given perspective adopted by a given subject (Weber's social scientist) who in turn develops a conceptual apparatus (most prominently ideal-types) in order to analyse how phenomena behave according to certain 'laws' (largely understood as patterns of regularity brought about by cause-effect relationships, etc.).[39]

Of course, Weber's methodological writings were more preoccupied with economics and history than jurisprudence, as per his own preoccupations. Moreover, his methodological reflections took place, remember, in the context of introducing the *Archiv's* new editorial policies to social scientists. It seems to me that these differences in the nature of the enquiry, which place law largely outside the scope of the cultural sciences Weber was concerned with, give us reasons to explain why Hart might have decided to deny his influence.

Weber admitted that the formal conception described above was not the only possible meaning of law.[40] Why then limiting its use to this specific use? I think Weber wanted to be cautious in maintaining the specificity of sociol-

---

[37] Michel Coutu, 'Weber Reading Stammler: What Horizons for the Sociology of Law?' (2013) 40 (3) *Journal of Law and Society* 356, 366.
[38] Max Weber, *Critique of Stammler* (The Free Press 1977) 133.
[39] Weber (n 9), 76.
[40] Coutu (n 37), 364–369.

ogy, and even of sociology of law, distinguishing them from jurisprudence or legal dogmatics.[41]

Hartian methodology, however, always required the presence of a kind of participant adopting an internal point of view without which law is not brought about as a social phenomenon at all.[42] By contrast, when developing his methodological thought, Weber took legal phenomena as existing independently of this relationship.

At this point it is useful to come back to Leiter's distinction between epistemic and moral values and its use in the analysis of the concept of a 'city'. I averred in the previous section that the analogy fell short of settling his discussion with Finnis. I submitted that the analogy failed to prove Leiter's point that the concept of law, *just as the concept of a city*, can be grasped and appraised solely through the application of epistemic criteria. My discussion on Weber's unelaborated take on law and legal phenomena gives me a vocabulary to argue why Leiter falls short of closing the debate: cities are not *like* law. They are not *analogous* to law.

For now, I have suggested Webearian reasons for Hart's reluctance to recognise Weber as a source of theoretical influence. Weber's social science is methodologically different from jurisprudence. The next section sees the problem from Hart's point of view. I will first briefly reconstruct Hart's vision on this problem as expounded in *The Concept of Law*. In Hart's understanding, the object law is *brought about* by certain participants (i.e., officials) without whom no legal object would exist. The relationship between objects and participants in the (re)production of legality is less distant than it is in Weber's social sciences.

4. HART'S DEPARTURE

Hart's most general contribution to the question 'what is law' is that the law is the union of primary and secondary rules. The usual story about what this union entails says that legal systems exist when two minimum sufficient and necessary conditions are met:

> On the one hand, those rules of behaviour which are valid according to the system's ultimate criteria of validity must be generally obeyed, and, on the other hand, its rules of recognition specifying the criteria of legal validity and its rules of change and adjudication must be effectively accepted as common public standards of official behaviour by its officials.[43]

---

[41] Ibid., 368.
[42] Hart (n 3), 101–110.
[43] Ibid., 116.

Nevertheless, it is not clear why Hart was so explicit in affirming the necessity and sufficiency of both conditions. In the case of the first condition, Hart was adamant that this is the only requirement ordinary citizens *need* to satisfy, regardless of whether they accept the rules of the legal system or not: 'they may obey each "for his part only" and from any motive whatever'.[44] As for the second condition, Hart says that 'officials must regard these common standards of official behaviour and appraise critically their own and each other's deviations as lapses'.[45] Legal systems are, then, brought about by the concurrence of the 'obedience by ordinary citizens' and 'the acceptance by officials of secondary rules as critical common standards of official behaviour'. Such duality is, for Hart, 'merely the reflection of the composite character of a legal system as compared with a simpler decentralised pre-legal form of social structure which consists only of primary rules'.[46]

Right after describing both conditions, however, Hart qualifies his claim in ways that almost completely deny that sufficiency and necessity are in fact features of the first condition. This part must be quoted at length:

> But where there is a union of primary and secondary rules, which is, as we have argued, the most fruitful way of regarding a legal system, the acceptance of the rules as common standards for the group may be split off from the relatively passive matter of the ordinary individual acquiescing in the rules by obeying them for this part alone. In an extreme case the internal point of view with its characteristic normative use of legal language ('This is a valid rule') might be confined to the official world. In this more complex system, only officials might accept and use the system's criteria of legal validity. The society in which this was so might be deplorably sheeplike; the sheep might end in the slaughter-house. But there is little reason for thinking that it could not exist or for denying it the title of a legal system.[47]

This is a strange way of presenting the problem. Of course, Hart's concern was not only with the formal validity of legal norms, but with their relationship to efficacy as well. Yet, the preceding quote puts a strong emphasis on the role of officials and on the normative attitudes *they* must adopt towards rules if a valid legal system is to be deemed as such. So, even in the 'extreme case' where only officials follow the directives of the legal system as the result of adopting the internal point of view, we may be, perhaps, in the presence of a legal system on the verge of a revolution, or one that is extremely fragile in its capacity to guide the citizens' behaviour. But we will be in the presence of an existent and valid

---

[44] Ibid.
[45] Ibid., 117.
[46] Ibid.
[47] Ibid.

legal system, nonetheless. Hart is explicit about this.[48] Hence, as depicted in the text of *The Concept of Law,* both conditions are not copulative and, to the extent that we distinguish validity and efficacy, the second condition suffices for bringing about a valid system.

I am not the only one drawing attention to this and to other concomitant problems, of course. After posing the question, 'Whose behaviour is structured by the operative rule of recognition?', Kramer answers that Hart's answer in sometimes 'a bit muddled'.[49] Kramer also quotes P M S Hacker who notes that Hart treats non-officials, or private persons, more like spectators than like participants.[50] Barczentewicz also gives a brief overview of the secondary literature discussing what exactly counts as an official. Lamond considers that the group is not limited to the judges,[51] Goldsworthy that senior legal officials alone count,[52] Raz in turn considers that only 'primary law-applying institutions' make the cut.[53] Barczentewicz's own take is closer to Raz's.[54]

Moreover, Barczentewicz notes that Hart suggested that 'it is the group of all legal officials of the system in question' that count as legal officials,[55] but that he subsequently 'lapsed into speaking about the courts only':[56] '[The rule of recognition] is in effect a form of judicial customary rule existing only if it is accepted and practised in the law-identifying and law-applying operations of the courts'.[57] Himma, by contrast, thinks that 'judicial officials are not the only participants whose behaviour and attitudes figure into determining the existence and content of the rule of recognition'.[58]

---

[48] Ibid., 103.
[49] Matthew Kramer, 'The Rule of Misrecognition in the Hart of Jurisprudence' (1988) 8 (3) *OJLS* 401, 406.
[50] P M S Hacker, 'Hart's Philosophy of Law' in P M S Hacker and Joseph Raz (eds), *Law Morality and Society: Essays in Honour of H.L.A. Hart* (Clarendon 1977) 23.
[51] Grant Lamond, 'The Rule of Recognition and the Foundations of a Legal System in Luís Duarte d'Almeida, James Edwards and Andrea Dolcetti (eds), *Reading HLA Hart's 'The Concept of Law'* (Bloomsbury 2013) 112.
[52] Jeffrey Goldsworthy, *The Sovereignty of Parliament: History and Philosophy* (OUP 2001) 238–243.
[53] Joseph Raz, *The Authority of Law* (OUP 2009) 108–111.
[54] Mikolaj Barczentewicz, 'The Illuminati Problem and Rules of Recognition' (2018) 38 (3) *OJLS* 500, 514.
[55] Ibid.; Hart (n 3), 117.
[56] Barczentewicz (n 54), 514.
[57] Hart (n 3), 256.
[58] Kenneth Einar Himma, 'Making Sense of Constitutional Disagreement: Legal Positivism, the Bill of Rights, and the Conventional Rule of Recognition in the United States' (2003) 4 *Journal of Law in Society* 149, 154.

So, the central role that Hart gives to 'officials' in his theory is 'both striking and curious'.[59] This is not only because Hart 'nowhere tells us just what an "official" is or how we recognize one',[60] something which has led scholars to discuss, for example, problems of circularity in Hart's jurisprudence.[61] The important role given to officials is also puzzling because in the 'more complex system' Hart is talking about in the quotation above, it could be one in which law is whatever the officials say it is.[62]

Simmons argues this would be a rather unfair interpretation of Hart, for Hart is adamant that, to use Simmons' example, an official accepting the rule of recognition requiring her to apply Acts of Parliament would be having the law wrong by applying one of such Acts on the basis that she does not agree with its content.[63] As it happens, Hart clearly distinguished validity from existence.[64] And yet, the predominance of the role of 'officials' in recognising and in bringing about law is manifest in Hart's jurisprudence, for it is *their* practice what counts as dispositive in determining the content of the rule of recognition and, therefore, in determining the sources that count as obligatory or permitted, which are, in turn, the ones that will ground the norms that they may eventually apply to concrete cases. It may be the case that such a system may lack efficacy and that it may disappear eventually due to its impossibility to guide the behaviour of citizens. But that is a different question: the point is that Hart is clear that what counts as necessary and sufficient for the identification and creation of law is that common public standards of validity criteria are accepted by officials.

This leave us with a quandary. Is it really the case that, in spite of Hart's explicit reluctance to admit the need for citizens to adopt the internal point of view, all that counts is official behaviour? Adler has affirmed this: '"For Hart, elite consensus defines law" … Officials, not citizens, are the recognitional community: that is, the rule of recognition supervenes on official actions, beliefs, judgements, etc., alone'.[65]

Gardner, however, suggested that the general obedience demanded from non-officials cannot merely consist of patterns of action compatible with legal

---

[59] Nigel Simmons, *Central Issues in Jurisprudence* (Sweet & Maxwell 2013) 158.
[60] Ibid.
[61] Kramer (n 49); Matthew Adler, 'Popular Constitutionalism and the Rule of Recognition: Whose Practices Ground U.S. Law?' (2006) 100 *Northwestern University Law Review* 719, 733.
[62] Simmons (n 59), 159.
[63] Ibid.
[64] Hart (n 3), 69.
[65] Adler (n 61), 733.

requirements even if these subjects do not realise that they are acting in conformity with the law. He first recognised that in Hart:

> ... the relevant custom, the one that makes the rule what it is, is not the custom of a population that can identified independently of it. There is no wider population, beyond the official users, who participate in making the rule by their cumulative attempts to follow it.[66]

But then, he added:

> This does not mean, of course, that Hart did not regard the existence of a legal system as also depending, in a different way, on the behaviour of a wider population. On the contrary... True, even for Hart, it can't be sheer coincidence that the general population stays, by and large, on the right side of the law. Some explanatory link between their conformity and the legal rules is required. Those who hold themselves out to be the officials of the legal system must be able to affect non-official behaviour by changing or applying the rules, or else they are not officials of the legal system.[67]

Gardner's view was that this 'shows just how little "social basis" a system of rules needs, in Hart's view, in order to qualify as a legal system'.[68] But Adler goes even further, I think for the right reasons. His contention is that 'it is pretty clear, as a matter of Hart exegesis ... that Hart believed official practice, not citizen or subject practice, to be constitutive of the rule of recognition and thereby to provide ultimate criterion of legal truth'.[69]

My view is that the disagreement is only apparent. The explanatory link that Gardner asks for is not one that is found in Hart, to the extent that such a link derives from an exegetical analysis of Hart's account. This is pretty clear, indeed, *as a matter of Hartian exegesis.*

So, the questions we are left with are, first, why would Hart be so stringent in this role allocation? And second, is this helpful in answering why Hart would refuse to acknowledge Weber as a source of inspiration?

I think Adler also gives a good answer to the first question. Hart's methodological commitment to descriptivism precludes any logical space for the idea that mere observers, subjects or citizens, have any in role in determining the content of the rule of recognition and, therefore, in determining what is or what is not law or legal.[70] Such descriptivism entails moral neutrality and the

---

[66] John Gardner, *Law as a Leap of Faith* (OUP 2012) 283.
[67] Ibid., 284.
[68] Ibid., 285.
[69] Adler (n 61), 733.
[70] Ibid., 734.

rejection of any justificatory aim. It entails objectivity. This stance is, as it is well known, explicit in Hart's *Postcript*:

> My account is *descriptive* in that it is morally neutral and has no justificatory aims: it does not seek to justify or commend on moral or other grounds the forms and structures which appear in my general account of law, though a clear understanding of these is, I think, an important preliminary to any useful moral criticism of law.[71]

This commitment provides the room Hartian positivism needs to say without contradiction, for example, that wicked systems of law, or systems that the entire citizenry regards as unjust, immoral, etc., are systems of law nonetheless. It also allowed Hart to rebuff Dworkin's interpretivist criticism to his theses on the bases that '[d]escription may still be description, even when what is described is an evaluation'.[72]

Adler makes this point nicely:[73]

> Identifying the rule of recognition as the ultimate, secondary rule accepted by the citizenry would preclude a legal system with an alienated citizenry, and would seem to make the rule virtually vacuous in less dysfunctional systems where most citizens are (rationally) ignorant of secondary legal matters.[74]

This is an elaborated way of saying that 'the sheep might end in the slaughter-house'.[75] However, from this point onwards, Hart cannot be Weberian anymore. Weber made his methodological commitments with a certain type of object in mind – those relevant for the social sciences, where economics and history were the most prominent examples. The nature (and I do not mean anything ontologically strong with the word) of economics and history is such that, under Weber's assumptions, the social scientist can still look at the world as something that is not brought about by her. Picking up on Leiter's example again, cities come about with a larger independence from the practice of the city dweller or the scientist seeking to come to terms with what a city is. Put differently, the existence of object city is less dependent on the Weberian social scientist's say-so of fiat than law is in Hart's system, which gives officials the capacity to actually bring about their object.[76]

---

[71] Hart (n 3), 240.
[72] Ibid., 244.
[73] Leslie Green in his introduction to the *Concept of Law* concurs.
[74] Adler (n 61), 734.
[75] Hart (n 3), 117.
[76] This, of course, within the limitations set by the ultimate criterion, namely the rule of recognition, for which 'there is no rule providing criteria for the assessment of its own legal validity'; Ibid., 107.

I want to finish with an example from a discussion on originalism and textualism which illustrates this point nicely. Scalia discusses the Supreme Court case *Church of the Holy Trinity v. United States*, in which this church subscribed a contract with an Englishmen to move to the United States so that he would take over as rector and pastor. The US Federal Government argued that the contract violated a federal statute that made it illegal for any person to:

> in any way assist or encourage the importation or migration of any alien ... into the United States, ... under contract or agreement ... made previous to the importation or migration of such alien..., to perform labor or service of any kind in the United States.[77]

The Circuit Court for the Southern District of New York decided against the church and sentenced it to pay a fine. The Supreme Court overturned the decision. The reason, in its central portion was:

> It must be conceded that the act of the [church] is within the letter of this section, for the relation of rector to his church is one of service, and implies labor on the one side with compensation on the other. Not only are the general words labor and service both used [in the statute], but also, as it were to guard against any narrow interpretation and emphasize a breadth of meaning, to them is added 'of any kind'; and further, ... the fifth section [of the statute], which makes specific exceptions, among them professional actors, artists, lecturers, singers and domestic servants, strengthens the idea that every other kind of labor and service was intended to be reached by the first section. While there is great force to this reasoning, we cannot think Congress intended to denounce with penalties a transaction like that in the present case. It is a familiar rule, that a thing may be within the letter of the statute and yet not within the statute, because not within its spirit, nor within the intention of its makers.[78]

Weber could not have explained the validity of this decision. Hart could. The first saw the universe of legality as 'naturally clearly definable [and valid] (in the legal sense!) for historical reality' because he was not thinking of law as the same kind of object as the objects of social sciences. Weber could not have deemed the Supreme Court's decision as valid, for Weberian participants do not have the kind of illocutionary power the Supreme Court is exercising in the case at hand. By contrast, given that the exegetical reading of Hart I have commented on here limits participants in the determination of what counts as legal to officials, and because officials do have the power to change their object by say-so or fiat, a Hartian interpretation of the case commented by Scalia would

---

[77] Antonin Scalia, *A Matter of Interpretation: Federal Courts and The Law* (Princeton 1997), 18–19.
[78] *Church of the Holy Trinity v. United States* (1892) SCOTUS 143.

not lead us to conclude that the Court was trespassing the limits of legality by clearly deciding against the letter of the statute (the only object Weber's social scientist could have had access to as part of what is 'naturally clearly definable'). By contrast, under this Hartian reading the Court was merely playing the game of law.

5. CONCLUSION

In the wording of the editors of this collection, my contribution to this collection has revolved around some of the following questions: 'ought jurisprudence be objective, and how can it become so? Should legal sources be objective, and how can they become so?' I have reflected on this question from the perspective of the distinction between facts and values as understood by Max Weber and H L A Hart. I argued that Hart and Weber shared a basic commitment to this distinction. This shared commitment permeates Hart to the point where authors have seen a Weberian undertowing in his work. Hart, nonetheless, never admitted such inspiration.

Secondly, Hart's reluctance to admit Weber's theoretical inspiration has not been properly theorised in the secondary literature.

Thirdly, I have suggested that Weber's methodology was concerned with a certain group of social sciences. Law was not one of them. Moreover, in some scattered remarks in his methodological writings he maintained a limited vision of what law is, in ways that separate legal phenomena from the same methodological treatments he gave to social sciences. I thus claimed that given the nature of the enquires each author focused on, Hart could have only followed Weber up to a certain point on pain of betraying his methodological commitment to descriptivism.

As I have stated, my explanation is based on an exegetical reading of Hart and on a reading of Weber's methodological work. These are certainly not the only ones available. I have not attempted here to take sides on many other discussions. My intention here has been merely, as my title indicates, to suggest a plausible explanation for Hart's reluctance to admit Weber's influence.

6. Objectivity of legal knowledge: The challenge of scepticism
Matti Ilmari Niemi

1. INTRODUCTION

Objectivity is a crucial issue when knowledge and its trustworthiness are at the centre of attention. In the field of law, both objectivity in the cognitive sense and the objectivity of values must be taken into consideration. Traditionally, objectivity has, in different ways, been both supported and rejected by well-known authors working in the realm of both legal philosophy and various areas of jurisprudence. Rejection embodies scepticism, which is treated as a wicked problem by the author of this chapter.

Sceptical attitudes towards the reliability of knowledge or values have been an essential feature of many schools of thought in relation to ethics and jurisprudence. Some of these attitudes are discussed below.

David Hume is treated here as a prominent figure whose original sceptical writings concerning knowledge in the areas of both sciences and ethics are well known. However, his later positive ethical approach is seldom noticed in the legal arena. In this context, the sceptical approach is an object of attention, but the positive approach is the cornerstone of the author's comprehension of the knowledge of law. Therefore, it is an object of specific attention and exploitation.

The author of this chapter argues in favour of the objectivity of legal knowledge in the frames of conventional legal dogmatics. Nevertheless, both knowledge of law and its objectivity are understood in a weak sense, in which respect, legal knowledge manifests as interpretation and reasoning. Answers to sceptical questions as well as criticisms of scepticism derive from this perspective.

2. TWO SENSES OF OBJECTIVITY

The problems of objectivity are general philosophical issues. The objective/subjective dichotomy nonetheless comprises two different dimensions, and perhaps two different senses. The first is the general approach while the second is a specific approach, relevant both to ethics and law.

The general approach – that is to say, cognitive and epistemic approach – refers to the problem of objectivity of knowledge. How is it possible to know about the world in an objective way? Knowledge should not be influenced by particular perspectives or personal or restricted group interests or evaluations.[1] This is, naturally, an important problem in all fields both of sciences and of humanities. Accordingly, it is also a crucial issue in jurisprudence. How is it possible to know about valid law in an objective way?

Objectivism is often contrasted with projectivism. Objectivism about a topic holds that judgements about it can be objective. Projectivism holds that judgements about a topic amount to merely objective-sounding expressions of attitudes or feelings. Our personal and internal attitudes or feelings are projected to appear as qualities of external objects.

The distinction between attitudes or feelings and their objects can be traced back to the philosophies of Hume and John Locke. Locke drew from *Galileo Galilei* the distinction between primary and secondary qualities, which he adopted as the basic epistemic concepts of his philosophy of science.[2] There are two kinds of qualities according to Locke. Only some qualities are external, which is to say that they constitute real aspects of the external world. Many manifestations of qualities are merely impressions of the mind. They are subjective experiences but not perceptions of facts.[3] This seems to be a root of the strong and influential positivistic dimension of Western philosophy.

The problem of objectivity in the second sense refers to values. This is an axiological problem, crucial in the field of ethics but, nevertheless, also important in the field of law. Does human society have objective values? Do we share as members of a society objective or common values? If we have objective values, what is their significance and role in legal dogmatics and in specific legal systems?

---

[1] This is the claim for independence of knowledge from the knower. The concept 'objectivity' has many meanings and senses. See Gonzalo Villa-Rosas and Jorge Luis Fabra-Zamora, 'Introduction: The Meanings of "Objectivity", Chapter 1 in this book. No doubt, the point of view adopted in this chapter is directed to objectivity about law instead of objectivity of law. As a matter of fact, valid law as the presumed object of knowledge cannot have any independent or separate existence, and therefore, law and justified knowledge of law coincide. See Jaap Hage, *Objectivity of Law and Objectivity about Law*, Chapter 2 in this book.

[2] Bertrand Russell, *The History of Western Philosophy and its Connection with Political and Social Circumstances from the Earliest Times to the Present Day* (George Allen & Unwin Ltd 1982) 585.

[3] John Locke, *An Essay Concerning Human Understanding* (Clarendon Press 1894) book II, chapters 1, 2 and 4, 175 and 178.

Humean emotivism is an important element of the background to value subjectivism, and was often utilised at the end of the 19th century and during the first half of the 20th century.[4] Subjectivism, in turn, is an important ally of legal positivism. Subjectivism takes into account that people express their personal attitudes, desires or feelings when making moral judgements.

In addition, the two aspects of the problem of objectivity are interconnected but, on the other hand, not mutually exclusive. It is reasonable to ask whether objective knowledge of values is possible and whether objective knowledge of law can be founded on values.

A school of jurisprudence can adopt different standpoints in relation to the two dimensions of objectivity. For instance, proponents of traditional natural law theory adopt both cognitive and value objectivism and take the view that objective and well-justified legal statements are founded on certain given and universal – i.e., objective – human values that are regarded as constituting practical reasonableness.[5] Proponents of legal positivism, on the other hand, adopt cognitive objectivism while usually rejecting the idea of objective values. They regard the validity of law as being based on certain social facts that form a part of a legal system, but not necessary on varying moral considerations and opinions.[6]

3. LEGAL POSITIVISM AND OBJECTIVITY

Social and separability theses comprise the two important characteristics of legal positivism.[7] They posit law as a matter of fact, as decisions or other social facts, and entail the view that there is not necessarily a connection between law and morals.

The social thesis is one of the cornerstones of the approaches of Hans Kelsen and H L A Hart. Kelsen saw legal rules, in the form of sections of statutes, as legal facts and as the content of the legislator's will.[8] For Hart, law appears in the form of the extant and valid rules of a legal system identified by the rule of recognition. He viewed the existence of a legal system as a social

---

[4] See e.g., the studies of E Westermarck, C L Stevenson and A J Ayer.

[5] See, e.g., John Finnis, *Natural Law and Natural Rights* (Clarendon Press 1980) 14.

[6] See, e.g., Jules L Coleman and Brian Leiter, 'Legal Positivism', in Dennis Patterson (ed.), *A Companion to Philosophy of Law and Legal Theory* (Blackwell Publishers 1996) 243.

[7] Ibid., 241.

[8] Hans Kelsen, *Pure Theory of Law* (University of California Press 1970) 73 and 79.

phenomenon.[9] The social thesis provides the foundation of cognitive objectivism adopted in legal positivism.

For Kelsen, legal rules as sections of statutes (essentially the legal 'ought' in the form of imputation) are the defined and extant objects of the statements of legal dogmatics. These statements are either true or false and, hence, they comprise value-free and objective descriptions of their objects. Moreover, Kelsen employs correspondence as the definition of truth. Accordingly, valid legal rules are social facts and a special branch of reality constituting the object area of legal knowledge.[10]

On the other hand, legal norms differ from observable reality. For Kelsen, existence means validity. The concept of a special kind of legal reality embodies the will of a lawgiver (in a non-psychological sense).[11] Law manifests itself in the decisions of the lawgiver. With the help of these philosophical points of departure Kelsen defended legal dogmatics as an acceptable branch of science but, at the same time, as one with independent features. The criteria for acceptability were, however, provided by philosophical positivism.[12] Furthermore, Kelsen's statements in respect of legal dogmatics leave no interpretative space in the form of evaluations. For instance, interpretative sentences containing principles of justice are doomed to be subjective.

Kelsen's theory of law adopts cognitive objectivity in a strong sense, as a reflection of philosophical realism. This strong conception of objectivity is the traditional and simple one in which objectivity means congruence between a judgement and its object. A judgement is objective if, and only if, it describes its object as a part of the world. If a judgement does not tell us about an object, it tells us about the speaker – in which case it is subjective.

---

[9] H L A Hart, *The Concept of Law* (2nd edn, Clarendon Press 1994) 201.

[10] Kelsen (n 8) 4 and Hans Kelsen, 'A "Realistic" Theory of Law and the Pure Theory of Law: Remarks on Alf Ross's On Law and Justice', in Luís Duarte d'Almeida, John Gardner and Leslie Green (eds) *Kelsen Revisited. New Essays on the Pure Theory of Law* (Hart Publishing 2013) 195–221, 196. See Monika Zalewska, Imputation as a Supervenience in the General Theory of Norms, Chapter 4 in this book.

[11] Hans Kelsen, *General Theory of Law and State* (Russell & Russell 1961) 30, 46 and 153, and Kelsen (n 8) 4, 72 and 76. I interpret the term 'norm', employed by Kelsen, to mean a rule compared with a principle.

[12] Humanities and social sciences were under great pressure in the light of the positivistic philosophy that held sway at the end of the 19th and at the beginning of the 20th centuries. Kelsen, like many other theorists, felt obliged to defend legal dogmatics as an acceptable branch of science. In addition, Kelsen found it necessary to transform legal dogmatics into a branch of science acceptable from the viewpoint of positivistic philosophy. See Kelsen (n 11) 4 and Kelsen (n 8) 1, 24 and 71. On the other hand, supporters of legal realism went much further in this way.

For Hart, the existence of legal rules or, rather, the existence of a certain legal system bears, on the one hand, social facts but, on the other hand, validity without ontological commitments as far as conventional behavioural rules are concerned. The existence of these rules is explained by reference to membership of a legal system. Hart views validity as a means of understanding language, which is basically a factual (and contingent) practice.[13] The criteria of validity, in turn, refer to certain rules of recognition adopted by a certain society at a certain time. These criteria may be reduced to a particular established practice of a people and society.[14] In essence, the existence of the rules of recognition means the existence of a certain practice of judges and other officials. Both Hart and Kelsen close the gap between 'is' and 'ought' but do this in different ways.[15]

Like Kelsen, Hart adopts a strong conception of objectivity but, nevertheless, in a weaker form, i.e., a statement is objective if, and only if, it is a statement about an object.[16] The grammatical meaning of a statement is the crux of the matter. In order to be objective, a statement has to give information about a defined object in a world other than that of the speaker's mind. On the other hand, no specific ontology or concept of truth is required.

Both the principal theses of legal positivism – i.e., social and separability theses together – entail drawing a qualitative distinction between law and morals: descriptions of valid law (or expressions of valid law) differ radically

---

[13] See, e.g., H L A Hart, 'The Ascription of Responsibility and Rights', in A Flew (ed), *Logic and Language*, first series (Blackwell Publishers 1960) 145; H L A Hart (ed.), *Essays in Jurisprudence and Philosophy* (Clarendon Press 1983) 23; and Hart (n 9) 94. The influence of the mature Wittgenstein on Hart is obvious here. That is why the phrase 'use in the language' (*Gebraucht in der Sprache*) is important in this respect. An existing practice can be seen as the core of Wittgenstein's idea. See Ludwig Wittgenstein, *Philosophical Investigations I* (Blackwell Publishers 1958) 43. At the level of legal issues, Hart interprets this approach as the thesis according to which a concept's meaning (content) is determined by its use (as a social practice). For the dynamic character of positive law, see also Kelsen (n 11) 399. On linguistic and historical point of view over objectivity of law, see Caroline Laske, 'Big Data Linguistic Analysis of Legal Texts – Objectivity Debunked?', Chapter 9 in this book.

[14] Hart (n 9) 101 and 109. On the crucial role of officials as the foundation of existence of a legal system, see Grant Lamond, 'The Rule of Recognition and the Foundations of a Legal System', in Luís Duarte and Andrea Dolcetti (eds.), *Reading H L A Hart's The Concept of Law* (Hart Publishing 2013) 110

[15] Both Kelsen and Hart define a crucial crossing point which belongs to the world of ought (*sollen*) and to the world of is (*sein*). Kelsen defines legal rules as existing facts with the content of ought. Hart defines the rule of recognition as a norm and, at the same time, an existing fact of a society. See Kelsen (n 8) 4.

[16] See Leonardo Marchettoni, 'From Hart to Dworkin via Brandom: Indeterminacy, Interpretation, and Objectivity', Chapter 7 in this book.

from moral evaluations. The existence of a legal rule is a social fact, but what is the character of morals?

I argue that legal positivism, at least plain-fact or exclusive positivism, presumes ethical subjectivism. A consistent proponent of this approach must view morals as a variety of different opinions, attitudes, feelings, or personal interests; i.e., subjective expressions of individual people, but not descriptions of a society.

This assumption is present in the major texts of positivists. The relativity of moral values in these texts means, in fact, different and contrasting personal moral evaluations, values or interests of different groups of persons but not values of societies, understood as shared values of the members of a society as the subjects of a legal system.[17]

4. ON HUME AND HIS LESSONS

Sceptical arguments against values, in terms of the way in which they are traditionally treated, have received wide attention in the field of ethics since Hume's days. Often, these arguments have been connected with philosophical positivism. It is no coincidence that value subjectivism enjoyed wide support in the first half of the 20th century, which was when philosophical positivism was at its peak. In the same way, ethical subjectivism lost support in step with the declined of philosophical positivism after World War II.

Hume presented a well-known sceptical analysis on values. He doubted the existence of virtues and vices in human actions:

> Take any action allow'd to be vicious: Wilful murder, for instance. Examine it in all lights, and see if you can find that matter of fact, or real existence, which you call *vice*. In which-ever way you take it, you find only certain passions, motives, volitions and thoughts. There is no other matter of fact in the case.[18]

Hume's view is that virtues and vices or goodness and badness are not real properties of actions or attributes in the real world – i.e., reality outside human conscience. In other words, there are no values that constitute primary qualities in reality. Instead, separately, there are human evaluations that constitute secondary qualities, which is to say that an act creates an impression in the mind

---

[17] I interpret the texts of Kelsen and Hart as expressing an emotivistic or subjectivistic view of morals. See Hans Kelsen (n 8) 63; Kelsen, 'Law, State and Justice in the Pure Theory of Law' (1947–48) *Yale Law Journal* 377–390, 377; Hart (n 9) 200; and Hart *Essays* (n 13) 82. See also Peter Morton, *An Institutional Theory of Law* (Clarendon Press 1998) 11, 194, 364 and 369.

[18] David Hume, *A Treatise of Human Nature* (P H Nidditch ed, Clarendon Press 1978) 468.

that entails its characterisation as either good or bad. These facts are the feelings of spectators in relation to an actor.[19] Accordingly, and despite structural similarities, there is a significant difference between the spheres of knowledge of nature, i.e., between natural sciences and ethics.[20] This is the essence of Hume's original and well-known approach.

According to Hume, knowing goodness and badness is not the same thing as describing the execution (i.e., external performance) of virtues and vices. To know your duty is one thing; to decide to do it is another. Knowledge does not exert direct influence on conduct, which is to say that reason alone can never be a motive for any action of the will.[21] Accordingly, talk of ethical reasoning and knowledge is not the same thing as qualities of human nature or actions. Therefore, it is not sustainable to deduce ought-statements (moral statements) from is-statements about human nature or the qualities of a human being.[22] This is Hume's famous guillotine.

What can we learn from Humean emotivistic and naturalistic ethics in the area of law? My intention is not to develop any kind of legal application of Humean philosophy. Instead, certain of his ideas, which are historically important, are worthy of notice and exploration.

Hume's original, sceptical arguments are clear and well-known. His negative approach is unambiguous. On the one hand, his moral philosophy provided a powerful and influential critique of traditional Aristotelian ethics that amounts to a critique of the belief in indubitable good and bad elements in human behaviour, i.e., the presumption that certain virtues and vices exist as natural and knowable qualities in human actions.

On the other hand, Hume's positive approach and proposal for a better philosophical foundation for ethics, provided later, is not so clear. Different conclusions can be drawn. I consider here two important and different conclusions as two different paths.

---

[19] Hume also paid attention to the motives and feelings of the actor. According to Hume, the ultimate object of praise and approbation is the motive of an action, but the external performance has no merit. Hume (n 18) 477.

[20] Hume describes the foundation of ethics as impressions (as reactions and feelings) of other people (i.e., spectators) caused by actions. Accordingly, moral distinctions are not derived from reasons or by reasoning. In a similar way, impressions and ideas caused by perceptions are the foundation of natural sciences. In both cases, there are important restrictions as limitations of the possibilities of human knowledge. These limitations are discussed in Hume's well-known sceptical arguments. The difference between ethics and natural sciences lies in the content of impressions and ideas. See Hume (n 18) 457 and 470.

[21] Ibid., 413. See A H Basson, *David Hume* (Penguin Books 1958) 88.

[22] Ibid., 469. See Basson, ibid., 94.

The first of these is grounded on philosophical positivism and naturalism. These starting points are adopted, for instance, in the context of Scandinavian legal realism which involves a sceptical attitude towards the existence of norms and legal concepts as starting points or reasoning.

The positivistic approach to knowledge entails the presumption that some kind of observable reality comprises an object of knowledge. Legal realists seek to rehabilitate legal knowledge within the realm of natural sciences, which is to say the sphere of acceptable positivistic science described by Hume as principles founded on impressions, ideas, and perceptions.

Scandinavian legal realism entails the view that the actual beliefs and attitudes of people or judges comprise the part of reality treated as the object of legal knowledge. In other words, Scandinavian realists have adopted both naturalism and emotivism in a similar manner to Hume. Following Hume, human evaluations taking place in the minds of people are treated as legal facts in this school of thought. They are psychological facts. Accordingly, legal facts can be reduced to psychological facts as parts of perceivable reality.

Alf Ross, as the leading scholar of Scandinavian realism, applied Axel Hägerström's positivistic philosophy in the area of law.[23] In his early theory, Ross defined people's behaviour attitudes as experiences, instead of rules or concepts, that constitute the objects of legal knowledge.[24] They were attitudes of citizens – essentially attitudes towards duty. However, in the context of legal dogmatics these attitudes had the content of legal statements. Accordingly, the reality of law appeared as psychological reality.

In his later theory, Ross defined the object of legal knowledge as the behavioural attitudes of judges. Nevertheless, the traditional practice of legal dogmatics could continue in the same way and with the help of the methods previously in use. There was no need for fundamental change in legal dogmatics on the basis of it objects being understood and defined in a new way. It was not necessary to move from legal dogmatics to empirical psychology, and legal knowledge could still be founded on conventional legal sources.[25] As a matter of fact, Ross insisted that knowledge as to the behavioural attitudes of judges can be identified by references to statutes, precedents and other conventional

---

[23] See Axel Hägerström, *Rätten och viljan* (Gleerup 1962) 42, 60 and 104, Axel Hägerström, *Till frågan om den objektiva rättens begrepp I* (Kungliga Humanistiska Vetenskapssamfundet 1917) 60 and Axel Hägerström, *Inquiries into the Nature of Law and Morals* (Almqvist & Wiksells 1953) xi and xii.

[24] Alf Ross, *Virgelighed og Gyldighed I Retslæren* (Levin & Munksgaard 1934) 101 and 106.

[25] Alf Ross, *Om Ret og Retfærdighed* (Nyt nordisk förlag 1953) 25, 29, 52, 56, 58 and 89.

legal sources. Accordingly, the traditional method of legal dogmatics was interpreted and explained in a new way.

According to Hume, vices and virtues are not qualities in human actions (or other facts that form part of observable reality) but perceptions and impressions in the mind based on feelings.[26] Accordingly, human evaluations as secondary qualities should be treated as individual and subjective experiences according to the basic principles of Humean positivism.

This is a manifestation of the restricted sphere of human knowledge in the area of morals emphasised by Hume.[27] On the one hand, ultimate reasons drawn from nature and reality as well as existing things stay out of the sphere of human perceptions. On the other hand, moral understanding stays out of the sphere of natural sciences. This is grounded on the narrow (i.e., positivist) conception of scientific knowledge adopted by Hume who regarded the foundation of scientific knowledge purely reflections or projections of experiences, i.e., as perceptions.[28]

As a point of departure, Hume seems to view evaluations as subjective experiences and objects of knowledge but not as elements of objective knowledge. Humean cognitive naturalism indicates that we can know about goodness or badness, but this knowledge is psychological knowledge – i.e., knowledge about how people react to other people's actions.

On the other hand, however, Humes's view is that people understand and explain moral distinctions in uniform ways by reference to their feelings. The reality of the virtue of an action lies in the fact that it produces feelings of moral approval in spectators. In other words, those spectators have moral sense.[29] Instead of being objects of knowledge – i.e., facts – values begin to appear as the content of knowledge. The focus is rather on the outcomes and circumstances of actions and people's motivations than on the observable feelings of those people.

Moreover, later, in the context of his positive approach, Hume also seems to treat these human evaluations as some special kind of objective knowledge or, at least, as a basis for objective ethical reasoning. Evaluations that depart from private situations and interests – i.e., from immediate feelings and impressions – and which chime with the feelings and impressions of other people are capable of expressing universal principles.[30] Therefore, ethical principles stand

---

[26] Hume (n 18) 469.
[27] Basson (n 21) 23.
[28] Hume (n 18) 66 and Basson (n 21) 27.
[29] Hume (n 18) 471 and Basson (n 21) 102. Here, Hume's utilitarian conclusions are not taken into account or followed. See Hume (n 18) 618, and David Hume, *An Enquiry Concerning the Principles of Morals* (Hacket Publishing Company 1983) 38.
[30] Hume (n 18) 618, and Hume (n 29, *An Enquiry*) 75.

in a position analogous to scientific principles in the arena of natural sciences. In other words, justified, acceptable and common feelings and attitudes can ground bear objective knowledge of goodness and badness and objective ethical reasoning. That which constitutes good is that which every informed and impartial spectator would approve of and hence, that which we do tend to approve of when we rid ourselves of purely personal prejudices and tendencies and try to work out what is right.[31]

Accordingly, objectivity in the field of ethics appears to be based on uniform and common feelings and attitudes of people. In this context these attitudes are not merely private or subjective feelings or reactions, or objects of knowledge as facts, but express common and justified – i.e., general and universal – attitudes as ethical principles.

Finally, Hume adopted a moderate approach in the field of ethics.[32] Knowledge based on common understanding – in essence, common feelings as to goodness and badness – appear as a special kind of weak knowledge.[33] Hume's later vision differs from the original one but primarily entails a different point of view.

What amounts to shared and well-justified attitudes towards different kinds of behaviour? This kind of knowledge or reasoning is imperfect and incomplete. It rather suggests and justifies than make certain statements or offers descriptions of facts. What kinds of action are treated as bad (i.e., forbidden) on the basis of good reasons? Good reasons refer to convincing and persuasive arguments for their badness. Accordingly, moral knowledge or reasoning is not certain or absolute.[34] Often, there are reasonable disagreements, and there can be many incompatible conclusions. Moreover, valid moral reasoning and conclusions can vary in respect of time and places. Different civilisations have different moral codes.[35] According to Hume, moral understanding is rather

---

[31] Charles R Pigden, Naturalism, in Peter Singer (ed.), *A Companion to Ethics* (Blackwell Publishers 1991) 428.

[32] Basson (n 21) 87.

[33] As a matter of fact, even knowledge in the field of natural sciences appears weak in Humean philosophy. The reason for this lies in the restricted character of all knowledge. Even knowledge of nature contains sceptical features and is uncertain. Nevertheless, the spheres of natural sciences and ethics are separate.

[34] Hume's ethical naturalism seems to contain a similar deduction from 'is' to 'ought' which is the target of his own critique. Virtues and vices, i.e., goodness and badness defined as existing feelings and as facts seem to contain both 'is' and 'ought' dimensions with a necessary, i.e., logical, connection. Hume, however, deconstructs this logical connection by means of convincing and justificatory reasoning. Logical deductions cannot be drawn from ethical principles where these constitute recommendations based on existing human feelings.

[35] Basson (n 21) 96.

a matter of taste than certain knowledge of given objects. Therefore, moral reasoning is not a matter of truth but of persuasion and justification. There is no given or absolute moral code or absolute moral reasoning or knowledge.

The weak character of moral knowledge, in Hume's conception, reflects weak objectivity. This conception provides a solid foundation for and gives rise to the weak conception of objectivity adopted here, whose development is needed in the area of law.

5. CRITICAL NOTES

Questions born of a sceptical stance tend to remain open. On a general level, it is difficult to provide entirely comprehensive answers to them. The discussion should be located firmly within the context of the branch of science or humanities at hand in order to master the problem of scepticism. On this specific level, we can discover whether the sceptical arguments put forward are plausible or worthy of notice.[36] In other words, we have to apply the arguments advanced in respect (in this case) of legal knowledge while keeping one eye firmly on the problem of objectivity.

Legal positivism is founded on a strong conception of objectivity which is in itself problematic in the sphere of jurisprudence.

First, it is misleading to present legal knowledge as a search for and description of existing rules as social facts in a society. Legal knowledge is not a matter of fact-finding or description but of comprehension of the legal system adopted in a particular society.[37] The detail – e.g., a section of a statute – can only be grasped properly in the light of the system as a whole. Interpretative recommendations amount to justified conclusions directly grounded on conventional legal sources as well as on principles and moral values of a society. In addition, the exploitation of legal concepts and systems is an essential dimension of legal knowledge. This is the case both in relation to jurisdiction and to legal dogmatics.

Second, knowledge of law manifests itself in the form of interpretation and not descriptions. Recognition of the applicable sources of valid law – such as particular sections of statute – is the first step in the process of interpretation and acquisition of legal knowledge rather than the outcome.

Third, in view particularly of powerful criticism presented by Ronald Dworkin – it is easy to see that the account of legal knowledge given by legal

---

[36] See Ronald Dworkin, 'Objectivity and Truth – You'd Better Believe it' (1996) *Philosophy and Public Affairs* 87–139, 89, 118, 120, 122 and 128.

[37] Therefore, I agree with Moreso when he criticises David Enoch's moral realism. See Josep Joan Moreso, 'Moral Objectivity without Robust Realism', Chapter 13 in this book.

positivists is too narrow. The valid law contained with a given legal system does not comprise only decisions of a legislator or certain strict rules, individualised beforehand with the help of a specific rule of recognition. It also comprises principles applied in different situations and cases in different ways depending on the specific details and circumstances of those situations and cases.[38] Principles appear as the common area of law and morals and embodiments of values. Both judges and legal scholars appear to regard principles as an aspect of conventional legal reasoning and interpretation. In addition, choices between alternative interpretations are informed either by principles or made on the basis of values. Legal interpretations are justified interpretations. Dworkin's famous appeal to principles challenged both the social and separability theses of legal positivism.

Accordingly, there is a necessary connection between law and morals.[39] Moral values often manifest themselves in the form of principles in the legal arena. In addition, even statutes and precedents – as the most important legal sources – can be seen as manifestations of values adopted in a given legal system and society. It is more realistic to regard statutes, for example, as applications and particularisations of values than as social facts. This is in line with the ultimate purposes of legislation and jurisdiction.

Fourth, value subjectivism often connected with and supporting legal positivism is not a tenable theory of values. Principles and many other substantial arguments used in an established way both in the context of particular legal systems and in the sphere of legal dogmatics are demonstrations of the objective values of a society. In addition, recognising statutes and precedents as manifestations of values supports the idea that societies have objective values. It is not possible that acceptable substantial legal arguments merely indicate personal evaluations, preferences, opinions or interests, or limited group interests. Competent legal knowledge – which is to say, advanced legal interpretation – implies objective evaluations.

The problems of Scandinavian realism, Ross' theories in particular, are apparent. It is not possible to acquire information on law by researching the actual attitudes or beliefs of citizens or judges. On the other hand, research into conventional legal sources, especially statutes and precedents, cannot produce information on the attitudes or beliefs of citizens or judges. Accordingly, by following Hägerström's original thinking, either legal dogmatics has to be abandoned as being an unacceptable science or the whole naturalistic enterprise has to be abandoned. Clearly the latter will be chosen here.

---

[38] Ronald Dworkin, *Taking Rights Seriously* (Harvard University Press 1977) 22.
[39] See Ronald Dworkin, *Justice in Robes* (the Belknap Press of Harvard University Press 2006) 34.

In addition, it is unwise to embark upon a process of 'naturalization' by seeking to reduce 'ought' statements (legal statements) to 'is' statements (those describing attitudes or beliefs). Indeed, this is an appropriate place to make use of Hume's guillotine.

As far as Hume is concerned, I have already argued against following his naturalism or emotivism. The idea of reducing ethics to human feelings is problematic, because it amounts to a hopeless attempt to transform legal dogmatics into a branch of science or even seek to pass off legal knowledge as scientific knowledge. Accordingly, the first path based on Hume's thinking is not the route adopted here. Nevertheless, the point that virtues and vices or goodness or badness are not properties of human action is worth positive consideration. It is wise to pay attention to the reactions of other people instead of the alleged properties of actions.

The second path founded on Humean philosophy is the route adopted here. More precisely, this approach is based on Hume's ideas concerning the weak character of ethical knowledge and argumentation relating to the significance of actions. In the same way, knowledge of law appears as weak knowledge. Such knowledge is not descriptions of given facts, but argumentative and creative reasoning founded on justifications, as well as interpretation and other substantive reasons for actions.

6. WEAK CONCEPTION OF OBJECTIVITY ADOPTED

6.1 Foundations of Weak Objectivity

I abandon the strong conceptions of objectivity described above. Instead, I will outline a weak conception of objectivity relevant and applicable in relation to legal knowledge. In addition to weakness, the adopted conception of objectivity also differs from the strong conception in other respects.[40]

The adopted conception of objectivity is weak because, in line with the stance adopted in this chapter, knowledge of law is weak by its nature. Knowledge about valid law does not appear as descriptions of any kinds of facts or other objects. Instead, knowledge of law manifests itself as appeals to the conventional legal sources of a legal system, to principles of justice,

---

[40] On different senses and strengths of objectivity, see Jan-Reinard Sieckmann, 'The Problem of Normative Objectivity', Chapter 11 in this book. The form of objectivity adopted in this chapter can be called a weak version of epistemic objectivity. The adopted point of view is internal. See also a reminiscent distinction between externalist (realist) and intentionalist theory of legal meanings examined by Maija Aalto-Heinilä, 'Can Legal Texts Have Objective Meanings?', Chapter 8 in this book.

to certain goals as embodiments of public policies, to the consequences of different interpretative options and to other substantive reasons as premises of legal interpretation.[41]

Accordingly, knowledge of law appears as interpretation – i.e., legal reasoning and the drawing of inferences from formal and substantive reasons – by which one arrives at the interpretative conclusions adopted. Objective legal knowledge means objective interpretation as well as objective reasoning.

Inferences arrived at on the basis of legal interpretation are not logical deductions but substantive reasoning that involves substantive considerations. This is clear in hard cases but the same holds true even in easy or routine cases to which no exceptional features or exceptional rules or principles apply. The easiness of a case can be understood only within the framework of the legal system as a whole.

The requirement for objectivity does not exclude interpretative creativity.[42] On the contrary, the use of substantive reasons in different ways in different situations underlines the significance of creativity in legal interpretation. In this respect, the demand for objectivity appears as a demand for neutral, disciplined and open reasoning. All arguments must be public and open to critical scrutiny. In this context, it does not suffice merely to identify the legal rule applied in a given situation or case.

The weakness of legal knowledge manifests itself in the form of specific features of legal interpretation. Instead of certain descriptions or noting clear facts, the function of interpretation is to persuade. A successful interpretation is a persuasive interpretation and it expresses rational justification of norms. This is the highest level of certainty available. The most convincing interpretation is that which persuades the audience that there are no good or more convincing reasons to reach other conclusion in the situation or case at hand. In addition, the final conclusion of interpretation often results from balancing arguments and counter-arguments against each other.[43]

Here we can lean on certain features of Hume's thinking along the second path. Legal knowledge is treated as argumentative reasoning. In addition, I will

---

[41] See Matti Ilmari Niemi, 'Form and Substance in Legal Reasoning: Two Conceptions' (2010) 23, 4 *Ratio Juris*, 479–492, 487. About strong and weak objectivity, see also Marchettoni (n 16).

[42] Objectivity explained as a requirement for acceptable knowledge points out the normative function and nature of the concept objectivity. See Villa-Rosas and Fabra-Zamora (n 1).

[43] See reasonable convergence as criterion of objective validity of norms, as far as norm adoption is concerned, in Sieckmann (n 40).

exploit the constructive conception of objectivity introduced by John Rawls.[44] Rawls' conception focuses our attention on the criteria of objective reasoning, on arguments and conclusions and their justifications instead of on entities or objects of knowledge. There is no need to assume that legal reasoning has any particular object or descriptive character. Even the concept of truth remains redundant. In other words, I adopt a conception of objectivity without objects. In this respect, I also draw on the thinking of Thomas Nagel.[45]

In order to be objective, reasoning must be at general level, impartial and unbiased, that is, free from particular interests. Furthermore, the following considerations apply in respect of such reasoning: (1) it must be characterised by the use of familiar terms and methods of reasoning; (2) it must aspire to arrive at well-justified conclusions; (3) the criteria and order of priority applied in respect of the arguments put forward must be given or known beforehand; (4) it must be clearly distinguishable from purely individualistic viewpoints; and (5) the notion of objectivity and its criteria applicable to the reasoning used must be common to reasonable persons. In short, objectivity entails the ability to depart from an individual point of view, and join the common and general discourse. Each professional and reasonable agent must recognise it as eligible legal reasoning.[46] In other words, objectivity is freedom from bias.[47] This is an expression of Hume's idea of evaluations departing from private situations and interests. The Kantian term 'objectivisation' also applies in this context.[48]

---

[44] John Rawls, *Political Liberalism* (Columbia University Press 1993) 110 and 115. See my approach to weak objectivity applied in legal knowledge and based on Rawls' thinking in Matti Ilmari Niemi, 'Objective Legal Reasoning – Objectivity Without Objects', in Jaakko Husa and Mark van Hoecke (eds) *Objectivity in Law and Legal Reasoning* (Hart Publishing 2013) 78.

[45] According to Nagel the 'objectivity of moral reasoning does not depend on its having an external reference' and that 'moral thought is concerned not with the description and explanation of what happens but with decisions and their justifications'. Thomas Nagel, *The Last Word* (Oxford University Press, 1997) 101. The difference between epistemological and ontological objectivity can also be exploited here. Epistemological objectivity does not entail ontological objectivity. See John Searle, *The Construction of Social Reality* (The Free Press, 1995) 63. See also Dworkin (n 39) 260.

[46] See Sieckmann (n 40).

[47] See Villa-Rosas and Fabra-Zamora (n 1).

[48] Immanuel Kant, *The Grounding for the Metaphysics of Morals* (Hackett Publishing Company 1981) 412. The Kantian idea of objectivisation is similar to Hume's approach on evaluations departing from private situations and interests. According to Kant, the objective level – i.e., the level of categorical imperatives – is reached by departing from the subjective level by means of rational reasoning.

How is it possible to achieve this? In the words of Nagel: 'How to combine the perspective of a particular person in the world with an objective view of the same world, the person and his viewpoint included?'[49]

My aim here is to show how the general criteria of objectivity set out above are applied in the legal arena. These criteria are, however, already familiar in that arena and have much in common with the general rules of legal reasoning outlined by Robert Alexy.[50] The function of the rules mentioned above can be seen as seeking to ensure the objectivity of legal reasoning and interpretation.

It is worth noting that the adopted weak conception allows for differing degrees of objectivity. An adequate moral or legal notion of objectivity is not an either/or matter. Judgements can be more or less objective, and more or less subjective; they can be more or less successful, and more or less convincing and credible.

The aim of the general criteria of the weak conception of objectivity is to secure ideal epistemic conditions that facilitate the achievement of correct reasoning and conclusions.[51] Hence, meeting the criteria promotes objectivity. In the field of law, ideal epistemic conditions refer to advanced and conventional methods of legal reasoning. Furthermore, they offer usable criteria of criticism.

Law refers to and regulates relations between persons and is situated at the level of society. The objectivity adopted here appears as inter-subjectivity, which is a crucial dimension of objectivity.

However, law is also an artificial and conceptual construct that is dependent on the members of a given society and on their conventions. As a normative and systematic whole, it is constituted by the members of the society as a whole. On the other hand, as an essential aspect of the society, law appears as a given matter from the viewpoint of the individual members of the society.

The general criteria of objectivity must be specified on the level of legal reasoning.

---

[49] Thomas Nagel, *The View from Nowhere* (Oxford University Press 1986) 3. In addition, according to Nagel, 'we are to rely less and less on certain individual aspects of our point of view, and more and more on something else, less individual, which is also part of us'. Nagel (n 49) 67. On this point, Kramer employs the terms 'epistemic objectivity' and 'transindividual discernibility'. See Matthew H Kramer, *Objectivity and the Rule of Law* (Cambridge University Press 2007) 46. His point of view is, nevertheless, different.

[50] See Robert Alexy, *A Theory of Legal Argumentation* (Clarendon Press, 1989) 187.

[51] See Jules L Coleman and Brian Leiter, 'Determinacy, Objectivity, and Authority', in Andrei Marmor (ed.) *Law and Interpretation, Essays in Legal Philosophy* (Clarendon Press, 1997) 263 and 272.

6.2 Specific Features of Objective Legal Interpretation

A strong commitment to official sources of law, in the form of statutes and/or precedents, is one obvious dimension of legal objectivity. Their existence and significance can be explained in many ways; for example, as social facts and as evidence of a lawgiver's will, as Kelsen saw it. In this context they constitute the primary manifestations of the conventions of a society, the shared values of its members and the policies that the society has adopted.[52] Accordingly, they are the primary manifestations of the valid law – i.e., basically, justice adopted in the society.

From the cognitive point of view, application of statutes and/or precedents strengthens legal knowledge. It advances legal certainty as a dimension of justice. On the other hand, the use of these legal sources engenders new questions as to the proper application of statutes or precedents and justified interpretations of them.

In the Western world, statutes and precedents represent the visible, primary and objective means by which a society expresses and imposes its norms and, at the same time, its values. As embodiments of these norms and values, statutes and precedents provide primary premises and a strong foundation for the objectivity of legal reasoning. As a matter of fact, they constitute the strongest foundation for objectivity in the area of law.

Applicable sections of statutes or precedents have to be taken into account. It is not acceptable to ignore them in the context of any valid process of legal interpretation or adjudication. On the other hand, unconventional interpretations or applications take place and well-justified *contra legem* interpretations or judgments are possible. In addition, discretion in the case of a gap in law has to be made. Statutes or precedents cannot provide a complete set of norms.

---

[52] Conventions are not defined here merely as formal decisions tied to certain procedures at the surface level of a legal system (i.e., in the narrow and positivistic sense). Instead, they are seen as reflections of conventions at a deeper level and in a broad sense. They are expressions, applications and adjustments of the principles of justice and values in addition to other factors that influence the content of law. Hence, it is natural to use these principles and values as the premises of legal reasoning besides sections of statutes and precedents. Adjustment also refers to reconciliation and compromises between opposing interests. Accordingly, it refers to the sufficient consensus of a society granting the acceptability of the adopted legal system (i.e., its legitimacy). Dworkin presupposes such a consensus although he criticises the positivistic idea of convention as the foundation of a legal system that was introduced by Hart and emphasised by Jules L Coleman. See Hart (n 9) 102, 109 and 116; Jules L Coleman, *The Practice of Principle* (Oxford University Press 2001) 75 and Ronald Dworkin, *Law's Empire* (Fontana Press 1986) 199 and 211. See also the semantic sting-argument introduced by Dworkin, in ibid., 45.

Affirmation of the strong position of statutes or precedents does not compel one to adopt any kind of positivism. Despite their crucial position, statutes and precedents are not enough in legal reasoning; much more is needed. Statutes and precedents do not constitute an exhaustive list of legal sources. Both formal and substantial reasons are employed, and they are used both in epistemic and creative ways. In the context of legal dogmatics, statutes and precedents offer neither necessary nor sufficient reasons for the conclusions. In addition to them, and sometimes instead of them, many other kinds of arguments are used and needed. Since many of these constitute substantive reasons and are context-dependent, it is not possible to exhaustively list all possible legal reasons beforehand or an unconditional hierarchy of them. In this strict sense, the rule of recognition introduced by Hart is not viable.[53] I take the view that legal relevance offers the only basis on which to restrict the sphere of legal reasons. Hence, the concept of law adopted here is both wide and open. It is not possible to impose a strict demarcation between legal and non-legal reasons or issues. All relevant reasons are legal reasons.

In addition to statutes, many kinds of precedents and principles, legal concepts and substantive reasons are applied, and a systematic approach is followed in the process of legal interpretation. On the other hand, consistent with the weak character of legal knowledge, no ontological or metaphysical dimensions of these concepts are adopted. Concepts are necessary elements of judicial understanding that also have an ordering role through which the structure of law and of a specific legal system may be understood.[54]

The order of priority in which different legal reasons are applied cannot be exhaustively determined beforehand in the abstract. At best, it is possible to identify a prima facie order. The ultimate weight and effect of different legal reasons varies in different situations and cases. Legal interpretations and applications are context-dependent. Exceptional interpretations and deviations from applicable statutes or precedents are possible. Interpretation is always needed, even in easy cases. Accordingly, it is justifiable to consider parts of statutes or precedents as primary rather than as exclusive reasons.[55]

---

[53] See Hart (n 9) 100. The rule of recognition is a useful and significant concept if a short and closed list of legal sources given beforehand is presumed. This is the case in the frameworks of legal positivism. If all relevant reasons are applicable and acceptable reasons in the context of legal interpretation, the rule of recognition is not viable.

[54] More closely about the employment of principles in legal interpretation as well as critique against it, see Triantafyllos Gkouvas, 'Rethinking the Legal Effect of Interpretative Canons', Chapter 10 in this book.

[55] For the argument that sections of statutes constitute exclusive reasons, see Joseph Raz, *The Authority of Law* (Oxford University Press 1979) 29 and 33.

From the viewpoint of objectivity, relevant legal reasons or acceptable conclusions are not enough. They have to be used in a conventional and acceptable way. By meeting the requirements of correct reasoning, we seek to secure its objectivity.

From the citizen's viewpoint, the objectivity of legal reasoning appears as *impartiality*. Normative standards apply in each society, to which a citizen appeals when he or she appeals to the law, independent of the standards or interests of certain persons or groups. Legal reasoning, as a response to this appeal, has to take place free from such distorting factors. This approach is generally linked with adjudication, the work of judges, but impartiality is also required of legal scholars.

By means of the concept of impartiality we can introduce two new qualifications of legal objectivity: first, those who interpret or apply the law must intend to do so objectively, and second, they must hold impartial positions. One must assume that scholars, in addition to judges, are not exempt from these requirements.[56]

In this sense, the demands of law are *impersonal*. The call for objectivity in the most important sense, is the ability to guarantee that the standpoint introduced is that of society at large and an embodiment of its values, not a personal opinion, evaluation, or another subjective or individual viewpoint. Objective interpretations are made by persons but, on the other hand, it is demanded that these interpretations are impartial and unbiased, that is, free from personal interests and evaluations.[57]

Even the use of relevant legal reasons and correct reasoning is not enough. I take it for granted that judges and scholars seek to use the best possible reasoning and arrive at the best possible conclusions. In Dworkin's words, true propositions of law are best constructive interpretations of a community's legal practice founded on the principles of justice, fairness and procedural due process.[58] In this context, the aim to achieve the most acceptable and objective conclusion – i.e., the most advanced expression of the law – is apparent.[59] This involves arriving at a standpoint that is not personal in nature but represents

---

[56] Objectivity *qua* impartiality when the focus is on the objectivity of law. See Kramer (n 49) 53.

[57] Greenawalt uses the term 'interpersonal force'. See Kent Greenawalt, *Law and Objectivity* (Oxford University Press 1992) 202.

[58] Dworkin (n 52) 225.

[59] See the virtue theory of objectivity provided by Amaya. Amalia Amaya, 'Virtue and Objectivity in Legal Reasoning', Chapter 14 in this book. Naturally, an objective, that is, an ideal interpretation for this part of reasoning, is made by human beings and, in this sense, it is an outcome and product of this kind of human and virtuous activity. The pursuit of objectivity is a human virtue. Even in this sense it is a matter of best possible legal reasoning.

the most reasonable and acceptable conclusion in the context of the society of which the person presenting the reasoning is a member. On this point, I appeal to the notion of the best possible interpretation put forward by Dworkin.[60]

According to Dworkin, a sufficient consensus and realisation of citizens' rights is possible by means of legal interpretations based on good legal reasons. Ideal reasoning, in which the best possible reasons are utilised, provides the best possible solutions and, in this weak sense, the only right answers. The imaginary perfect judge *Hercules* can always provide such reasoning and solutions.[61] Accordingly, real human judges and scholars, even at their best, merely produce incomplete reasoning and conclusions. On the other hand, they reach for the perfect ones.

Legal knowledge is weak, and, in practice, it is not possible to reach the level of perfect reasoning or to take into consideration all possible reasons relevant in a situation or a case. In other words, it is not possible to put justice into effect in a perfect way, but it is worth trying to achieve this. By means of objective reasoning it is possible to present good reasoning and arrive at good conclusions by searching for the best possible ones.

7. CONCLUSIONS

This chapter has discussed the idea that the objectivity of legal knowledge is grounded on valid methods of interpretations. However, legal knowledge is understood in the weak sense. The concepts 'moderate' or 'pragmatic legal cognitivism' might be adopted here. No doubt, this is a substantive view on law and legal knowledge.[62] This approach resembles the positive approach to ethics adopted by Hume. The adopted conception of knowledge and objectivity is used as to ground the defence against the challenge posed by scepticism. Moreover, the criticism of certain schools of jurisprudence is grounded on this approach. Both the value scepticism of legal positivism and the cognitive scepticism of Scandinavian legal realism are called into question. On the other hand, the strong conception of knowledge adopted by legal positivism is also challenged.

---

[60] See Dworkin (n 52) 338, 379 and 411. Even the notion that there can be one ascertainably correct answer to any legal questions, put forward by Dworkin, can be interpreted as the best possible answer. In other words, there is always a best justified answer. See Dworkin (n 38) 279 and Dworkin (n 39) 41. About Dworkin's view on legal interpretation, see Marchettoni (n 16).

[61] See Dworkin (n 38) 105, Dworkin (n 52) 239 and Dworkin (n 39) 42.

[62] See Hector A Morales-Zúñiga, 'Is Legal Cognitivism a Case of Bullshit?', Chapter 3 in this book.

Objective legal knowledge appears as objective interpretation – i.e., conclusions are inferred from premises by judges and legal scholars. Accordingly, legal knowledge denotes the process of deriving conclusions from legal reasons. In this process statutes and precedents play the most significant role, as primary premises, and legal reasons. As formal reasons, they earn this position because they indicate the principles of justice and values adopted in a society as the basis of its legal system. They are not, however, sufficient reasons. Directly applicable substantial reasons are also needed and used.

The task of both judges and legal scholars is to put into effect the adopted justice and values in the best possible way. This job can be done with the help of objective legal interpretation.

PART II

OBJECTIVITY AND LEGAL INTERPRETATION

7. From Hart to Dworkin via Brandom: Indeterminacy, interpretation, and objectivity

Leonardo Marchettoni

In *The Concept of Law* H L A Hart aims to explain the idea of obligation in law and states that obligations are fundamentally connected with social practices: our practices include current settled dispositions to act in certain ways. Practice becomes the source of a duty to behave according to a given pattern. However, this simple explanation opens the door to a vast array of problems. In fact, recourse to practice must be qualified. Obligations lie on a substratum of empirical regularities but are not reducible to them: as Hart says, there are some specific features of obligations that cannot be captured by an account in terms of empirical regularities. In particular, the aspects pertaining to the so-called internal point of view require the reference to something like an abstract norm.

The introduction of abstract norms beyond empirical regularities raises the problem of defining the relationship that puts the former in relation to the latter. However, carrying out this task proved to be very difficult. Furthermore, in hard cases, when the law seems indeterminate, the lack of a satisfying account of the relation between norms and regularities results in the recourse to a kind of discretionary power on the part of the judges. In such cases the same practice, so to speak, breaks down, showing the perspectival nature of norms.

The problem of the indeterminacy of norms is one of the shortcomings of Hart's theory that triggered Dworkin's criticism. Dworkin argues that the determinacy of law does not fail even in hard cases, because each judge takes part in an interpretive enterprise of reconstructing the content of law according to the values of the community.

In this chapter, I try to shed new light on the Hart-Dworkin debate by re-reading it against the background of Robert Brandom's theory of the social institution of norms. First, I compare Hart's conception of practice to Brandom's and contend that Brandom's theory, as expounded in his seminal *Making It Explicit*, manages to avoid Kripke-style arguments to the effect that every rule is exposed to the perils of indeterminacy. Brandom's subsequent work turns to a new model of concept determination that centres on the activity of unfolding the content of the norms that implicitly governed our past practices. This last conception, in my opinion, shows significant points of contact to Dworkin's and can be put forward as an attempt to provide a new solution to the problem of the objectivity of law.

A last caveat is in order. My chapter is not a piece of exegesis. While I aspire to be faithful to Hart's and Dworkin's texts, there are surely lots of hermeneutical subtleties that I cannot take in due account. My aim is of a more theoretical nature. For this reason, I will not consider Dworkin's first attempt to criticise Hart, as expounded in the seminal papers collected in *Taking Rights Seriously*.[1] After all, there is certainly no shortage of excellent reconstruction of the entire Hart-Dworkin debate.[2]

1. HART ON OBLIGATIONS, RULES AND RECOGNITION

In the fifth chapter of *The Concept of Law*, Hart begins to lay out his personal views on the law. After having criticised Austin's gunman model in the previous chapter, the time has finally come to expound an alternative picture. His overall strategy is clear. Hart argues that, despite its errors, Austin's theory departed from the correct assumption that 'where there is law, there human conduct is made in some sense non-optional or obligatory'.[3] The problem with Austin is that he confused 'being obliged to do something' and 'having an obligation to do something'.[4] The first statement has a psychological import: it expresses the beliefs and motives that explain the agent's conduct. The second, on the other hand, has a completely different nature. It requires something, for the existence of which beliefs and motives are neither sufficient nor necessary: it requires the presence of an obligation.

In turn, obligations cannot be accounted for in predictive terms; they are not reducible to the probability of being sanctioned.[5] Obligations are conceivable only where there are social rules capable of giving normative force to certain types of behaviour. However, not all rules generate a corresponding obliga-

---

[1] Ronald Dworkin, *Taking Rights Seriously* (Harvard University Press 1977).
[2] For example, see Scott J Shapiro, 'The "Hart–Dworkin" Debate: A Short Guide for the Perplexed' in Arthur Ripstein (ed), *Ronald Dworkin* (CUP 2007).
[3] H L A Hart, *The Concept of Law* (2nd edn, Clarendon Press 1994), 82.
[4] Ibid.
[5] Ibid., 83ff. More on this in Leonardo Marchettoni, 'Norma, obbligo e sanzione. Una rilettura di alcune nozioni giuridiche a partire dalla pragmatica di Robert Brandom' (2017) 17 *Diritto & Questioni Pubbliche* 251.

tion, since rules of etiquette do not seem to bring about obligations or duties.⁶ According to Hart, to talk about obligations there must be three further requirements: (1) the rules must be supported by a 'serious social pressure' towards conformity, which leads to verbal criticism of those who deviate or even to physical sanctions (henceforth, *seriousness*); (2) the rules are believed to be necessary to the maintenance of social life (*necessity*); (3) since obligations may conflict with the agent's wishes, they 'are thought of as characteristically involving sacrifice or renunciation'.⁷ Therefore, the corresponding rules must be seen as prevailing over the agent's preferences (*overridingness*). *Necessity* and *overridingness* are related to what Hart calls 'the internal point of view' and implies that obligations may provide a *reason* for behaviour.

I have retraced in some detail Hart's train of thought in this part of *The Concept of Law* in order to introduce the first point of my argument: according to Hart, legal obligations presuppose rules that exhibit both an *empirical* – that is, *external* – dimension and some additional characteristics – *seriousness, necessity, overridingness* – which are not merely external. Obligations depend on social rules, which are basically accountable for in terms of regularities but requires the occurrence of some specific features that cannot be captured in this way. The external dimension invites a dispositionalist interpretation, as long as dispositions are seen as related to the social import of rules.⁸ But talk of empirical regularities cannot express the other adjunctive features that distinguish the norms that generate obligations from general social rules, namely *seriousness, necessity* and *overridingness*. More specifically, it cannot capture the *internal point of view* because it leaves no room for the introduction of considerations of the motivating force of rules, it does not recognise them as reasons.⁹ Therefore, obligations are analysable as empirical regularities *plus* certain specific features that are, at least *prima facie*, non-reducible to dispositional discourse.

To incorporate these further aspects, we must go beyond the simple model of rules as empirical regularities and approach the realm of norms. In fact, the idea that obligations provide *reasons* for behaviour requires that we introduce abstract norms – distinct from sets of empirical regularities – capable of motivating agents. This reveals the greatest problem of post-Hartian legal philosophy, namely that of specifying which relationship empirical regularities

---

⁶ Hart (n 3) 86.
⁷ Ibid., 87.
⁸ I assume that dispositions are intrinsic resources that make a given agent capable, in a given situation, of performing a given task in a given way. So, talk of dispositions presupposes the obtaining of empirical regularities, since every agent that possesses a disposition *d* in the situation *s* will behave according to the same pattern.
⁹ Hart (n 3) 89–90.

bears to norms. It is fair to say that Hart was unable to solve this problem. The rigid dichotomy between the external and the internal points of view is a clear symptom of such failure.

The problems of Hart's solution are immediately apparent in the case of his theory of the rule of recognition. Hart says that 'For the most part the rule of recognition is not stated, but its existence is *shown* in the way in which particular rules are identified, either by courts or other officials or private persons or their advisers.'[10] This statement means that with reference to the rule of recognition there is no possibility of distinguishing an abstract norm from the empirical regularities through which officials manifest *their* acceptance and understanding of it. The internal dimension of the rule collapses on the external one for the obvious reason that, since the rule of recognition is an *ultimate* rule,[11] the introduction of an abstract norm distinct from the practice would have opened the problem of judging about the congruence between the rule and practice. So, there is a difficulty regarding the proper way to manage the distinction between the external and the internal dimension of the rules.

Evidently, such a conception poses a number of problems, because, as it has been pointed out,[12] it is not at all clear in which way a rule whose content is defined by the dispositions of a proper subset of citizens could determine the extension of the set of valid primary rules. In fact, Hart's rule of recognition cannot exert any normative force. This shortcoming, in turn, leads to the 'perspectivality' of the rule of recognition. The problem is the following. When Hart discusses the issue of the uncertainty of the rule of recognition, he must conclude that 'when courts settle previously unenvisaged questions concerning the most fundamental constitutional rules, they *get* their authority to decide them accepted after the questions have arisen and the decision has been given'.[13] In other words, judges decide according to their understanding of the matter and let their authority fill up the void created by the uncertainty of the rule and by the normative inertia of the practice.

This problem represents a case in point of the kind of indeterminacy that Hart discusses in the seventh Chapter of *The Concept of Law*. To these pages, therefore, I turn my critical attention.

---

[10] Ibid., 102, italics in text.
[11] Ibid., 105.
[12] Scott J Shapiro, 'What is the Rule of Recognition (and Does it Exist)?' in Matthew D Adler and Kenneth Einar Himma (eds), *The Rule of Recognition and the U.S. Constitution* (OUP 2009)
[13] Hart (n 3) 153, italics in text.

2. HART ON THE INDETERMINACY OF NORMS

In the previous section, I argued that according to Hart legal rules are a particular kind of social rules. They lie, as it were, on a substratum of empirical regularities. However, empirical regularities are not sufficient to produce obligations, as obligations involve three more specific requirements, namely *seriousness*, *necessity* and *overridingness*. The latter two characteristics are particularly important, because they introduce what Hart calls the internal point of view, that is, the idea that a merely external consideration of the empirical regularities associated with rules is not enough to capture how agents may feel constrained by the motivating force of norms.

The dichotomy between the external and the internal point of view, and between empirical regularities and abstract norms is problematic, because it is not easy to explain the relationship between the two terms. Since there is no principled way to connect norms and regularities, a problem concerning the perspectival character of the law may arise. In the case of the rule of recognition this problem is related to the fact that there is no supreme instance that can judge in case of disagreement between officials, so the decisions derive their normative force from the authority of the issuer. This kind of problem, however, is not very different from the familiar troubles associated with the so-called indeterminacy of the law.

This issue is the specific target of the seventh Chapter of *The Concept of Law*. Hart's purpose in this chapter is to delimit the ways in which the law can be indeterminate. Indeed, according to Hart, the indeterminacy of the law is not global but can be circumscribed. In most cases, the application of the law seems to be straightforward and, as a result, there does not seem to be any problems with determinacy. The goal of discriminating between easy and hard cases can be pursued through a proper analysis of the causes of indeterminacy. There are, Hart says, two general devices used in order to communicate general standards of conduct: legislation and precedent.[14] The shortcomings of the first device depend on the semantic limitations of the general terms employed in it, since general terms cannot accommodate either the infinite complexity of the fabric of facts, or the indeterminacy of our aims.[15] On the other hand, the drawbacks of precedent are related to the impossibility of extracting, from previous examples, any definite rule that may constrain subsequent decisions of

---

[14] This bipartition reminds me of the way in the fifth chapter Hart introduces the rule of recognition, by saying that it may consist in a list of texts or in a set of general characteristic possessed by the primary rules. See Hart (n 3) 94–95.

[15] Ibid., 134–35.

courts.[16] When unforeseen cases arise, judges must play a creative role, issuing new law, which can settle still unanswered questions. However, Hart also says that such a predicament is not ubiquitous, because in most situations the law offers determinate rules, which do *not* require officials and private individuals to make 'a fresh judgment from case to case'.[17]

It is important to understand the exact reasons behind the failure of determinacy. As I said, Hart thinks that, in most situations, general terms work quite well. In these cases, there is no doubt about their use. They are 'plain cases', that is, cases that do not require any interpretive effort, in which 'the recognition of instances seems unproblematic or "automatic"'.[18] However, there are also hard cases, in which the 'agreement in judgments as to the applicability of the classifying terms' breaks down.[19] In such cases, hermeneutic canons offer no guidance, since 'these canons are themselves general rules for the use of language, and make use of general terms which themselves require interpretation'.[20] As a consequence, we must relinquish the comfort of general terms and rely on the second device listed above, namely precedent. Faced with a situation where there is no previous agreement on the applicability of a general term, the interpreter of the law can only use the plain case as an authoritative example. But the recourse to this strategy involves the attribution of a discretionary power. Indeed, the interpreter 'chooses to add to a line of cases a new case because of resemblances which can reasonably be defended as both legally relevant and sufficiently close'.[21] Such a power is discretionary because there cannot be a general agreement on the correct way to complete the list of items subsumed under the relevant general term. Otherwise, we would fall back in some plain case. But this also means that there is no common practice, as this seems to presuppose a wide agreement among practitioners.

The foregoing discussion should serve the purpose of making clear that Hart links failures of determinacy to the lack of a common practice. This point is especially important in light of the previous section: the predicament is basically the same as in the case of the rule of recognition. Lack of a common practice means lack of agreement on the correct way of interpreting the rule. The main difference is that in the case of the rule of recognition we have no abstract norm distinct from practice, whereas in the case of primary rules abstract norms do not cover hard cases: in both situations we have that the

---

[16] Ibid., 128–29.
[17] Ibid., 135.
[18] Ibid., 126.
[19] Ibid.
[20] Ibid.
[21] Ibid., 127.

commonality of practice cannot be ensured by the content of the norms and we must fill up the normative voids.

Judicial discretion in the case of indeterminacy of primary norms is the counterpart of the recourse to authority that settles issues previously not foreseen at the level of secondary norms. In both cases, the perceived uncertainty of the law opens up a discretionary space to interpreters, because in such cases there is no law that can constrain their evaluations. Therefore, we end up with the following chain: the lack of common practice implies indeterminacy – in the sense of inability of the law to resolve the question definitively – which in turn implies failure of objectivity. Thus, for the transitivity of implication, the lack of common practice implies failure of objectivity. Finally, by contraposition, objectivity implies common practice.

The overall upshot is that Hart's brand of positivism, to the extent that it advances a practice theory of law, connects lack of common practice to failures of objectivity. Hart, by linking the need for judicial discretion to an absence of agreement, opens the door to doubts about the objectivity of law. Such qualms require criteria that separate cases where the law dictates what should be done from cases where the law is silent. Hart fulfils this task by distinguishing between plain cases and hard cases, that is, between cases where there is a wide agreement on the practice to be followed, and cases where no such agreement exists.

3. THE PROBLEM AND DWORKIN'S ATTEMPT TO SOLVE IT

The discussion in the seventh Chapter of *The Concept of Law* highlights the crucial issue behind the weakness of Hart's model. Hart considers abstract norms that are nonetheless related to empirical regularities. But this relationship is left underdetermined. So, there is no way to ensure common practice. It follows the indeterminacy, both at the level of primary rules and at the level of the secondary ones, where the rule of recognition cannot exert any normative force to define the boundaries of valid law.

As it is widely known, Dworkin attempts to fill in the gaps in Hart's story by providing a different account of legal practice. Dworkin maintains that the same distinction between plain and hard cases is the consequence of a misconception of the nature of law. This misconception is rooted in a 'semantic view' according to which what law depends on some set of specific criteria.[22] To the semantic theories of law, Dworkin opposes his 'interpretivist' conception, which is based on two assumptions: (*a*) that the practice of law has some point

---

[22] Ronald Dworkin, *Law's Empire* (Fontana 1986) 31ff.

'that can be stated independently of just describing the rules that make up the practice'[23] and (*b*) that the requirements of the practice are sensitive to its point.

Once the interpretative conception is embraced, the possibility of distinguishing between cases in which judges apply the existing law and cases in which judges create new law out of their discretionary power disappears, because the work of judges is always a kind of constructive interpretation aimed at finding the best solution to the cases on which they have to decide. Judges are required to carry out a holistic interpretation of previous law and to extend that body in a way that is sensitive to *their* understanding of its point – actually, to their understanding of the understanding of its point entertained by the *community* to which they belong – in relation to the content of the case they are to decide. A momentous consequence is that there is no real problem about the indeterminacy of the law. The judges try to find the best interpretation of the existing law, that is, the interpretation that answers the questions posed by the case. Therefore, their activity is, in some sense, incompatible with the very idea of the indeterminacy of law.

The example of Dworkin's conception shows that the risk of indeterminacy can be avoided if the ties that link objectivity and practices are severed. In Hart's view the problem of indeterminacy and lack of objectivity arose from the attempt to ground the norms in social rules, practices, and empirical regularities. Hence, the problem of ensuring the normative force of rules and their effectiveness in demarcating valid law and facts referred to by the law. Dworkin can claim to dodge this shortcoming by positing the existence of an objective set of normative elements that orient judges' practices. In this way, objectivity is no longer a metaphysical property: it does not derive from the fact that there is, after all, something inside the law that dictates what must be done. Rather, it becomes a *pre-theoretical* assumption – in the sense of an assumption required by the normative and social conception of interpretation Dworkin calls for.[24]

This latter point becomes evident if we look at Dworkin's famous chain novel model.[25] Dworkin in *Law's Empire* argues that the efforts of judges can be assimilated to the act of continuing a chain novel: the judge is like a writer that sets to her/himself the task of completing in the best way a story started by other authors. The judge aims to find the best solution to the cases she/he has to decide by constructing the best interpretation of the previous law. But which normative standard the interpretation must satisfy is something that has to be chosen by the judge. Of course, another judge can correct his/her predecessor's

---

[23] Ibid., 47.
[24] On Dworkin's attitude to objectivity, see also Thomas Bustamante's essay in this volume.
[25] Dworkin, *Law's Empire* (n 22) 225ff.

interpretation. What is impossible to find is something like a definitive standard, that is, a set of criteria that is not subject to further correction.

When we see the whole matter in this regard, we can conclude that the respective positions of Hart and Dworkin are not all that far apart. Hart thinks that judges use discretionary powers in hard cases. Dworkin thinks that in all cases judges strive to find the best interpretation of the law. The second statement does not necessarily contradict the first. The key point is to understand whether use of discretion is necessarily at odds with Dworkin's idea that judges should decide cases in light of the best interpretation of the existing law.

4. RETHINKING NORMS AND OBJECTIVITY

In the preceding sections, I have recalled some familiar issues of Hart's and Dworkin's conceptions of norms and interpretation. In the first two sections, I argued that Hart's theory of legal rules conceives of them as based on empirical regularities plus some specific requirements, particularly what I have called *necessity* and *overridingness*, which illustrate the aptitude, on the part of a given norm, to provide reasons capable of motivating behaviour. Hart, however, proves to be unable to manage such dichotomy. He is forced to posit two different levels, the level of empirical regularities and the level of abstract norms, without explicating which relationship obtains between them. As a result, in so-called hard cases, he must conclude that judges are guided by their discretion because they run out of law.

On the contrary, Dworkin maintains that judges are always constrained by the law, even in the most difficult and novel cases. In his opinion what binds the judges is their interpretation of the best reconstruction that their community provides of the law. The judges aim for a constructive interpretation that can put the existing law in the best light. Therefore, there is no discretion on their part, because their decisions follow the content of law.

My suspicion is that Hart's and Dworkin's respective positions become not so distant if we read them correctly. This fact could emerge more clearly if we try to reformulate the entire question in a different manner. The starting point is the relationship between regularities and norms. I said that Hart cannot explain how abstract norms relate to empirical regularities. Post-Hartian legal philosophers explored several possibilities: reduction, supervenience, rational determination, grounding.[26] In the end, the situation is not so different from

---

[26] See, among many, Andrei Marmor, *Social Conventions from Language to Law* (Princeton University Press 2009); Mark Greenberg, 'How Facts Make Law' (2004) 10 *Legal Theory* 157; George Pavlakos, 'The Metaphysics of Law: From Supervenience to Rational Justification' in Bartosz Brożek, Antonino Rotolo and Jerzy Stelmach (eds), *Supervenience and Normativity* (Springer 2017).

that of the well-known rule-following problem: as Wittgenstein and, later, Kripke made clear, a set, however vast, of data cannot dictate the answer to the question of how to apply a rule in a previously unanswered case and, on the other side, the content of rules is not always 'transparent' to their interpreters. The same moral applies to judges: decisions in 'hard' cases are always discretionary, in the sense of not necessarily being reducible to the application of a pre-existing norm – because the content of the norm itself does not provide detailed operational instructions – nor to the extension of a previous sequence of examples – because the past cases do not dictate the solution of the new ones.

Perhaps, to solve this conundrum, it may be useful to turn our gaze to a different perspective. My suggestion is Robert Brandom's theory of the social institution of norms.[27] In the first chapters of his masterpiece, *Making It Explicit*,[28] Brandom introduces the basic elements of his conception of *sapience*. Sapience is what distinguishes human beings from merely sentient beings. It can be expressed as a kind of subjection not only to natural laws but also to inferentially articulated norms. But this does not mean that sapience is a kind of abstract essence that only agents of a given type possess. On the contrary, Brandom stresses that the possession of sapience is rather a matter of exhibiting certain practices that, in principle, can be shared by any agent.

Taking this normative starting point calls for an extensive discussion of the nature of norms and of the traditional problem of rule-following. The first chapter of *Making It Explicit* is indeed devoted to outlining a theory of norms capable of addressing the rule-following paradoxes. The difficulty here is clearly in explaining how the act of behaving according to norms can be accounted for in a way that preserves the existence of facts regarding what counts as the correct application of a rule.

First, Brandom, in the footsteps of Wittgenstein's *Philosophical Investigations*, criticises the 'regulist' (Platonist) view, according to which the normativity of intentionality presupposes the existence of explicit rules, because it entails the unfortunate consequence of an infinite regress of interpretations.[29] Brandom then takes into consideration the 'regularist' theory, that is, the view that explains the existence of norms through regularities of behaviour or dispositions towards action. The problem with this proposal is

---

[27] The following pages are based on Leonardo Marchettoni, 'Brandom's Theory of the Institution of Norms' (2014) 2 *Philosophical Inquiries* 37 and Leonardo Marchettoni, 'Brandom on Norms and Objectivity' (2018) 19 *Critical Horizons* 215, to which I refer for further details.

[28] Robert B Brandom, *Making It Explicit: Reasoning, Representing, and Discursive Commitment* (Harvard University Press 1994).

[29] Ibid., 18–26.

that any finite sequence of behaviour is consistent with an infinite number of possible continuations, and thus that behaviour could accord with an infinite number of rules; this makes it impossible to distinguish between correct and incorrect performances.[30]

The upshot of these first two stages suggests that, in order to make sense of the idea of the normative character of intentionality, we need an account of norms that steers a middle course between the Platonist and the regularist views, that is, an account that replaces explicit norms with norms *implicit* in practice. Brandom's solution to the problem of following a rule centres on the idea that we can explain the existence of rules if we focus on our activity of treating performances as correct or incorrect.[31]

The failures of the regularist approach and of what Brandom calls 'communal assessment theories'[32] suggest that there is no way to express the normativity of intentionality without referring to norms.[33] We must therefore accept that the normative vocabulary is non-reducible and non-replaceable even if norms emerge from non-normative facts. Brandom assumes that the fact that the institution of norms is a consequence of our judgments and assessments of value, and hence cannot be accounted for in a language devoid of normative terms, does not entail these judgments and assessments being themselves describable in 'purely physical terms.'

Following this path, Brandom is led to an explanation of normative facts that takes normative statuses of performances – i.e., statuses of performances in relation to their correctness or incorrectness – to be instituted by our practical attitudes, i.e., by our treating certain performances as correct or incorrect. Normative attitudes are assessments, 'assignments to performances of normative significance or status, as correct or incorrect according to some norm'.[34] In turn, assessments are basically noting more than dispositions to sanction, i.e., to reward appropriate and punish inappropriate performances, as Brandom

---

[30] Ibid., 26–29.

[31] Brandom's account is probably akin to the social account of rules given by Jaap Hage in Chapter 2.

[32] Brandom is referring to the theories of Kripke and others – Saul Kripke, *Wittgenstein on Rules and Private Language* (Blackwell 1982); Crispin Wright, *Wittgenstein on the Foundations of Mathematics* (Duckworth 1980) – according to which the failure of both Platonist and regularist accounts leads us to the conclusion that the normative character of rule-following can only be explicated in the context of the practice of a given community. In response, Brandom asserts that communal assessment theorists make an illicit reference to normative notions such as 'expert' or 'authority'.

[33] Brandom (n 28) 45–46.

[34] Ibid., 35.

acknowledges.³⁵ The interdependence of practice and value assures us that, where we encounter the same attitudes, we will also find the same statuses. At the same time however, since attitudes cannot be described in naturalistic terms, since the very idea of sanction makes recourse to normative notions, the stronger claim that normative statuses supervene on merely natural facts does not follow.

As a consequence a three-tier construction is achieved: the base layer is represented by non-normative phenomena such as the regularities of behaviour; the second level includes our subjective normative attitudes; finally the third tier contains objective normative statuses – that is, the performance statuses in relation to their correctness or incorrectness. However, Brandom argues that the fact that normative statuses are instituted by practical attitudes does not exclude that the former are objective. On the contrary, one of Brandom's primary purposes is to provide a characterisation of semantic norms that leaves room for objectivity. In turn, this feature requires us to be sensitive to the distinction between the content of norms, that is, what *is* correct according to the rules, and our conception of norms, that is, what we *take* to be correct according to them.

It is fair to say that Brandom's notion of objectivity is somewhat peculiar. According to the standard account 'Objectivity may be taken to be equivalent to mind-independence in the sense that, in general, the objective facts about the world are what they are independently of whatever people happen to believe or desire.'³⁶ Therefore, it requires something like a view from nowhere.³⁷ Instead, Brandom regards the objectivity of conceptual content as 'the way in which its proper applicability is determined by how things are in such a way that anybody and everybody might be wrong in taking such a content to apply in particular circumstances'.³⁸ Thus, whereas within the traditional approach, the question of objectivity is analysed regardless of practice, Brandom suggests an approach in which objectivity is connected to the authority structure implicit in the social practice of claiming.

On this basis, we could try to identify two notions of 'objectivity': a strong and a weak one.

---

    ³⁵ Ibid., 34ff.
    ³⁶ James Ladyman, 'Ontological, Epistemological, and Methodological Positions' in Theo AF Kuipers (ed), *General Philosophy of Science: Focal Issues* (North Holland 2007) 307
    ³⁷ For a far more detailed analysis of the concept of 'objectivity', see the Introduction to this volume. On objectivity and mind-independence, see also Chapter 2 by Hage.
    ³⁸ Brandom (n 28) 529.

Strong Objectivity (*SO*): a given conceptual content is strongly objective = it is independent of people's beliefs, desires, and so on.

Weak Objectivity (*WO*): a given conceptual content is weakly objective = its proper applicability is determined by how things are in such a way that everybody might be wrong in taking it to apply in particular circumstances.

Objectivity, in Brandom's sense, is strictly related to authority and responsibility because the creation of the dialogical structure that makes objectivity possible depends on the way in which autonomous subjects are nonetheless responsible to the authority of the norms instituted in the course of the practice. This explains why an entire community can be wrong about the application of a given norm: because such application does not conform to the content – reconstructed by an independent observer – of the rule socially instituted.

All this does not imply the existence of a privileged perspective. The idea is rather, as Brandom explains in the last Chapter of *Making It Explicit*, that defining the parameters of correctness is entirely up to the interpreter who attempts to reconstruct the discursive scorekeeping practices. According to Brandom, the norms that establish when it is correct for an agent to attribute a given doxastic commitment to someone else are not available in advance as a set of explicit principles, 'but are implicit in the particular practices by which we understand one another in ordinary conversation'.[39] Furthermore, since the external interpretation of a linguistic community is not qualitatively different from the ordinary scorekeeping activity, 'There is never a final answer as to what is correct; everything, including our assessments of such correctness, is itself a subject for conversation and further assessment, challenge, defense, and correction'.[40]

Since there are no mind-independent criteria of correctness, objectivity becomes perspectival.[41] Conceptual contents can only be specified from some perspective and there is no common content passing from the point of view of a given speaker to that of the others,[42] therefore, the proper application of concepts in a given circumstance varies according to the perspective of each speaker. This entails a corresponding variability of the criteria governing the correct applicability of conceptual contents: the appropriate application of contents in response to the way things actually are can be determined in different ways by different speakers. In sum, what conceptual contents are at stake is a matter of interpretation.

---

[39] Ibid., 646.
[40] Ibid., 647.
[41] Ibid., 606.
[42] Ibid., 600.

Some critics have argued that Brandom does not offer a satisfactory answer to the problem of the objectivity of content.[43] This criticism may seem reasonable if we think of Brandom's characterisation of our dialogical interactions as games of giving and asking for reasons, which carry with them a very complex structure within which anaphoric chains, deictic mechanisms, *de re* and *de dicto* ascriptions should ensure a correspondence between what it is said and how things really stand in the world. However, the crucial point, in my view, is that Brandom account given in *Making It Explicit* dispenses with the idea of agents sharing some substantive item. All that matters is that there is a structure that makes it possible to distinguish the different perspectives of each speaker. This structure is common to all practitioners, who can thus share conceptual contents. No other item is shared by them. What are the consequences for the explanation of communication? To discuss this point, it may be useful to read what Brandom says in his reply to Habermas. The gist of Brandom's answer is that 'mutual understanding in the strong sense Habermas is insisting upon is *not* required for the undertaking of joint projects'.[44] Brandom's social perspectivism could represent a problem for communication only if the latter were seen as a process of mutual understanding in which agents get in touch with each other. But the conception of communication that emerges from Brandom's writings is not based on the idea that communication consists in making exactly the same moves – this task could be possible only if we postulated some universal norm – but rather in the ability to synchronise different movements.

In his later works Brandom has highlighted that conceptual norms are never complete, that is, they are always liable to further determination, by means of the acts of later performers. Brandom describes this process of never ending re-shaping of the reality via redefinition of the concepts employed as a kind of recognition, which involves different traditions, rather than different individuals.[45] This process, however, is not left to the autonomy of subjects but also depends on their responsibility to the attitudes of others because, even if each subject is autonomous in that she/he can choose the norms which she/he abides

---

[43] See, among many, Jürgen Habermas, 'From Kant to Hegel: On Robert Brandom's Pragmatic Philosophy of Language' (2000) 8 *European Journal of Philosophy* 322; Bob Hale and Crispin Wright, 'Assertibilist Truth and Objective Content: Still Inexplicit?' in Bernhard Weiss and Jeremy Wanderer (eds), *Reading Brandom: On Making It Explicit* (Routledge 2010).

[44] Robert B Brandom, 'Facts, Norms, and Normative Facts: A Reply to Habermas' (2000) 8 *European Journal of Philosophy* 363, italics in text.

[45] Robert B Brandom, *Reason in Philosophy: Animating Ideas* (Harvard University Press 2009) 103–104.

by, she/he is nonetheless responsible to the content of these norms, which is not up to her/him.

Indeed, if authority and responsibility must be completely symmetrical, the authority of conceptual contents over the activities of practitioners has to be balanced by the reciprocal authority of practitioners over those contents. This means that the practice of acknowledging commitments consists not only in the process of applying conceptual contents, but also in the process by which they are determined. This process develops over time and involves both retrospective and prospective dimensions. Whereas in *Making It Explicit* Brandom emphasised the *synchronic* perspectivity of conceptual content, which is a consequence of the '*symmetry*' of state and attitude between ascriber and the one to whom a commitment is ascribed',[46] in his later works he stresses its *diachronic* instability, which is a consequence of the symmetry between recogniser and recognised. In this way, he is adding a new dimension of 'perspectivity,' since the same content of concepts evolves over time, in response to the variable relations of authority.

In such a way, according to Brandom, a new mechanism for determining the conceptual content arises, characterised by a form of weak objectivity: the application of concepts does not follow predefined rules, which are independent from praxis but, so to speak, emerges from the practice itself, in the sense that deciding which performances are correct and which are not depends on the varying ways in which the previous tradition is rebuilt. As a consequence, the conceptual contents are both determined and determinable.

5. HART, DWORKIN, AND BRANDOM

In its essence, the debate between Hart and Dworkin hinges on two different ways of conceiving of the role of the judges. According to Hart, in hard cases judges perform a creative role, filling up the lacunae of the existing law out of their discretion. Their resulting decisions form new law because they are 'covered' by the authority of the issuers. Therefore, law is not objective, in the sense that what the law requires in a given situation is not predetermined in advance of judicial activity. On the contrary, Dworkin maintains that, even in hard cases, judges do not perform a creative role. Instead, they must accomplish a constructive interpretation of the existing law, which highlights in the best possible way what the law requires. Therefore, there is no shortage of law: the law is already there, waiting for the judge to bring it to light. In this sense, the law is objective: in any case there is an objective answer on the part of the law.

---

[46] Brandom, *Making It Explicit* (n 28) 600, italics in text.

Put in these terms the two positions seem to differ in that they employ different meanings of 'objectivity'. Hart adopts a strong notion of objectivity: law is objective when it provides a definite answer, independent from judicial discretion, to questions about which law can be applied in a given case. Dworkin seems to adopt a weaker notion of objectivity: in Dworkin's jargon the law is objective in the sense that it can be reconstructed in the best possible way. Objectivity is not something independent from practices; instead, it is a pre-theoretical property, which we must employ in our account of the practice itself. The practice is qualified by the interpreter's attempt to provide the best reconstruction of the legal system. But such an attempt is conceivable if and only if this system is built around objective values. Thus 'best' and 'objective' are linked: some values can be said objective because we can question whether the account given is the best possible, and, on the other side, we can question whether a given account is the best in so far as such evaluation stands against a set of objective values.

If this is so, perhaps we can try to adapt Brandom's weak notion of objectivity to Dworkin. The idea is roughly the following: Dworkin urges us to reconstruct the activity of applying the law as an activity aimed at the best. But aiming for the best means that the entire community of interpreters may be wrong and that a single interpreter may claim to correct their mistake. On the other side, there are no definitive interpretations, since each interpretation is subject to further assessment and scrutiny. This situation leads to a kind of pluralism, which is both synchronic, because there are many different interpreters, and diachronic, because each interpreter may be corrected by her/his inheritors.

It is worth noticing that in recent years Brandom has tried to apply his ideas to the case of the determination of legal concepts, taking up the framework already developed by Dworkin. More precisely, Brandom proposes to read Dworkin's famous chain novel metaphor in the context of his model of conceptual content determination.[47] The aspect that Brandom finds most problematic in Dworkin's approach is precisely the way in which he introduces the normative parameter on the basis of which each judge must continue the work of his predecessors. The main problem is that it is not clear in what sense one legal interpretation can be called 'better' than another.

One could try to solve the problem by calling on the metaphysical independence of values: the best interpretation is the one that is objectively true, the one that captures the metaphysically independent values involved in it.

---

[47] Robert B Brandom, 'A Hegelian Model of Legal Concept Determination: The Normative Fine Structure of the Judges' Chain Novel' in Graham Hubbs and Douglas Lind (eds), *Pragmatism, Law, and Language* (Routledge 2014).

Instead, Brandom believes that the sense of the Dworkinian metaphor can be grasped by his own model of recognition of content without conjuring up problematic metaphysical assumptions. Applied to law, this model implies that every judge, when he/she comes to draw on past cases in order to decide the new ones must undertake a work of reconstruction of the conceptual contents involved. Through this activity he adds new conceptual determinations, while at the same time becoming *accountable* to the authority of past uses of these concepts. But on the other hand, he is projecting his authority on future uses, which will also contribute to marking the evolution and enriching the contents involved with further determinations. In this way, a perfect symmetry between past and future and between active and passive recognition is achieved, which illuminates the diachronic structure and the constitutively unsaturated character of legal concepts.[48]

At the same time, Brandom's lesson is also important because it provides us with a 'link' between Hart and Dworkin. The first point to be noted is that Brandom's theory of the social institution of norms provides a compelling account how objective – in the weak sense – norms get instituted by the subjective attitudes of practitioners. This account calls into question aspects of the social pressure norms engender and the motivating force they exert, so it can be used to connect Hart's external and internal dimension.[49] Moreover, one of the consequences of Brandom's weak conception of objectivity, as I tried to show in the previous section, is that conceptual content gets perspectival. This, in turn, entails that the unity of practice breaks down according to the different understandings. This is not so different from Hart's claim that when we run out of abstract rules, we must avail ourselves of our discretion and go ahead. The impossibility of a common practice follows from the absence of common content and forces a 'perspectivisation' of norms.

In fact, Hart's judge is not so far off from Dworkin's. The difference lies in the space that divides discretion from the attempt to reconstruct the whole legal system. This room is reduced if we think of the latter as something which does

---

[48] It can be noted, in passing, that this way of reconstructing the relationship between law and interpreters seems in tune with the 'protestant' attitude towards interpretation that Dworkin displays in *Law's Empire*. On these themes, see also Thomas Bustamante, 'Revisiting the Idea of Protestant Interpretation: Towards Reconciliation between Dworkin and Postema' in Thomas Bustamante and Thiago Lopes Decat (eds), *Philosophy of Law as an Integral Part of Philosophy. Essays on the Jurisprudence of Gerald J Postema* (Hart 2020).

[49] It would be interesting to see how Hart's *seriousness*, *necessity* and *overridingness* can be explained, in the context of Brandom's model, by taking second-order provisions into account. Unfortunately, I cannot pursue this project here. Some elements that may be useful in this regard can be found in Marchettoni, 'Brandom's Theory of the Institution of Norms' (n 27).

not respond to objective – in the strong sense – values but as an activity which depends on our variable routes and that therefore may be performed in several ways, which cannot be ranked in a definite manner.

6. CONCLUSION

In this chapter, I tried to shed new light on the Hart-Dworkin debate by employing some ideas from Brandom's repertoire. I started from Hart's account of legal obligations, highlighting that his conception is trapped between the external dimension of norms – that is, their being based on a substratum of empirical regularities – and the internal dimension – which is related to their attitude to become reasons for action. I have argued that this distinction engenders a dichotomy that cannot be easily managed. The upshot is Hart's idea that in hard cases judges must compensate the lacunae of the existing law with their discretion, since abstract norms do not provide any guidance to practice.

Such shortcomings prompted Dworkin's criticism to the effect that Hart's conception does not capture the interpretative dimension of juridical activity. According to Dworkin judges perform a constructive role, trying to build up a comprehensive image of the overall legal system and deciding hard cases following the principles they obtain from their interpretation.

Dworkin's approach contrasts with Hart's in that it seems to postulate a set of objective values that guide the activity of judges. However, if we choose to read Dworkin's model as a reminder of the interpretive work done by the judges, discarding the idea that the best interpretation is the single one faithful to metaphysically independent values, we can soften the difference with Hart. In fact, I have argued that much of this difference depends on the notion of objectivity employed. In order to stress this point, I have proposed to turn one's attention to Brandom's theory of the social institution of norms, contending that Brandom makes recourse to a weak concept of objectivity. This concept can be fruitfully adapted to the legal domain, thus establishing a link between Hart's and Dworkin's models, and redefining the very meaning of the question of the objectivity of law.

8. Can legal texts have objective meanings?
Maija Aalto-Heinilä

1. INTRODUCTION

The question about the objectivity of law can be asked at many different levels and about many different features of law. For example: is law objective because it is based on sound moral views? Or because it treats people in an objective way? Or because it is mind-independent? Or because it is based on rules that are objectively ascertainable?[1] In this chapter I understand the problem about objectivity of law in this way: what accounts for the possibility that there can be correct and incorrect interpretations of legal texts? If the problem is formulated in this way, it is natural to answer it by saying that a legal text must have a *meaning* that is in some sense objective and constraining.[2] But this of course raises the further question, what is meaning, and how can it be objective?

I will examine two different answers to the question of meaning that have been put forth in legal theory, both of which claim to provide the kind of constraint to legal interpretation that the objectivity of law requires. The first answer (propounded e.g., by Michael S Moore) is the *external* (or *realist*) theory of meaning, in which the world somehow directly, causally, determines

---

[1] For different dimensions of the objectivity of law, see, e.g., Kent Greenawalt, *Law and Objectivity* (Oxford University Press 1995) 3–7, and Matthew Kramer, *Objectivity and the Rule of Law* (Cambridge University Press 2007) 2–99. A thorough introduction to the many facets of objectivity is provided in the introduction to this volume.

[2] As Robert Brandom puts it:
  [T]he idea that there is a difference between exercising normative authority by appeal to *law* and simply exercising *power* in its name depends on the possibility of distinguishing applications of the law that are rationally justifiable in virtue of the *meanings* of the concepts that articulate the law and those that are not.
Robert Boyce Brandom, 'A Hegelian Model of Legal Concept Determination', in Graham Hubbs and Douglas Lind (eds), *Pragmatism, Law and Language* (Routledge, 2014) 19–20 (emphases added). Brandom's views are extensively discussed in Chapter 7 of this volume.

the meanings of our words without the speakers' intentions, beliefs or conventions affecting the matter. The task of the interpreter is then to investigate the 'real' nature of the referents of our words, with the help of the latest scientific theories; law is objective to the extent that those theories accurately describe reality. The second theory of meaning (whose most radical advocate is Stanley Fish) makes meaning depend on the speaker's or author's *intention*: without somebody's intending something by words, they are just 'dead' marks on a paper or soundwaves in the air. The author's intention becomes thus the constraining element and provider of objectivity to the meaning of a legal text.

I try to show that both views, if taken as wholesale explanations of meaning (and not as only highlighting some aspects of meaning in some cases), are deeply puzzling: they assume a sort of 'sideways on'-perspective into language and the world that seems incoherent if we try to think through what it means.[3] The exposure of the incoherence of such a viewpoint lies at the heart of Ludwig Wittgenstein's philosophy (at least according to a certain way of understanding it).[4] Thus, Wittgenstein plays a crucial role in my criticisms of the external and intentional theories of meaning. At the end of the chapter, I discuss whether Wittgenstein's philosophy can offer any constructive insights into the theory of legal interpretation and the problem of objective meanings, or whether it can serve only the critical role of pointing out confusions. I suggest that Wittgensteinian insights might be useful in some limited contexts when the question of meaning arises – if, for example, the interpreter is asked to think about the 'ordinary' meanings of words.

Before embarking into the debate about meaning, I try to briefly answer a challenge that has been brought against this whole enterprise – that is, the enterprise of using philosophy/philosophers of language to solve or illuminate

---

[3] The expression 'sideways-on' is used, e.g., by Martin Stone, in 'Theory, Practice and Ubiquitous Interpretation: The Basics', in Enrique Villanueva (ed.), *Law: Metaphysics, Meaning and Objectivity* (Editions, Rodopi, 2007) 170. My approach is very much inspired by Stone's general outlook on problems that arise in philosophy of law and by his understanding of Wittgenstein (see, e.g., Martin Stone, 'Focusing the Law: What Legal Interpretation is Not', in Andrei Marmor (ed.) *Law and Interpretation: Essays in Legal Philosophy* (Oxford University Press 1995, 31–96.)). Stone also discusses Stanley Fish's views, as I do in this chapter. However, Stone's target is the 'early' Fish, who emphasized the role of *readers* and interpretive communities in the formation of meaning (see e.g., Stanley Fish, *Is There a Text in This Class?* (Harvard University Press 1980) 109, 171), whereas I discuss here Fish's more recent views that focus on the role of author's intention.

[4] This understanding is perhaps more typical of the 'New Wittgensteinian'-scholars, rather than more traditional readings of Wittgenstein (see Alice Crary and Rupert Read (eds), *The New Wittgenstein* (Routledge 2000)).

legal theoretical problems.[5] Some legal philosophers have, namely, claimed that philosophy of language in general, and Wittgenstein's philosophy in particular, is of little or no relevance – or even detrimental – to law and legal theory. For example, Michael Green believes that 'the influence of the philosophy of language on the philosophy of law has been largely negative. Philosophers of law would have been better off if the philosophy of language had been set aside entirely.'[6] However, Green is mostly criticising attempts to answer the big question 'What is law?' by analysing linguistic practices. His main point, briefly put, is that the practice of employing the word 'law' is not the same as the practice of law; or that a theory of meaning does not decide which theory of law – natural law, realism or positivism – is the correct one.[7]

I agree with Green in that theorising about meaning cannot, at least alone, decide the fundamental question of what law is. However, I am not here interested in the nature of law as such, but simply assume that whatever law is, it is typically expressed in some authoritative *texts*; and in the legal practice, it is not uncommon that the question of what those texts mean arises. This naturally leads to the question of what we mean by 'meaning', which is a philosophical rather than a legal question. Legally binding sources do not define what meaning, in general, is (although they may define what some individual term in a legal text means and may even say something about the required methods of interpretation[8]). Thus, in this narrower context – the context of legal interpretation – it is in my view legitimate to turn to theories of meaning that have been advanced in philosophy of language, and to think about their relevance to the actual practice of interpretation. Although in this chapter I criticise Moore's and Fish's views about meaning, I agree with them in that philosophical discussion about meaning is not pointless for legal theory.

Green himself admits that philosophy of language might be of some use in the context of legal interpretation but thinks that Wittgenstein's philosophy is not.

---

[5] I would like to thank the anonymous reviewers for pointing out to me the need to discuss this challenge.

[6] Michael Steven Green, 'Dworkin's Fallacy, or What the Philosophy of Language Can't Teach Us about the Law' (2003) 89 *Virginia Law Review* 1897, 1946.

[7] Ibid., 1919–1924.

[8] The UN *Vienna Convention on the Law of Treaties* (1969) is a good example: in article 2 (*Use of terms*) some key terms of the Convention are defined; and in article 31, paragraph 1, a general rule of interpretation of international treaties is given: 'A treaty shall be interpreted in good faith in accordance with the ordinary meaning to be given to the terms of the treaty in their context and in the light of its object and purpose.' Vienna Convention on the Law of Treaties (adopted 23 May 1969, entered into force 27 January 1980) vol. 1155 United Nations Treaty Series 331. Available at: https://legal.un.org/ilc/texts/instruments/english/conventions/1_1_1969.pdf (Accessed 14 January 2022).

Likewise, Brian Bix[9] and Scott Hershovitz[10] have claimed that Wittgenstein's philosophy has little or no relevance to legal theory or practice. Simply put, according to these critics, Wittgenstein is irrelevant because he is concerned with *different issues* than philosophers of law. However, it is noteworthy that these critics focus mostly on Wittgenstein's remarks on *rule-following*, and on the debate that arose after Saul Kripke's controversial sceptical reading of them.[11] This debate, which is about how there can be correct and incorrect applications of even the simplest mathematical rules, is, according to Green, about a more fundamental issue than law: it is about the possibility of human intentionality in general. Thus, it is no more relevant to law than to all human action.[12] According to Bix, Wittgenstein's rule-following discussion occurs at a different level of abstraction than the discussion concerning legal rules:[13] and according to Hershovitz, it is about different kind of rules than legal rules.[14] Wittgenstein's examples of rules were simple mathematical or linguistic rules (such as '+2' or rules for the use of colour terms) about which there is fundamental agreement, and which are followed unreflectively. To the contrary, law is a reflective activity that is characterised by disagreement rather than agreement, at least in adjudication.[15] Therefore, as Hershovitz puts it, 'it is misguided to apply Wittgenstein's remarks to law ... [they] occur at too basic a level to advance debates within jurisprudence'.[16]

The claim that Wittgenstein's philosophy is irrelevant to legal theory cannot, of course, be countered *in abstracto*, but only by actually applying Wittgenstein's philosophy and trying to show, as one goes along, that it is not irrelevant or misguided. The success of this application cannot be evaluated beforehand. At this point I will only make a few remarks. First, the mere fact that some philosopher talks about different matters than those at hand is not,

---

[9] Brian Bix, 'The Application (and Mis-Application) of Wittgenstein's Rule-Following Considerations to Legal Theory', in Brian Bix, *Law, Language and Legal Determinacy* (Clarendon Press 1993) 36–62, and Bix, 'Cautions and Caveats for the Application to Wittgenstein to Legal Theory', in Joseph Keim Campbell, Michael O'Rourke and David Shier (eds), *Law and Social Justice* (MIT Press 2005) 217–29.

[10] Scott Hershovitz, 'Wittgenstein on Rules: The Phantom Menace' (2002) 22(4) *Oxford Journal of Legal Studies* 619–40.

[11] Saul Kripke, *Wittgenstein on Rules and Private Language: An Elementary Exposition* (Blackwell 1982).

[12] Green (n. 6) 1946.

[13] Bix, 'The Application (and Mis-Application) of Wittgenstein's Rule-Following Considerations to Legal Theory' (n 9) 49.

[14] Hershovitz (n 10) 635–6.

[15] Bix, 'The Application (and Mis-Application) of Wittgenstein's Rule-Following Considerations to Legal Theory' (n 9) 48–9; Bix, 'Cautions and Caveats for the Application to Wittgenstein to Legal Theory' (n 9) 220–221; Hershovitz (n 10) 640.

[16] Hershovitz, ibid.

in itself, an argument against employing that philosopher's ideas. Not seeing essential similarities or illuminating analogies between two different things might just be due to lack of philosophical imagination. Second, as I see it, the most important legacy Wittgenstein left us is the *way* he did philosophy, and not so much what he said about any particular issue, such as rule-following. The Wittgensteinian method, which enjoins us to think of concrete, everyday examples and to remind ourselves of the obvious, can, in my view, be fruitfully applied wherever philosophical puzzlements arise. Legal philosophy is no different from any other branch of philosophy in this sense – it contains difficult theoretical problems in connection with which Wittgenstein-inspired reminders of some simple everyday facts might be useful. The problem of meaning, in particular, is such a problem, to which I shall finally turn.

2. SEMANTIC EXTERNALISM

To repeat, the problem posed in this chapter is whether legal texts can have objective meanings that can in principle constrain the interpreter. One answer that has been suggested to this problem is applying the *externalist* or *realist* theory of meaning also to legal terms. I will first briefly introduce semantic externalism and then its application to legal interpretation.

The basic idea of the external theory of meaning is often presented with Hilary Putnam's famous slogan 'Meanings just ain't in the head!'[17] This means that what some word means is not determined by the mental contents of the user of that word (the beliefs, descriptions, pictures, theories etc. that she may associate with the word). Words refer to things in the world; and this relation is external to us – a direct connection between language and the world without the speaker's mental states mediating between them. For example, the meaning of the word 'water' is determined by what water is really like, and not by our beliefs about what water is like (as Putnam's famous 'Twin Earth' example is supposed to show).[18] Thus, a consequence of semantic externalism is that 'successful referring is possible even in a situation where nobody knows the necessary and sufficient conditions for belonging to the extension of the expression, or is able to recognize reliably whether the expression applies or not'.[19]

---

[17] Hilary Putnam, 'The Meaning of Meaning', in *Mind, Language and Reality. Philosophical Papers, Vol. 2.* (Cambridge University Press 1975) 227.
[18] Ibid., 223–5.
[19] Panu Raatikainen, 'Philosophical Issues in Meaning and Translation', in A Aejmelaeus and P Pahta (eds), *Translation – Intepretation – Meaning.* Studies Across Disciplines in the Humanities and Social Sciences 7. (Helsinki Collegium for Advanced Studies 2012) 165.

But how can there be this direct connection between language and the world? Another famous proponent of externalism, Saul Kripke, has developed a 'causal chain theory' to explain this. His answer is that the physical environment causes people to respond linguistically to its stimuli. For example, when people encountered a new interesting metal, they 'baptized' it 'gold'. After this original baptism or introduction of the name, the meaning is passed on to subsequent users of the word. The meaning of the word 'gold' is the same for new speakers as for the initial baptisers in so far as the former learn it from the latter (through maybe a long chain of speakers) and in so far as they intend to use the word as it was used by those who initially named the substance.[20] Thus, not all the speakers of a language have to be 'baptizers' who are directly acquainted with the meaning of a word; shared meanings are possible because of 'linguistic division of labour' – a subset of speakers passes meaning on to other speakers.[21]

This is a very simplifying picture of Putnam's and Kripke's ideas (who could be called the 'founding fathers' of externalism); what interests us more are the applications of these ideas in legal theory. The most famous advocate of 'K-P- semantics' in the sphere of law is undoubtedly Michael S Moore, so I will focus here on his formulations.[22] Instead of externalism or K-P- semantics Moore sometimes talks of a 'realist' or a 'causal' theory of meaning, but

---

[20] See Saul Kripke, 'Naming and Necessity', in Donald Davidson and Gilbert Harman (eds), *Semantics of Natural Language* (D Reidel Publishing Company 1972) 298–303. Because the intentions of speakers are important for Kripkean 'causal' theories, Speaks raises the question whether they can be distinguished from (what Speaks calls) 'mentalist' theories. See Jeff Speaks, 'Theories of Meaning', in Edward N Zalta (ed.), The Stanford Encyclopedia of Philosophy (Fall 2017 Edition), https://plato.stanford.edu/archives/fall2017/entries/meaning/, section 3.2.1.) (Accessed 2 October 2018).

[21] Putnam (n 17) 228.

[22] The term 'K-P-semantics' (Kripke-Putnam semantics) is used by Moore e.g., in his 'Can Objectivity be Grounded in Semantics?', in Enrique Villanueva (ed.), *Law: Metaphysics, Meaning and Objectivity* (Editions Rodopi, 2007), 235–60. Other legal philosophers who advocate externalism include e.g., David Brink (see his 'Legal Theory, Legal Interpretation and Judicial Review' (1988) 17(2) *Philosophy and Public Affairs* 105–48, and 'Semantics and Legal Interpretation (Further Thoughts)' (1998) Vol II *Canadian Journal of Law and Jurisprudence* 181–91), and Ori Simchen (see his 'Meta-semantics and Objectivity', in Enrique Villanueva (ed.), *Law: Metaphysics, Meaning and Objectivity* (Editions Rodopi 2007) 216–34.)

the idea is the same in all of them – that the relation between words and their meanings is external to the intentions or conventions of speakers:

> A realist theory asserts that the meaning of 'death', for example, is not fixed by certain conventions. Rather, a realist theory asserts that 'death' refers to a natural kind of event that occurs in the world.[23]

> [T]he 'causal' theory [...] holds that the existence of 'natural kinds', or sets of objects in the world that share certain essential properties, causes us to refer to those objects by a common name. [...] The causal theory begins with a fact about the world [...] it takes the meaning of a word to be fixed by the nature of the thing referred to.[24]

This view is based on the idea that there is a world that exists independently of our linguistic conventions, and that it contains, among other things, natural kinds, i.e., collections of particulars that share certain essential properties. In short, Moore's theory of meaning presupposes metaphysical realism. This realism extends to the meaning of legal and moral terms also; that is, a Moorean semantic externalist believes that there are moral and legal 'kinds':

> kinds such as contracts and law exist in the world irrespective of us thinking that they exist and words like 'contract' used in propositions of law, and words like 'law' used in legal theory, take their meaning from the nature of these kinds and not from conventional guides to usage.[25]

Moore attempts to give a naturalist analysis of legal kinds: they are not some strange metaphysical entities but reducible to natural properties (Moore dubs himself a 'reductionist naturalist'[26]). It is not necessary here to go into the details of Moore's complex theory; the basic idea is that there are some natural 'base properties' upon which moral and legal properties supervene. More specifically, moral and legal kinds are reducible to disjuncts of those base properties that causally explain certain undisputed facts, e.g., people's moral beliefs or judges' behaviour. The mode of explanation is the same as 'functionalism' in philosophy of mind, where, when explaining what e.g., 'intentions' are, 'all that is needed are the physical states making up the base properties,

---

[23] Michael S Moore, 'A Natural Law Theory of Interpretation' (1985) 58 *Southern California Law Review* 277, 294.
[24] Michael S Moore, 'The Interpretive Turn in Modern Theory: A Turn for The Worse?' (1989) 41 *Stanford Law Review* 871, 876.
[25] Moore, 'Can Objectivity be Grounded in Semantics?' (n 22) 258.
[26] Michael S Moore, 'Legal Reality: A Naturalist Approach to Legal Ontology' (2002) 21(6) *Law and Philosophy* 679.

the behaviour to be explained, and causal roles for the set of physical states that intentions are'.[27]

A curious feature of Moore's realist theory of meaning is the role it gives to *experts* in specifying meaning. If meaning is determined by how the world really is (and not by what we think about the world), then those who know most about some kind – e.g., death – also know most about its meaning. Thus, '[t]he meaning of a word like "death" is only to be found in the best scientific theory we can muster about the true nature of that kind of event';[28] likewise, the meaning of 'malice' or 'contract' is given 'by the best theory we can think of as to the nature of the things referred to'.[29] Best theories are provided by experts in the field; so speakers should have 'linguistic deference'[30] to them if they want their words really refer to what they intend them to refer to (to the 'real thing' and not to some mistaken conception about it).

To summarise, according to Moore's realist theory of meaning law is objective because the terms that express the law have referents in reality that exist independently of our beliefs about them, and that give meaning to legal terms and truth-value to legal propositions irrespective of our subjective thoughts about the matter. According to Moore, externalism is not just a philosophically correct theory of meaning, but also one adopted in everyday thinking and talking: we are all 'hopelessly realist in our metaphysics',[31] and therefore the realist or causal theory is '*the* theory presupposed by the intentions with which we speak in everyday life'.[32] If this were not the case, it would, according to Moore, be hard to make sense of disagreements and debates about the real nature of e.g., water. Genuine disagreement presupposes something *about* which it is, something that exists independently of our conceptions about it; and the external theory of meaning, with its concomitant metaphysics, is (so the argument goes) the only theory that can make sense of the ordinary, everyday phenomena of disagreement.

What implications does this theory of meaning have for legal interpretation? Simply, that 'judges should use the realist theory of meaning'.[33] That is, law-appliers should guide their interpretations 'by the real nature of the things to which the words refer and not by the conventions governing the ordinary

---

[27] Ibid., 686. See also Michael S Moore, 'Law as a Functional Kind', in Robert P George (ed.), *Natural Law Theory. Contemporary Essays* (Oxford University Press 1992) 188–242.
[28] Moore, 'A Natural Law Theory of Interpretation' (n 23) 300.
[29] Ibid., 337.
[30] This term is from Simchen 'Meta-semantics and Objectivity' (n 22) 224.
[31] Moore, 'A Natural Law Theory of Interpretation' (n 23) 327.
[32] Ibid., 322.
[33] Ibid., 301.

usage of those words'.[34] In this way judges' actions not only conform to the demands of the (supposedly) correct philosophical theory about meaning, but also to the demands of rule of law. The ideal of rule of law demands things such as separation of powers, predictability of decisions, substantive and procedural fairness and efficiency of adjudication.[35] According to Moore, the realist theory of meaning best protects these values because he thinks it is, as we saw, the view about meaning we presuppose in our everyday lives. The idea here is that the rule of law virtues, like predictable decisions and procedural fairness, require that judges adopt, as far as possible, the same theory of meaning as ordinary speakers (which include both legislators and the citizens who are subject to laws); in this way the judges can be said to follow legislators' intentions and also fulfil the reasonable expectations of ordinary citizens.

How should one assess Moore's externalism? Obviously, there is a lot that makes sense in it, if it is understood in a common-sensical way: we surely are realists in our everyday metaphysics (it would be impossible to do almost anything if we constantly doubted the existence of the external world around us); and of course we take many of our words to be linked to our surroundings and being meaningful just because they are linked to it (e.g., indexicals like 'this' or 'here'). However, the theory raises many questions. For example, if judges sometimes argue about the 'real nature' of e.g., brain-death, do they not have to rely on the quite ordinary language in the course of doing so (language whose individual words can be correctly used without knowledge of the latest scientific theories)? Does not even a new and unexpected scientific discovery that profoundly changes our beliefs need to be expressed by using ordinary words whose meanings are shared by the linguistic community? How can the causal theory explain the meanings of other terms than those naming 'natural kinds' – is the only function of words to *refer* to some external things?

Most importantly, how can the beliefs and conventions of speakers be irrelevant when we are talking about *institutional facts* (such as someone being a judge, or some piece of paper being money)?[36] Such institutions do not exist 'out there' independently of human conventions, waiting to be discovered and named, but cease to exist as soon as people collectively stop believing in them

---

[34] Ibid., 287.

[35] See ibid., 313–18.

[36] This last worry is voiced also by Dennis Patterson, in his 'Realist Semantics and Legal Theory' (1989) Vol II *Canadian Journal of Law and Jurisprudence* 2, 176–7. For an overview of criticisms of semantic externalism, see Luca Gasparri and Diego Marconi, 'Word Meaning', The Stanford Encyclopedia of Philosophy (Spring 2016 Edition), Edward N Zalta (ed.), https://plato.stanford.edu/archives/spr2016/entries/word-meaning/, section 3.3 (Accessed 2 October, 2018), and Speaks, 'Theories of Meaning' (n 20), section. 3.2.

and stop, e.g., treating someone as having authority to decide disputes, or some piece of paper as having value.[37]

It is equally strange to think that we could all along have been *mistaken* about the real nature of, say, contracts. Realism about 'legal kinds' allows for the theoretical possibility that despite the mutually accepted convention of treating certain signs and actions as constituting a binding contract, some expert could show us to have been totally ignorant of what contracts really are; their real metaphysical essence is independent of all conventions. But do the parties who dispute whether there was a contract between them ever frame their dispute as being about the real metaphysical essence of contracts? Does it make sense to think of solving such disputes by appealing to an expert who gives a naturalistic analysis of the relevant concepts (such as 'agreement' or 'fairness' or 'reasonable') and reduces them to some disjuncts of base properties that causally explain people's behaviour? A naturalistic analysis of legal concepts may be interesting from the point of view of some other discipline, but I find it hard to see what relevance it has in actual disputes when people disagree about what should be done.

The basic Wittgensteinian worry about semantic externalism is this: What can it *mean* that 'we begin with a fact about the world', or that 'the world causes us to refer to objects by a common name'? What kind of viewpoint should we be able to have in order to pronounce such claims about the relation between language and the world? It is as if we could grasp the entirety of our language, on the one hand, and the world as such, on the other hand, and see how they directly interact without language-users' beliefs and conventions having anything to do with it.[38] But all attempts to imagine 'the world as such' have to be formulated by having recourse to our ordinary language (if there is any*thing* that we are imagining); and on the other hand, our ordinary language is so interwoven into the external world and human practices that to try to conceive it abstractly, as something that stands against the world (and possibly gives

---

[37] As Searle puts it, 'we continue to maintain institutional entities and institutional facts in existence by continually representing them as having that form of existence'. John R Searle, 'Meaning as a Biological and Social Phenomenon', in Richard Schantz (ed.), *Prospects for Meaning* (de Gruyter 2012) 566. Social facts are discussed in Chapter 2 of this volume.

[38] Wittgenstein puts it nicely:
Your question refers to words; so I have to talks about words. You say: the point isn't the word, but its meaning, and you think of the meaning as a thing of the same kind as the word, though also different from the word. Here the word, there the meaning. The money, and the cow you can buy with it. (But contrast: money, and its use.)
Ludwig Wittgenstein, *Philosophical Investigations* (G.E.M. Anscombe tr, Blackwell 1996), §120.

a completely distorted picture about the world), is impossible, at least to me. I cannot see how we could detach ourselves from our ways of conceptualising the world so as to be able to make the kind of claims that the external theory of meaning requires us to make. For example, as Wittgenstein has famously shown, the supposedly fundamental and primitive meaning-endowing acts of 'baptism' make no sense unless one presupposes the existence of language with fixed meanings. In his so-called private language argument Wittgenstein points out that naming something is a complex language-game that requires e.g., that there is a category for the thing named, that we know the meanings of words like 'this' and 'is', and that certain conventional ways of understanding facial expressions and bodily gestures are in place.[39]

But, to conclude, these problems result only if externalism is taken to be a *wholesale* theory of meaning – if the possibility of naming things and making discoveries about those things is thought to represent the origin and essence of *all* instances of meaning. If externalism is taken to describe only one language-game (the scientific investigation of the nature of reality) that takes for granted the existence of other language-games with their fixed meanings, some of the above objections lose their force.

3. INTENTIONALISM

If we reject semantic externalism as the answer to the problem about the objectivity of law, what other possibilities are there? The polar opposite of externalism (which denies that speakers' intentions and beliefs play any role in constituting meaning) is a theory that can be called *intentionalism*.[40] Its most radical proponent is Stanley Fish.[41] According to him, texts or utterances have no meaning unless they are 'animated' by somebody's intention: 'Words alone, without an animating intention, do not have power, do not have semantic shape, and are not yet language.'[42]

---

[39] Ibid., §257–261.

[40] This sub-chapter partly draws on Maija Aalto-Heinilä, 'Fairness in Statutory Interpretation: Text, Purpose or Intention?' (2016) 1 *International Journal of Legal Discourse* 1, 193–211, and Maija Aalto-Heinilä, Seppo Sajama and Niko Soininen, 'The Bankcrupcy of the Intentional Canon of Interpretation' (2020) 51 *Rechtstheorie* 3, 279–89.

[41] There are less radical forms of intentionalism, most notably Paul Grice's (see his *Studies in the Ways of Words* (Harvard University Press 1989)). However, I think that in Grice's case, too, intentions fail to have the explanatory role they are supposed to have (and the most important thing for meaning turns out to be 'general usage' (ibid., 222)) Unfortunately there is not room to discuss Grice's views here.

[42] Stanley Fish, 'There is No Textualist Position' (2005) 42 *San Diego Law Review* 629, 632.

This kind of intentionalism does not allow a distinction between what *words* mean and what some *author* means by them. Words have *no* meaning apart from the speaker's or author's intention; and the author can make them mean whatever she wants. As Fish puts it, 'words cannot refuse the intention assigned them [...] Theoretically, nothing stands in the way of any string of words becoming the vehicle of any intention'.[43] Even an utterance like 'gleeg gleeg gleeg', according to Larry Alexander and Saikrishna Prakash, 'means what the speaker intended it to mean, even if to others it sounds like nonsense'.[44] Thus, meaning and *communication* of meaning are two different things – according to Fish, 'failure to communicate a meaning does not mean that it was not intended'.[45]

Intentionalism has been defended by pointing out that if somebody uses a word that has several different meanings – such as the English word 'bank' – then the only way to find out which meaning is in question is to resort to the speaker's or author's intention.[46] Intentionalists also claim that if two or more people are disagreeing about what the correct meaning of some word in a given text is – say the word 'bay' in the sentence 'I took the boat out on the bay' – then the disagreement can only be about the author's intention.[47] In other words, intention is supposed to be the thing that restricts interpretation (and thus the thing that accounts for the objectivity of meaning). The following quote summarises well Fish's intentionalism:

> If interpretation is to be rational and not arbitrary there must be something to be interpreted, something prior to the interpreter's efforts, something the interpreter is trying to get right, something in relation to which an interpretation can be rejected. What could that something be? There are only two possibilities: the text and the intention of the author. But the text isn't really a possibility because a text doesn't become a text – the vehicle of a message – until the assumption of purposive design, of intention, is in place; take that assumption away and the text dissolves into a mass of shapes [...] that mean nothing and, because they mean nothing, can be made to mean anything.[48]

---

[43] Ibid., 634.

[44] Larry Alexander and Saikrishna Prakash, 'Is that English you're Speaking – Why Intention Free Interpretation is an Impossibility' (2004) 41 *San Diego Law Review* 967, 978.

[45] Fish (n 42) 634.

[46] Alexander and Prakash (n 44) 974–5; Steven Knapp and Walter Benn Michaels, 'Not a Matter of Interpretation' (2005) *San Diego Law Review* 651, 654.

[47] 'The possibility of interpretative disagreement – disagreement about what a text means [...] – is entirely dependent upon our treating the text as an expression of its author's intent.' (Knapp and Michaels, ibid., 662).

[48] Stanley Fish, 'Intention is All There is: A Critical Analysis of Aharon Barak's Purposive Interpretation in Law' (2008) 29 *Cardozo Law Review* 1109, 1114.

Obviously, if no text has meaning without an 'animating intention', this applies to legal texts, too. So the task of the legal interpreter is to find out the intention of the legal text's author. But now the question naturally arises: where and how can we find the author's intention? Fish, on the one hand, tries to evade this question by saying that it is not the business of intentionalists to try to provide an answer to it. According to him, intentionalism is not a *theory* of interpretation, nor a *method* that can be applied; it is simply a necessary truth about what any text means – it means what its author intends.[49] On the other hand, Fish does say something about where *not* to look for the author's intention. One should not try to see inside the author's head and identify intentions with some mental states or processes:

> Much of the criticism of intentionalism stems from the mistaken notion that it requires looking into people's heads, but it requires nothing of the kind. It may be odd to say so, but intentionalism has nothing to do with psychology.[50]

By this Fish means that interpretation (legal or otherwise) does not require a theory of mind and knowledge about which of the speakers' synapses are firing on what side of the brain, etc.[51]

Another non-starter in the search for the author's intention is to construct a 'reasonable author' and ask how he or she would intend a given text. According to Fish, 'rather than being an interpretive device, [the reasonable author] is a device brought in when interpretation has failed'.[52] It may sometimes be advisable to invent an author and ask what this hypothetical person would have meant – e.g., if all efforts to find out the intention of the real author have failed – but at the moment of doing this one is, according to Fish, no longer interpreting the text but 're-writing' it.[53]

Where can the real intention be found, then? The only piece of advice Fish gives is that we just need to do 'good old-fashioned empirical inquiry' in the course of which we put together pieces of evidence and on the basis of them build an account of the author's intention.[54] When interpreting a legal text, this means things like investigating the legal history of the text and the purposes that legislators, given their role in that particular institutional setting, might have had for producing that text.[55]

---

[49] Ibid., 1113–15.
[50] Ibid., 1131.
[51] Ibid.
[52] Ibid., 1132.
[53] Ibid., 1133.
[54] Ibid., 1141.
[55] Ibid., 1131.

This sounds perfectly reasonable. However, when we put it together with the intentionalist account of meaning, things become very problematic. If no text means anything apart from someone's intention, and if intentions can be found by means of empirical evidence (which does not, however, mean psychological-medical scrutiny of the author's brain), what can this evidence be if not *other texts* – floor speeches, committee reports, newspaper articles, letters, interviews, etc.? But if the evidence consists of other texts, how can we know what they mean? Do we not have to find out their underlying intentions with the help of yet other texts? And does this not lead to an endless regress of texts and intentions? How can we make any progress in the process of interpretation? What is the criterion for having solved the meaning of a text? It seems that at some point we either have to rely on something other than texts, or else the meaning of some texts has to be taken as given – as simply understood without appeal to anything else.[56]

As we saw, Fish talks of the institutional role of the legislator; grasping this role and the tasks and expectations connected with it supposedly helps the interpreter to begin (and sometimes also end) the process of legal interpretation. Yet at the same time Fish insists that an author can give any meaning she wants to a sign ('language can take on any meaning an intender wishes'[57]); she does not have to respect the demands of 'ordinary' or 'public' language. Public language is only an arbitrary convention, and the intending agent is 'free to ignore it':

> That is, an author who wishes to intend something need not bind herself to the word-meaning correlations found in the public language of the day, although she may choose to do so for political or sociological reasons. She can say 'dogs' and mean 'dogs, lions, pigs and snakes;' she can say 'dogs' and mean Newton's Third Law; she can say (or write) 'dogs' and mean anything she likes.[58]

But if this is the case, how does the specification of the author's institutional setting (and other contextual knowledge) help the interpreter? If anyone can mean whatever they want with their words, does not legal interpretation then become mere guessing what legislators may have meant (if public meanings

---

[56] Dennis Patterson makes a similar point when he claims that interpretation is parasitic on understanding; and he also draws on Wittgenstein's philosophy in his criticisms of Fish. However, Patterson's target is the 'early Fish' who emphasised the reader's creative role in the formation of meaning (see n 1). See Patterson, 'Interpretation in Law' (2005) 42 *San Diego Law Review* 685, and Patterson, 'The Poverty of Interpretive Universalism: Toward the Reconstruction of Legal Theory' (1993) 72 *Texas Law Review* 1.
[57] Fish (n 48) 1122.
[58] ibid., 1123.

constrain them in no way)? What kind of constraint can such a view of meaning provide for interpretation? On the other hand, even if it were possible to mean whatever one wants with familiar words, would this make any difference to our actual practices? If you want to argue with someone, convince her, command her, etc., you must use language that the other person understands (i.e., our ordinary, public language). Private meaning-changing intentions are totally irrelevant in ordinary communication.

The most puzzling thing about intentionalism is the claim that 'intentions come first, words with meanings second'.[59] What can it mean that the intentions of speakers precede meaningful uses of language? Doesn't the formulation, or identification, of an intention – i.e., recognising the intention as something that gives *this* and not *that* meaning to a sign – presuppose, as Wittgenstein puts it, 'a language full-blown (not some sort of preparatory, provisional one)'?[60] As we saw, Fish's example of this ability to give whatever meaning we want to words is a speaker who uses the word 'dog' to refer to Newton's Third Law.[61] But here the speaker is operating with an already existing language and is using it as the foundation upon which she builds a code-language. This code could be taught to someone (with the help of the shared, public language); here, the ordinary meanings of words presuppose intentions and not the other way round.

In fact, it is not so clear whether we can just like that change the meanings of familiar words. How would this happen in practice? Wittgenstein provides a nice illustration of such an attempt:

> If I say 'Mr Scot is not a Scot', I mean the first 'Scot' as a proper name, the second one as a common name [...] – Try to mean the first 'Scot' as a common name and the second one as a proper name. – How is it done? When *I* do it, I blink with the effort as I try to parade the right meanings before my mind in saying the words. – But do I parade the meanings of the words before my mind when I make the ordinary use of them?
> When I say the sentence with this exchange of meanings I feel that its sense disintegrates – Well, *I* feel it, but the person I am saying it to does not. So what harm is done?[62]

This, in my view, shows how even if we operate with an existing language, it is not clear what it would mean to privately just *switch* meanings. The attempt to do so seems to lead to disintegration of sense, rather than to new meanings. On the other hand, even if the intender 'blinks with effort' as she tries in her mind

---

[59] Ibid., 1137.
[60] Wittgenstein, *Philosophical Investigations* (n 38), §120.
[61] Fish (n 48) 1123.
[62] Wittgenstein, *Philosophical investigations* (n 38) 176.

to give new meanings to familiar words and while doing so feels the sense of the whole sentence to disintegrate, what harm is done? As I see it, by this Wittgenstein tries to point out that in ordinary communication it is irrelevant what goes on in the person's mind, as long as both parties to communication operate with the common, everyday language. And especially in the context of legal interpretation, it is surely an absurd starting-point that the legislator perhaps made some private changes of meaning when it wrote a law, even though it uses quite ordinary words. How could behaviour be guided by texts whose meanings were up to each writer's, or interpreter's, own decisions?

And if we try to imagine not the switching of meaning but creating meaning *ex nihilo* to something that does not yet have it – such as a naming a private sensation by a mere act of 'intending' – it is even less clear what it is that we are supposed to imagine. This is what Wittgenstein tries to show in his famous 'private-language argument'. Briefly put, Wittgenstein's point is to remind us (as we saw when discussing externalism) that naming something is a complex language-game that presupposes a lot of things. For example, if one tries to name a private sensation with the name 'S', one needs the word 'sensation' – which belongs to our ordinary, shared language – in order to name a *sensation*.[63]

In short, if we try to imagine intentions or acts of naming that do not presuppose any existing shared language, it becomes unclear what we are imagining. The sense of Fish's radical intentionalism (according to which intentions come first, words with meanings second) disintegrates when we think through what it would really mean.

4. A WITTGENSTEINIAN ALTERNATIVE?

We have discussed two theories of meaning as possible answers to the question of whether legal texts can have objective meanings. Both Moore's realism and Fish's intentionalism, if taken as general theories of meaning, were shown to be problematic: they both assume that we could somehow detach ourselves completely from our ordinary language and could grasp the essential natures of various 'kinds', or speakers' private intentions, as conceptually prior to language. But the attempt to make such conceptual separation throws us back to our ordinary language, for we can talk about the metaphysical essences, or intentions behind words, only with the language that we now have. In short, language, as a whole, cannot be compared to some external yardstick.

But, to repeat, these problems arise only if externalism and intentionalism are taken to be theories about meaning *in general*. It is not to say that in adju-

---

[63] Ibid., §261.

dication, judges never consult experts when they need to know, e.g., whether some species fulfils the criteria of being 'endangered'; or that they never think about what the intention of the legislator was when they passed a statute. It is only to say that all this happens in and presupposes language full-blown, not some preparatory one.

Wittgenstein's philosophy was employed in the course of criticising these two theories (as general theories of meaning). Does adopting a Wittgensteinian view about language mean that we can never say anything general about meaning? Are not all such attempts doomed into the same incoherent 'from sideways on'-position? Must we fall completely silent about meaning and just let 'language speak for itself'?[64] Not necessarily. Surely, following the Wittgensteinian path all the way through, we must say that a *theory* of meaning is strictly speaking impossible, if by a 'theory' we mean a generalisation supposed to apply to the whole of language that is pronounced from an external viewpoint. But this does not preclude the possibility of reminding ourselves how we *use* words like 'meaning', 'to mean' and 'to understand' in our language. These are ordinary words about which we can ask: '[W]hat is the criterion for an expression's being meant *thus*? What should be regarded as a criterion of the meaning?',[65] or 'What shows that [a child] really understands [a] word?'[66] Thus, the following quotes from Wittgenstein should not be understood as capturing his 'theory' of meaning, but as reminders of what we regard as the criterion of meaning in our everyday use of language, and as pointing out some connections *within* language – i.e., pointing out relationships between linguistic expressions:

> I want to say the place of a word in grammar is its meaning.
>
> But I might also say: the meaning of a word is what the explanation of its meaning *explains*. [...]
>
> The explanation of the meaning explains the use of the word.
>
> The use of a word in the language is its meaning.[67]

If these reminders do not strike one as immediately obvious, it is useful to think of concrete examples – of cases of teaching the meaning of a word to someone, and cases of evaluating whether someone really understands a new

---

[64] Ludwig Wittgenstein, *Philosophical Grammar* (Rush Rhees ed, Anthony Kenny tr, University of California Press 1978) 40–41.
[65] Ibid., 45.
[66] Ibid., 64.
[67] Ibid., 59–60.

word.[68] And it is especially useful to think of other words than those naming 'natural kinds' – words in connection with which the externalists' idea of *pointing* makes no sense. For example, the word 'perhaps':

> How does a child learn the use of the word 'perhaps'? It may repeat a sentence it has heard from an adult like '*Perhaps* she will come'; it may do so in the same tone of voice as the adult. (That is a kind of game). In such a case the question is sometimes asked: Does it already understand the word 'perhaps' or is it only repeating it? – What shows that it really understands the word? – Well, that is uses it in particular circumstances in a particular manner – in certain contexts and with a particular intonation.[69]

In this case the teaching consists simply of talking to the child: using the word in the contexts and sentences in which it is ordinarily used (and using various bodily gestures and expressions and tones of voice that ordinarily go with these sentences); and gradually the child learns to do *the same*. Sometimes, in connection with other words and other learners, we may use other methods of teaching: we may point to a sample (e.g., to a red patch of colour), or make a drawing, or translate the word into another language. Although meaning can be taught and explained in these and multifarious other ways, what is noteworthy is that we do *not* teach meaning by saying that is identical with the learner's private intentions (i.e., that she can give whatever meaning she wants to it – unless we are playing some kind of game), nor by saying that the meanings we teach are really only hypothetical approximations of the real meanings (whose knowledge requires familiarity with the latest scientific theories).

Wittgenstein's remarks on rule-following – that, as we saw, have occupied the central stage in Wittgenstein's applications to legal theory – are, in my view, fruitfully understood as simple reminders of what we regard as criteria that someone has understood the meaning of a word. The teaching of the meaning of some word has been successful if the learner repeatedly *does* something with the word successfully: uses it in a way that others recognize as meaningful and react correspondingly.[70] Grasping meaning is to be immersed

---

[68] '[A]lways ask yourself: How did we *learn* the meaning of this word ("good" for instance)? From what sort of examples? in what language-games?' (Wittgenstein, *Philosophical Investigations* (n 38) §77.
[69] Wittgenstein, *Philosophical Grammar* (n 64) 64.
[70] See Wittgenstein, *Philosophical Investigations* (n 38) §143–45.

in a practice or following a rule; and for there to be genuine rule-following, there must be a regular custom:

> Is what we call 'obeying a rule' something that it would be possible for only *one* man to do, and to do only *once* in his life? This is of course a note on the grammar of the expression 'to obey a rule'.
> It is not possible that there should have been only one occasion on which someone obeyed a rule. [...] – To obey a rule, to make a report, to give an order, to play a game of chess, are *customs* (uses, institutions).[71]

Again, it is important to notice that this is put forth as a note on the *grammar* of the expression 'to obey a rule'; so the justification for claiming that the idea of a rule presupposes regularity – repeated cases of doing *the same* – is simply that this is what we *call* rule-following. For us, it makes no sense to talk of a rule that is obeyed only once or that consists of doing something different every time (unless the rule is 'do something different every time').

What about disagreements about meaning, which are typical in hard legal cases? As we saw, both externalists and intentionalists claim to be able to make perfect sense of them: they both have something other than mere practices and conventions to settle disputes about the meaning of some word. For the realist, the correct meaning is determined by the 'real' nature of the world, for the intentionalist, author's intention decides the matter. Does not Wittgenstein's outlook on meaning lead to the conclusion that 'human agreement decides what is true and what is false',[72] i.e., to relativism? However, as was already pointed out, even those realist theorists who disagree about the true nature of something have to be able to formulate their competing views in a common language; likewise, the interpretation that correctly captures the author's intention has to be expressed in a language that others understand, if the interpretation is to convince anyone (or if there is to be so much as a conversation about the correct interpretation). So, in the end disagreements presuppose that we agree in the *language* we use: there has to be a shared framework ('form of life') within which disputes can arise.[73]

This is not to say that there are never any confusions or uncertainty about meaning. It is just to say that when faced with such uncertainty, the rest of language will remain fixed – the meanings of all of our words cannot be doubted simultaneously, the doubt can never be universal. Language is needed as the medium of doubt. But what do legal interpreters do when faced with such doubt about the meaning of some word? If we reject the externalist and intentionalist

---

[71] Ibid., §199.
[72] Wittgenstein, *Philosophical Investigations* (n 38) §241.
[73] Ibid.

theories of meaning, are Wittgenstein's insights of any use for her, or for the theorist who describes what is going on in such cases? To be reminded that the interpreter has to express her doubt in a language that she cannot, as a whole, doubt, will probably not help her to move forward. So do we have to concede the point made by Green, Bix and Hershovitz, that Wittgenstein's concerns were indeed so different and so abstract (or basic) that they are of no use to the actual legal practice, or to the theoretical problem about the objectivity of law?

I think that Wittgensteinian insights (or platitudes) about language may be of *some* use in the context of law. Dennis Patterson has applied Wittgenstein's idea by identifying the unquestioned framework (within which disputes may arise) with the *forms of argument* that lawyers use when they try to justify a legal decision.[74] Patterson's idea is this: judges (and other law-appliers) often disagree about how some legal text should be interpreted. But they do not disagree about the *possible ways* of interpreting legal texts. These ways are inculcated in them in the course of legal training, and they can be called the 'grammar' of law. The grammar stays in place and exerts normative force by being actually used and applied by the legal participants:

> Legal norms are objective to the degree the forms of argument continue to be recognized as legitimate forms of legal justification. The forms of argument are a culturally endorsed form of legal appraisal. They 'exist' only to the extent they continue to be employed by the 'caste of lawyers'.[75]

There is of course not a uniform set of argumentative forms that is used everywhere, but nevertheless enough overlapping similarities between various sets that warrants Patterson's point: even if disagreements arise in the practice of law, there is considerable regularity and uniformity in the appropriate ways to respond and solve those disagreements. Certain ways of arguing are *recognised* and *treated as* legitimate and others as not. Even if 'the grammar of law' is not a mechanical procedure for arriving at correct answers, it does exclude certain responses and arguments as inappropriate, and is constraining in this sense.

Wittgenstein's reminders can be concretely useful if the legal interpreter employs the form of argument, or canon of interpretation, that is usually called the *textual* canon. This is a rule of legal interpretation that probably exists in some form in all legal systems that have written laws. The textual

---

[74] Many other legal theorists have also been influenced by Wittgenstein; see the collection of essays *Wittgenstein and Law* (Dennis Patterson ed, Ashgate 2004).

[75] Dennis Patterson, 'Normativity and Objectivity in Law' (2001) 43 *William and Mary Law Review* 325, 356. The role of canons of interpretation in legal reasoning is discussed in Chapter 10 in this volume.

rule typically enjoins the interpreter to follow the *ordinary* or plain meaning of the legal text.[76] Of course, understanding some text according to its ordinary meaning often requires no special effort and just happens unreflectively. But, as Wittgenstein points out, we do not always have a clear overview of how our language actually works and need to be reminded of it, even though we are fully competent speakers in the everyday life.[77] Thus, thinking about the ordinary meaning may sometimes require conscious reflection. This means, for example, thinking about the following questions: How is this word actually used, in what situations and contexts? How would I teach the meaning of this word to someone? How did I learn it? How would I explain what it means? Of course, this kind of investigation into the ordinary meanings of words does not help to answer the further question, how should the case be decided. But it is a preliminary step in reaching the decision – usually there is a strong presumption for interpreting legal texts according to their ordinary meanings, and good reasons are required for going against this presumption. Wittgenstein does not help us in giving those reasons, but he might help us in clarifying the thing – ordinary meaning – that might sometimes, in the name of justice or reasonableness, be ignored.[78]

5. CONCLUSION

In this chapter, the starting-point was the question whether legal texts can have objective meanings that can constrain the interpreter. This led to the further question of what meaning, in general, is. My main task was to examine two answers to this question: semantic externalism and intentionalism, especially as they have been used in legal theory. I tried to point out, often with the help of Wittgenstein, what difficulties these theories contain, at least if they are understood to be giving the essence of meaning, and not as reminders of how we *sometimes* proceed when we are puzzled about the meaning of some legal term. As general theories of meaning, they presuppose a language-independent access to the world as such, or to meaning-endowing intentions; but how could we have such access without language?

However, no proper alternative was given in place of these discarded theories. Wittgenstein's philosophy is not well suited for such a task; he is more interested in 'destroying houses of cards' and clearing the ground, rather than

---

[76] According to the *Black's Law Dictionary*, the 'textual approach' means 'interpretation to the clear and ordinary meaning or words in a text'. https://thelawdictionary.org/textual-approach/ [accessed 13 December 2021].
[77] Wittgenstein, *Philosophical Investigations* (n 38), §122, 127.
[78] About empirical, rather than armchair, methods of investigating ordinary meanings, see Chapter 9 in this volume.

building substantive philosophical theories.[79] But his lasting legacy is to urge us to pay closer attention to how language ordinarily functions, to concrete examples of using and teaching, to the actions with which words are interwoven. This method may help to solve some puzzles about meaning also in the legal context. But Wittgenstein's philosophy does not help to decide the big, difficult questions of philosophy of law or legal adjudication, such as what law in general is, or what the interpreter should, in the name of justice, do after she has specified the meaning of some legal text.

---

[79] Wittgenstein, *Philosophical Investigations* (n 38), §118.

9. Big data linguistic analysis of legal texts – objectivity debunked?
Caroline Laske

1. INTRODUCTION

The essence of Western legal traditions, based on the concept of the rule of law, lies in the neutrality and generality of the scope of its system and its legislation. The law is said to be justified if it is verifiably general, neutral and impartial; it must be perceived as rational and meaningful. To that extent it is governed by the concept of objectivity, the character of which lies in the ability to consider or represent facts, information, etc., without being influenced by subjective elements such as particular perspectives, value commitments, community bias or personal interests, feelings or opinions, to name just a few relevant factors. In the present chapter, objectivity in law will be discussed in relation to its cognitive aspect, that is, as a characteristic of rational knowledge, which in the area of law, makes a legal system and its legislation meaningful.

This chapter is less a treatise of jurisprudence on objectivity, and more a discussion of (linguistic) methodologies that can be instrumental in revealing (intertextual) meanings in texts and – in our context – highlight objectivity, or the lack of it, in legal texts. I am less concerned with what Reiss and Sprenger call 'objectivity as faithfulness to facts'[1] and as described by Jaap Hage in his contribution to this book. Nor am I dealing with theories of meaning, such as semantic externalism and (radical) intentionalism, as discussed by Maija Aalto-Heinilä in the previous chapter. My argument evolves around semantic objectivity as the result of convention: the use of language and specific terms is deemed objective when it corresponds to the convention determined by the uses given by most speakers of a given group. The objectivity of the use of language and specific terms in a given situation can in turn be evaluated in relation to its conventional use. However, semantic objectivity in this sense

---

[1] Julian Reiss and Jan Sprenger, 'Scientific Objectivity', *The Stanford Encyclopedia of Philosophy* (Fall 2014 Edition), E N Zalta (ed.), URL: http://plato.stanford.edu/archives/fall2014/entries/scientific-objectivity/ accessed 20 June 2022.

does not mean that the conventional use of language and meaning is intrinsically free from bias. I will argue that language cannot be entirely neutral but is always the result of encoding meanings in particular contexts. Big data linguistic analysis provides tools to reveal contextualised encoding of meanings, both in the context of intersubjective agreement of the use of language, as well as in that of highlighting biases.

This chapter is structured in two main parts. Following the introduction, the next section sets out the adopted understanding of what constitutes language, meaning and the assessment of both in relation to context, following the systemic functionalist approach. Also included in this section is an overview of corpus linguistics tools and methodologies that enable the analysis of language and meaning in their textual context. The chapter then dicusses two corpus linguistics studies. Both offer insights into how meanings were constructed and how the extent to which semantic objectivity can be relied upon in the interpretation or understanding of legal texts could be evaluated. The first study concerns the quest for 'ordinary' meanings in relation to legal interpretation by judges in US courts and how corpus linguistics can contribute empirical information to questions of meaning and semantic objectivity for judges in their interpretive tasks. The second study examines the evolution of a contract law concept diachronically and as encoded in the language. It allows us to retrace and understand the process of intersubjective agreement of the use of language and how it has defaulted in relation to impartiality.

2. LINGUISTICS

2.1 Language, Meaning and Context

A central aspect of law is its intrinsic and deep-level link to language, in particular to the use of written language. The underlying premise is that language, as an act of communication, stresses the function, notably the social function, of the use of language when people interact with each other. Consequently, language is an indicator of how meanings are encoded and decoded in a given situation. These processes can be revealed through big data linguistics analysis. Legal language fulfils several functions, the most important of which is probably to achieve justice by 'producing legal effects by speech acts'.[2] Matilla further identifies a function of legal language as the transmission of legal messages, strengthening the authority of the law and maintaining order in society, reinforcing the team spirit of the legal profession and, lastly, linguistic

---

[2] Heikki Mattila, *Comparative Legal Linguistics. Language of Law, Latin and Modern Lingua Francas* (Ashgate 2013) 41.

policy goals.³ The law and its practices have realised acts through the use of language. This is grounded in the law's historical traditions, its normative nature, prescriptive and performative functions and the basic premise that the letter of the law is supreme. To that extent it is one of the quintessential areas where the theory speech acts of Austin and Searle reveals all its significance.

If we accept semantic objectivity as an underlying premise in law, in the case of written legal texts whether in the form of legislation, statutes or case law, the legal language reveals, among others, how this objectivity is encoded and decoded. Studying the legal language and how meanings are formed in that particular context enables us, inter alia, to ascertain aspects such as intersubjective agreement of the use of language, as well as partiality. There is a need to 'measure' such aspects empirically, rather than just according to our intuition. Text and terminological analysis using big data methodologies, such as electronically held corpora and linguistics concordance software, allows us to gain better empirical insight into how meanings are encoded, while simultaneously supplying textual context. If combined with a diachronic approach, we will also learn of historical usages from periods of which we have little linguistic experience. This highlights how semantic objectivity in law can be relative, influenced by time and place, but it will also provide the contextual information that can help us evaluate objectivity at a given moment in relation to its own time and place. The corpus linguistics approach does not preclude other approaches such as, for example, discourse analysis. On the contrary, the two could be used as complementary tools, which is particularly relevant in assessing partiality and biases.

In this chapter, meaning is not to be understood in a structuralist sense,⁴ but rather from a pragmatic view that stresses the social function of the use of language. This systemic functional linguistics, as first adopted by Michael Halliday in the 1980s,⁵ offers an account of language as it is used in actual social situations and is, in this sense, always concerned with the meaning, communicative functionality and rhetorical purposes of language. At the heart of systemic linguistics is the understanding of the communicative properties of

---

[3] Ibid., Chapter 2, 41–86.

[4] Ferdinand de Saussure, *Cours de linguistique générale* (Payot & Rivages 1916/2005).

[5] Also called systemic functional grammar or systemic linguistics. The standard reference work is: Michael Halliday, *An Introduction to Functional Grammar* (Edward Arnold 1985/1994); see also Caroline Laske, *Law, Language and Change. A Diachronic Semantic Analysis of* Consideration *in the Common Law* (Brill 2020) Chapter 3; Caroline Laske, 'Translators and Legal Comparatists as Objective Mediators' in Jako Husa and Mark Van Hoecke, *Objectivity in Law and Legal Reasoning* (Hart Publishing), 213–28, at 214–17.

written and spoken texts of all types (why a text means what it does and why it is valued as it is), as well as the understanding of the relation between language, on the one hand, and culture, community, social grouping and ideology, on the other.[6]

For functional linguists, language appears to have developed and is used for three purposes, which Halliday has called metafunctions:[7]

(i) Ideational *metafunction* encodes meanings of experience which realise field of discourse ('experiential meanings'). This metafunction refers to the use of language to represent experience and construct a view of reality with the various categories language offers to talk about real-world happenings. There are three main constituents of the ideational metafunction: processes (typically expressed as verbs identifying entities and states of affairs), participants (typically expressed as nouns identifying entities), and circumstances (typically expressed as adverbs or prepositional phrases acting to provide some context to the first two elements).

(ii) *Interpersonal metafunction* encodes meanings of attitudes and relationships which realise tenor of discourse ('interpersonal meanings'). This metafunction refers to the use of language to represent interaction between speakers, the way they construct and fill social roles, adopt and/or express attitudes/points of views, form relationships and alliances and so on. A speaker can adopt four basic interpersonal positions (which can be complicated, qualified and extended): declarative (offering information), interrogative (demanding information), imperative (commands in relation to action or response rather than information) and offer (willingness to supply action and response).

(iii) *Textual metafunction* encodes meanings of text development which realise mode of discourse ('textual meanings'). This metafunction refers to the use of language to organise the experiential and interpersonal meanings into a coherent, connected and unified entity. The most prominent textual function in this context is what has been termed the 'theme' which indicates the angle or the point of departure adopted by the speaker. Themes can be subdivided into simple, multiple, topical, interpersonal or textual themes. The rest of the clause is called 'rheme'.

From the simple examples listed in Annex 1, we can see how meanings are encoded in what linguists call 'text', which is a piece of language in use that can be of any length and in either written or spoken form. It is 'language that is

---

[6] Halliday (n 5) xxi.
[7] Examples for each metafunction is listed in Annex 1 below.

functional'.[8] A text, in this sense, is a coherent collection of meanings appropriate to its context. The way the text's meanings are combined gives the text its texture and the text's structure rests on the mandatory structural elements used in the combination of these meanings. Encoding the meaning depends on two surrounding contexts: the *'context of culture'* refers to the general outer cultural environment in which a text occurs. This context includes elements such as conventions of address, politeness, discourse etc., which shape meanings within a particular culture. The context of culture has been described 'as the sum of all the meanings it is possible to mean in that particular culture'.[9] Within that general context of culture, there is an inner layer, which functional linguists have named the *'context of situation'* and which refers, as the term indicates, to the specific situation in which a text occurs and in which meanings are formed. This context includes 'the things going on in the world outside the text that make the text what it is'.[10] A study of the extra-linguistic levels of context of culture and context of situation will show how meanings are encoded and will reveal the (social) function of the use of language.

Furthermore, the lexical and/or grammatical analysis considers the elements in the language and describes how they function. By moving beyond traditional grammar classification of words and by considering the function they play, we can shine a very different light onto the meanings and realities they represent. Firth[11] famously said: 'You shall know a word by the company it keeps.' Observing the interaction between the lexical and grammatical patterning reveals how different meanings of a specific word tend to associate with different patterns. Grammar and lexis do not operate independently and as separate systems, but together as a single system.[12] For example, words with specialised legal meanings 'behave' differently from the same words in general language contexts.

For a better insight into how the parameters explained above apply to a particular text, it is necessary to examine language and meaning in their textual

---

[8] Michael Hallida and Ruqaiva Hasan (eds), *Language, Context and Texts: Aspects of Language in a Social Semiotic Perspective* (Deakin University Press 1985).

[9] David Butt, Rhonda Fahey, Susan Feez, Sue Spinks and Colin Yallop (eds), *Using Functional Grammar: An Explorer's Guide* (Macquarie University 2000) 3.

[10] Ibid., 4.

[11] John Rupert Firth, 'A Synopsis of Linguistics Theory 1930–1955', in *Studies in Linguistic Analysis* (Philological Society 1957) 1–32, at 11.

[12] John Sinclair, *Corpus Concordance Collocation* (OUP 1991) 103; see also Adele Goldberg, *Constructions: A Construction Grammar Approach to Argument Structure* (University of Chicago Press 1995); Stefan Gries and Dagmar Divjak, 'Behavioral Profiles: A Corpus-based Approach Towards Cognitive Semantic Analysis' in Vyvyan Evand and Stéphanie Pourcel (eds) *New Directions in Cognitive Linguistics* (John Benjamins 2009) 57.

context. The use of corpus linguistics methods is ideal for this sort of empirical approach, as it allows for systematic analysis of authentic evidence.

2.2 Corpus Linguistics

Corpus linguistics work as a method of exegesis on the basis of detailed searches of words and phrases in multiple contexts and among large volumes of texts, goes back as far as the Middle Ages, when biblical scholars manually indexed the words of the Holy Scriptures.[13] Subsequently, it has also been practised by literary scholars[14] and lexicographers.[15] The first computer-generated concordance tools appeared in the 1950s, when it took 24 hours to process 60,000 words and used punched-card technology for storage! Modern corpus work, as we know it today, emerged in the 1980s and 1990s.

Enquiries using digitally held corpora allow for access to large bodies of texts of naturally occurring language, that can be searched electronically, according to given criteria with a few mouse clicks, providing information on the data that is both quantitative and qualitative, and is empirical rather than intuitive. Our own intuition of the relative frequency of words, phrases and structures can be little more than vague and general. And while we may be conscious about the frequency of lexis, it is highly unlikely that we have any precise intuitions about the frequency of grammatical categories. Corpus linguistics methodologies can be purely descriptive and ideologically neutral but can also be used in discourse analysis and coupled with critical approaches.[16] This is best done by undertaking a diachronic linguistic and semantic analysis using corpus linguistics methodologies. Besides providing an empirical basis for studying language in use, corpus work also has a heuristic function to the extent that the analysis of the material systematised in a corpus generates new knowledge. By using algorithm-based analytical tools, the researcher may find him/herself confronted with results that were unexpected.

---

[13] Michel Albaric, 'Hugues de Saint-Cher et les concordances bibliques latines (XIII-XVIII siècles)' in Louis Jacques Bataillon, Gilbert Dahan and Pierre Marie Gy (eds), *Hugues de Saint-Cher (+1263), bibliste et théologien: Etudes réunies* (2004) 467.

[14] E.g., Andrew Becket, *Concordance to Shakespeare* (G.G.J. and J. Robinson 1787).

[15] E.g., Samuel Johnson, '*Dictionary of the English Language: in which The Words are deduced from their Originals, and Illustrated in their Different Significations by Examples from the best Writers*'; Ancestor of the OED (first published in 1884 as unbound fascicles) *A New English Dictionary on Historical Principles; Founded Mainly on the Materials Collected by The Philological Society.*

[16] Kieran O'Halloran, 'Critical Discourse Analysis' in James Simpson (ed.) *The Routledge Handbook of Applied Linguistics* (Routledge 2011) 109.

Besides statistical information, linguistic concordance tools allow for search terms to be placed within their textual context (KWIC[17] lines), which in turn reveal the patterns associated with particular uses of the search term. If we study the communicative functionality of language, it may be more productive to look at patterns first, rather than at meaning in an isolated fashion. If a word has several meanings or its meaning has shifted over time, we will find a tendency for each meaning to be associated most frequently with different patterns, consequently words which share a pattern also tend to share aspects of meaning.[18] This approach dismantles the traditional distinction between grammar and lexis.[19] Sinclair argues that the two do not operate independently, as separate systems, but together, as a single system: lexical items cannot be described without reference to their grammatical patterning; meaning is dependent upon grammar and vice versa; all grammar patterning is dependent upon lexical choice. Sinclair reverses the common (Chomskyan) assumption that grammatical generalisation arises from an underlying rule and believes such generalisations to be derived from the observation and extrapolation of experience:

> The new evidence suggests that grammatical generalizations do not rest on a rigid foundation, but are the accumulation of the patterns of hundreds of individual words and phrases. The language looks rather different when you look at a lot of it at once.[20]

Work on electronically held corpora with linguistics software obviously offers the perfect basis for observations of language in use.

A corpus is usually defined as a systematic collection of naturally[21] occurring texts of both written and spoken language that has been computerised. It

---

[17] Concordance lines are most commonly displayed in the so-called pre-set KWIC format. 'Key Word in Context' shows the search term in its context as found in the original text. These can then be sorted according to the words to the left and right of the search term and, hence, provide an excellent overview of the type of contexts in which the search terms occur.

[18] Examples of this are given in Susan Hunston and Gill Francis, 'Verbs Observed: A Corpus-driven Pedagogic Grammar' in (1998) 19(1) *Applied Linguistics* 45–72.

[19] Of the traditional split between 'grammar' and 'lexis', Sinclair wrote:
> In the explicit theoretical statement of linguistics, grammatical and lexical patterns vary independently of each other. In most grammars, it is an assumption that is obviously taken for granted ... Equally, it is rare for a dictionary to note the common syntactic patterns of a word in a particular sense.

John Sinclair (1991) 103.

[20] Ibid., 100.

[21] Natural language, as opposed to artificial or constructed language devised for international communications, computer programming or mathematical purposes, is

offers the empirical basis for carrying out systematic linguistic investigations on authentic evidence. The fact that it is held digitally and searchable electronically offers possibilities that are not otherwise available. Yet, the corpus linguistics methodologies only make sense if a corpus is designed in such a way that it forms a representative basis for making generalisations about a language as a whole or as defined by the underlying premises of the research. The overall corpus design is conditioned by the methods of text sampling and sampling decisions made by the researcher whether conscious or (in part) unconscious. Only a well-defined conception of what the sample is intended to represent will subsequently allow for choices to be evaluated as to the adequacy or representativeness of the corpus. It is less a question of sample *size* and more one of being representative for the range of text types in the target population (the latter of which has to be defined in turn) and for the range of linguistics distribution in the population.

Biber[22] has developed a very comprehensive set of principles for achieving 'representativeness' in corpus design, which will not be repeated here. His main message is that corpus design is cyclical, the bottom-line being: 'that the parameters of a fully representative corpus cannot be determined at the outset'.[23]

He has represented this process schematically as follows:

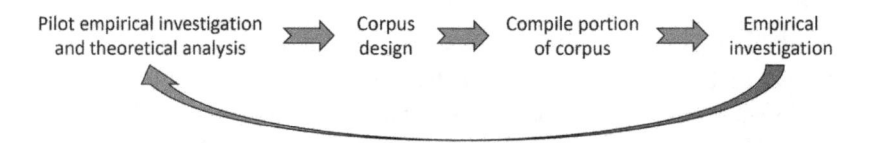

Pilot empirical investigation and theoretical analysis → Corpus design → Compile portion of corpus → Empirical investigation

Figure 9.1   *Biber's cyclical process to achieve 'representativeness' in corpus design*

The following sections will discuss two studies in which the use of corpus linguistics tools have contributed to a better grasp of how meanings were constructed and how to evaluate the extent to which semantic objectivity can be relied upon in the interpretation or understanding of legal texts.

---

language that has evolved naturally, is hereditary and in extended use (see definition in the OED).

[22]   Douglas Biber, 'Representativeness in Corpus Design' in (1993) 8(4) *Literary and Linguistic Computing* 243–57.

[23]   Ibid., 256.

3. CORPUS LINGUISTIC STUDIES

3.1 Interpreting Ordinary Meanings

The first study deals with the quest for 'ordinary' meanings in relation to legal interpretation by judges. In their ground-breaking paper *Judging Ordinary Meaning*, Lee and Mouritsen[24] report on how corpus linguistics tools and methodologies can contribute empirical information to questions of meaning for judges in their interpretive tasks. Among the examples they discuss features the seminal 'no-vehicles-in-the-park' rule that figures in the Hart-Fuller debate.[25] The issue centres around what constitutes 'vehicle'. As Lee and Mouritsen[26] point out, we are faced with a continuum of meanings that evolve around the notion of 'carrier' in the sense of transporting someone or something, such as bicycles, pushchairs, mopeds, cars etc., but what about a wheelchair, a mower, a wheelbarrow or a war memorial that includes a tank. Similarly, cats and dogs can be considered as carriers of diseases. Much has been written about the original debate, which will not be repeated here. Of interest is how corpus based methodologies can help to assess the meaning in issues such as theorised by the Hart-Fuller debate.

In the quest of ascertaining the ordinary meaning of a term in legal language, we can resort to etymology or dictionary definitions. However, this restricts the search to mere semantic meanings. A big data approach involving corpora of naturally occurring texts will offer considerably more quantitative, qualitative and contextual information on pragmatic meanings and uses in naturally occurring language environments. In the case of diachronic corpora, it also allows us to trace historically the evolution of language usages and meanings. In law, the use of texts that are not contemporaneous is common. Diachronic corpora are particularly relevant to revealing semantic shifts of meanings across time which, in law, can represent several decades or even centuries between the drafting of legislation and its application in the courts.

Lee and Mouritsen have adopted this approach in their examination of the meaning of 'vehicle' in relation to the no-vehicle-in-the-park rule. They chose

---

[24] Thomas Lee and Stephen Mouritsen, 'Judging Ordinary Meaning' in (2018) 127(4) *The Yale Law Journal* 788–1105; the author of this paper only gives a short overview of Lee and Mouritsen's findings. For their latest paper on the subject, see Thomas Lee and Stephen Mouritsen, 'The Corpus and the Critics' in (2021) *University of Chicago Law Review* (forthcoming).

[25] H L A Hart, 'Positivism and the Separation of Law and Morals,' in (1958) 71 *Harvard Law Review* 593, at 606–15; Lon Fuller, 'Positivism and Fidelity to Law - A Reply to Professor Hart' in (1958) 71 *Harvard Law Review*, 630, at 662–9.

[26] Thomas Lee and Stephen Mouritsen (n 24) 800–802.

the News on the Web (NOW) corpus for contemporary language uses and the Corpus of Historical American English (COHA) – the latter also covers the period of the Hart-Fuller debate. Both corpora were built at Brigham Young University.[27] It could be argued, for the sake of completeness, that the corpora should include a wider variety of English – the COHA only includes American English texts – and that a separate legal corpus ought to be added to ascertain how specific words were used by judges and legislators in the past. Admittedly, Lee and Mouritsen write from the pragmatic perspective of US judges and the primacy of the *ordinary* meaning rule. To that extent their choice is defendable, but in the context of the interpretation of legal texts, it can sometimes be interesting to also examine concordance data from legal text corpora.

In their study of the collocates[28] of 'vehicle', Lee and Mouritsen have found, in both the contemporary and the historical corpora, that the automotive use of vehicle predominated, signposted by collocates such as (in the NOW corpus) 'motor', 'car', 'fuel', 'gas', 'fuel-efficient', 'gasoline' etc.[29] Presumably, the lists of collocates for an 18th century corpus or a 14th century corpus would be very different. If we look for meaning in the 21st century or even in 1958 when Hart and Fuller engaged in their debate, we can argue that the ordinary meaning of 'vehicle' in the no-vehicle-in-the-park rule is likely to refer to motorised vehicles The collocation data is further interesting by its absences of, for example, 'airplane' as a motorised vehicle,[30] or bicycle as a non-motorised vehicle. The NOW corpus data includes no references to 'airplanes', 'bicycles', 'roller skates', 'toy automobiles' that would raise, according to Hart, the disputed question of what should be included in the definition.[31] The concordance tool confirms these findings. Of 100 randomised concordance/KWIC lines[32] of 'vehicle' from the NOW corpus, 91 referred to

---

[27] *NOW Corpus*, BYU, http://corpus.byu.edu/now, contains 7.1 billion words of data from web-based newspapers and magazines from 2010 to the present time. The corpus grows by about 140–160 million words of data each month (from about 300,000 new articles), or about 1.8 billion words each year.

COHA, BYU, http://corpus.byu.edu/coha, is the largest structured corpus of historical English. It contains more than 400 million words of text from the 1810s–2000s and is balanced by genre decade by decade (both accessed 23 June 2022).

[28] In the BYU corpora and related resources, collocates are defined as words that occur near a given search word (node).

[29] Thomas Lee and Stephen Mouritsen (2018) 788–1105, at 837–40.

[30] The 'airplane' example was actually invoked in the US Supreme Court case *McBoyle v United States*, (1931) 283 U.S. 25, 26-27.

[31] H L A Hart (1958) 607–8.

[32] 'Key Word in Context' (n 17).

'automobiles', the others include a bus, ambulance, cargo-ship, jet-ski and some metaphorical uses.[33]

Lee and Mouritsen did not use a clusters tool in their study, probably because it appears to have been unavailable with the corpora they chose. It would have meant downloading the corpora and using a separate concordance software package that included a clusters tool. Such tools allow for the most frequent two- or three-word pattern around the search term to be shown by clustering the words immediately to the right or left of the search term and then rank these results by frequency, range or probability. It would provide further contextual information, such as for example, the likelihood that 'vehicle' can be found to cluster with 'park' and what words it is most likely to cluster.

From this brief outline of the results Lee and Mouritsen have reported,[34] we can observe how the use of corpus linguistics tools and methodologies have provided us with data, which suggests that the meaning of 'vehicle' is to be understood with reference to 'automobile'. To the extent that the data was constructed empirically based on language in use, it is a move away from linguistic intuition and an advance towards semantic objectivity.

While Lee and Mouritsen were concerned with seeking the ordinary meaning of the language of the law with the assistance of corpus linguistics methodologies, the next section will discuss the use of these methodologies in a study on the development of legal concepts and the corresponding terminological evolution and usages.

3.2   Specialised Terms and Meanings

This research was not concerned with the quest for ordinary meanings but rather with the formation of specialised terms and meanings and how these evolved from everyday language usages, comprehensible to the ordinary man, to highly technical legal jargon. In other words, its aim was not to seek the ordinary meaning of everyday language words placed in a legal interpretive context, but rather to gain a deep level understanding of specialised and technical legal terminology by comprehending the etymological, terminological and historical aspects of terms, the use of which may appear obscure to a point where we cannot easily retrace its origin. By studying the evolution of legal concepts diachronically and as encoded in its language, we can retrace and

---

[33]   Thomas Lee and Stephen Mouritsen (n 24) 841.
[34]   Besides the study of *vehicle*-in-the-park, Lee and Mouritsen also examined ordinary meanings in the following cases *Muscarello v United States* (1998) 524 U.S. 125 (*'carrying* a firearm'); *Taniguchi v Kan Pacific Saipan, Ltd.* (2012) 566 U.S. 560 (*'interpreter'* in the sense of translator); *United States v Costello* (7th Cir. 2012) 666 F.3d 1040 (*'harbouring* an alien').

understand the process of intersubjective agreement of the use of language and where it has defaulted in relation to impartiality.

If we return for a moment to the premise stipulated at the beginning of this chapter, we remember that language, as an act of communication, encodes meanings in accordance with the socio-political, cultural and historical contexts in which they are uttered. Similarly, the language used in particular in legal proceedings is the product of these contexts and a reliable indicator of them, as well as of the way laws are created, practiced and interpreted. There is continuous interaction between the way laws create meaning in language and how language creates realities in law.[35] Consequently, studying the language means gaining a better understanding of the contexts and the realities of the law, including prior legal-discursive traditions relating to concepts such as the rules of law, social control, political power, objectivity, consistency, transparency etc.

Diachronic terminological studies using corpus linguistics methodologies and tools can contribute to understanding how legal concepts have created meanings in language and how some terminology has evolved alongside the corresponding concepts. What will be outlined here briefly draws on results from a diachronic study that examined certain aspects of medieval contract law in England (mainly the concept of consideration) to show the interaction of law and language.[36] Doctrines, like the concept of consideration, appear in today's perception so well anchored in contract law and in our legal minds, that we may find it difficult to imagine its development took a tortuous and at times haphazard path, stretching over several centuries. Yet, to understand this process is to better understand the law as it is today. This allows for an evaluation of the contexts (e.g., social control, political repression, objective justice etc.) and the prior legal-discursive traditions that contributed to the formation of specific laws and legal concepts. The study as such was not concerned with objectivity in law, but the methodology it adopted is relevant in the context of ascertaining objectivity in law from a linguistics point of view.

---

[35] Mark Van Hoecke and Mark Warrington, 'Legal Cultures, Legal Paradigms and Legal Doctrine: Towards a New Model for Comparative Law' first published 1998, reprinted in Maksymillian Del Mar, William Twinning and Michael Giudice (eds), *Legal Theory and the Legal Academy*, The Library of Essays in Contemporary Legal Theory, vol. III (Ashgate 2010), at 535.

[36] All the results of the study are published in: Caroline Laske, *Law, Language and Change. A Diachronic Semantic Analysis of* Consideration *in the Common Law* (Brill 2020). The project was financed by the Flemish Research Fund FWO.

3.3 The Common Law Concept of Consideration

The customary law aspect of the English common law is characteristic of its evolution ever since its formation under Henry II's reign (1154–1189). It was never interrupted by a codification movement as had been the case in continental Europe. It evolved primarily through organic adaptations, rather than *tabula rasa* changes: innovation was a process of nudging boundaries, extending legal categories to let new legal actions through the back door. Similarly, the legal language was governed mainly by how it was spoken and written by judges and handed down through the law reports. Terminological and register boundaries were shifted through the natural language use in the courts of law. The need for new terms designating emerging legal concepts was rarely satisfied by introducing neologisms or setting out legal definitions. Instead, everyday vocabulary gradually evolved into specialised terminology, signposting autonomous legal concepts in concordance with the evolution of legal conceptual thinking. The main exceptions were Latin and some fixed Anglo-French phrases and terminology.

The concept of making informal promises legally enforceable was non-existent at the time when exchanges were made solely on an executed basis. Until the 14th century, an informal (i.e., unwritten and unsealed) undertaking or promise was not legally binding unless something had already been given in exchange (*quid pro quo*). In that case, it was an act of debt or exchange. It involved the proprietary notion of an executed exchange or debt and evolved around the fiction that the lender was claiming what belonged to him, rather than what the object of the promise was. The flourishing of trade, especially the expansion beyond the borders of England, had meant that people relied more and more on informal promises. As the case law shows, judges were increasingly confronted with requests for legally enforcing genuine undertakings and promises – a new form of legal action became necessary. The concept that a legal action can be raised on a broken promise was entirely absent before that time. Between the late 14th century and the 17th century, a shift away from the proprietary notion towards a promissory notion can be observed in the case law. This is also reflected in the terminology, which settled hesitantly. In the medieval case law reports, we can observe the use of words such as 'cause', '*causa*', 'occasion' and '*quid pro quo*', which is confusing as that last term was specifically associated with actions of debt.

But making informal promises actionable raised the question of the limit beyond which promises can no longer be considered as legally enforceable. The modern contract law doctrine of offer and acceptance, as the moment when a promise becomes binding, was unknown then. This is the root of the so-called concept of consideration, spelling out the circumstances in which the promise was made as the motivating reason for making the promise. The requirement is to show that something must have been given or promised in exchange, and that the promise must be 'met with' or 'supported by' some element of consideration or return for the promise. Once it could be established that a promise had been made 'in (good) consideration of X' but had not been honoured, it was actionable in a court of law. There was no further requirement for the plaintiff to show that a contract had been made. In order to follow how the word 'consideration', which came from general language usages, shifted along a continuum of meanings towards a highly specialised legal meaning, it was necessary to examine the uses of 'consideration' diachronically and as the term occurred in the case law.

3.4 Diachronic Corpus Analysis

The sources used to constitute the corpus and sub-corpora were the case law reports that can be found in the Year Books and the early Law Reports.[37] These are presented in both their original language (Latin, Anglo-French, Middle/Early Modern English) and an English translation undertaken by the editor at the time of the publication of the material. Most texts were written in two, sometimes three languages (Anglo-French, Middle/Early Modern English, Latin), though one language usually dominated. The majority of the original language sources were in Law French and passages in Middle/Early Modern English tended to be transcripts of declarations made by one of the parties to the action. All lexical and proximity searches were undertaken only on the main original language body of texts from the Anglo-French and Middle/Early Modern English sources; all Latin passages, (English) translations, editors' footnotes and introductions, or other editorial explanations etc. were disregarded. The searches took into account the different Anglo-French and Middle/Early Modern English spellings and the technique for covering all varieties had to be adapted to each document.

The diachronic analysis revealed the evolution of the conceptual perception, on the one hand, and the corresponding semantic shifts, on the other. The aim was to evaluate the concordance between the historical and conceptual development of 'consideration' and the way the relevant terms and vocabulary were used, changed and shifted throughout this evolution, most notably the increased abstraction and technicality of both the concept and the language. The search term around which the study centred was 'consideration', the main results of which will be reported here. But other terms were also studied

---

[37] 15th to early 19th centuries. A detailed list of the sources can be found in Annex 2. All texts are accessible via the database of HeinOnline: www.heinonline.org (accessed 23 June 2022).

(not reported here), including debt, covenant, *quid pro quo*, cause, assumpsit, promise and contract. These figured as search terms in KWIC concordance lines, as well as in proximity searches and their choice was made on the basis of contemporary contract law jurisprudence or thinking. The aim was to further single out terminological pointers that would provide more information on the register variations.

The results confirmed tendencies sufficiently definite to show a concordance between the hesitant and at times confused development of the concept of consideration and the terminology used in discussions of the issue in case law. It also revealed the many proposals and attempts that were made before legal thinking settled on the terminology as we know it today. Of particular interest is the observation that while certain aspects of the new legal action were already established and confirmed in subsequent cases, the terminology still lingered behind and remained on well-trodden paths. While the legal mind was progressing along a path of new ideas, the intersubjective agreement of the use of the language expressing such innovations remained conservative.

The corpus was structured into four main sub-corpora with the following timespans; the criteria for the cut-off point in time for each sub-corpus was dictated by the evolutionary process of the legal concept of consideration:

- late 14th/15th century corpus: for the period before the concept of consideration was established; this was the time when the shift happened from primarily proprietary thinking to that of promissory exchange.
- 16th century corpus (Tudor, mainly Elizabethan era): for the period when the concept of consideration materialised in the case law.
- 17th century corpus (mainly early Stuart era): for the period when the concept was well established.
- mid-18th/early 19th century corpus: for a series of cases decided by Lord Mansfield and his colleagues when the idea of consideration as a moral obligation was defined.

For the purposes of studying the register of the language and in order to highlight the shift from general to specialised language use, the context provided by the concordance lines was grouped into four main types of language uses for the purpose of this study:

(i) general language meaning/use:
     This is language comprehensible to the ordinary man.
     e.g.: 'The court's decision was made in consideration of all the facts.'

(ii) general language meaning but use in a legal context:
This is also comprehensible to all, but the legal context in which this language occurs adds legal meanings that may only be picked up by those with some legal training.
e.g.: 'The payment was promised in consideration of the marriage to his daughter.'

(iii) specialist/technical/abstract meaning and use:
This language is abstract to a point that its meaning can no longer be understood by a non-specialist.
e.g.: 'The instrument imported a prima facie consideration.'

(iv) Latin uses.

There is, no doubt, some overlap between the different groups and the categorisation may appear somewhat artificial at times, but for the purpose of this study, it is essential to group concordance lines together for evaluation.

The main pointers to the use of technical language can be observed in the interaction between the lexical and grammatical patterning, because every meaning of a specific word will tend to have different patterns. Grammar and lexis do not operate independently and as separate systems, but together as a single system.[38] Words with technical meanings 'behave' differently from the same words in general language contexts. In our example (iii) above we find 'consideration' as a full noun rather than in the causal link phrase of 'in consideration of' that is typical for general language usages.

The diachronic approach of the study has revealed a shift in the semantic content of the term 'consideration' in the English case law between the late 14th and the 19th centuries. General language uses of 'consideration', as represented by the black part of the stacked columns in Figure 9.2 below, fall substantially with time. In the earlier sources, it is used in the sense of the court or the judges 'taking (something) into account' when reaching a decision. From the late 16th century, this use is less frequent: it falls to a 13 per cent share. It is interesting that the context of these general language concordance lines in

---

[38] John Sinclair, *Corpus Concordance Collocation* (OUP 1991) 103; see also Adele Goldberg, *Constructions: A Construction Grammar Approach to Argument Structure* (University of Chicago Press 1995); Stefan Gries and Dagmar Divjak, 'Behavioral Profiles: A Corpus-based Approach Towards Cognitive Semantic Analysis' in Vyvyan Evand and Stéphanie Pourcel (eds), *New Directions in Cognitive Linguistics* (John Benjamins 2009) 57.

the 16th century corpus is almost exclusively in Middle English. It only occurs three times in Anglo-French. This suggests that the increased specialisation of legal language appears to have happened in Anglo-French rather than Middle English.

The principal semantic shift in the use of the term 'consideration' took place during the 16th century. We can observe two main changes. First, there is an increased use of the collocation 'in consideration of' as a causal conjunction between the two elements or events necessary for striking a contractual agreement. While this particular collocation could be used in any situation of exchange, the textual context clearly shows that we are dealing with specialist and technical matters of the law. It is a relatively restricted set of vocabulary concerned with legal instruments and persons, payments, indenture, estate etc., in exchange of mainly marriage and other family matters. In other words, both the meaning and function of the collocation is in a general language sense, but it is the lexical and semantic context that is highly technical.

Second, as we move from the 16th and into the 17th centuries, we find 'consideration' in technical uses. The lexical variety of its textual context is relatively poor and semantically restricted. The term consideration tends to be combined with a limited set of words, which is indicative for the use of specialised language. Furthermore, it appears as a full noun in a function of participants, accompanied by adjectives and prepositions, and associated with material processes. The term can also be found as a one-word sentence, where the word is between two full-stops and thus charged with conceptual meanings. All these grammatical pointers put the word consideration in prime positions within the clauses, a position where it appears in its own right and as a sign-post for a concept rather than as a mere causal link between two other prime elements. It is in this sense that the word is used in a way akin to a concept.

As we come to the decisions taken by Lord Mansfield and his fellow judges between the mid-18th century and early 19th century, we have a very different situation. The language is Modern English and had already been the subject of the Great Vowel Shift, inflectional simplification and Johnson's linguistic standardisation. It means that the use of language and terminology is a lot more structured. Mansfield's concept of consideration as moral obligation, rather than as just an element to be given 'in exchange' to make a contract legally enforceable, leads to the use of terminology that was absent prior to the Mansfield cases. The term 'consideration' clusters and collocates more with words such as 'promise' and 'moral'. The effort to introduce a notion of moral obligation into contract formation, akin to the civil law tradition, came together with the attempt to shift the intersubjective agreement of the use of language relating to the concept of consideration. This push for conceptual change on the part of Mansfield and some other judges ultimately failed and the semantic shifts reverted back to the notion of pure exchange without moral obligation.

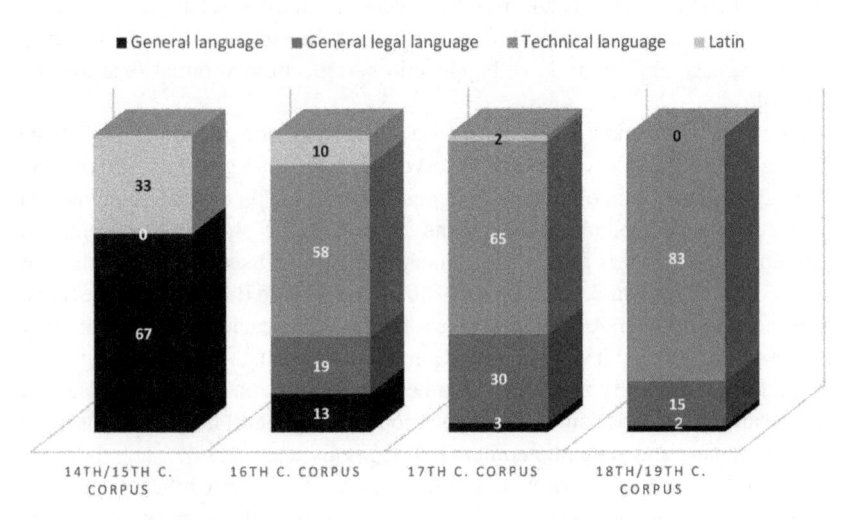

Figure 9.2   Language register for 'consideration'

Figure 9.2 shows how in the use of the terminology that encodes the concept of consideration, we have shifted along a linguistic continuum from '*consideration*' as a general concept to '*in consideration of*' in a general context (black), to '*in consideration of*' in a specifically legal context, though still within a general language understanding (dark grey), to '*consideration*' as the linguistic expression of a legal concept (grey). As the concept gained in stature, so did its position as an autonomous concept. This was reflected in the use of the term 'consideration' no longer solely in the context of a causal connector but as a stand-alone noun and cover-term for the conceptual thinking of how to make informal agreements enforceable. The term 'consideration' stood hitherto for a legal concept that has continued to evolve to the present day.

4.   CONCLUSIONS

In Alice's Wonderland, Humpty Dumpty admits that he can choose language to mean whatever he wants it to mean. We have recently entered an era where these sorts of self-appointed meanings have become prevalent. Corpus-based methodologies and tools provide data that can reveal semantic prosody and manipulation of meanings, which, in turn, inform us on the presence or absence of elements such as semantic objectivity and biases.

In both studies reported in this chapter, the corpus-based methodologies and tools provide empirical information about contexts, which in turn improve knowledge about ordinary meanings, legal language and legal concepts. Lee and Mouritsen's study used corpus-based methodologies to search for pragmatic natural language uses in relation to the search for ordinary meanings in the context of judicial interpretation. In a recent case involving President Trump having allegedly violated the constitution by accepting foreign money at his hotel, a corpus linguistics study on the meaning of 'emolument' was submitted to the court, though not on behalf of either party.[39] Predictably highly charged because of its political context, Cunningham (Georgia State University) and Egbert (Northern Arizona University) were able to supply linguistic information on the 'behaviour' of the word emolument that could inform the debate on whether Trump's acceptance of foreign money at his hotel was contrary to the constitution. Cunningham and Egbert have described corpus linguistics as a 'scientific method'. While it uses large amounts of data from which quantitative and qualitative information can be extracted that can contribute to a certain semantic objectivity in the understanding of language, the approach inevitably also involves some subjective elements due to choices of corpora, linguistics tools, measurements and interpretation of data etc.

The second study reported above on the terminology in relation to the concept of consideration provides data that reveals the evolution of terminology for the purpose of getting a better understanding of its etymological, terminological and historical content. One of the basic premises of the concept of semantic objectivity in law is that the legal language needs to be precise and unambiguous, so that the law is generally ascertainable and transparent, and that, for example, partiality and ulterior motives cannot be easily be hidden. By studying the evolution of legal concepts diachronically and as encoded in its language, we can retrace and understand where the process has defaulted in relation to semantic objectivity and impartiality.

Whatever linguistic methodology we use to evaluate objectivity in law, it may be relevant to not just rely on theoretical constructs and linguistics intuition, but also on a pragmatic approach that can offer some empirically ascertained data. But to the extent that human choices need to be made in relation to data selection and interpretation of results, objectivity can only ever be measured against the relative subjectivity of these choices. It may illustrate that language is never neutral, that it is always pregnant with socio-political, ideological and economic contents, and that, in particular in areas such as the law, idealised meaning is constructed, the objectivity of which is an illusion.

---

[39] *Maryland v Trump*, brief of *Amici Curiae*; USCA4 Appeal: 18-2486, Doc: 27, filed: 01/29/2019.

ANNEX 1 – EXAMPLES FOR HALLIDAY'S METAFUNCTIONS

(i) Ideational Metafunction / Experiential Meanings:

An example of the simplest clause constituent structure:

The train	departs
(participant)	(process)

The dog	barked
(participant)	(process)

This becomes more elaborate when other participants are added:

My uncle	missed	the train
(participant)	(process)	(participant)

Or circumstance is added:

The train	departs	at six o'clock
(participant)	(process)	(circumstance)

My uncle	missed	the train	by five minutes
(participant)	(process)	(participant)	(circumstance)

(ii) Interpersonal Metafunction/Interpersonal Meanings:

There are many elements that indicate interpersonal meanings. Here are few examples:

- mood (order, apologise, invite, reject, describe etc.): Sit down! Please be seated.
- modal auxiliary: will (inclination/futurity), can (ability/possibility), should or have to (obligation); e.g. I will collect her. I could go and collect her after work. You should go to the station now!
- use of pronouns: I, you, we, our, your; e.g. Before we begin, I would like to like to set out the main stages of our trip together.

(iii) Textual Metafunction/Textual Meanings:

Example illustrating how the organisation of a text informs the textual meaning:

THEME	RHEME
My dog	chased the cat all around the garden.
The cat	was chased all around the garden by my dog.
All around the garden,	the cat was chased by my dog.

ANNEX 2 – LEGAL SOURCES

Year Books/Law Reports and Other Sources:

All sources listed here are electronically accessible via the database of HeinOnline (www.heinonline.org). Beside every title below, each click to access the documents in question has also been listed.

(i) Selden Society Publications:

HeinOnline – Selden Society Publications and the History of Early English Law – Selden Society Publications – Selden Society (Annual) Series

- Year Books of Henry VI, 1 Henry VI A.D. 1422 (50 Selden Society)
- Year Books of 10 Edward IV and 49 Henry VI A.D. 1470 (47 Selden Society)
- Reports of Cases by John Caryll, part I, A.D. 1485–1499 (115 Selden Society)
- Select Cases in the Council of Henry VII (1485–1509) (75 Selden Society)

(ii) English Reports

Full Reprint: HeinOnline – English Reports, Full Reprint

- Volume 72 Eng. Rep. The English Reports – King's Bench Division containing
  - Bellewe (1585): LES ANS DU ROY RICHARD LE SECOND. Collect 'Ensembl' Hors les Abridgments De Statham, Fitzherbert et Brooke. Per RICHARD BELLEWE, de Lincolns Inne. 1585.
  - Keilwey (1688): REPORTS d'ascuns CASES (qui ont evenus aux temps dy Roy Henry le Septieme de tres heureuse memoire, & du tres illustre Roy Henry le huitiesme, & ne sont comprises deins les livres des Terms & Ans demesmes les Roys.) Seliges hors des papiers de ROBERT KEILWEY, Esp.; par JEAN CROKE, Sergeant al Ley, Jades Recorder del City de Londres & Prolocuteur del meason des Communes es derniers jour du rege de la Royne Elisabeth. 1688.
    Ovesque les Reports d'ascuns Cases prises per le Reverend Juge *Guilleaume Dallison* un des Justices del Bank le Roy, au temps de la Reyne *Elisabeth* & per *Guilleaume Bendloe* Serjeant al Ley au temps de la mesme Royne; touchants la construction de divers Acts de Parliament par equitè.

La tierce Edition embellie de pluis que deux milles References aux autres livres cybien Ancient que Moderne de la ley, *Jamais* uncore imprimès.

- Moore (1688): CASES Collect and Report per Sir Fra. Moore, Chevalier, Serjeant del Ley. Imprime and Publie per l'Original jadis remainent en les maines de Sir GEFREY PALMER, Chevalier and Bar., Attorney-General a son Tres-Excellent Majesty le Roy Charles le Seond. Le Seco Edition. 1688.

- Volume 73 Eng. Rep. The English Reports – King's Bench Division containing:
  - Benloe (1661): Les REPORTS de GULIELME BENDLOES Serjeant de la Lay: Des Divers Resolutions et Judgments donne par les Reverendes Judges de la Ley: De certeine Matieres en la Ley en le Temps del Raigne de Roys et Roignes Hen. VIII., Edw. VI., Phil et Mar. et Elisab. Avec que Autres Select Cases en la Ley adjudges et resolves en le Temps del Regne de Tresillustres Roys Jaques et Charles le premier: Jammais par cy devant imprimee. Publies en le XIII au de Treshaut et Renosmes Charles le Second Par le Grace de Deiu Roy d'Angleterre, Scoce, Fr. et Irel. Le Restituteur et Conservateur de la Ley. 1661
  - also containing in English translation: Dyer, volumes 1, 2 and 3; Brook's new cases; these were disregarded.

- Volume 123 – Eng. Rep. The English Reports - Common Pleas containing:
  - Benloe (1689): Les REPORTS de GULIELME BENLOE, Serjeant del Ley, Des divers PLEADINGS et CASES en le COURT del COMON-BANK, en le several Roignes de les tres Hault & Excellent Princes, le ROY HENRY VII., HENRY VIII., EDW. VI., & le ROIGNES MARY & EIZABETH. 1689
  - Dalison (1689): Les REPORTS des divers SPEICAL CASES Adjudge en le COURT del COMON BANK en les Reignes de les tres hault & Excellent Princes HEN. VIII. EDW. VI. et les Reignes MAR. & ELIZ. Colligees par GULIELME DALISON un des JUSTICES Del BANK le ROY. London, 1689.
  - Anderson, vols. 1 and 2 (1664): Les REPORTS du Treserudite EDMUND ANDERSON, Chivalier, Nadgairs, Seigniour CHIEF JUSTICE del COMMON-BANK. Des mults principals CASES ARGUES & AGJUGES en le temps del jadis ROIGN ELIZABETH

cibien en le COMMON-BANK come devant touts les Juges de cest Poialme, colligees & escries per luy mesme & imprimees per l'Original ore remaneant en les maines des Imprimeur. London, 1664.
- Savile (1688): Les REPORTS de Sir JOHN SAVILE, Chevalier, Nadgairis Baron de l'Exchequer, de Divers SPEICAL CASES cybien en le COURT de COMMON Bank, come L'EXCHEQUER en le Temps de ROYNE ELIZABETH. London, MDCLXXXVIII.
- also containing in English translation: Brownlow and Goldesborough, vols. & and 2; Hutton; Bridgman; these were disregarded.

- Volume 81 – Eng. Rep. The English Reports – King's Bench Division containing:

  - Rolle (1675): Les REPORTS de HENRY ROLLE Searjeant del' Ley, de divers CASES en le COURT del' BANKE le ROY. En le Temps del' REIGN de ROY JAQUES. Colligees par luy mesme & Imprimees par L'Original. 1675.
  - Palmer (1721): The REPORTS of SIR JEFFREY PALMER, Knight and Baront; ATTORNEY GENERAL to His Most Excellent Majesty, KING CHARLES the SECOND; The Second Edition. 1721
  - also containing in English translation: Bulstrode; this was disregarded.

(iii) **Mansfield & co cases: (in alphabetical order) – HeinOnline – English Reports, Full Reprint – Eng. Rep. reference**

Atkins v Banwell (1802) 2 East 505, or 102 Eng. Rep. 462
Atkins v Hill (1775) 1 Cowp. 284, or 98 Eng. Rep.1088
Barnes v Hedley (1809) 2 Taunt. 184, or 127 Eng. Rep. 1047
Barrell v Trussell (1811) 4 Taunt. 117, or 128 Eng. Rep. 273
Brooks v Haigh (1840) 10 Ad & E. 323, or 113 Eng. Rep. 124
Clarke v Shee (1774) 1 Cowp. 197, or 98 Eng. Rep. 1041
Cooper v Martin (1803) 4 East 77, or 102 Eng. Rep. 759
Earle v Oliver (1848) 2 Ex. 71, or 154 Eng. Rep. 410
Eastwood v Kenyon (1840) 11 Ad. & E. 438, or 113 Eng. Rep. 482
Exeter Corporation v Trimlet (1759) 2 Wils. K.B. 95, or 95 Eng. Rep. 705
Flight v Reed (1863) 1 H. & C. 703, or 158 Eng. Rep. 1067
Grenville v Da Costa (1797) Peake Add Cas. 113, or 170 Eng. Rep. 213
Haigh v Brooks (1839) 10 Ad & E. 309, or 113 Eng. Rep. 119
Hawkes v Saunders (1782) 1 Cowp. 289, or 98 Eng. Rep. 1091
Hayes v Warren (1731) 2 Strange 933, or 93 Eng. Rep. 950
Holliday v Atkinson (1826) 5 B. & C. 501, or 108 Eng. Rep. 187
Jestons v Brooke (1778) 2 Cowp. 793, or 98 Eng. Rep. 1365
Lee v Muggeridge (1813) 5 Taunt. 36, or 128 Eng. Rep. 599
Lindon v Hooper (1776) 1 Cowp. 414, or 98 Eng. Rep. 1160
Littlefield v Shee (1831) 2 B. & Ad. 811, or 109 Eng. Rep. 1343
Martyn v Hind (1776) 2 Cowp. 437, or 98 Eng. Rep. 1174 (1776) 1 Dougl. 142, or 99 Eng. Rep. 94
Mawson v Stock (1801) 6 Ves. Jun. 300, or 31 Eng. Rep. 1062
Mayor Yarmouth v Eaton (1763) 3 Burr. 1402, or 97 Eng. Rep. 896
Meyer v Haworth (1763) 8 Ad. & E. 467, or 112 Eng. Rep. 916
Montefiori v Montefiori (1762) 1 Black. W. 363, or 96 Eng. Rep. 203
Moses v Macferlan (1760) 2 Burr. 1005, or 97 Eng. Rep. 676
Munt v Stokes (1792) 4 T.R. 561, or 100 Eng. Rep. 1176
Nightingal v Devisme (1770) 5 Burr. 2589, or 98 Eng. Rep. 361
Paynter v Williams (1833) 1 C. & M. 810, or 149 Eng. Rep. 626
Pillans and Rose v Van Mierop and Hopkins (1765) 3 Burr. 1663, or 97 Eng. Rep. 1035
Price v Neal (1762) 1 Black. W. 390, or 96 Eng. Rep. 221
Randall v Morgan (1805) 12 Ves; Jun. 66, or 33 Eng. Rep. 26
Rann v Hughes 1778 (1778) 4 Bro. P.C. 27, or 2 Eng. Rep. 18 7 T.R. 350, or 101 Eng. Rep. 1014
Reech v Kennegal (1748) 1 VEs. Sen. 123, or 27 Eng. Rep. 932
Shadwell v Shadwell (1860) 9 C.B. (N.S.) 159, or 142 Eng. Rep. 62

Smith v Bromley (1760) 2 Dougl. 696, or 99 Eng. Rep. 441
Stock v Mawson (1798) 1 Bos. & Pul. 286, or 126 Eng. Rep. 907
Tate v Hilbert (1793) 2 Ves. Jun. 111, or 30 Eng. Rep. 548
Thomas v Thomas (1842) 2 Q.B. 851, or 114 Eng. rep. 330
Thornton v Illingworth (1824) 2 B. & C. 824, or 107 Eng. Rep. 589
Trueman v Fenton (1777) 2 Cowp. 544, or 98 Eng. Rep. 1232
Wells v Horton (1826) 2 Car. & P. 383, or 172 Eng. Rep. 173
Wendall v Adney (1803) 3 Bos. & P., 247 at 250, or 127 Eng. Rep. 137
Weston v Downes (1778) 1 Dougl. 23, or 99 Eng. Rep. 19
Willliams v Moor (1843) 11 M. & W. 256, or 152 Eng. Rep. 798
Wing v Mill (1817) 1 B. & Ald. 104, or 106 Eng. Rep. 39

10. Rethinking the legal effect of interpretive canons[1]

Triantafyllos Gkouvas

Determinative answers to legal questions are rarely the result of directly applying a single rule to the facts of a case. More often than not, success in an exercise of legal reasoning is measured by how the arguments used purport to explain the interaction between different sources of law 'vying' for recognition of their legal relevance. The complexity of this interaction is often compounded when interpretive norms or conventions such as codified or doctrinally established canons of statutory construction anchor judicial reasoning to a deliberative perspective which often appears to clash with contrary indicia of ordinary linguistic meaning and legislative intent. Crucially, despite their being widely advocated as interpretive 'rules of thumb' for clarifying the ordinary meaning of statutory texts, suspicion, both scholarly and official, abounds as to the number and nature of cases where their use disguises or suppresses the subjective, if not bluntly law-making, dimension of legal interpretation. The bulk of jurisprudential scholarship on the use of such canons usually prefaces the questions of their legitimacy and objective purport with formal digressions into the nature and scope of their interaction with statutory provisions. This interaction is commonly approached as concerning the metaphysical question of when and how the contribution made by a statutory provision to the content of the law—or, equivalently, its legal effect[2]—is modified, as a matter of legal fact rather than as a matter of unilateral judicial choice, by interpretive norms whose pedigree is either statutory or common law.

---

[1] This chapter has benefitted immensely from discussing many of the issues raised with Lisa Burton Crawford, Tom Campbell, Julie Debeljak, Patrick Emerton, Jeff Goldsworthy, Jan Mihal, Dale Smith, David Tan Dar Wei, and Kevin Walton. Research and writing of it have been generously supported by the Australian Research Council (ARC) within the parameters of the ARC Discovery Project 'Construing Statutes: The Interaction Between a Statute's Linguistic Content and Principles of Statutory Construction'.

[2] I shall treat the notions of 'legal effect' and 'contribution to the content of the law' or 'legal content' as by and large equivalent.

Whereas their orthodox justification often tends to restrict their role to that of 'presumptions about what an intelligently produced text conveys',[3] cases abound where their actual implementation or invocation in the context of judicial argumentation seems aimed at protecting underenforced values against legislative encroachment. What makes these cases jurisprudentially challenging is that, more often than not, the purposeful protection of these values comes at the price of adopting an interpretation which appears so linguistically strained and radical that it attracts the charge of arrogating to the judges the power to practically rewrite existing law by channelling their jurisprudential values and intuitions through the deceitfully objective lens of construction canons. Cases where statutory canons are pleaded as an impartially[4] granted license to radically depart from a statute's linguistic meaning can serve as an occasionally fuzzy[5] but generally identifiable border between those canons which purport to modify the legal content of statutes and those which merely indicate the objective legal content that a statute already has.

In the first section, I will provide a brief overview of the controversy sparked by the judicial application of interpretive canons and codify available distinctions made by legal scholars in the context of evaluating the legal effect of these canons. In the second section I will explore two 'conservative' approaches, one epistemological and one normative, to the question of whether interpretive canons have the power of modifying the legal effect of ordinary legislation or constitutional provisions. Despite their incommensurable premises both approaches adopt a similarly deflationary stance on the role of canons in legal reasoning. In the third section I will spell out the premises and implications of a distinctly metaphysical account of how interpretive canons can interact with legal norms independently of their actual use by 'canon-friendly' judges. The basic idea is that the recognition of a distinct role for interpretive canons presupposes a tighter connection between the intrinsic properties of these canons and the sources of law (statutes, constitutional provisions, administrative decrees etc) whose legal content they affect.

---

[3] Antonin Scalia and Bryan Garner, *Reading Law: The Interpretation of Legal Texts* (Thomson West 2012) 70.

[4] For how impartiality as a virtue and as criterion matters for ascriptions of objectivity see in this volume Gonzalo Villa-Rosas and Jorge Luis Fabra-Zamora, 'Introduction: The Meanings of "Objectivity"'.

[5] Fuzziness can even affect canons traditionally thought as 'normative'. For instance, the US Supreme Court oscillates in its description of the federalism canon as being about how Congress should act and how Congress is presumed to act. For this point and the accompanying references see Thomas Bennett, 'The Canon at the Water's Edge' (2012) 87 *N.Y. Uni. Law Rev.* 207, 212.

1. BACKGROUND CONTROVERSY AND DISTINCTIONS

Contemporary scholarship offers different routes for demarcating the borderline in the universe of statutory and constitutional law cases where interpretation as the clarification of legal meaning shades into creative, subjectively contoured modes of interpretive reasoning.[6] Interpretive canons—both linguistic[7] and substantive[8]—weigh much heavier on the interpretive scale in the sense that they appear to counsel judges to mobilize their jurisgenerative powers well beyond ascertaining the meaning of authoritative legal texts for the sake of realizing normative values often incorporated in other parts of the law. Such canons occupy a spectrum ranging from general norms enjoining the exercise of principled discretion in balancing competing policies in light of the practical outcomes of different interpretive choices to what is known in the Anglo-American systems as 'clear statement rules' which require an explicit statement on the face of the statutory text to rebut a policy presumption usually created for the sake of protecting constitutional rights and structures.[9]

---

[6] For the distinction between clarifying and creative processes of interpretation see Jeffrey Goldsworthy, 'Implications in Language, Law and the Constitution' in Geoffrey Lindell (ed), *Future Directions in Australian Constitutional Law* (Federation Press 1994) 150–84. Goldsworthy further refines this distinction by subdividing creative interpretation into supplementary and rectifying variants. The former variant regards the supplementation of a pre-existing legal meaning to resolve indeterminacies, whereas the latter variant regards alterations in the legal meaning of statutory provisions that occur in the process of purposefully correcting or improving the law.

[7] Some linguistic canons usually thought to be purely syntactical are applicable by way of normative argument regarding the value at stake. For instance, the purpose of the maxim '*inclusio unius est exclusio alterius*' (the inclusion of the one is the exclusion of another) is to emphasize that statutes should not be casually construed to mandate changes not specified by the language chosen.

[8] Substantive canons such as the rule of lenity, the avoidance canon, and the presumption against extraterritorial application of domestic laws, to name a few, provide interpretive guidance by bearing upon the substance or subject area of the legal instrument being interpreted. Avoidance canons which counsel judges to avoid an interpretation of a statute that actually jeopardizes its constitutionality are more often than not applied in ways that conflict with the linguistic meaning of statutes pushing courts 'to yield results that, for political or other reasons, may well have lain beyond the legislature's intended reach'. David Shapiro, 'Continuity and Change in Statutory Interpretation' (1992) 67 *N.Y. Uni. Law Rev.* 921, 960. Shapiro bases the justification of this interpretive 'transgression' on the claim that judges 'have a unique responsibility to accommodate change to a complex and relatively stable structure of rules and principles' (ibid).

[9] Such canons abound in federal states. *See* John Manning, 'Clear Statement Rules and the Constitution' (2010) 110 *Colum. L. Rev.* 399, 406–7; *see also* William

Karl Llewellyn, a prominent American legal realist, based his classic critique of canon-based interpretation on the premise that the scholarly and judicial adoption of interpretive canons was jurisprudentially, rather than simply doctrinally, flawed. His critique was based on the claim that the pragmatic nature of law-making is such that it renders their use radically indeterminate.[10] Similar, if not more scathing, remarks can also be found in the work of contemporary legal realists. Proponents of legal realism will often resist the temptation of accommodating a meaningful role for statutory canons on the grounds that their users 'presume that the courts are observers rather than participants, and that a statute is primarily a linguistic artifact, rather than a mechanism for allocating resources and deploying force'.[11] Equally disparaging has been the treatment of these canons by major proponents of legal pragmatism such as Richard A Posner who dismisses the utility of time-honoured canons by asserting that 'they are fig leaves for decisions reached on other grounds'.[12]

Against this background of suspicion different distinctions have been propounded for the sake of bestowing a distinct role on interpretive canons. A prominent division advocated by Lawrence Solum suggests that canons should be divided into canons of interpretation—in the strict sense—and canons of construction. Whereas the former are rules of thumb aiming at summarizing pre-existing regularities in the epistemic process of discovering the legal content of a statute or constitutional provision, canons of construction are 'rules of law' in the technical sense that they purport to modify or shape the legal effect given to statutes.[13] Other proposed distinctions apply different criteria of division. Cass Sunstein maps the canon universe into four basic functional categories, namely, those that clarify statutory meaning, those that illuminate interpretive instructions from the legislature, those that

---

Eskridge, Jr. and Philip Frickey, 'Quasi-Constitutional Law: Clear Statement Rules as Constitutional Lawmaking' (1992) 45 *Vanderbilt Law Rev.* 593.

[10] Karl Llewellyn, 'Remarks on the Theory of Appellate Decision and the Rules or Canons About How Statutes are to be Construed' (1950) 3 *Vanderbilt Law Rev.* 395. Llewellyn contrasts 28 canons and counter-canons with a view to showing that there are two opposing canons on almost every point. For a similar critique originating from another leading legal realist of the early era see Max Radin, 'Statutory Interpretation' (1930) 43 *Harv. L. Rev.* 863.

[11] Richard Edward Rubin, 'Modern Statutes, Loose Canons, and the Limits of Practical Reason: A Response to Farber and Ros' (1992) 45 *Vanderbilt Law Rev.* 579.

[12] *Continental Cas. Co v. Pittsburgh Corning Corp.*, 917 F.2d 297, 300 (7th Cir. 1990). *See* also Richard A Posner, 'Statutory Interpretation—in the Classroom and in the Courtroom' (1983) 50 *U. Chi. L. Rev.* 800 and James C Thomas. 'Statutory Construction when Legislation is Viewed as a Legal Institution' (1966) 3 *Harv. J. on Legis.* 191.

[13] *See* Lawrence Solum, 'The Interpretation-Construction Distinction' (2010) 27 *Const. Comment.* 95.

promote better law-making, and those that serve a judicial, constitutional, or common-sense substantive purpose.[14]

Given that appeals to function evoke both normative and descriptive uses it remains unclear what could determine whether the function of a canon is merely epistemic (objective)[15] or creative (subjective) in a particular case. In response to this concern Stephen Ross distinguishes 'descriptive' from 'normative' canons on the basis of the legal realist rationale that the former '[involve] *predictions* [emphasis added] as to what the legislature must have meant'.[16] On a different reading of the same distinction Kenneth Bamberger preserves the use of normative canons in the narrow context of semantic ambiguity noting that 'normative canons draw on a range of values derived elsewhere to resolve legislative ambiguity'.[17] A more dynamic division is the one advocated by William Eskridge and Philip Frickey between 'substantive policy canons' embodying public policies drawn from the Constitution, 'textual canons' postulating conventions of grammar and syntax, linguistic inferences and textual integrity and 'extrinsic source canons' directing the interpreter to authoritative sources of linguistic meaning and legislative intent. The game-theoretic vision animating this division treats these canons as part of an interpretive regime serving both rule-of-law purposes such as clarity and predictability and coordination purposes such as distributing certain decisional power to the courts and signalling judicial preferences for specific policy priorities.[18]

2. EPISTEMIC AND REGULATIVE CANONS

The assumption legitimately conveyed by the title of this chapter is that under some conditions interpretive canons can have a robustly metaphysical impact in the sense that they can essentially figure in the explanation of when and why the legal effect of *another* legal provision is modified because of its interaction with a canon. The title appears to license a heterodox understanding of interpretive canons as the 'metaphysical culprits' for the modification of the legal effect of other legal provisions. That being said, it would be inexcusably

---

[14] Cass Sunstein, *After the Rights Revolution: Reconceiving the Regulatory State* (Harvard University Press 1990) 150–56.

[15] For an instructive distinction between the ontological objectivity of law and the epistemic objectivity about law see, in this volume, Jaap Hage, 'Objectivity of Law and Objectivity about Law'.

[16] Stephen Ross, 'Where Have You Gone, Karl Llewellyn? Should Congress Turn Its Lonely Eyes to You?' (1992) 45 *Vanderbilt Law Rev.* 561.

[17] Kenneth Bamberger, 'Normative Canons in the Review of Administrative Policymaking' (2008) 118 *Yale L. J.* 64, 72.

[18] William N Eskridge, Jr. and Philip Frickey, 'The Supreme Court, 1993 Term—Foreword: Law as Equilibrium' (1994) 108 *Harv. L. Rev.* 23, 97–108.

hasty to shoulder and defend this strong hypothesis without acknowledging the explanatory virtues of metaphysically less demanding approaches to the same phenomenon of interaction between canons and other legal provisions. This is not to say that these approaches lack a distinct metaphysical background. What makes them count as metaphysically 'mute', so to speak, is the fact that they do not account for the legal relevance of interpretive canons by way of assigning to them a distinct metaphysical role over and above the metaphysical role of social and normative facts. Their legal relevance is settled directly and solely by reference to general premises about how non-legal facts make legal facts, that is, facts about the obtaining of legal obligations and rights.

In what follows I will lay bare the premises of two prominent approaches to how interpretive canons interact with ordinary legal norms in a way that bypasses the ordinary concern about the judicial overdetermination of their purpose. This is a step preparatory to the next and final section where I will attempt to sketch a more radical approach to how interpretive canons can be taken to affect the content of the law. Each of these two approaches features two distinct variants which rest on competing general theories of legal metaphysics concerning the way in which non-legal facts make law. What ties them under the same generic approach is the way they individuate the role of interpretive canons. The first approach is broadly epistemological in the sense that it treats interpretive canons as objective evidence for what the law already requires.[19] Both variants of this approach decline to acknowledge any distinct metaphysical role for interpretive canons. The second approach is normative not in a strictly legal or jurisprudential but in a political-institutional sense. Both variants of this approach treat interpretive canons as reflecting a certain normative conception of what makes the division of labour between the legislative and judicial institutions institutionally desirable.

According to the first epistemological approach textual canons such as *ejusdem generis* or substantive canons such as the avoidance of unconstitutional interpretations of statutes are judicially crafted or codified rules of thumb for discovering what the law *already* requires independently of the

---

[19] Treating interpretive canons as epistemic tools is not identical with treating them as mind-reading tools. The 'epistemic' and the 'intentional' are distinct notions much in the same way that knowledge is not, at least obviously, reducible to understanding. The former has as its object *facts* that the "knower" invokes as reasons for settling various practical and theoretical questions. The latter has as its object *attitudes* (including, of course, intentions) held by 'other minds' to which the 'understander' attributes certain propositional contents. In sloganesque terms, facts are creatures of *reason*, whereas attitudes (intentions) are creatures of the *mind*. For a critique of treating interpretive canons as mind-reading tools, and, more broadly, of treating the interpretation of linguistic meaning as a mind-reading process see Jamie Blaker, 'A Statute's Meaning Need Not Be Its Law'(2018) 46 *Fed. L. Rev.* 455.

fact that these canons are judicially adopted or statutorily entrenched. The first variant of this approach is distinctly positivist in the sense that it treats such canons as mere burden-allocators or tiebreakers[20] allowing interpreters of a legal text to draw inferences about the actual or reasonably attributable content of legislative intention. The positivist allure of this variant is due to the implied role of descriptive facts about legislative intention as the principal determinants of the content of the law. The only contribution of interpretive canons consists in their elucidating the law-making impact of such facts about legislative intention. In other words, and despite appearances, they do not operate as vehicles for smuggling the perspective of the judge into the inventory of determinants of the content of the law.

The classic application context of such epistemic canons comprises cases where there are two equally plausible readings of a statute. The application of the relevant canon will proclaim the 'winner' considering the overall balance of available evidence. An apt illustration of this case can be found in an influential understanding of the canon of constitutional avoidance in the jurisprudence of the US Supreme Court. The Court's current avoidance doctrine is marked by a conflict over how far the statute's meaning can be stretched for the sake of rescuing its constitutionality. On one understanding of the canon, prominently defended by Justice Antonin Scalia, the avoidance canon is merely an interpretive tiebreaker.[21] The canon thus serves the same function as the baseball rule that a tie goes to the runner—it provides a default rule for discerning legislative intent. For tiebreaking avoidance, the range of plausible meanings attributed to statutory language must remain within the remit of what the legislature may be taken to have intended it to have. That is, the judicial interpreter must first determine that a statutory provision is capable of more than one meaning and only then can she use the avoidance canon to decide which meaning does not contradict the intention one may reasonably impute to the legislature. At any rate, the epistemic understanding of constitutional avoidance remains consonant with the broadly positivist idea that the content of the law is determined by facts that are directly or indirectly related to what the legislature intended to convey by way of enacting a statute.

A non-positivist variant of the same epistemological approach holds that interpretive canons are indicative of the normative impact of law-making

---

[20] It should be kept in mind that a tiebreaker canon is an epistemically rebuttable presumption which does not always necessitate a result. Sometimes the party burdened with establishing the contrary may succeed at responding to this burden by advancing persuasive arguments that the statutory text, legislative history, or statutory purpose is inconsistent with the presumption established by the canon. *See* Antonin Scalia and Bryan Garner, *Reading Law: The Interpretation of Legal Texts* (Thomson West 2012).
[21] Ibid.

facts—facts about the sayings, doings and mental states of law-making officials—on our legal obligations and rights. Mark Greenberg is the most prominent proponent of this view which he directly ties to his general theory of law also known as the 'moral impact theory of law'.[22] Greenberg enlists interpretive canons in the array of factors that are epistemically but *not* juris-generatively relevant, which is to say that, unlike the actions of law-making institutions, they do not change the content of the law by way of changing the morally relevant circumstances that obtain at the time of the enactment of a new statute. In this context he mentions the example of canons of statutory interpretation instructing that textual ambiguities be resolved in favour of Native Americans and veterans. According to the moral impact theory of law, Greenberg explains, 'these canons are *ways of taking into account* [emphasis added] the United States's moral debts to Native Americans and veterans, respectively'.[23] His view is that what these canons do is to draw the attention of the courts to pre-existing and *independently legally relevant* objective moral reasons such as the moral debt of the state to certain communities. It is these reasons rather than the actual application and/or endorsement of the respective canons that shape the effect that the enactment of a statute has on the content of the legal rights and obligations of members of these special communities.[24]

The second approach is politically normative in the sense that it treats interpretive canons as mirroring an ideal division of institutional labour between legislative and judicial institutions. The basic idea is that, in the circumstances specified by the canons, objective reasons of effective institutional design empower courts either to make new law within the constraints set out by both the canon and the statutory text or to modify the application of an existing law to a particular case in accordance with the direction provided by the canon. In either case the role of interpretive canons is regulative in the sense that it allows courts to modulate the regulative effect of existing legislation on the basis of considerations of institutional design.[25]

---

[22] Mark Greenberg, 'The Moral Impact Theory of Law' (2014) 123 *Yale L. J.* 1288.
[23] Ibid., 1333.
[24] Greenberg ascribes general scope to this approach noting, ibid., that:
[o]ther canons and interpretive doctrines can be understood in similar ways. The rule of lenity and the doctrine of avoiding absurd results are obvious examples. The Moral Impact Theory also understands linguistic or textual canons as rules of thumb for working out the moral consequences of statutes.
[25] It should not come as a surprise that both variants of the regulative approach I am about to detail are derivative of a broadly positivist understanding of how facts make law. The key to understanding the compatibility between the regulative (rather than epistemic) role assigned to interpretive canons and the positivist grounds on which this assignment is licensed is the implicit allegiance of both variants to a sharp distinction between the bindingness of legal norms (legal normativity) and the aspirational

The first variant of the regulative approach targets the validity of legal norms in the sense that it demarcates the context in which a statute or a part thereof may be judicially invalidated *ex nunc*. It suggests that in cases where the linguistic content of a statute clashes with the instructions of an interpretive canon, the latter represents a direction to the court to *uno actu* repeal the canon-inconsistent norm and make new law in accordance with the constraints encoded by the canon. Until the court actually sets out to formulate a new, canon-compatible legal rule, the previous, canon-inconsistent rule remains legally valid. Judicial declarations of invalidity are exercises of what Joseph Raz calls 'directed powers'.[26] These powers are rules of change[27]—not rules of recognition—which confer a law-making power to the court to *uno actu* repeal the canon-inconsistent norm and make new law in accordance with the constraints encoded by the empowering canon. Until the court actually sets out to formulate a new, canon-compatible legal rule, the previous, canon-inconsistent rule remains legally valid.[28] To understand why interpretive canons cannot,

---

requirements of institutional design (political normativity). Regardless of whether it results in the creation of new legal norms or the disapplication of a pre-existing legal norm to a particular case, the regulative effect of interpretive canons is entirely a function of *descriptive* facts about how a court *actually* decides to proceed in a particular case. Prior to its actual response there is no legal fact of the matter as to whether the court's response is legally mandated to validate the instructions of a canon or whether the legal norm whose content or application is targeted by a particular canon remains legally valid.

[26] Following Joseph Raz's authoritative definition, a directed power is:
a law-making power coupled with a duty to use it, and to use it to achieve certain objectives and only them, regardless of whether or not this power is limited in the corresponding way…Directed powers are the paradigmatic case of the law providing for its own development. Here we find the law providing reasons for the introduction of new legal rules, yet those are not part of the law until enacted by the empowered authority.

(Joseph Raz, 'The Inner Logic of The Law' in Joseph Raz, *Ethics in the Public Domain: Essays in the Morality of Law and Politics* (rev. edn, Clarendon Press 1996) 238–53, 242).

[27] According to H L A Hart's original formulation of this concept:
[t]he simplest form of such a rule is that which empowers an individual or body of persons to introduce new primary rules for the conduct of the life of the group, or of some class within it, and to eliminate old rules…it is in terms of such a rule, and not in terms of orders backed by threats, that the ideas of legislative enactment and repeal are to be understood.

(H L A Hart, *The Concept of Law* (2nd edn, P A Bulloch and J Raz, (eds), Clarendon Press, 1994) 95). Another example of a rule of change is the stipulation that superior courts may overrule precedents established by inferior courts.

[28] Joseph Raz (n 25) highlights this point noting, at 250, that:
[t[here is then a uniquely correct solution to the case, but it is not law until given legally binding force by the court. Until then it may be the case that the law

on this view, produce any change in the legal effect of a statutory provision *prior* to the court's imprimatur—that is, prior to the court's actual application of the canon in a particular case—we need to take into account the normative-institutional rationale[29] that licenses the ability of the courts to change the law by following guidelines set by the law itself. Provided that, in more-or-less exceptional cases, judicial decisions can be taken to establish binding rules of law either in virtue of an entrenched doctrine of precedent[30] or simply by the force of judicial custom, there is room for arguing that judicial institutions are more apt at crystallizing certain linguistic and moral considerations into binding precedential or customary rules than legislative organs.[31]

A less 'intrusive' variant of the regulative approach does not focus on the combined invalidating-cum-law-making effect of the application of interpretive canons but on the mode of applying canon-inconsistent legal provisions to particular cases. Instead of repealing and creating a new legal rule, courts are portrayed as taking the circumstances outlined in a canon to license the disapplication or modified application of an otherwise legally valid rule to the case at hand. This is not a directed judicial power to make new law but a manifestation of what the common law parlance describes as the power of equitable override. The disapplied legal rule retains its validity and its unmodified application to other cases remains possible. The operative premise in this approach is that despite their formulaic nature legal rules are defeasible for the logically compelling reason that law-makers are not omniscient nor endowed with impeccable foresight that can anticipate the proper legal treatment of any future case.[32] Accordingly, courts are better placed to address the occasional

---

imposes a duty on the court to establish a new legal rule, but that rule is no more legally valid prior to the courts' decision than is a piece of subordinate legislation, which an official has a legal duty to enact, legally valid before its enactment.

[29] Héctor Morales-Zúñiga formalises this institutional rationale as the institutional counterpart of a discursive right to justification. See, in this volume, Héctor Morales-Zúñiga, 'Is Legal Cognitivism a Case of Bullshit?'

[30] These doctrines do not have overriding legal force. As Raz (n 25) notes, '[i]n common-law jurisdictions, and perhaps in all precedent-recognising legal systems, legal doctrines governing the use of the directed powers of the courts are defeasible to a particularly high degree'.

[31] For a critical account of assimilating judicial with philosophical reasoning see Jeremy Waldron, 'Judges as Moral Reasoners' (2009) 7 *Int. J. Const. Law* 2. For a reconciliatory argument see Christopher Eisgruber, 'Should Constitutional Judges Be Philosophers?' in Scott Hershovitz (ed), *Exploring Law's Empire: The Jurisprudence of Ronald Dworkin* (Oxford University Press 2006) 5–22.

[32] As Frederick Schauer remarks, the institutional rationale that permits the judicial modification of the scope of application of positive law is that;
legal rules, if literally or faithfully followed, will sometimes generate outcomes that are absurd, silly, unfair, unjust, inefficient, or in some other way suboptimal.

frictions or impasses we encounter when the actuality of governance by law provides compelling moral, rational or prudential reasons to resist the mechanical application of abstract legal requirements. When confronted with such unfortunate circumstances, Frederick Schauer suggests:

> the applier of a rule putatively takes the occasion of application not to revise the rule, but instead to make an exception for just the case at hand...the original rule persists in largely unrevised form, save the specific exception that is made for exactly this case.[33]

3. CANON-BASED MODIFICATION AS SUPERVENIENCE

The distinguishing mark of the previous two approaches is their accommodation of interpretive canons within available schemes of jurisprudential theorizing that also apply to cases that do not involve the interaction of legal provisions with canon-based instructions. Such cases are part of common

---

When such unfortunate consequences occur as a result of the inevitable over- and under-inclusiveness of rules, advanced legal systems commonly provide a mechanism by which legal decision-makers may ameliorate the harsh consequences of necessarily coarse rules.
(Frederick Schauer, 'Is Defeasibility an Essential Property of Law?' in Jordi Ferrer Beltrán and Giovanni Battista Ratti (eds), *The Logic of Legal Requirements: Essays on Defeasibility* (Oxford University Press 2012) 77–88, 7).

[33] Ibid., 79. The most common formula for accommodating the defeating effect of certain considerations on positive law takes the form of an *exception* to the existing rule. This is a position explicitly defended both on pragmatist and semantic grounds. Following the former approach Richard Posner has claimed that courts always retain the ability to add 'ad hoc exceptions' to existing and exceptionless rules for the practical reason that so doing is often institutionally desirable or useful; see Richard Posner, 'The Jurisprudence of Skepticism' (1988) 86 *Mich. L. Rev.* 834. H L A Hart follows the latter approach arguing that not only can a defeasible rule still be a rule, but also that the list of exceptions cannot be exhaustively specified in advance (H L A Hart, *The Concept of Law*, n 26, 128). An alternative formula has been recently developed by Hrafn Asgeirsson. His *Pro Tanto* view about legal content holds that occasional gaps between the content of statutory provisions and the contribution these provisions make to the content of the law are not symptomatic of changes in the *pro tanto* legal content—which directly corresponds to the communicative content—of statutory rules but rather of changes in the all-things-considered legal effect of the interaction of the reasons for action provided by these rules with other legal-normative considerations. He takes this legal effect to be equivalent with the legal obligations and rights that obtain as a result of the statutory reasons that remain undefeated in the aftermath of that interaction (see Hrafn Asgeirsson, 'Can Legal Practice Adjudicate Between Theories of Vagueness?' in Geert Keil and Ralf Poscher (eds), *Vagueness and Law: Philosophical and Legal Perspectives* (University Press 2016) 95–126.

practice in legal systems which have constitutionally or statutorily entrenched rights[34] or value clauses and a concomitant practice of strong or weak judicial review.[35] In this final section I will venture a step forward by showcasing the assumptions and critically evaluating the implications of an alternative approach that invites the introduction of extra-jurisprudential insights. The basic idea is that the interaction between interpretive canons and positive law is not a distinct type of metaphysical relation but *supervenes*, nonetheless, on some of the intrinsic properties of the related entities. Such relation of supervenience is not in and of itself capable of objectively making it the case that the law has this or that content. Rather it purports to mirror in a metaphysically reliable way the process by which the content of the law can change as a matter of metaphysical and not just empirical or semantic fact.[36] Most importantly, for the purposes of this volume chapter, this alternative approach paves an alternative avenue for partly resisting, though not vindicating, the thought that interpretive canons are simply doctrinally sanctioned crystallizations of the evaluative mindset and/or values of judges.

In its most standard use by analytic philosophers the notion of supervenience serves to describe relations or patterns of co-variation between (sets of) properties, relations or, even, entire possible worlds. Generally speaking, a superven-

---

[34] A hybrid case is introduced by *limitation clauses* which are an integral part of most modern international and domestic charters of rights. As opposed to construction canons such as the canon of constitutional avoidance or canons enjoining the rights-consistent interpretation of statutes, limitation clauses purport to modify the legal effect of constitutional or statutory *rights themselves* rather than the legal effect of rights-infringing statutes. Some charters of rights feature a single overarching limitation clause applicable to all rights, whereas others contain a series of limitation clauses applicable to specific rights or clusters of rights. Following Grégoire Webber's classification of limitation formulas, charters of rights vary in the degree of guidance they provide with respect to how rights are permissibly limited. Some stipulate the permissible ends according to which a right may be limited (public health, morals, the prevention of disorder or crime) whereas others rely on an open-ended reference to a 'free and democratic society' without further specification (see Grégoire Webber, *The Negotiable Constitution: On the Limitation of Rights* (Cambridge University Press 2009) 2).

[35] *See* Michael Giudice, 'The Regular Practice of Morality in Law' (2008) 21(1) *Ratio Juris* 94–106.

[36] For how the relation of supervenience can also be utilized to account for the co-variation between conditions and normative consequences in the application of legal norms see, in this volume, Monika Zalewska, 'Imputation as a supervenience in the General Theory of Norms'.Whereas Zalweska's approach aims at capturing a principled co-variation between the *descriptive* and the normative in law, my approach aims at capturing the co-variation between the *ontological* (the role of legal validity in how law can change) and the normative (the modification of the legal-normative effect of legal provisions by canons).

ience relation holds between a set of properties A and a set of properties B just in case no two things can differ with respect to their A-properties without also differing with respect to their B-properties. To borrow an example from a theoretically adjacent discourse it is close to common ground to say that the ethical supervenes on the natural. Roughly, this amounts to saying that it is impossible for two possible worlds to be identical with respect to how they are naturally configured but differ with respect to their proximity to a moral ideal or code of standards. This relational pattern is fit for describing the potential effect that changes in one domain may have on the constituents of another domain. In the present example, any change in the natural properties of a clearly demarcated circumstance in a possible world cannot fail to be accompanied by changes in what is morally best or right to do all things considered.

The application of this framework to the interaction between interpretive canons and positive law is made possible thanks to the versatility of the relation of supervenience. A promising feature of this formal relation is that it is not only used in the context of elucidating co-variation patterns involving different types of properties. It can also be used to carve the distinction between internal and external relations at its joints. As I will explain further downstream the interaction between interpretive canons and legal norms can be modelled in the likeness of a metaphysically internal relation. This is a type of relation that holds exclusively in virtue of the properties of its relata. This is to say that there is no metaphysically distinct relation of, say, *modification of the legal effect* of a statute by an interpretive canon that obtains *over and above* the properties of the statute and the canon involved. Supervenience is ideally fit for representing this type of interaction in a metaphysically modest but, nonetheless, non-perspectival way.[37]

Bridging the gap between talk of internal relations and talk of supervenience relations requires the injection of some additional premises. Both David Armstrong and David Lewis have sought to explain the nature of internal relations in supervenience terms.[38] Internal relations like the relation of *being taller than* supervene on the intrinsic features of their relata such that the nature of these relata guarantees that the relation obtains. For example, if I am 6'1" and Mary is 5'11", I am taller than Mary. All that there needs to obtain for the predication of the relation of being taller than to be true in our case is for

---

[37] By non-perspectival I mean mind-independent in the qualified sense that matters in our discussion. In other words, judicial reasoning is often, and not without good reason, portrayed as cloaking its conclusions on the content of the law under the veil of objectively reporting legal obligations and rights that obtain independently of the judgments that represent them.

[38] David Armstrong, *Universals: An Opinionated Introduction* (Westview Press 1989) 43; David Lewis, *On the Plurality of Worlds* (Blackwell 1986) 62.

me and Mary to have the heights indicated above. Nothing beyond our heights needs to obtain for it to be the case that this relation holds. This is precisely the sense in which Armstrong famously claimed that internal relations are an 'ontologically free lunch'. In his words, 'they are not an addition to the world's furniture', hence they 'are not the sort of relations we should be focussing on in ontology'.[39] Conversely, the relation of my standing at a distance of 3 meters from where Mary sits does not supervene on our intrinsic properties. Nothing about what makes us the persons we are figures essentially in the explanation of our relation. Spatiotemporal and comparative—both qualitative and quantitative—relations[40] are standard cases of external relatedness where the truth of the respective claims depends on a relational *tertium quid* rather than on the intrinsic properties of the relata.

Keeping analogies in sight, we could describe the modifying impact of an interpretive canon on the content of a legal provision as an internal relation holding between a source of legal content,[41] say, a statute, and a modifying canon in the presence of which and under some specifiable conditions the legal content of a statute is different from what it otherwise would have been. In more formal terms, we could then argue that the relation of legal effect modification is a two-place relation holding between a statute S and a modifying canon M. Omitting time and location subscripts for the sake of simplicity this relation can be expressed by a relational predicate **R (S, M)**. Claims about this relation entail that when such modification occurs there must exist two distinct sources of legal content, namely, a statute and a modifying canon. Consequently, a supervenience claim about the obtaining of this two-place relation would be that the relational predicate **R (S, M)** supervenes on the intrinsic properties of its relata, namely, the statute S and the modifying canon M. In the slogan language of supervenience, the same thing can be asserted as follows:

No two sources of legal content can differ with respect to whether one alters the legal effect of the other without also differing with respect to the intrinsic properties of either or both.

---

[39] David Armstrong, A World of States of Affairs (Cambridge University Press 1997) 87 and 92 respectively.

[40] Peter Simon and Fraser MacBride, 'Relations and Truthmaking' (part I, Peter Simons) (2010) 84 *Proc. Aristot. Soc. Suppl. Vol.* 199.

[41] By 'source of legal content' I simply mean a representational vehicle (rule, principle, mental state) that carries legally relevant information. Assuming, as I believe we still can, that cognitivism remains the standard approach to the semantics of legal discourse, the nature of such information is by and large propositional.

A plausible specification of this claim would be that the legal-effect-altering relation between a statutory provision and a modifying canon supervenes on the modifying canon's *legal validity* rather than on its subjective application by a judge.[42] Legal validity, in other words, is that legality-conferring property that makes a canon count as a source of legal content that is capable of interacting in impactful ways with other sources of legal content such as statutes. This formulation acquires the shell of what is commonly described in general metaphysics as a *super-internal* relation.[43] As Karen Bennett defines the term, '[a] superinternal relation is one such that the intrinsic nature of only *one* of the relata—or, better, one side of the relation—guarantees not only that the relation holds, *but also that the other relatum(a) exists and has the intrinsic nature it does* [emphasis added]'.[44] This is a rather strong claim: it says that wherever a relation of legal effect alteration obtains, it obtains in virtue of the intrinsic nature of *one* of the relata, namely, the modifying canon *and* that the modified provision makes its particular contribution to the content of the law.

To illustrate the force of this claim, we may consider the case of a legal system where there applies an interpretive canon to the effect that statutory provisions be interpreted in accordance with a human rights instrument. A prominent case of this sort is section 3(1) of the Human Rights Act 1998 currently in force in the United Kingdom. This requirement reads:

So far as it is possible to do so, primary legislation and subordinate legislation must be read and given effect in a way which is compatible with the Convention rights.

The prevalent view is that this requirement is a typical instance of a modifying canon such that any statutory provision deemed to be in violation of

---

[42] Appeals to the "legal-content-role" of the legal validity of modifying canons can have a broader scope depending on how one construes the property of being legally valid. For instance, appeals to the nature of law as a coherent system of norms can also be proxy for more traditional invocations of legal validity. Dale Smith makes a suggestion that lies within the vicinity of such an approach noting that '[o]ne option is to treat the correct interpretation of a provision as determined, at least in part, by how well competing interpretations cohere with other relevant legal norms. Such a proposal appears particularly well-suited to taking seriously the interaction between a statutory provision and other legal norms.' (Dale Smith, 'Is the High Court Mistaken about the Aim of Statutory Interpretation?' (2016) 44 *Fed. L. Rev.* 227, 255).

[43] I think it would be misleading to characterize the relation of legal effect alteration as a simply internal relation. The legal validity, *ergo* existence of the modifying canon is the minimal supervenience base for it to be the case that on a particular occasion a statutory provision makes a particular contribution to the content of the law.

[44] Karen Bennett takes grounding to be a typical instance of this type of relation. See Karen Bennett, 'By Our Bootstraps' (2011) 25 *Philos. Perspect.* 27, 32.

a Convention right is subject to the effect of section 3(1).[45] To appreciate the modal force of the relation of the canon enshrined in section 3(1) to other statutory provisions all we need to do is to suppose that section 3(1) has been repealed by another statute enacted by the Parliament. Before this repeal and because of the validity of section 3(1), the affected statutory provision was taken to make a particular contribution *S* to the content of the law. After the repeal, section 3(1) has undergone an intrinsic change as it has ceased to be legally valid, which amounts to saying that it has ceased to have the shell of a legal rule of the UK legal system and therefore it has ceased to legally exist. Consequently, one could also assume that upon the repeal of section 3(1), the affected statute has also undergone an intrinsic change but not of the same kind as section 3(1). In other words, the affected statute remains legally valid but is now taken to make a different contribution *D* to the content of the law. Switching to the meta-language of supervenience one could say that the intrinsic change in the existence status of the modifying canon is exclusively accountable both for the fact that it is no longer the case that section 3(1) alters the legal effect of the statutory provision *P and* for the fact that *P* has intrinsically changed such that it now makes a different contribution *D* to the content of the law. Differently put, the same supervenience motto appears to obtain, namely, that the provision *P* and section 3(1) cannot differ with respect to whether section 3(1) alters the legal effect of *P* without also being the case that section 3(1) has ceased to legally exist.[46]

The main feature of this approach is that it ventures to analyse the modification of the legal effect of statutory provisions by other source-based rules or principles in terms of the legal validity, hence the 'legal' existence rather than the judicial application of the latter. If the modifying canon were not legally valid,[47] the statutory provision would not be affected and would have a dif-

---

[45] Lord Irvine, 'The Impact of the Human Rights Act: Parliament, the Courts and the Executive' [2003] *Public Law* 308. For a deflationary take on the British jurisprudence spawned by s. 3(1), see Aileen Kavanagh, 'Unlocking the Human Rights Act: The "Radical" Approach to Section 3(1) Revisited' (2005) 3 *Eur. Hum. Rights Law Rev.* 259.

[46] It is a further question whether we could establish the same co-variation pattern if the invalidation of s. 3(1) is not the result of a repeal but of an amendment of its own legal content. Such an amendment would amount to the invalidation of the previous modifying provision and its simultaneous replacement with a new one.

[47] It is a further substantive question whether an interpretive canon is legally valid in the requisite robust sense only if it is properly codified—as often is the case—or, conversely, if it is adopted and applied by judicial and administrative institutions. At any rate, the former stricter condition cannot, on pain of inconsistency, apply to common law systems where the majority of such canons remains uncodified, yet prominently relevant for statutory and constitutional interpretation.

ferent intrinsic nature, namely, it would make a different contribution to the content of the law. Whereas a supervenience analysis falls short of providing a full metaphysical explanation of how two properties or two internally or super-internally related entities are related, it can signal an important metaphysical constraint in the case of relations between objects. If the relation of two objects has a supervenience base it necessarily follows that their relation is a function of the *intrinsic* rather than extrinsic properties of both or either one of the relata. In our case this also means that if the relation of legal effect modification has a supervenience base, both the validity of the modifying canon and the legal content of the modified statutory provision must be *intrinsically* borne by these entities. The crucial point is that super-internality is such that the intrinsic nature of the modifying canon suffices to also guarantee the intrinsically borne legal content of the modified provision. Consequently, the preceding analysis entails that the intrinsicality of the legal content of a legal provision is a function of the fact that another provision is legally valid, namely, *legally existent*.

What follows from the latter claim? We have already seen that if the relation between a legal provision and a modifying canon supervenes on the latter's *existence*, then the contribution that the modified provision makes to the content of the law—namely, its legal effect—is an *intrinsic* rather than empirically contingent aspect of the provision. In other words, this contribution is attributable to the modified provision by virtue of the intrinsic profile of the modifying canon, namely, its legal validity or, equivalently, existence. But what is it for an object's intrinsic properties to be guaranteed by the intrinsic nature of *another* object? At this point we may avail ourselves of Gideon Rosen's association of intrinsicality with grounding. The basic intuition is that a property F is intrinsic if and only if whether x is F depends entirely on how things stand with x and its parts and not on x's relations to things distinct from x. On the basis of this remark Rosen suggests that 'F is an intrinsic property *iff*, as a matter of necessity, for all x: If x is F in virtue of $\phi(y)$—where $\phi(y)$ is a fact containing y as a constituent—*then y is part of x* [emphasis added]; and If x is not-F in virtue of $\phi(y)$, then y is part of x.'[48]

Returning to the legal case, the latter definition yields a metaphysically robust proposition: if the intrinsic possession of the legal content of a statutory provision is grounded in the fact that the modifying canon legally exists, then the content of the modifying canon is *part of* the legal content of the statutory provision! In other words, *if* the supervenience hypothesis holds, we are

---

[48] Gideon Rosen, 'Metaphysical Dependence: Grounding and Reduction' in Bob Hale and Aviv Hoffmann (eds), *Modality: Metaphysics, Logic, and Epistemology* (Oxford University Press 2010) 109–35, 112.

committed to the following two claims: (a) the legal content of a statute is *intrinsically* borne by the statute, (b) the intrinsic possession of legal content is *grounded* in the existence of a modifying canon, and (c) (b) entails that the modifying canon is part of the statutory provision's legal content.

Becoming jointly committed to these claims is obviously an impressively robust jurisprudential choice. Whereas supervenience hypotheses are usually invoked in the context of deflating or postponing one's engagement with the exploration of deeper metaphysical truths, the strict application of this hypothesis to the case of legal effect modification results in a set of very strong jurisprudential claims whose defence cannot be merely premised on the modal force of a supervenience claim. To see why it becomes intuitively very difficult to jointly shoulder and defend these claims it is worth specifying the implications of each one of these three claims.

With regard to the intrinsicality of legal content, the basic point is that if a legal provision's contribution to the content of the law is an intrinsic property of that provision, then whatever type of content—semantic, communicative or other—it turns out to be it must be intrinsically borne by the provision. For instance, suppose that a jurisprudential theory submits that the legal content of a statute is the content the legislature communicates by way of its enactment.[49] If the legal content of a statute is its communicative content, it follows that the communicative content of a statute must be *intrinsically* borne by the statute. This amounts to saying that the communicative content of the statute is determined by the thinker's or speaker's individual intrinsic mental properties.[50] Consequently, in the legal case linguistic expressions and/or thoughts would not be taken to bear any semantically and/or conceptually interesting relations to worldly things or events precisely because their subjects (speakers, thinkers, agents) can competently access the relevant truth-conditions for their words or

---

[49] An alternative hypothesis would be to say that the legal content of a statute is its semantic content. This claim would also be subject to an internalist constraint such that to be competent with a legal expression's linguistic meaning would to be in a 'legally proper' internal cognitive state that enables one to identify its extension in any possible world on the basis of *a priori* reflection alone. Presumably, this 'legally proper' cognitive state would be a manifestation of the legislature's actual rational, reference-fixing or communicative dispositions.

[50] Subjective theories of communicative content take actual mental states to be the constitutive determinants of speaker meaning. See, e.g., Paul Grice, *Studies in the Way of Words* (Harvard University Press 1989); Stephen Schiffer, *Meaning* (Oxford University Press 1972); Stephen Neale, 'Pragmatism and Binding' in Zoltan Gendler Szabó (ed), *Semantics versus Pragmatics* (Oxford University Press 2005); and Kent Bach, 'The Top10 Misconceptions about Implicature' in Betty Birner and Gregory Ward (eds), *Drawing the Boundaries of Meaning* (John Benjamins 2006) 21–30.

concepts *independently of* their relation to external facts (social and physical environment).[51]

Whereas it is theoretically defensible to associate somehow the communicative content of a legal source with the legislature's actual, subjective state of understanding, it would be rather odd to premise that claim on the implications of a hypothesis about how the legal content of legal provisions supervenes on the existence of some interpretive canons. The intrinsicality of semantic or communicative content—also known as narrow content—is already a robustly substantive theory of content individuation which rests on an internalist understanding of how mental states or linguistic entities come to have their contents. In the present case, this commitment would, for instance, *ipso facto* exclude from consideration the plausibility of what is commonly termed 'objective communicative content' which claims that a statutory provision's linguistic content consists of the information that a reasonable member of the intended audience would take the legislature as intending to convey via the words used in the provision.[52] The latter objective variant of communicative content is obviously externalist, hence its legal relevance would be denied simply by

---

[51] Strictly speaking, whereas mental events can be determinants of both narrow linguistic and narrow mental content, it is worth emphasising that internalism about semantic content is conceptually and methodologically distinct from internalism about communicative content. The former is a theory of linguistic content individuated by syntax broadly construed: meanings are intrinsic properties of expressions which are in turn placed in the head. As James McGilvray aptly summarises the point 'the domain of syntax includes all locally determined, intrinsic features of linguistic mental events' (James McGilvray, 'Meanings Are Syntactically Individuated and Found in the Head' (1998) 13 *Mind Lang.* 225, 243). The latter is a reductionist theory of linguistic content: linguistic content just is a form of mental content which is linguistically conveyed by what a speaker says. Consequently, a subjectivist conception of communicative content is also an internalist conception of mental content. The idea will roughly be that communicative content is solely determined by what the speaker intends to communicate, or equivalently, by what is in the speaker's head.

[52] Objectivism about legal content is a jurisprudential variant of content externalism: it holds that legal content is taken to be determined by legislative intentions properly communicated by legal-semiotic means (e.g., the enactment of a statute), in other words, by those mental states that can be reasonably ascribed to the mind of the legislators by the audience to which the enactment of the latter is communicated. See, e.g., Jeffrey Goldsworthy, 'Moderate and Strong Intentionalism: Knapp and Michaels Revisited' (2005) 42 *San Diego L. Rev.* 669; Richard Ekins, 'Interpretive Choice in Statutory Interpretation' (2014) 59 *Am. J. Jurisprud.* 1; Scott Soames, 'What Vagueness and Inconsistency Tell Us about Interpretation' in Andrei Marmor and Scott Soames (eds), *Philosophical Foundations of the Language in Law* (Oxford University Press 2011) 31–57 and Andrei Marmor, 'Truth in Law' in Michael Freeman and Fiona Smith (eds), *Current Legal Issues: Law and Language* (Oxford University Press 2013) 45–61.

virtue of the supervenience claim about the nature of dependence of legal content on the existence of modifying canons.

Secondly, the claim that the intrinsic possession of legal content by a modified statutory provision is *grounded* in the existence of the modifying canon has a further robust consequence: a change in the legal content of the modifying provision can produce a change in the legal content of the modified statutory provision. This is a direct implication of applying the notion of grounding to facts about the possession of an intrinsic property by a certain thing. As explained above, to say that the intrinsic possession of legal content is grounded in the existence of a modifying canon just is to say that the legal content of the modifying canon is *part of* the statutory provision's legal content. In other words, the legal content of the modifying canon is a *mereological component* of the legal content of the provision whose legal effect it modifies. Pushing this claim a bit further we could say that, *if* the supervenience hypothesis holds, the modification of the legal effect of a legal provision by another law simply consists in the *re-composition* of the legal content of that provision through the incorporation of the legal content of the modifying canon into the legal content of the thereby modified provision.

This claim moves well beyond the much weaker claim that the determinants of the legal content of the modifying and the modified provision are interconnected in a way that leads a change in the *determinants* of the legal content of the modifying provision to produce a change in the *determinants* of the legal content of the modified provision. The latter case is an instance of what may be termed 'meta-semantic holism'[53] which falls short of what would qualify as the central case of meaning holism. It is precisely the latter, full-fledged variant that the supervenience hypothesis invites. It does so by making the interaction between the modifying and modified provision a one-to-one rather than a one-to-many relation. More precisely, the semantic effect of this claim acquires a perspectival flavour.[54] This is to say that the legal *content*—and not

---

[53] For the distinction between first-order and meta-semantic holism see Henry Jackman, 'Descriptive Atomism and Foundational Holism: Semantics between the Old Testament and the New' (2005) 21 *ProtoSociology* 7.

[54] In general, the phrase 'normative perspective' purports to capture those features of an individual or collective agent's normative judgments, values, and the like on which the truth of *further, derivative* judgments about what one ought or has reason to do, think or feel depends. The relevant relation between a normative perspective and perspectival propositions is that of *logical entailment*. This is a non-normative, at least in any robust sense, relation holding between the propositions expressed by the respective judgments. Sharon Street outlines the role of entailment in perspectival normative judgments noting that:

> [q]uite apart from whether we think a given set of values is correct, in other words – indeed, even if we aren't clear yet on what it is for a set of values to be

just the truth conditions—of a legal utterance in the context where a modifying canon applies depends on the features of that context.

To see how this could play out we may recall section 3(1) of the UK Human Rights Act according to which '*so far as it is possible to do so, primary legislation and subordinate legislation must be read and given effect in a way which is compatible with the Convention rights*'. The contextually relevant feature of section 3(1) will be the *linguistic or substantive (normative) viewpoint*[55] of the modifying canon such that to assert, for instance, that, as a result of the operation of section 3(1), the legal content of a statutory provision is S is to assert that *from the normative viewpoint of section 3(1)*—or, equivalently, *from the normative viewpoint of the Convention*—it is the case that S.[56] Differently put, the metaphysical claim that the legal content of the modifying canon is a mereological part of the legal content of the modified provision can be semantically translated into the claim that the linguistic or normative viewpoint conveyed by the modifying canon is part of the legal content rather than the truth conditions of the modified provision.

By concluding this section, I hope to have demonstrated that, despite its initial appeal as an alternative model for accommodating their legal relevance, a supervenience-based understanding of the legal effect of interpretive canons is not as metaphysically modest as the standard rationale for resorting to supervenience-based arguments would suggest. In other words and somewhat counterintuitively, an unreserved application of the supervenience model can

---

    correct – we can nevertheless think about and discuss what *follows*, as a purely logical and instrumental matter, from a given set of values in combination with the non-normative facts.
(Sharon Street, 'Constructivism in Ethics and Metaethics' (2010) 5 *Philos. Compass* 363, 367). It is a further metasemantic question whether the perspective-dependence of normative judgments is a consequence of the way the *content* or, conversely, the *truth-conditions* of a normative judgment are determined by the relevant perspective. In the former case normative judgments are treated as indexically anchored to a given perspective, whereas in the latter case the same type of judgment is treated as metasemantically perspectival. For this distinction see Karl Schafer, 'Constructivism and Three Forms of Perspective-Dependence in Metaethics' (2012) 89 *Philos. Phenomenol. Res.* 69, 69–71, and John MacFarlane, 'Nonindexical Contextualism' (2009) 166 *Synthese* 231.
   [55] The labels 'linguistic' and 'substantive' correspond to linguistic and substantive canons.
   [56] It bears emphasizing the relevant normative viewpoint which figures in the content of the modified provision is not the set of standards of the European Convention on Human Rights but the domestic modifying provision under s 3(1) *which incorporates* the Convention's standards. Otherwise, we would be led to the radically different claim that the modifying canon is not s 3(1) but directly the entire Convention *regardless of* its domestic statutory entrenchment.

be metaphysically inflationary in the case of what determines the content of the law. As it turns out, jurisprudential appeals to supervenience may not after all, or at least, not in every case, immunize the truth of legal statements from appeals to the normative mindset of those who are vested either directly or indirectly with the task of making law. This is not a devastating blow to attempts at preserving the objectivist or non-perspectival allure of legal talk and thought. It is rather an indirect acknowledgment that the mental can be *objectively* relevant for the truth of legal statements on condition that its relevance be fixed by certain metaphysical truths about how non-legal facts make law. Accordingly, legal supervenience, so to speak, may be part of the set of such metaphysical truths and may point the way towards adjudicating in a principled way the disagreement between objectivists and subjectivists about legal content. The only caveat that I would add to this possibility is that it is objectivity rather than subjectivity that comes at a greater price precisely because appeals to its importance tend to significantly increase the load of legal-ontological commitments one needs to shoulder.

PART III

OBJECTIVITY AND PRACTICAL REASONING

11. The problem of normative objectivity
Jan-Reinard Sieckmann[1]

1. CONCEPTIONS OF OBJECTIVITY

Normative objectivity, I understand, is the objective validity of norms; that is, validity in the sense that every reasonable agent must accept the respective norm as valid and, hence, must apply and follow it. A weaker form of objectivity implies that the claim to validity of a certain norm is defensible; that is, that every reasonable agent must accept that one may claim this norm to be valid. Objective validity is not a fact that one could discern directly, but can only be established by means of normative justification. In the first place, normative justification will aim at objectivity in a stronger sense. Perhaps, however, all one can achieve is weak objectivity of normative judgements in the sense of defensibility. In any case, objectivity in this sense requires a form of rational justification.

From these conceptions of objectivity regarding normative justification, other meanings of objectivity must be distinguished.[2] One can speak of objectivity with regard to objects, statements, sentences, or persons. In general, objectivity is opposed to subjectivity. Objects of the external world, but also abstract or ideal entities are distinguished from subjective attitudes or experiences of individuals. Accordingly, statements might be called objective if they refer to external objects, and subjective if referring to experiences or attitudes of individuals. Objective validity of statements means that they state facts, and are true, correct, or rationally justified, whilst subjective validity means validity for those who believe or accept them. Sentences can be called objective if, according to their semantic structure, they are capable of being true or false. By contrast, they are subjective if they express (not describe) personal attitudes

---

[1] I would like to thank Muhammad Ali Safdar for corrections and improvement on the English language.

[2] See, e.g., Joseph Raz, *Engaging Public Reason* (Oxford University Press 1999) 118–60; Andrei Marmor, *Positive Law and Objective Values* (Oxford University Press 2001) 112–34; also Gonzalo Villa-Rosas and Jorge Luis Fabra-Zamora, and Jaap Hage in this volume.

towards certain matters. Persons are called objective if they are disposed to judge objectively, and subjective if they are inclined to follow their own attitudes, disregarding objective facts.

Normative justification is concerned with the validity of norms as expressed in normative sentences or speech acts. In this respect, objectivity can be classified into different types as semantic, ontological (also called metaphysical), or epistemic.[3] Semantic objectivity means that the respective sentences or speech acts have referential character; that is, according to their semantic structure, they refer to facts, and hence can be qualified as true or false. This is the case if they have the structure of propositions, which can be displayed by 'that'-clauses. That is, one can transform such statements in the form 'It is the case that ...'.

Ontological objectivity means the existence of objects independently of their perception or recognition, that is, things are what they are independently of how we take them to be. Regarding sentences, ontological objectivity means that a sentence refers to an object that actually exists, independently of the thoughts or attitudes of the speaker. Accordingly, moral judgements or, more generally, normative judgements correspond to some fact in an observer-independent external world. With regard to the law, ontological objectivity implies that there exist right answers as a matter of law. This is a thesis of metaphysical realism. In contrast, anti-realism denies the existence of facts outside and independently of the views of someone.

Epistemic objectivity (also called methodological, justificatory, or discourse objectivity) means that sentences can be verified or justified as objectively valid. Hence, a sentence can actually be qualified as true or false, and any reasonable agent must accept its validity. Epistemic objectivity thus amounts to a normative justification in a strict sense. However, there might exist other types of normative justification, for example, procedural justification, which does not presuppose the truth of the warranted judgement. The strict claim to epistemic objectivity of normative judgements is difficult to justify, although some discourse theorists try to support it by transcendental-pragmatic arguments.[4] Nevertheless, universal reasonable acceptance may serve as a regulative idea, or as a criterion for the critique of normative claims. A weaker and incomplete form of epistemic objectivity is correctness in the sense that any

---

[3] See also Raz (n 2) 130; Marmor (n 2) 113.
[4] Karl-Otto Apel, *Transformation der Philosophie* (Suhrkamp 1973); Jürgen Habermas, *Die Einbeziehung des Anderen* (Suhrkamp 1996); Carlos Santiago Nino, *The Ethics of Human Rights* (OUP 1991); Robert Alexy, *Theorie der juristischen Argumentation* (2ed. (with a new postscript), Suhrkamp 1991); ibid., *Recht, Vernunft, Diskurs* (Suhrkamp 1995).

reasonable agent must accept a certain position as free of mistakes.[5] These are positions of cognitivism. Non-cognitivism denies that sentences can be verified or can be objectively valid. Intermediate positions hold that some norms can be recognized as valid, whilst others can only be claimed to be valid through subjective judgements.

The strongest form of objectivity combines all three forms of objectivity.[6] Other combinations are semantic and ontological objectivity without epistemological objectivity, which implies the existence of a normative reality not cognitively accessible, and semantic and epistemological objectivity without ontological objectivity, which is suggested by constructivist theories.[7]

A crucial issue is the semantic objectivity of norm sentences. It implies that norm sentences are used to state norms, more precisely, to state the existence or validity of norms. It is not clear whether norm sentences can be interpreted this way. A well-known distinction is that between norms and normative propositions. Norms are said to be prescriptive, and not capable of being true or false. Normative propositions are defined as stating that according to a normative system S the respective norm is valid. Accordingly, they are regarded as descriptive,[8] and hence objective in the semantic sense. However, they are not normative, for they merely state that certain criteria of membership in a particular system are met. By contrast, a genuine normative statement expresses that something ought to be done, without making this statement only relative to a particular system. In this sense, genuine normative statements are absolute, and system-relative normative propositions are not really normative.

We have to conclude then that the suggested juxtaposition of norms and normative propositions limits semantic objectivity to descriptive language and excludes already semantically the possibility of normative facts and genuine normative statements. This disregards the differences between the internal expressions of participants of the discourse and the external statements of observers. In addition, it also disregards the difference between normative arguments as the input of argumentation and normative judgements stating the result of an argumentation. The internal point of view requires that normative

---

[5] A special case of this weak epistemic objectivity is the defensibility of a normative claim. It requires not only that a certain position is arrived at without mistakes but includes also that without mistake one can claim this position to be normative and hence binding on others. For example, a certain life plan may be defensible. Still, this does not justify the claim that everyone should live according to this view.

[6] See Raz (n 2) 130.

[7] See Cristina Lafont, 'Moral Objectivity and Reasonable Agreement' (2004) 17 *Ratio Juris* 27–51.

[8] Georg Henrik von Wright, *Norm and Action* (Routledge 1963) 104–6; Carlos E Alchourrón and Eugenio Bulygin, *Normative Systeme* (Alber 1994) 205.

statements can be made in a genuine normative sense, not only as a description of the content of a particular system of norms.

2. NORMATIVE ARGUMENTS, STATEMENTS, AND JUDGEMENTS

I am interested in normative objectivity in the sense of the rational justification of norms. This issue cannot be discussed without a clear understanding of what is the structure of the justification of norms.[9] Only on this basis, one can address the further questions of whether normative claims have semantic, ontological, or epistemological objectivity.

2.1 Types of Normative Speech

Regarding the structure of normative justification, it is of crucial importance to observe the difference of two levels of argument, that of introducing arguments to be balanced against each other, and that of statements of the results of such a balancing.[10] This distinction is well known since Dworkin's thesis that rules and principles are logically distinct types of norms, which play different roles in legal argumentation.[11] Despite widespread critiques and some deficits in Dworkin's distinction of rules and principles,[12] the distinction of two types of logically distinct norms is sound and necessary for any analysis of the structure of normative argumentation. In this line of argument, one should distinguish between normative arguments and normative assertions or judgements.[13] The core of normative justification consists in the balancing of normative arguments, the result of which are normative judgements as to which norm is definitively valid.[14]

---

[9] Justification of norms is quite a different issue than that of legal interpretation, which presupposes or at least does not question the validity of the interpreted norm. On the objectivity of legal interpretation Nicos Stavropoulos, *Objectivity in Law* (OUP 1996).

[10] Jan-Reinard Sieckmann, *Regelmodelle und Prinzipienmodelle des Rechtssystems* (Nomos 1990) 83; ibid., *The Logic of Autonomy* (Hart 2012) 13–17.

[11] Ronald Dworkin, *Taking Rights Seriously* (Harvard UP 1978) 22–28.

[12] See Sieckmann 1990 (n 10) 54–62.

[13] One might regard both terms as synonymous. However, whilst assertions claim truth, which excludes incompatible assertions, it seems that normative judgements do not exclude diverse judgements of other agents, but only claim to be recognized as correct by other agents.

[14] Sieckmann 2012 (n 10) 70–84. As far as I can see, this model is not used in the ongoing discussion on moral realism or objectivity in morals. See, for example, John McDowell, *Mind, Value, and Reality* (Harvard University Press 2002);

In addition, at both levels of argument, that of introducing normative arguments and that of stating its results, one must distinguish:

- the direct use of norm sentences of the form 'One ought to X', which might express a normative argument or a normative assertion,
- genuine normative statements of validity 'It is valid that one ought to X', which can express validity as an argument or definitive validity of the respective norm, and
- descriptive statements about such normative expressions.

For example, one might argue that smoking in public places should be prohibited because it affects other people. On the other hand, one might argue that smoking in public places should be allowed because it is an expression of freedom. Thus, one offers normative arguments for one or the other solution. None of these arguments claims to state what is actually or definitively prohibited or permitted in public places. Both make claims or demands of what ought to be recognized as obligatory, prohibited, or permitted:

(1) One should not be allowed to smoke in public places.
(2) One should be allowed to smoke in public places.

In this case, one offers a direct normative argument. In addition, one can make statements regarding the validity of arguments (statements of validity as an argument). For example, one can state the character as a normative argument at a meta-level:

(3) There is an argument that one should not be allowed to smoke in public places.
(4) There is an argument that one should be allowed to smoke in public places.

Such normative arguments or statements about normative arguments are about what one should accept as the result of the argumentation but do not purport to state this result. This result, that is, a statement of what definitively or actually ought to be done, follows only from a balancing of the competing arguments,

---

Ruth Shafer-Landau, *Moral Realism. A Defence* (Clarendon Press 2003); Michael Moore, *Objectivity in Ethics and Law* (Ashgate/Dartmouth 2004); Gerhard Ernst, *Die Objektivität der Moral* (2 ed., mentis 2009); Tatjana Tarkian, *Moral, Normativität und Wahrheit* (mentis 2009); Franz von Kutschera, *Wert und Wirklichkeit* (mentis 2010); Torbjörn Tännsjö, *From Reasons to Norms* (Springer 2010); Markus Rüther, *Objektivität und Moral* (mentis 2011). One finds distinctions of prima facie or pro tanto-norms and strictly valid or absolute norms. These approaches, however, grasp only part of the structure of moral justification.

determining which of the arguments gets priority, and the conditions of this priority. Such a result might be:

(5) One should definitively not be allowed to smoke in public places if other people are present.

Again, one can make a meta-level statement regarding the validity of the respective norm:

(6) It is definitively valid that one should not be allowed to smoke in public places if other people are present.

I will call such statements with a genuine normative character, normative judgement. Normative judgements may directly express a norm, implicitly stating its definitive validity (direct normative statement), or they may explicitly state its definitive validity (statement of definitive validity). In both cases, the speaker expresses a normative position and does not merely describe an argument. Within an argumentation, this position refers to the issue of whether a certain norm should be accepted as valid. Following this position, one will express also a first order-norm as to what should definitively be done. All these expressions are contributions with which one participates in a practical discourse.

By contrast, one might – as an observer[15] – describe what is argued or stated:

(7) It is argued that one should not be allowed to smoke in public places.
(8) It is argued that one should be allowed to smoke in public places.
(9) It is stated as definitively valid that one should not be allowed to smoke in public places if other people are present.

Such statements are descriptive. They may occur in a practical discourse, but do not, however, carry a normative claim.

2.2 Objectivity of Normative Arguments, Judgements, or Statements

It is important to distinguish normative arguments, normative judgements, and normative statements also regarding the issue of objectivity. Distinguishing

---

[15] The perspective of a participant is hence that of someone making and justifying normative judgements, an observer is abstaining from normative judgement. As to the distinction of the perspectives of participants and observers see also Robert Alexy, *The Argument from Injustice* (OUP 2002) 25.

necessary recognition, correctness, and truth, one can state the following definitions of objective validity:

(1) A normative argument is objectively valid if each reasonable agent must recognize it as a valid normative argument.

Or,

(2) A normative argument is objectively valid if each reasonable agent must recognize the statement of its validity as an argument as correct.

Or,

(3) A normative argument is objectively valid if the statement of its validity as a normative argument is true.

Correspondingly,

(4) A normative judgement that one should do something is objectively valid if each reasonable agent must recognize it as a valid normative judgement.

Or,

(5) A normative judgement that one should do something is objectively valid if each reasonable agent must recognize the statement of definitive validity of the respective norm as correct.

Or,

(6) A normative judgement that one ought to do something is objectively valid if the statement of the definitive validity of the respective norm is true.
(7) A normative statement that it is definitively valid that one ought to do something is objectively valid if it is true.

By contrast to normative judgements and genuine normative statements, descriptive statements about norms refer to empirical facts, for example, that a norm is advanced as an argument or that it is stated as definitively valid, and hence can be qualified as objectively valid or true just as any other descriptive statement according to the empirical facts it refers to. The problem of normative objectivity exists regarding normative arguments, judgements, or statements. It has two aspects: One is the general issue of whether truth, correctness, and the rational necessity to accept something as valid are equivalent. In this chapter, I will assume that they are and disregard the difference between truth, correctness and rational necessity.[16] The other aspect is what are the conditions in which a normative statement can be qualified as objectively valid in the sense that each reasonable agent must recognize it as valid.

Regarding normative arguments, it is important to note that they are meant to start normative argumentation, not to state its result. Thus, they do not purport to state what actually is to be done, that is, they do not claim to state normative facts. Accordingly, they lack semantic objectivity but are merely legitimate claims of autonomous individuals. By contrast, the other types of normative expressions have propositional structure and hence are objective in semantic respect. Accordingly, the semantics admits genuine normative judgements or statements claiming to state normative facts, and hence, that the respective proposition is true, whether this claim can be epistemically justified or not.

3. OBJECTIVITY REGARDING NORMATIVE JUSTIFICATION

As mentioned above, the problem of whether normative justification can establish that norms are objectively valid cannot be answered without a clear understanding of the structure of normative justification. A crucial thesis of this analysis is that normative justification is possible only within a framework of the balancing of normative arguments, that is, by autonomous reasoning.[17] The validity of norms depends, hence, on the judgements of autonomous agents. These judgements must comply with formal requirements of autonomous reasoning, which must be observed in order to make normative justification possible and do not result from balancing normative arguments. However, these requirements must be founded on the analysis of autonomous reasoning.

The idea of autonomous reasoning excludes fundamentalist positions as well as scepticism about norms. Autonomous reasoning is incompatible with a view that accepts a foundation of normative validity beyond and independently of autonomous judgements. It is also incompatible with the view that no norms can be objectively valid, for autonomous reasoning might show that certain norms must be accepted as valid by any reasonable agent.

---

[16] As to the distinction of truth and justified belief, Marmor (n 2) 140. Rational necessity may be more than justified belief. Still, one might distinguish it from truth.
[17] See also Sieckmann 2012 (n 10) 13.

3.1 Justification by Balancing Normative Arguments

The structure of autonomous reasoning is defined by the balancing of normative arguments. The balancing of competing normative claims is the core of the justification of definitively valid norms. Such claims constitute normative arguments. The result of the balancing is bound by these arguments though it is not completely determined by criteria applicable by means of logical inferences. Therefore, balancing includes an autonomous decision. Also, a normative judgement is based on a decision. The resulting structure of the justification of norms, normative decisions, or judgements reveals the structure of autonomous reasoning, that is, the justification of normative judgements by means of the balancing of normative arguments. These judgements are at the same time free but also required by normative arguments and are, in this sense, autonomous.[18] Thus, the balancing of normative arguments is the core of autonomous reasoning and also – since it is the only way of substantially justifying norms[19] – of normative justification.

Three issues of the justification of norms must be distinguished. First, how to establish normative arguments by means of claims put forward by autonomous agents. Second, how to get from normative arguments to autonomous judgements. Third, how to get from autonomous judgements to normative statements about objectively valid and binding norms.

As to the first issue, the validity of normative arguments is established by autonomous agents by putting forward these arguments. Autonomous agents have the normative power to make interest-based claims valid as normative arguments. Denying this competence would make impossible any attempt of normative justification. There are restrictions of this competence. In particular, claims must be universalizable in order to constitute a normative argument. That is, it must be possible for any other autonomous agent to accept this claim as a normative argument. But given this condition, claims of autonomous agents constitute valid normative arguments. They do not include normative statements. However, statements regarding the validity of these arguments refer to facts – that is, claims made by autonomous agents – and can be true or false. Accordingly, such statements are objective in a semantic and ontological sense and can be objectively valid in an epistemological sense.

As to the second issue, autonomous agents also have the normative power to form normative judgements based on the balancing of normative arguments.

---

[18] Sieckmann 2012 (n 10) 17.
[19] Another, non-substantive type of justification is proving certain normative assumptions to be necessary conditions of the possibility of normative justification. As to this type of a priori-justification Nino (n 4); Alexy 1995 (n 4) 133ff.

Autonomous reasoning will not be possible without recognizing this competence. Again, certain restrictions apply, in particular requirements of rational balancing. If these requirements are met the judgement is rationally justified. However, it is a subjective judgement, expressing the normative opinion of the respective agent. Such individual normative judgements do not express facts; they are not objective in an ontological or epistemological sense. However, they are objective in a semantic sense, that is, it is not meaningless to judge them as true or false. Nevertheless, one cannot justify regarding them as true, for this would imply the claim to objective validity for any autonomous agent, which, however, cannot be justified on the basis of the individual judgement of a particular autonomous agent. Only a statement of validity regarding the normative view of this particular agent would be objectively justified.

As a consequence, regarding the issue of bindingness, autonomous justification by individual agents provides only the starting point for the construction of the objective validity of norms. Autonomy implies that autonomous agents may make their own judgements of what they think is correct. The agents may, however, hold incompatible normative views as to which norm ought to be accepted as valid, and their autonomous judgements may diverge. The problem of the objective validity of normative judgements is how to overcome a divergence between competing individual judgements in order to establish a commonly binding norm that everyone must reasonably accept.

3.2   An Example

Subsequently, the structure of normative justification will be outlined. An example will help to illustrate the structure of normative justification. A typical normative problem is whether smoking should be permitted in public places. The problem may be resolved in different ways. One possible solution is the norm:

N1: Smoking is permitted in public places
Different arguments may be advanced in favour of this norm, in particular, the interests of smokers in enjoying this aspect of their lives, or interests in raising the capacity to work by smoking. The contrary norm is:

N2: Smoking is forbidden in public places
This norm can be supported by other arguments, for example, the interests of non-smokers in clean air, in avoiding health risks, and in a safe environment. The corresponding normative arguments can be presented as the principles of individual liberty, efficiency, well-being, health care, and the protection of the environment. Thus, a balancing of interests and of the corresponding normative arguments is required. Some people may believe that N1 should be valid,

others that N2 should be chosen, some may favour a compromise, for example, that smoking ought to be forbidden in closed public rooms but permitted in the open air. The decision will depend on what is achieved respecting the fulfilment of the competing principles, and what relative weight is to be assigned to these principles respecting the degree of their fulfilment or non-fulfilment in the case at hand.

The relative weight of competing for normative arguments in a concrete case is defined by the extent to which the fulfilment of one of them is necessary to justify a certain loss of fulfilment of the conflicting argument. The greater the relative weight, the more that will be required for the fulfilment of the competing claim. The problem is how to determine the relative weight of normative arguments. There are no fixed criteria for the attribution of relative weight to conflicting arguments. If there were, one could apply these criteria directly instead of engaging in a balancing of conflicting arguments, and the process of balancing would then be redundant and without justificatory force. If there is a case of genuine or autonomous balancing, the relative weight of the arguments depends on the judgement of the person doing the balancing. Hence, the balancing of normative arguments essentially requires a personal judgement. It is an expression of autonomy.

The determination of which norm is definitively valid will also have to take into account the normative views of other people.

For example, if many people, including smokers, think that one should not smoke in public, this will itself constitute a reason to think that the prohibition of smoking (N2) is the correct solution.

Thus, the balancing will depend on the normative views of the agents involved. Accordingly, balancing normative arguments is a reflective process in which individuals take into account their normative conceptions. Based on this normative material, consisting of conflicting arguments and individual normative conceptions of the agents involved, a solution must be found as to which norm ought to be definitively valid. It is important to distinguish this mutually reflective process from the simple process of balancing arguments. Whereas the simple balancing of arguments can be analysed in terms of an optimisation model applied by a single agent, the mutually reflective balancing of individual normative conceptions is more complex. It cannot be done by a single agent alone, and there is no clear criterion that guides the reflective process.[20]

---

[20] The process of inter-subjective reflection must follow the rules of rational practical discourse (see Alexy 1991 (n 4)). However, in general these rules do not determine a particular result of the discourse. Also, it is not guaranteed that these rules are followed in a real discourse. However, this is of no concern regarding the requirement of inter-subjective reflection as a condition of objective validity.

Summing up, balancing decisions resolve a conflict between normative arguments by establishing a priority among these arguments and a corresponding norm as the result of the procedure of balancing. There are no positive, pre-determined criteria from which the correct result could be inferred. Instead, the result of balancing is established by the judgement of an autonomous agent. Since there are no criteria that can adjudicate between diverging judgements, a solution can only be found in a rational argumentation among agents with different normative views. This argumentation may lead to a reasonable agreement as to which norm ought to be accepted as valid. Whatever arguments are used, however, there is no guarantee that reasonable people will reach such an agreement.

This openness of the balancing of normative arguments raises doubts as to the claims to correctness and bindingness that can be made regarding a norm recognized as valid. If one must acknowledge at least the possibility of reasonable disagreement, how can one hold any position to be the correct one? And how can one regard a commonly accepted solution as binding on its addressees?

4. OBJECTIVE VALIDITY AND INDIVIDUAL AUTONOMY

A crucial problem of normative justification is the relation between objective validity and individual autonomy. Self-legislation – the basic idea of autonomy – is the determination of the validity of norms by autonomous agents themselves. Normative validity seems to be essentially subjective. The problem is not the existence of reasonable disagreement but the impossibility to justify norms independently of their acceptance by autonomous individuals.

The idea of moral autonomy suggests that autonomous beings have the right to live according to their moral convictions.[21] It implies that an autonomous person must not be subjected to a norm that he or she rejects as morally wrong. Accordingly, the normative validity of a norm cannot be established without the consent of the norm addressees if these are autonomous agents. An autonomous agent can make moral judgements according to certain standards of reasonableness, for example, consistency, empirical correctness, universalization. A moral judgement or norm is a judgement that claims correctness in an

---

[21] This conception of moral autonomy must be distinguished from autonomy as the capability to act self-determinedly, that is, to have a free will, autonomy as the capability to recognize the moral law, and autonomy as the right to act according to this law. As epistemic criteria are not sufficient to determine the moral law, at least not in all substantive matters, moral autonomy cannot be restricted to acting according to the moral law discovered by reason.

absolute sense, that is not only relative to a certain empirically defined system of norms.

Normative theories based on the idea of moral autonomy raise problems if they are connected with a claim to objective validity.[22] By objective validity of a norm, I mean that this norm can correctly be stated as valid.[23] A statement is correct only if it is rationally justified; that is, if every reasonable person must accept this statement as correct by standards of rationality.[24] By contrast, subjective validity of a norm means that a norm is believed to be valid by someone and, thus, is valid in an individual normative conception, or is valid from a certain point of view. Validity is used here in a normative sense, meaning that the norm should be applied and followed by its addressees.[25] If a norm is objectively valid in this normative sense it can be said to be binding on its addressees. Hence, objective validity has two implications: an epistemological one, that a norm is rationally justified, and a normative one, that it is binding on its addressees.

One problem of a normative theory based on moral autonomy is that it must refer to the consent of reasonable people as an objective of normative justification, if not as a criterion of validity. However, actual consent will often not be obtained, and even when it is, this actual consent might be erroneous and cannot guarantee the correctness of the consented judgement. On the other hand, an ideal consent, which is obtained under conditions that exclude mistakes, cannot be achieved and, thus, cannot be applied as a criterion of the validity of norms. Moreover, even if consent was achieved, it could not establish a binding norm, as anyone could change his or her view and hence invalidate the consent. In order to exclude such a change of normative views, there must be normative criteria that restrict autonomous decisions. The standards of reasonableness that autonomous agents must fulfil, do not contain such restrictions, for they are of formal character and do not have immediate substantive implications. If, on the other hand, there were substantive restrictions, the moral autonomy of reasonable agents would be curtailed. If moral autonomy consisted only in the recognition of the moral law, one might wonder whether

---

[22] See Hilary Putnam 'Are Moral and Legal Values Made or Discovered?' (1995) 1 *Legal Theory* 5.

[23] One might even say that it can be stated as a normative fact. 'Fact' is used here as the meaning of a true statement, not necessarily restricted to the empirical world.

[24] A reasonable person is one who is able to make autonomous decisions according to standards of rationality. Standards of rationality are, in the first instance, logical consistency and empirical evidence. Whatever else is required by rationality depends on a conception of rationality. The model of normative justification suggested here might be combined with diverse conceptions of rationality.

[25] See Sieckmann 1990 (n 10) 99.

talking of autonomy made sense at all. At least, the recognition of the moral law would render the criterion of consent superfluous.

The problem is how the objective validity of a norm can be established within autonomous morality. Only one particular aspect of this problem shall be discussed here. According to the idea of moral autonomy, the objective validity of a norm requires the consent of the norm addressees, or perhaps even of all reasonable people.[26] However, a complete reasonable consensus on normative matters will often not exist. The question then is whether an alternative is available to the criterion of reasonable consensus. This, I suggest, is the criterion of reasonable convergence.

5. OBJECTIVE VALIDITY AND REASONABLE CONVERGENCE

Substantive definitive validity of a norm implies not only that this norm is the result of a successfully completed argument, but also that this norm ought actually to be applied and followed and, hence, is binding on its addressees. The justification of such statements must ensure that this claim to bindingness is justified. It must show that each reasonable agent must accept the claim to bindingness that is at issue as legitimate, although he might not accept the proposed norm in substance.

From this, certain necessary conditions for justifying statements of substantive definitive validity of a norm follow.

(1) An autonomous judgement stating the norm in question is required.
(2) The judgement must stem from correct individual reasoning.

That is, the justification of the judgement offered by the agent in question must comply with the requirements both of correct balancing and the reflection of the diverse normative conceptions of all autonomous agents concerned. These requirements apply already to statements of definitive validity in the procedural sense. In addition, the justification for the bindingness of a particular norm has two further conditions:

(3) In procedural respect, a discursive justification is required, including not only individual reflection but also a mutual, inter-subjective reflection on the part of the autonomous agents involved in their respective normative judgements. Thus, the agents must ask which norm ought to be

---

[26] See Alexy 1995 (n 4) 131; Habermas (n 4) 49; Jan-R. Sieckmann, 'Richtigkeit und Objektivität im Prinzipienmodell' (1997) 83 *ARSP* 23.

accepted as binding with regard to the situation of diverging normative views.

(4) In substantive respect, the norm in question must be supported by a reasonable convergence of autonomous agents in their judgements coupled with their need to have a commonly binding norm.

The need for a discursive justification follows, for no one can individually determine which norm is binding on other autonomous agents. In order to achieve this, a compromise between diverging normative positions in one's own individual normative conception will not suffice. No other agent must accept norms as binding that are only the product of another individual's judgement. Of course, people might agree by chance on what ought to be recognized as definitively valid and hence, as a binding norm. If, however, there is no agreement, then the judgement of one individual, even if made after consideration of all the relevant arguments, cannot be binding on other agents. This follows from the principle of autonomy, which requires that autonomous agents shall not be subject to the judgement of other agents. Thus, there emerges an important constraint on autonomous reasoning:

(T1) An autonomous agent cannot determine by his normative judgement alone which norms are collectively binding.

As a consequence, and in addition to a complete individual balancing of arguments, a discursive justification is required in order to correctly make statements of definitive validity and bindingness. Norms cannot be established as binding by monological reasoning alone. Rather, all autonomous agents involved must be included in the procedure of argumentation, mutually taking into consideration the individual normative judgements of all participants. This is necessary not only in order to acquire information about the interests and normative views of the agents involved, but also because a claim to the bindingness of the norm cannot be justified without reflexive reference to the normative conceptions of all autonomous agents concerned.[27]

For example, the smoker and her opponent have to take into account the normative judgements of each other, and they have to form a normative conception on the question of which norm ought to be definitively valid regarding this situation of dispute.

Moreover, these conceptions must be judged according to their rational acceptability and to the weight that should be given to them.

---

[27] This reflexive process aims also at removing bias and hence approximating objectivity. On objectivity as freedom from bias see Villa-Rosas and Fabra-Zamora (n 2) in this volume.

For example, one might question whether the judgement of a smoker is affected by an addiction to smoke that stands in the way of rational judgement. On the other hand, this addiction might establish a special urgency of the smoker's interest that must be taken into account also at this second-order level of balancing.

In summary, among the individual normative judgements, one must distinguish inter-subjectively reflected conceptions from individual normative conceptions that are not based on inter-subjective reflection. Inter-subjectively reflected conceptions may be called normative conceptions in a strict sense – or moral conceptions, as distinct from personal ethics.

The inter-subjectively reflected normative judgement is a judgement of the higher order. It is still an individual judgement, for everyone will hold his own view, which can diverge from that of other agents. The definitive normative claim of such judgements is still restricted to the requirement that other agents ought to recognize the respective norm as definitively valid or, at a higher level, that such a claim be recognized as definitively valid. It may have some independence and stability where changes in individual normative judgements are concerned, for a change in the normative judgement of one individual may, even in his view, not affect the normative judgement based on inter-subjective reflection. But inter-subjective reflection does not yet support a normative statement of substantive definitive validity of the form $VAL_{DEF\text{-}SUBS}N$.

Substantive definitive validity, or bindingness, of a norm can be established if the proposed norm is supported by the criterion of reasonable convergence, presupposing, in addition, that the need for a commonly binding norm can be justified. Reasonable convergence means that, based on rational arguments, the definitive validity of a particular norm is accepted by an increasing majority of the agents. This requires not only a majority but also that no counter-arguments are at hand that might reverse the majority, and hence one can expect that further discourse will lead to an increasing majority. One might define reasonable convergence as follows:

(RC)   A normative judgement is supported by reasonable convergence if a rational discourse leads to a tendency to accept this norm as definitively valid.

A reasonable convergence precludes the claim that an incompatible norm could be binding as well. If, in addition, a commonly binding norm is needed, reasonable agents must accept that this norm is stated to be binding on all its addressees, including those who reject this norm in substance. Thus, it justifies a claim to bindingness.

(T2)   A norm may be claimed to be binding if it is supported by reasonable convergence of autonomous agents, and in addition, a commonly binding norm is needed.

One should note, however, that this justification only *permits* proponents of a norm to claim this norm to be binding on all its addressees. It does not exclude that opponents claim this norm to be wrong. Thus, what can be stated as definitively valid is the permission to claim a norm to be binding, in the case that the conditions for claims of bindingness are met.

6.   SUMMARY

The issue of whether the objective validity of norms can be justified requires to be clear as to the model of justification presupposed. According to the model of autonomous reasoning, justification of norms requires the balancing of normative arguments. This implies distinguishing between normative arguments, judgements, and statements.

Normative arguments are justified by the normative competence of autonomous agents to establish such arguments. Normative arguments are not objective in semantic, ontological, or epistemic respect, but statements as to their validity as an argument are. Their justification does not correspond to moral realism, but after they have been established as valid, their validity as a normative argument is a normative fact.

Normative judgements state the result of the balancing of normative arguments. They are objective in semantic respect, but not in ontological and epistemic respect. For they represent the individual normative view of an autonomous agent. Regarding objective validity, they are objectively valid only as normative arguments demanding that other agents recognize the respective norm as definitively valid.

Normative statements of the respective type of validity of a particular norm are objective in semantic and ontological respect. In epistemic respect, what seems to be justifiable, as objectively valid, is the permission to apply a particular norm as binding on its addressees, including its opponents, if a commonly binding norm is necessary and the respective norm is supported by reasonable convergence of autonomous agents.

Any plausible account of the objective validity of norms hence requires a differentiated approach, which must reflect the structure of normative justification.

12. Why do legal philosophers (perhaps correctly) insist on moral objectivity while dismissing metaethical inquiry?[1]

Thomas Bustamante

1. INTRODUCTION

In his legal and moral philosophy, Ronald Dworkin defended the view that value objectivity does not depend on any metaethical determinant. We need no reductive argument to account for the propositions we use in ordinary moral argument. Metaethical arguments to establish the truth or falsity of a first-order moral claim cut no ice, for they are both mysterious and unacceptable when we look at them from the internal point of view of the participants in moral discourse. According to Dworkin, metaethical arguments are based on a fallacy, for it is impossible to describe the nature of morality from an Archimedean point of view, which attempts to explain values and moral propositions with non-evaluative concepts.[2]

Although this claim is controversial and may appear too strong, even amongst lawyers, weaker versions of this argument are influential for most legal philosophers interested in moral theory. Joseph Raz, for instance, claims that the supervenience thesis, which requires that moral predicates supervene on non-moral ones, fails to provide an account of the objectivity of values or

---

[1] The mature version of this chapter was concluded during a Global Research Fellowship at New York University, during the Academic Years of 2020–2021 and 2021–2022. I have received funding from the Fulbright Commission (for the Research Fellowship) and from the National Council for Scientific Development (CNPq), which has granted me a Permanent Research Fellowship since 2013 (Grants # 423696/2018-1 and 306284/2020-0). I would like to thank, in addition to those institutions, the editors of this volume (Gonzalo Villa-Rosas and Jorge Fabra-Zamora) for the helpful critical comments in the first draft of this chapter.
[2] Ronald Dworkin, 'Objectivity and Truth: You'd Better Believe it' (1996) 25 *Philosophy & Public Affairs* 87; Ronald Dworkin, *Justice for Hedgehogs* (Harvard UP 2011).

an intelligible explanation of the emergence of particular moral norms. The intelligibility of values is achieved, instead, by circular explanations in which part of the explanation of specific values and evaluative practices is provided by other values we already master. On Raz's view, 'we commonly learn to apply evaluative predicates and concepts by example, through their association with other predicates or concepts, mostly with other evaluative properties and concepts'.[3]

These holistic accounts of objectivity are especially important for lawyers who do not think that a reductive justification of moral values is available, inasmuch as they must also recognize that moral judgments are pervasive in legal reasoning and that part of the explanation of the legitimacy of legal decisions is dependent on the objectivity of these judgments. This explains the title of this chapter: legal philosophies such as Dworkin's and Raz's, probably the most influential nowadays, tend to insist on moral objectivity while dismissing metaethical inquiry.

This scepticism towards metaethics is at the root of one of Dworkin's most provocative contentions, which is the thesis that 'lawyers and judges are working political philosophers of a democratic state'.[4]

It comes as no surprise that philosophers with an expertise in metaethics have resisted these assertions about the role of the lawyers, as the heated exchange between Dworkin and Simon Blackburn exemplifies. According to Blackburn, Dworkin's scepticism about metaethics is a symptom of a more general failure of legal scholars to understand the intricacies of proper philosophical thought. Perhaps the following comment can illustrate this point:

> I begin to think that [Dworkin's] real agenda is not cognitivism or realism or objectivity, but rather the need to defend a kind of arid legal intellectualism. Lawyers are happy with certain sources of authority: texts, and the best theories of them. They cannot happily work with emotions, instinct, imagination and culture. And that in turn may be, to echo Dworkin's words, part of what makes their incursions (there are honorable exceptions, of course) into philosophy so wearying, pointless and unprofitable, and the prominence they get such an indicator of the leaden spirits of our age.[5]

---

[3] Joseph Raz, *Engaging Reason* (OUP 1999) 221.
[4] Dworkin, *Justice for Hedgehogs* (n 2) 414.
[5] Simon Blackburn, 'Commentary on Ronald Dworkin's "Objectivity and Truth: You'd Better Believe It"' (1996) Brown Electronic Article Review Service (Bears), https://www.brown.edu/Departments/Philosophy/bears/9611blac.html accessed 23 June 2022.

This excerpt reflects not only a power struggle between a lawyer and a metaethics scholar, but also a controversy on the concept of objectivity and a more general disagreement about the character of moral philosophy.

I will attempt to defend in the next sections that, in their exchange with metaethical philosophers, lawyers can have a plausible claim. Lawyers need a conception of objectivity to affirm or reject the moral judgments that they make in their professional practice, and I will argue that we can rely on a methodological concept of objectivity to satisfy the legitimacy requirements of adjudication. If this is correct, we do not need more than an internal and non-Archimedean theory to understand the nature of morality. My argument is presented in the following steps. In the second section, I expound the dominant view about the presence of moral arguments in adjudication, which is found in two influential traditions of jurisprudence. I argue that a common commitment to moral objectivity is an important feature of legal practice, no matter which account we accept to determine the nature of law. In the third section, I attempt to specify a concept of objectivity that can play a role in legal argumentation, to show why lawyers and jurisprudence scholars are suspicious of metaphysical concepts. Finally, in the fourth section, I try to make sense of the claim that the prevailing methods of legal reasoning are more likely than metaethical investigations to provide a satisfactory understanding of moral facts.

2. THE LAWYER'S DEPENDENCE ON THE OBJECTIVITY OF MORAL ARGUMENT

Despite the jurisprudential controversies about legal ontology, legal scholars tend to reach a uniform verdict about the use of moral considerations in the practice of adjudication. When arguing about the nature of law, they are usually classified as positivists or non-positivists, and the gist of their theoretical disagreement concerns the type of facts which are said to provide the foundations of valid laws. Positivists ground the validity of legal propositions in social facts. At the source of the validity of a legal norm there would be a rule of recognition specifying certain features the possession of which is taken as a conclusive test for identifying a norm as part of the legal system.[6] Non-positivists, in turn, claim that social facts are not in themselves capable of establishing legal validity, inasmuch as moral considerations would also have a part to play. According to Dworkin, the leading exponent of contemporary

---

[6] H L A Hart, *The Concept of Law* (2nd edn, OUP 1994) 94.

non-positivist jurisprudence, law is an interpretive social practice whose content inherently depends on moral facts.[7]

Nonetheless, this theoretical disagreement usually masks an agreement about the role of morality in legal reasoning, since most legal positivists do not claim that social facts are the only kind of considerations that can be employed in court as a ground for a legal decision. The reasoning undertaken by lawyers and judges is often infused with moral judgments. On the non-positivist view this is fairly obvious: statutes, precedents and authoritative legal pronouncements are regarded as 'pre-interpretive facts' whose content is unintelligible without an interpretive moral judgment.[8] Dworkin regards legal practice as 'interpretive' because he holds that the right way to read it is to understand the meaning of its rules according to a moral point that justifies the practice while also explaining its political and institutional history.[9] But he is not alone in the thought that moral judgments are pervasive in legal reasoning. On the legal positivist camp, many lawyers are equally committed to moral reasoning. Although legal positivists regard the law as autonomous from morality, they tend to accept that the content of the law is frequently underdetermined. Legal reasoning comprises more than a reasoning to determine the content of the law, either because the law unintentionally leaves a gap, in which the scope of one's actual obligation is not fully determined, or because the law itself contains a number of 'principles of discretion' that authorize courts to further develop the law.[10] On the standard positivistic view, 'there is much more to legal reasoning than applying the law, and the rest is ... quite commonly straightforward moral reasoning'.[11] Legal reasoning is a form of reasoning that has 'valid legal norms among its major or operative premises, but combines them non-redundantly in the same argument with moral or other merit-based premises'.[12]

It comes as no surprise that the mainstream legal theorists in these two traditions are not impressed by scepticism. The sceptic about social rules is depicted as a 'disappointed absolutist',[13] and the sceptic about moral objectivity as a 'disappointed philosophical realist'.[14] Both Raz and Dworkin have

---

[7] Ronald Dworkin, *Taking Rights Seriously* (2nd print, Harvard UP 1978); Ronald Dworkin, *Law's Empire* (Harvard UP 1986).

[8] Dworkin, *Law's Empire* (n 7) 65–68.

[9] Ibid., 47.

[10] Joseph Raz, 'Legal Principles and the Limits of Law' (1972) 81 *Yale LJ* 823, 846.

[11] Joseph Raz, *Ethics in the Public Domain* (OUP 1994) 332–333.

[12] John Gardner, 'Legal Positivism: 5 ½ Myths' (2001) 46 *American Journal of Jurisprudence* 199, 216.

[13] Hart, *The Concept of Law* (n 6) 139.

[14] Andrei Marmor, 'An Essay on the Objectivity of Law' in Brian Bix (ed) *Analyzing Law: New Essays in Legal Theory* (OUP 1998) 3.

reasons to believe, therefore, in the objectivity of morality and evaluative concepts.

Why are lawyers so anxious to resolve the difficult problem of the objectivity of morality? Part of the answer is that the objectivity of morality is not only a question of theoretical interest. It is, in addition, a practical commitment embedded in the professional practice of adjudication. With some exceptions,[15] legal philosophers subscribe to the thesis that it is a constitutive feature of law that it claims legitimate authority for itself.[16] The law 'rests this claim, in part, on the objectivity of characteristic modes of reasoning and the normative judgments they produce'.[17] According to Postema,

> We demand objectivity of our moral and legal discourse for very fundamental practical reasons. ... We expect moral and legal norms to guide action and through this guidance inter alia to coordinate our social interaction. ... We look to these norms not only for guidance and coordination, but also for justification, or at least legitimacy. ... This is why we demand objectivity of our moral and legal discourse. It is not merely a welcome side-benefit of objectivity; it is objectivity's *raison d'être*.[18]

It seems to be the case, therefore, that a central aspect of legal reasoning *depends* on the possibility of objectivity of moral judgments. As the editors of this volume showed in their thoughtful Introduction, the concept of objectivity

---

[15] Kenneth E Himma, 'Law's Claim to Legitimate Authority' in Jules Coleman (ed) *Hart's Postscript: Essays on the Postscript to 'The Concept of Law'* (OUP 2001) 271.

[16] See esp. Joseph Raz, *The Authority of Law* (OUP 1979); Joseph Raz, *The Morality of Freedom* (OUP 1986); Raz, *Ethics in the Public Domain* (n 11) 210; Joseph Raz, *Between Authority and Interpretation* (OUP 2009). The thesis that the law claims legitimacy is different from the thesis that the right way to determine the content of the law is through a reasoning process that incorporates evaluative judgments. Normative positivists and legal formalists tend to accept the latter while rejecting the former. See, for instance, Frederick Schauer, 'Formalism' (1988) 97 *Yale Law Journal* 509; Frederick Schauer, *Playing by the Rules: A Philosophical Examination of Rule-Based Decision-Making in Law and in Life* (OUP 1991); Jeremy Waldron, 'Normative Positivism' in Jules Coleman (ed) *Hart's Postscript: Essays on the Postscript to 'The Concept of Law'* (OUP 2001) 410; Liam Murphy, 'The Political Question of the Concept of Law' in Jules Coleman (ed) *Hart's Postscript: Essays on the Postscript to 'The Concept of Law'* (OUP 2001) 371; Neil MacCormick, 'A Moralistic Case for A-Moralistic Law?' (1985) 20 (1) *Valparaiso University Law Review* 1. See also Scott Shapiro, *Legality* (Harvard UP 2011) 234–258, as interpreted in Thomas Bustamante, 'Book Review' (2012) 33 *Legal Studies* 499. An interesting feature of these interpretive accounts is that they ground their claim to a-moralistic adjudication in a moral argument about the legitimacy of political institutions and the proper modes of legal reasoning.

[17] Gerald J Postema, 'Objectivity Fit for Law' in Brian Leiter (ed) *Objectivity in Law and Morals* (OUP 2001) 99, 101.

[18] Ibid., 115.

performs a *normative function*, and our trust in judges and officials in a binding legal system is primarily dependent on our reliance in their capacity to deliver objective and unbiased decisions in legal cases. There seems to be, therefore, no legitimacy without objectivity.[19]

3. METAPHYSICAL AND METHODOLOGICAL CONCEPTIONS OF MORAL OBJECTIVITY

Nevertheless, the discussion in the previous section leaves an important question unanswered: are lawyers justified in their claims to moral objectivity? The answer depends on the concept of objectivity we have in mind.

In order to establish a sense of objectivity appropriate for domains like law and morality, Marmor distinguishes between 'metaphysical' objectivity, which requires a 'truth of the matter consisting in the fact that there is an object with properties corresponding to its description',[20] and 'logical' (or 'discursive') objectivity, which is satisfied with the possibility of *ascribing* truth values to the statements of a class.[21] The difference between the metaphysical and the logical (or discursive) concept of objectivity is that only the former is committed to a correspondence theory of truth and a reductive description of 'an object in the world'.[22] Logical objectivity, in turn, is compatible with a pluralistic conception of truth or with philosophical traditions that 'allow for the validity or truth of statements which are not descriptive (or reducible to descriptive) statements'.[23]

---

[19] Gonzalo Villa-Rosas and Jorge Luis Fabra-Zamora, 'Introduction: The Meanings of "Objectivity"', in this volume.

[20] Andrei Marmor, 'Three Concepts of Objectivity' in Andrei Marmor (ed) *Law and Interpretation: Essays in Legal Philosophy* (OUP 1995) 177, 181.

[21] Ibid., 178, 186–187. In a more recent republication of his article, Marmor has substituted the label 'logical' objectivity by 'discursive' objectivity. Andrei Marmor, 'Three Concepts of Objectivity' in *Positive Law and Objective Values* (OUP 2001, 112–134). It must be noticed that Marmor distinguishes, in addition, a third notion of objectivity, which he calls 'semantic' objectivity. On this account, 'the objective-subjective dichotomy is basically a characterization of a given speech. Roughly, a statement is semantically objective if and only if it is a statement about an object; and it is a subjective statement if and only if it is an aspect of one's self, that is, about some mental state of the subject making the statement'. Ibid, 113. In the argument I provide in the following lines, the semantic dichotomy between objectivity and subjectivity is not important, inasmuch as all participants can agree that the controversy about the possibility of objectivity in law is a controversy about the object or subject matter of our inquiry.

[22] Ibid., 185.

[23] Ibid., 186.

The point of distinguishing between a metaphysical and a logical sense of objectivity is to dissociate objectivism from moral realism. Once the logical concept of objectivity is available, it becomes possible to insist on the objectivity of moral assertions even if one accepts an anti-realist metaethical theory. Projectivism, constructivism, fictionalism, expressivism, and perhaps other metaethical isms become suitable candidates for delivering objective moral statements.

Nevertheless, despite its analytical consistency, the concept of logical objectivity appears too weak to satisfy the requirement of legitimacy that motivates lawyers to insist on the objectivity of their moral judgments. When lawyers argue for the objectivity of morality, they are looking for more than the logical concept of objectivity and less than its metaphysical sense. Consider, for instance, the following excerpt from Dworkin:

> I see no point in trying to find some general argument that moral or political or legal or aesthetic or interpretive judgments *are* objective. Those who ask for an argument of that sort want something different from the kind of arguments I and they would make for particular examples or instances of such judgments. But I do not see how there could be any such different arguments. I have no argument for the objectivity of moral arguments except moral arguments, no arguments for the objectivity of interpretive judgments except interpretive arguments, and so forth.[24]

This fragment makes it evident that Dworkin rejects the reductive explanations that would be required by the metaphysical concept of objectivity. But in his view the logical concept is in no better shape, for he thinks that we still need more than an Archimedean concept of objectivity whose point is to rescue some metaethical theories from their sceptical practical consequences. Instead of a stipulative concept to make sense of ordinary moral statements while maintaining the second-order assertion that there are no 'real' moral truths or that what seems to be a moral truth is actually something else, Dworkin is postulating, like the majority of lawyers, a *methodological* concept of objectivity.

This methodological objectivity, to repeat, is not grounded in any metaphysical view. A true metaphysical argument about morality would have to be an Archimedean argument. It would have to be both austere, in the sense that 'it does not rely even on very general or counterfactual or theoretical positive moral judgments', and neutral, in the sense that 'it takes no sides in substantive moral controversies'.[25] But Dworkin is convinced that no metaethical argument possesses these features. He comes to the controversial conclusion that metaethics is based on a mistake, because we can neither find moral properties

---

[24] Ronald Dworkin, *A Matter of Principle* (Harvard UP 1985) 171.
[25] Dworkin, 'Objectivity and Truth: You'd Better Believe It' (n 2), 92.

in the universe, which are supposed to make a causal impact on human beings, nor give up our entrenched convictions about the existence of moral norms. It would be unintelligible, for instance, to claim that we all err about the nature of our moral judgments or that we are confused about the status of our moral claims.[26] All sceptical metaethical positions, according to Dworkin, can be broadly classified as either a form of 'error theory'[27] or a variant of 'status scepticism',[28] which claims that when properly analysed (from a second-order or metaphysical point of view) the moral facts to which we appeal in our ordinary arguments are actually the projection of emotions, or attitudes, or feelings, or desires, or something else. But he claims that they are all unintelligible and implausible. The reason for this unintelligibility stems from a similar source: they are all trying to find a causal explanation for moral facts, i.e., they are trying to reduce moral facts to some prior fact which determines its status, and when they find out that no such causal explanation is available and no such prior facts exist, they are driven to external scepticism because of their flawed methodological ambitions. Moral values, on Dworkin's view, cannot be either affirmed or denied with these metaphysical theories, since they all fail to understand that values and moral norms belong to a metaphysically independent domain.

Dworkin's argument relies on Hume's distinction between facts and values, but unlike the Humean trend in metaethical inquiry he does not infer from this that moral truths do not exist. They do not exist as part of the causal world, in which the laws of science apply. But there is nothing that should prevent us from believing that they exist in a different domain. If this is the case, perhaps a hermeneutic theory can do a better work, as Dworkin suggests in his account of truth in the domain of value. 'The truth of any true moral judgment', he argues, 'consists in the truth of an indefinite number of other moral judgments. And its truth provides part of what constitutes the truth of any those others'.[29] We must apply, therefore, an integrated moral epistemology, which is all we need to gain access to values and moral truths. On Dworkin's holistic account of values, 'all true values form an interlocking network', in which 'each of our convictions about what is good or right or beautiful plays some role in supporting each of our other convictions in each of those domains of value'.[30] But right after proposing this test for our interpretive convictions about values, he deflates his claim to truth and adds that he means with this 'to describe method, not metaphysics', i.e., he means to explain 'how you must proceed if truth is

---

[26] Ibid.
[27] Dworkin, *Justice for Hedgehogs* (n 2) 46–49.
[28] Ibid., 50–66.
[29] Ibid., 117.
[30] Ibid., 120.

your agenda'.[31] Although sometimes this optimism about the objectivity of moral judgments can be confused with moral realism, it can only adjust to this label if it is somehow reinterpreted as an *ungrounded* realism,[32] or if realism is redefined as *itself* a moral theory.[33]

The relevant notion of objectivity in the lawyer's account of morality must therefore be both 'moderate' and 'domain-specific'. It must reject metaphysical objectivism in two ways: on the one hand, the account of objectivity favoured by Dworkin seems to be 'moderate' precisely in the 'weak' sense of objectivity suggested by Robert Brandom and employed by Marchettoni, in this book, to make sense of Dworkin's critique of Hart's advocacy of discretion in judicial reasoning.[34] On the other hand, as Postema explains, 'the case for a methodological approach to objectivity' does not resort to any metaphysical thesis; 'it depends, rather, on the domain-specific nature of the notion of objectivity', which is 'precisely what partisans of metaphysical objectivity reject'.[35]

When lawyers argue for the objectivity of moral judgments, they either claim that metaphysical descriptions of morality are self-contradictory,[36] or they hold that they are 'orthogonal to the central questions of the objectivity of the discourse'[37] and can only work if they provide 'illuminating summaries of central aspects of our practices', which are 'accountable to our practices, rather than our practices being accountable to them'.[38] Metaphysical descriptions of the 'true nature' of morality are at worse impossible[39] and at best subsidiary[40] or irrelevant[41] for the practice of moral interpretation. Instead of searching for the 'source' or the 'grounds' of the normativity of values and normative concepts, asking questions from an external viewpoint, the most influential contemporary legal philosophers tend to think that the explanation of normativity must be internal to normative practices.[42]

---

[31] Ibid., 121.
[32] Ronald Dworkin, *Religion without God* (Harvard UP 2013) 15.
[33] Matthew Kramer, *Moral Realism as a Moral Doctrine* (Wiley-Blackwell 2009).
[34] Leonardo Marchettoni, 'From Hart to Dworkin via Brandom: Indeterminacy, Interpretation, and Objectivity', in this volume, esp. section 4.
[35] Postema, 'Objectivity Fit for Law' (n 17), 133.
[36] Dworkin, 'Objectivity and Truth: You'd Better Believe It' (n 2); Dworkin, *Justice for Hedgehogs* (n 2).
[37] Postema, 'Objectivity Fit for Law' (n 17), 129.
[38] Raz, *Between Authority and Interpretation* (n 16) 227–228.
[39] Dworkin, 'Objectivity and Truth: You'd Better Believe It' (n 2); Dworkin, *Justice for Hedgehogs* (n 2).
[40] Postema, 'Objectivity Fit for Law' (n 17).
[41] Jeremy Waldron, *Law and Disagreement* (OUP 1999) 164–187.
[42] Joseph Raz, *From Normativity to Responsibility* (OUP 2011) 99.

The methodological concept of objectivity required for justifying moral arguments comprises the notion of 'epistemic objectivity', i.e., the claim that people can be objective about certain features 'if they are, in forming or holding opinions, judgments, and the like, about [certain] matters, properly sensitive to factors which are epistemically relevant to the truth or correctness of their opinions or judgments'.[43] But there is more. It encompasses, in addition, a type of 'domain objectivity', which recognizes not only 'certain structuring features' common to different domains,[44] but also some special responsibilities in the inquiry inside its own domain.[45]

Consider, for instance, Raz's account of domain objectivity. A domain is objective if it satisfies 'a whole range of criteria' which 'define the discipline to which objective thoughts are subject'.[46] Although Raz does not provide an exhaustive list of these criteria, he gives us some important assumptions: the possibility of knowledge condition, which means that 'only if a domain is objective can it express knowledge, or be said to be about something that one can have knowledge of'; the possibility of error condition, which requires that it remains possible to think that things are of a certain type without that being the case; the possibility of epistemic objectivity, which implies a 'capacity to avoid bias, or other emotional distortions'; the relevance condition, which requires that a domain contains 'facts or other considerations which are reasons for believing that they are or are likely to be true or correct'; the independence condition, which requires a 'reality which exists independently of our knowledge'; and the single reality condition, which means that a domain of thought only can be objective if submitted to the constraint that 'thoughts constitute knowledge only if they all can be explained as being about a single reality'.[47]

Among the conditions of objectivity stated above, the relevance condition occupies a prominent position. Depending on the domain of thought the 'reasons for holding a thought to be true or false are of a large variety of kinds'.[48] It is the set of features of the domain which accounts for the appropriateness of the reasons in such domain. The objectivity of a domain need not presuppose 'either a priori or self-evident or incorrigible understanding' of the reasons which are relevant in the domain. It is satisfied, instead, with

---

[43] Raz, *Engaging Reason* (n 3), 119.
[44] Postema, 'Objectivity Fit for Law' (n 17), 105.
[45] Raz, *Engaging Reason* (n 3), 122–123; Postema, 'Objectivity Fit for Law' (n 17), 105–107.
[46] Raz, *Engaging Reason* (n 3), 123.
[47] Ibid., 123–126. It is an open question whether Raz needs the last condition: the single reality condition, which seems to be indeed a metaphysical criterion of objectivity. Other legal philosophers, like Dworkin, would explicitly deny it.
[48] Ibid., 124.

the assumption that the thoughts which belong to this domain 'allow for the application of judgments based on reasons' and 'that there can be reasons of an appropriate kind'.[49]

Although one might object that some of Raz's criteria are metaphysical, which would allow one to hold that he is implicitly committed to the metaphysical concept of objectivity, there is still a sense in which they are all internal to the domain to which they apply.[50] Raz believes that the attempt to classify objectivity criteria as semantic, metaphysical or epistemic concepts misses the important point that these criteria are 'interdependent, and that at the most fundamental level these stipulated concepts are not useful'.[51] The important point is that to establish the objectivity of a moral judgment we need to make it an *intelligible* and acceptable norm, and this intelligibility requires: (1) 'appropriate experience, or learning from (or about) those who have experience'; (2) explanation of the point of a rule or a value, which need not be a point external to itself; and, (3) a network of mutually supporting moral propositions.[52]

4. IN DEFENCE OF THE LAWYERS

Probably most metaethics philosophers will not be impressed by the lawyers' arguments for moral objectivity. To retort to Dworkin's claim to moral objectivity, for instance, they might respond that he is trying to find an easy way to moral realism, i.e., to 'combine a commitment to realism with a certain lack of anxiety about the status and standing of morality', and that he has no right to this position.[53] They might claim, to justify this conclusion, that Dworkin cannot hold that metaethics is inconsistent without committing a performative contradiction, since this claim should be read as a second-order metaphysical argument instead of a first-order moral position.[54] Dworkin's theory would be

---

[49] Ibid., 125.
[50] Ibid., 131.
[51] Ibid., 130.
[52] Ibid., 174.
[53] Sarah McGrath, 'Relax? Don't Do It! Why Moral Realism Won't Come Cheap' in R Shaffer-Landau (ed) *Oxford Studies in Metaethics, Volume 9* (OUP 2014) 186, 187.
[54] Michael Moore, 'The Interpretive Turn in Modern Theory: A Turn for the Worse?' in *Educating Oneself in Public: Critical Essays in Jurisprudence* (OUP 2000), 335, 407–423; Kenneth Ehrenberg, 'Archimedean Metaethics Defended' (2008) 39 *Metaphilosophy* 508; Nick Zangwill, 'Commentary on Ronald Dworkin's "Objectivity and Truth: You'd Better Believe It"' (1996) *Brown Electronic Article Review Service (Bears)*.   https://www.brown.edu/Departments/Philosophy/bears/9612zang.html accessed 23 June 2022.

just another metaphysical theory, even if it claims that there is some property in moral values that makes them unintelligible without further moral judgments.

Nonetheless, a defender of methodological objectivity may reply that this objection has no bite. Even if it is correct, the claim to a *non-reductive* theory of moral objectivity remains unharmed. Raz, for instance, is not bothered if you like to call his value theory metaphysical.[55] What matters for him is that it is hopeless to try to identify values and their sustaining practices in value-free terms: 'There is no way we can capture the variety and nuance of various concepts of values and disvalues except in evaluative terms.'[56] Even if it is possible to explain, from a metaphysical point of view, the 'inescapability of normativity' or the 'hold reasons have on us', we lose the 'ability to explain' the concept of normativity if we go outside it.[57] Even when we talk about the basic goods or more general values, we can neither claim that they are self-evident nor be satisfied with the view that they are not derivative, as some natural law philosophers sustain.[58] In effect, Raz presents the following response to Finnis's claim that basic values – like life, knowledge, aesthetic experience, play, religion, and the like – need not be 'derived' because their value is self-evident:

> While it is true that the basic goods cannot be reduced to other goods, it is possible that they can be explained.... These explanations, if available, will be circular in that they will explain evaluative concepts using evaluative concepts. We know that the fundamental concepts all thought relies on cannot be explained in a non-circular way, but some wide circles have explanatory power.[59]

I think that this holistic explanation of moral values is what lawyers need to satisfy the objectivity requirement. Whether or not this method amounts to Dworkin's ambitious thesis of the 'unity of value', which tries to define values in a way that avoids conflicts among them,[60] it certainly is enough to vindicate at least a more nuanced version of it, which accepts only that 'basic ethical principles are interconnected', in the sense that 'the content of every such

---

[55] Joseph Raz, *The Practice of Value* (OUP 2002) 26.
[56] Ibid., 23.
[57] Raz, *From Normativity to Responsibility* (n 42) 99.
[58] John Finnis, *Natural Law and Natural Rights* (2nd edn 2011) 35.
[59] Joseph Raz, 'Value: A Menu of Questions' in John Keown and Robert P George (eds) *Reason, Morality and Law: The Philosophy of John Finnis* (OUP 2013) 13, 18.
[60] Ronald Dworkin, 'Do Values Conflict? A Hedgehog's Approach' (2001) 43 *Arizona Law Review* 251, 256.

principle is indeed partly constrained and determined by the content of every of other such principle'.[61]

If one interprets this as a metaphysical claim, an important aspect of Dworkin's argument about the metaphysical independence of value is preserved: the objection to a 'colonial philosophy', which tries to explain the status of moral propositions by reducing it to something else.[62]

We can come back, thus, to the exchange between Dworkin and Blackburn quoted at the outset of this chapter. When it comes to the reasoning process one needs to adopt to argue for moral claims, there is an important measure of agreement between Dworkin and Blackburn. According to Blackburn, 'There is only one proper way to take the question "On what does the wrongness of cruelty depend?": as a *moral* question with an answer in which no mention to our actual responses properly figures.'[63]

Both Dworkin and Blackburn seem think, therefore, that moral norms must be defended with statements *internal* to morality. Where does their disagreement reside? The problem of Blackburn's quasi-realism, for Dworkin, is that it still distinguishes between 'internal' statements of moral participants and 'external' statements of philosophers. Dworkin and Blackburn adopt different perspectives on how to make these moral judgments intelligible. While the latter still believes that we can have an external explanation of the status of these judgments, which can be a metaphysical explanation because it need not make any moral-evaluative assertions to provide this complete explanation, the former is sceptical of any explanation that cannot be shared from the internal point of view of the participants in moral practice. The problem of Blackburn's account, for Dworkin, is that it 'must find some external statements' to explain the nature of moral assertions in causal terms, otherwise it will not have a metaethical position that can antagonize Platonism and the other moral theories Blackburn criticizes.[64] In order to provide an argument against metaethical theories that allegedly fail because they describe moral facts as 'mind-independent', Blackburn must characterize his own position as 'external' and 'descriptive' as well: 'If Blackburn is to preserve projectivism as a distinct metaethical position, he must find something stronger to defend: the statement that "there are no moral properties", only "attitudes" among "real states of affairs", seems intended to provide this'.[65]

---

[61] Matthew Kramer, 'Working on the Inside: Ronald Dworkin's Moral Philosophy' (2013) 73 *Analysis* 118, 122.
[62] Dworkin, *Justice for Hedgehogs* (n 2) 9.
[63] Simon Blackburn, *Essays in Quasi-Realism* (OUP 1992) 172–173.
[64] Dworkin, 'Objectivity and Truth: You'd Better Believe It' (n 2), 111.
[65] Ibid., 112.

Yet according to Dworkin this is an explanation in which we, as committed participants in ordinary communicative practices, cannot believe:

> It makes no sense for us to treat our moral convictions as only projections of emotions rather than as reports of mind-independent moral facts unless we have already decided that there are no mind-independent moral facts for our convictions to report, and we cannot believe that there are no such mind-independent facts because we cannot believe (for example) that genocide would cease to be wicked if no-one thought it was or if no one projected a disapproving emotion toward its occurrences.[66]

In a sense, this argument can be classified as a nuanced form of pragmatic argument, since Dworkin is claiming that Blackburn's explanation fails because it cannot be accepted from the point of view of the practice. There is a *priority* of the practice in the definition of what counts as a good moral argument, or a good theoretical argument about the character of a moral proposition. Dworkin's theory of morality, like his theory of law, is part of a more general theory of responsibility (which includes a theory of moral responsibility and a theory of political responsibility), as we can learn even from his earliest writings.[67] According to Dworkin, part of our moral responsibilities, as theorists, is to construct an account for the objectivity of the moral propositions that we hold. It is 'irresponsible to try to do without such a theory'.[68] It is because of this need to make our moral philosophy *coherent with our practices* that Dworkin thinks that Blackburn cannot be happy with the thought that when we stake a moral claim we can merely 'interpret ordinary moral claims as projections without violence to logic'.[69] According to Dworkin, 'the difficulty we have in accepting that solution is not that we wish to continue uttering certain sentences, but that we cannot abandon the substantive moral position we now use those sentences to assert'.[70]

Dworkin's response to Blackburn's quasi-realism looks like a familiar philosophical argument which has been presented by Mackie in defence of his error theory: the so-called 'queerness argument'. According to Mackie, we should

---

[66] Ronald Dworkin, 'Reply by Ronald Dworkin' (1996) *Brown Electronic Article Review Service (Bears).* https://www.brown.edu/Departments/Philosophy/bears/9704dwor.html accessed 23 June 2022.

[67] Dworkin's most central submission in 'Hard Cases', for instance, is that his jurisprudence is part of a doctrine of political responsibility, which requires that 'political officials must make only such political decisions as they can justify within a political theory that also justifies other decisions they propose to make'. Dworkin, *Taking Rights Seriously* (n 7) 87.

[68] Dworkin, *Justice for Hedgehogs* (n 2) 8.

[69] Dworkin, 'A Reply by Ronald Dworkin' (n 66).

[70] Ibid.

avoid asserting truth-value to moral propositions because to consistently hold that there are moral facts, we would have to commit to the implausible metaphysical view that there are entities in the world with 'qualities or relations of a very strange sort, utterly different from anything else in the universe'.[71]

In a sense, Dworkin's response to Blackburn adopts a similar strategy. Dworkin's argument is a version of Mackie's queerness argument in the opposite direction. While Mackie claims that moral facts would be strange entities because they are assumed to have properties very different from everything else in the universe, or at least everything else that we know about, in a way that would be awkward for us to accept, Dworkin thinks that the queerness lies in explaining moral judgments as if they were simply projections of emotions. Some of the implicit commitments of Blackburn's projectivism cannot be made explicit, because the participants of moral argument cannot understand their own moral judgments in the way it explains. Dworkin believes that Blackburn fails to make moral judgments *intelligible to moral judgers*. It is because of this difficulty that he claims that what we cannot accept is the *theory* that denies the existence of independent moral facts.

If Dworkin is right, it appears that Blackburn's moral theory is plausible only for as long as it remains incomplete, i.e., for as long as it refrains from delivering the external explanation Blackburn says it is the job of philosophy to provide. When we look at morality from the inside, we must concede that Blackburn captures well the *relational* aspect of moral propositions. Like Dworkin, he acknowledges that moral agents explain and justify their moral judgments with other moral arguments. But as soon as his metaethical explanation of the character of moral norms is made explicit, it becomes clear that this explanation cannot be integrated into the ordinary views that as participants of moral practices we must accept. Blackburn regards philosophy and practice as two distinct language games that employ different concepts, and there is little that one can learn from the other. The concepts that make the vocabulary of the philosopher cannot be used in practice, on the pain of making our moral convictions unintelligible. If a philosopher retains her own first-order views about particular moral problems, she will be forced to conclude that the second-order theory ceases to be a plausible argument about the status of moral norms. Dworkin concludes that we must reject it because we cannot believe in this explanation without contradicting some of our convictions that are most deeply held.

It seems to be clear that if Mackie's argument can qualify as a genuine philosophical argument, so does Dworkin's. The arguments that Dworkin or other lawyers might employ to defend their position about objectivity are not

---

[71] J L Mackie, *Ethics, Inventing Right and Wrong* (Penguin Books 1977), 38.

'wearying, pointless and unprofitable'.[72] Lawyers seem to have a case for the objectivity of the moral claims they need to make in their professional practice, and perhaps it is a sound case. It may even be true that lawyers have a *privileged perspective* from which one can understand moral claims. I believe, in fact, that this might be the thought behind Dworkin's suspicion (or, as some might say, his quietism) about metaphysical questions. Moral questions, like legal questions, need to be answered in a certain way, which requires for the moral agent an attitude of taking responsibility for some judgment. Any questions about the nature of morality, of the kind that philosophers purport to make with their metaethical theories, need to be answered with the same kind of judgments and responsibilities. On many occasions, lawyers are better positioned than moral philosophers because they look at moral questions from a practical angle or point of view, which allows us to understand them in a better way. Here is a typical Dworkinian argument for this view, put forward by one of Dworkin's most faithful disciples:

> It is in legal argument that the most consistent, coherent and advanced systematization of real moral argument takes place. Law goes backward from cases to abstraction; moral philosophy usually goes the other way. Most academic professional moral philosophers are not particularly versed in law. Yet almost any hypothetical example that a moral philosopher thinks up will have occurred in real time at a real place and very careful (first order) thought will have been put into resolving the problem. ... Showing a moral philosopher only some of the hundreds of thousands of reported cases of the Anglo-American courts of the past three hundred years ought to be sufficient. The philosopher would discover that for every seemingly clear legal or moral rule, some human being, somewhere in the world, will throw up a situation that is new and baffling to solve. Judges and lawyers will consider the moral arguments for an ultimate proposition either way.[73]

This explains why Dworkin thinks that lawyers are 'working political philosophers'.[74] Dworkin believes that philosophy should be integrated into our ordinary arguments, which constitute a central aspect of our ordinary practices (including institutionalized and political practices). Despite the fierce resistance that Dworkin has offered against most strands of pragmatism, either in law or in philosophy,[75] one can find, as I argued above, some important traces of pragmatism in his accounts of truth and objectivity in morality and law.[76]

---

[72] Blackburn, 'Commentary on Ronald Dworkin's "Objectivity and Truth: You'd Better Believe It"' (n 5).
[73] Stephen Guest, *Ronald Dworkin* (3rd edn, Stanford UP 2013) 5.
[74] Dworkin, *Justice for Hedgehogs* (n 2) 414.
[75] See Ronald Dworkin, *Justice in Robes* (Harvard UP 2006).
[76] Hillary Nye, 'Staying Busy While Doing Nothing? Dworkin's Complicated Relationship with Pragmatism' (2016) 29 *Canadian Journal of Law and Jurisprudence*

There seems to be at least one sense in which Dworkin can be regarded as endorsing a kind of pragmatism in his account of moral objectivity. Dworkin seems to fit into the description of 'fundamental pragmatism' in the sense that Robert Brandom employs the term. He is in part a pragmatist because he assumes a conception of moral objectivity according to which our theories should be tested in practice, for it is the practice of moral argumentation that provides 'the ultimate criteria of adequacy according to which the success of that theoretical enterprise is to be assessed'.[77] He is a 'fundamental pragmatist' because he tacitly endorses the view that *knowing-how* to use moral concept takes an 'explanatory priority' over *knowing-that* moral concepts mean such and such. As a fundamental pragmatist, Dworkin must commit to the view that 'explicit theoretical beliefs can be made intelligible only against the background of implicit practical abilities'.[78] Given the *concreteness* and richness of the moral problems that figure in the ordinary business of adjudication, lawyers tend to be especially well trained in the discipline of making moral judgments and synthesizing moral claims, concepts and arguments in a network of values and practical directives.

The objectivity of moral judgments is purchased, in this account, not by making representations that match moral facts that pre-exist in the world, but instead by a discursive process in which moral contents are treated as *rational claims* in social and normative practices. Rationally assertible moral concepts, in this account, are those that can play the role of premises and conclusions in an inferential network of mutually supporting concepts. When a language-user employs these concepts, she takes them as reasons for further judgments and for inferences and actions based on them, and if she uses the concept correctly she becomes entitled to a social recognition of its force by the other participants in the discourse. By using concepts to describe moral norms in a 'game of giving and asking for reasons', she undertakes a *commitment* to place herself under the authority of these norms, i.e., to become liable to assessment under these norms. She becomes *responsible* for her judgments, while at the same time *entitled* to a social recognition of its correctness by other language-users. The social source of objectivity for the kind of moral judgments lawyers need to make in their professional practice is found in these mutual commitments and entitlements within a community of speakers, who endorse similar con-

---

71; Thiago L Decat, 'Inferentialist Pragmatism and Dworkin's Law as Integrity' (2015) 1 *Erasmus Law Review*, 14; Thomas Bustamante, 'Law, Moral Facts and Interpretation: A Dworkinian Response to Mark Greenberg's Moral Impact Theory of Law' (2019) 32 *Canadian Journal of Law and Jurisprudence* 5.

[77] Robert Brandom, *Perspectives on Pragmatism* (Harvard UP 2011) 59.
[78] Ibid., 65.

cepts and also employ them as premises and conclusions in the same game of giving and acknowledging reasons.[79]

I believe that this account of the relationship between theory and practice explains the dominant trend among legal philosophers to search for a *methodological*, rather than metaphysical, conception of objectivity. If we turn to legal history and to the arguments of prominent English lawyers likes Edward Coke and Matthew Hale, for instance, we can see that this view of moral objectivity has important similarities with the practice of seventeenth century common law lawyers, and that some of the arguments these lawyers deployed to sustain that the common law has a 'distinctive' rationality (which they called an 'artificial' reasoning) are analogous to the arguments that the contemporary legal philosophers quoted in this chapter employ in defence of their conception of moral objectivity. According to classical common law jurisprudence, the law could not be conceived of as a plain historical fact. The classical common lawyer's notion of the 'artificial reason' of law implied that 'only in the process of argument, regarding concrete cases, in open court subject to reasoned challenge, is the law to be found and forged'.[80] The law's reason was *internal* to law.[81] The jurisprudence of common lawyers required a 'refined skill of combining a grasp of general principles with a full appreciation of the significance

---

[79] Robert Brandom, *Articulating Reasons: An Introduction to Inferentialism* (Harvard UP 2003) 189–196. It is interesting to notice, in support of the interpretation advocated here, a series of attempts to interpret Dworkin's claim to objectivity in legal reasoning along these lines. See Leonardo Marchettoni, 'Brandom on Norms and Objectivity' (2018) 19 *Critical Horizons* 215–32; Marchettoni, 'From Hart to Dworkin via Brandom' (n 34); Thiago L Decat, 'Inferentialist Pragmatism and Dworkin's Law as Integrity' (n 76); Thiago L Decat, *Racionalidade, Valor e Teorias do Direito* (D'Plácido 2015); Thomas Bustamante, 'Revisiting the Idea of Protestant Interpretation: Towards Reconciliation between Dworkin and Postema' in Thomas Bustamante and Thiago L Decat (eds) *Philosophy of Law as an Integral Part of Philosophy: Essays in the Jurisprudence of Gerald J. Postema* (Hart Publishing 2020), 113–139; Thomas Bustamante, 'Is Protestant Interpretation an Acceptable Attitude Toward Normative Social Practices? An Analysis of Dworkin and Postema' (2021) 66 *American Journal of Jurisprudence* 1–25; Mathias Klatt, *Making the Law Explicit: The Normativity of Legal Argumentation* (Hart Publishing 2008). For a powerful argument that attempts to apply Brandom to law but suggests that Dworkin fails to address Wittgenstein's regress argument in the interpretation of rules, see Gerald J Postema, '*A Similibus ad Similia*: Analogical Thinking in Law' in Douglas Edlin (ed), *Common Law Theory* (Cambridge UP 2007), 102–33. For a response, see Thiago L Decat, 'Some Inferentialist Remarks on Postema's Conception of Analogical Thinking in Law' in Bustamante and Decat, *Philosophy of Law as an Integral Part of Philosophy*, 159–180.

[80] Gerald J Postema, 'Classical Common Law Jurisprudence (Part II)' (2003) 3 *Oxford Univ Commonwealth Law Journal* 1, 8.

[81] Gerald J Postema, 'Editor's Introduction' in Gerald J Postema (ed) *Matthew Hale on The Law of Nature, Reason and Common Law* (OUP 2017) xv, xxvi.

of particular circumstances'; it provided the 'concrete conditions of social life' in which these principles should be interpreted and applied.[82]

In a previous work, I described the rationality of common law, which claims to be distinguished from the 'natural reason' of philosophers, theologians, and scholastic natural lawyers, in the following sense:

> Classical common lawyers were suspicious of metaphysical formulae and undertook an effort to avoid transcendental arguments about morality, justice or the nature of law. The reason behind classical common law was a form of 'artificial reason' in the sense that it was a reasoning *in the law*, with little room for 'external' principles imported from second-order philosophy. If the historical series of decisions, customs and institutional materials extracted from legal practice failed to give one an uncontroversial solution to a given argument, the job of the lawyer was not to consult 'universal moral sources, as a natural lawyers might do, but rather to look longer, harder and deeper into the accumulated fund of experience and example provided by the common law'.[83]

Perhaps these common law lawyers were not entirely clear about the status of moral assertions and lacked a general account of objectivity in morality. In effect, they needed an artificial reason for law, understood as a special form of practical reasoning, because they thought that abstract moral principles (which they understood as 'natural law') and morality in general were indeterminate and thus incapable of guiding our action. But they were on the right track. They acknowledged that practical reasoning is not about excavating brute facts, and that transcendental arguments about the nature of our judgments are disappointing and sometimes describe our moral judgments in terms that do not make sense to ourselves. This explains why they thought, and many legal philosophers still think today, that a methodological account of objectivity in practical reasoning does a better job.

5.   CONCLUSION

Our analysis shows that Blackburn's quote at the introduction of this chapter is unfair.[84] There is much that lawyers can contribute to philosophy, even if they turn out to be wrong about their usual metaethical quietism. It makes sense not only for lawyers but also for rational agents participating in social practices

---

[82]   Ibid., xlviii–xlix
[83]   Thomas Bustamante, 'Precedent in the Common Law Tradition' in Mortimer Sellers and Stefan Kirste (eds), *Encyclopedia of the Philosophy of Law and Social Philosophy* (Springer 2021), 2, https://doi.org/10.1007/978-94-007-6730-0_541-1. The quote inside this fragment is from Gerald J Postema, 'Classical Common Law Jurisprudence (Part I)' (2002) 2 *Oxford Univ Commonwealth Law Journal* 155, 179.
[84]   See text above n 5.

like politics and moral discourse to abandon the ambitious assumptions of metaphysical objectivity while still maintaining a methodological account of objectivity to test the soundness of our claims. To be honest, I would not be surprised if you come to believe that lawyers have, in the end of the day, the best method to answer some real philosophical questions, and a respectful account of the kind of objectivity that we need to provide a public justification for our moral views.

13. Moral objectivity without robust realism[1]

J. J. Moreso

1. INTRODUCTION

David Enoch has written one of the most powerful and original defences of moral realism.[2] Many things make his book a vital contribution to philosophical reflection on morality and metaethics. In the introduction to his studies of Bentham, H. L. A. Hart attributes to the father of utilitarianism an extraordinary combination of a fly's eye for detail and an eagle's eye for illuminating generalizations, applicable to broad areas of social life.[3] Well, *mutatis mutandis*, the same can be said of Enoch's book. On the one hand, his attention to detail is exemplary, and the main text, together with his footnotes, is replete with arguments and counterarguments about the most intricate questions of contemporary metaethics. On the other hand, this attention to detail is combined with a broad vision for etching on our philosophical horizon a well-delimited and prominent place for reflection on morality, established in a vigorous defence, and founded on the existence of moral facts and properties which are not natural entities, nor reducible to them, and which ground the truth of moral judgements, independently of the beliefs and attitudes of humans beings.[4]

---

[1] This chapter derives from a Spanish-language ancestor: J. J. Moreso, 'Objetividad moral sin realismo robusto. Comentarios sobre Enoch', Discusiones (2015) 16, 191-222. My work has benefited from two research grants: DER2016-80471-C2-1-R from the Spanish Government, and 2017 SGR 00823 from the Generalitat of Catalonia.

[2] David Enoch, *Taking Morality Seriously. A Defense of Robust Realism* (Oxford University Press 2011). The numbers enclosed in round brackets in the text refer always to this book.

[3] H. L. A. Hart, *Essays on Bentham. Jurisprudence and Political Philosophy* (Oxford University Press 1982) 4.

[4] Other recent defences of non-naturalist moral realism, albeit different in many respects from Enoch's, are provided by Russ Shafer-Landau, *Moral Realism: A Defence* (Oxford University Press, 2003) and Ralph Wedgwood, *The Nature of Normativity* (Oxford University Press, 2007).

It is also true that, in the book, Enoch reveals a propensity for more radical philosophical positions, as he himself recognizes: 'As you may have noticed, I have the philosophical temperament of an extremist' (115). However, since I myself do not have such a philosophical temperament, but rather one that is – so to speak – more ecumenical, in this chapter I shall try to defend what seems to me to be a solid argument for the objectivity of morality, and criticize what seem to me to be inconclusive arguments for non-naturalist moral realism.

But first, a brief presentation of the book. It has ten chapters. The first is an introduction and an explanation of the motives that drove its development. Chapters 2–5 develop an argument for robust moral realism. Chapters 6–9 provide refined replies to possible objections to the foregoing argument. And Chapter 10 concludes the book.

I will not deal with the second half of the book, dedicated to responding to possible objections to Enoch's position. Chapter 6 contains some very skilled discussions of the acceptability or not of suspicious metaphysical entities. Chapter 7 presents the epistemological objection: the problem of explaining the correlation between our normative beliefs and normative truths, which are independent of our beliefs. Chapter 8 deals with the objection from the persistent presence of moral disagreements. Chapter 9 deals with the problems posed by motivation and the internal or external nature of normative reasons. Enoch concludes with a chapter where he tries to present the advantages of his position, and where he very honestly reveals the points in his argumentation in which he has less confidence, and about which he still harbours doubts.

I shall deal, instead, with the arguments whereby Enoch defends and argues for the constructive part of the book: the fundamental theses that characterize his philosophical approach. That is, with the argument of Chapter 2, according to which non-objective conceptions of morality, together with a very plausible normative thesis, which he calls IMPARTIALITY, imply unacceptable moral judgements in cases of disagreements and interpersonal conflicts. And also with the argument of Chapter 3, according to which normative truths are indispensable for practical deliberation, which is not optional for us, and such indispensability justifies ontological commitment to non-natural moral facts and properties, as part of our ontological furniture. Chapter 4 says that the two previous theses – the thesis of objectivity and the ontological thesis of the deliberative indispensability of the normative – while not implying robust moral realism, do make it the most plausible metaethical position. Chapter 5 then tries to show that it is not possible to obtain that result with fewer ontological commitments, since more ontologically parsimonious positions cannot ground deliberative indispensability.

I shall proceed as follows. In section 2 I present the argument from objectivity. In section 3 I try to show the force of this argument, which I find especially perspicuous. In section 4 I reconstruct the argument from the deliberative indispensability of the normative. In section 5 I express my doubts about the need to embrace such a robust ontological commitment, and in section 6 I conclude.

2. OBJECTIVITY FROM THE ARGUMENT FROM IMPARTIALITY

The argument is the following. Suppose that one afternoon my friend Pablo and I are in Madrid, and we decide to spend the evening together, but he proposes to go to the theatre to see *The House of Bernarda Alba* by Federico García Lorca, while I prefer to go to a concert by the violinist Julia Fischer. Pablo and I have not seen each other for a long time, and we want to spend the evening together. There is no reason why either of us should cede to the other's preference (such as it being the last programmed performance of this play, which has superb reviews and will never be performed again, or likewise for the concert). Then we would impose some solution in line with what Enoch (19) calls IMPARTIALITY, according to which:

> In an interpersonal conflict, we should step back from our mere preferences, or feelings, or attitudes, or some such, and to the extent the conflict is due to those, an impartial, egalitarian solution is called for. Furthermore, each party to the conflict should acknowledge as much: Standing one's ground is, in such cases, morally wrong.

The solution could be to draw lots, or to decide that since we are in Madrid, which is Pablo's city, we shall go to the theatre, and when we meet in my city, Barcelona, it will be my turn to decide. But whatever the solution, IMPARTIALITY seems to be an unquestionable moral principle: in matters of mere preferences, all preferences are worth the same.

Then, the argument continues, if cases of moral disagreement were of this sort, and the disagreement between Pablo and I arose because Pablo wanted to go to a basketball game and I wanted to go to a bullfight, IMPARTIALITY would also hold, and both sides should be disposed to withdraw our respective preferences. However, suppose that Pablo considers inflicting acute pain on animals to be immoral.[5] And he thinks, therefore, that going to a bullfight to

---

[5] Because he is a consequentialist, who takes into account the interests of animals among the relevant consequences, like Jeremy Bentham, *An Introduction to the Principles of Morals and Legislation* (Athlone Press 1970, original ed 1789) 281 and his contemporary followers, like Peter Singer, *Animal Liberation* (HarperCollins 1975) or, among others, Jesús Mosterín, *¡Vivan los animales!* (Debate, 1998) and Pablo de Lora, *Justicia para los animales* (Alianza 2003). Or less committedly, because he thinks, like Kant, that cruelty to animals diminishes the moral sensitivity of humans:

enjoy watching animals suffer is immoral. Then, would Pablo have a reason to withdraw his point of view? It seems not. It seems that, on the contrary, he should stand his ground and, perhaps, try to convince me to abandon my insensitivity until I understand that it is wrong to attend the bullfight. In this case IMPARTIALITY does not work, just as it does not work if Pablo and I disagree about which is the quickest way to get to Madrid's Teatro Real from Paseo de Recoletos at a certain time of day: by taxi or by public transport. Since there is a right answer about that matter of fact, IMPARTIALITY is of no help here, nor is it *rational* to follow its rule.

The author uses these ideas to argue that positions in metaethics which equate moral judgements with expressions of personal preference are false, and should therefore be rejected. Those positions which hold that the truth of moral judgements depends on the response that we human beings – given our beliefs and attitudes – give when confronted with a moral problem, are clear candidates for such a refutation. Enoch (27–40) takes care to show that not all views that make moral judgements dependent on humans' reactions are vulnerable to this objection. There are positions, like the view of constructivists who hold that the relevant response is the one which human beings would give in ideal conditions, or some especially sophisticated forms of expressivism which insist that some of our responses are *unique* and permit a convergence of judgement. Given that some of these positions will be discussed in section 4, we can now deal with the rejection of openly subjectivist positions, which make morality depend on our actual attitudes and feelings. In order to carry this out, Enoch (25) formulates a position which is extreme in the sense that (almost) no one would defend it in contemporary metaethics,[6] which he calls *caricaturized subjectivism*: 'Moral judgments report simple preferences, ones that are exactly on a par with a preference for playing tennis or for catching a movie.'[7]

'He who is cruel to animals becomes hard also in his dealings with men. We can judge the heart of a man by his treatment of animals.' *Immanuel Kant, Lectures on Ethics*, P. Heath and J. B. Schneewind (ed. and trans.) (Cambridge University Press 1977, original ed 1784–1785) 212.

[6] Although this is true in contemporary analytic metaethics, in my academic environment, in analytic philosophy of law, as conducted in Spanish and Italian, this position is still defended by important authors. See Eugenio Bulygin, *Essays in Legal Philosophy*, Carlos Bernal, Carla Huerta, Tecla Mazzarese, José Juan Moreso, Pablo E. Navarro and Stanley Paulson (eds) (Oxford University Press 2015) ch 19. and Riccardo Guastini, 'Dei rapporti tra liberalismo e non-cognitivismo' (2012) 2 *Teoria Politica* 137–142.

[7] These are the examples that Enoch uses to argue his case, and which I have replaced with attending the theatre or a concert.

And the following is the argument for the refutation, which – as can be seen – is an instance of *reductio ad absurdum* (25–26):

(1) Caricaturized Subjectivism. (For *Reductio*.)
(2) If Caricaturized Subjectivism is true, then interpersonal conflicts due to moral disagreements are really just interpersonal conflicts due to differences in mere preferences. (From the content of Caricaturized Subjectivism.)
(3) Therefore, interpersonal conflicts due to moral disagreements are just interpersonal conflicts due to differences in mere preferences. (From 1 and 2.)
(4) IMPARTIALITY, that is, roughly: when an interpersonal conflict (of the relevant kind) is a matter merely of preferences, then an impartial, egalitarian solution is called for, and it is wrong to just stand one's ground.
(5) Therefore, in cases of interpersonal conflict (of the relevant kind) due to moral disagreement, an impartial, egalitarian solution is called for, and it is wrong to just stand one's ground. (From 3 and 4.)
(6) However, in cases of interpersonal conflict (of the relevant kind) due to moral disagreement often an impartial solution is *not* called for, and it is permissible, and even required, to stand one's ground. (From previous section.)
(7) Therefore, Caricaturized Subjectivism is false. (From 1, 5, and 6, by *Reductio*.)

A metaethical premise, caricaturized subjectivism, and a premise of normative ethics, IMPARTIALITY, together imply a consequence that contradicts (6), the plausible premise that in cases of moral conflicts it is correct to stand one's ground, and so, by *reductio*, we may conclude that non-objectivist positions in ethics are false.

3. VINDICATING OBJECTIVITY

In my opinion, Enoch's argument is a good and conclusive one. It suffices that some of our interpersonal conflicts should be resolved by something like IMPARTIALITY, and that IMPARTIALITY never helps in our moral conflicts. If that is so, then non-objectivist metaethical views should be rejected because they fail to account for this feature of our morality.

As should become clear, objections to Enoch's argument try to cast doubt on the distinction between interpersonal conflicts concerning mere preferences and interpersonal conflicts for moral reasons. Moreover, they try to show that there are cases of non-moral interpersonal conflicts where IMPARTIALITY should not be applied, while there are cases of moral interpersonal conflicts where IMPARTIALITY should be applied.[8]

Let us look at two examples from Wedgwood that try to show that Enoch's distinction is inadequate in this way. First, a case of a non-moral disagreement in which it is not reasonable to abandon one's position: 'Suppose that you are on a committee that awards a certain art prize, and you have a deep disagreement with the other committee members.'[9] This is a disagreement whose origin is not moral but rather aesthetic. But it would not be morally wrong to stand your ground and publicly express your disagreement.

Clearly Wedgwood is right about this. But it is not clear why this argument tells against Enoch. For one thing, Enoch takes great care to say that there are many cases of interpersonal conflicts in which IMPARTIALITY does not prevail: this principle prevails only in conflicts that concern mere preferences and when there are certain circumstances of the context that do not lead to another solution. For another, in the case of the art prize, either there are principles of aesthetic value – as I myself am inclined to accept – and so there are no reasons to abandon what we believe to be correct, or else there are not, in which case this conflict may be about mere preferences, and hence should be decided by IMPARTIALITY.

The second example – a case of a conflict with a moral origin where it makes sense to renounce one's position – is, I think, of greater interest:[10]

> Enoch's example of an interpersonal conflict due to moral disagreement involves the moral importance of avoiding cruelty to dogs (p. 23). But suppose you are involved in a disagreement about an issue of this kind – say, about whether fox hunting should be banned by law. If there is no prospect of either side's persuading the other to change their view, it seems right for everyone to agree to settle the conflict by means of a democratic procedure, even though everyone agrees that there is a high chance that the outcome of this democratic procedure may be morally suboptimal.

---

[8] Manne and Solbel criticize Enoch with these arguments and propose an alternative strategy, which consists in holding that we should stand our ground when the conflict is sufficiently important, independently of whether its nature is of mere preferences or moral, Kate Manne and David Sobel, 'Disagreeing About How to Disagree' (2014) 168 *Philosophical Studies* 823–834. I think, for the reasons given by Enoch, 'In Defense of Taking Morality Seriously: Reply to Manne, Sobel, Lenman, and Joyce' (2014) 168 *Philosophical Studies* 853–865, in his reply, that this strategy does not work.

[9] Ralph Wedgwood, 'Book Review: Taking Morality Seriously. A Defense of Robust Realism. By David Enoch (Oxford: Oxford University Press, 2011)' (2013) 63 *The Philosophical Quarterly* 389–393, at 390.

[10] Ibid., 391.

Here again Wedgwood is right insofar as it seems correct to defer to the democratic majority on the case's solution. But, again, this does not tell against Enoch. We can accept that the fox hunting case is a case of disagreement with a moral origin, yet no one – not even after the democratic decision – has any reason to abandon their moral position. On the contrary, we expect the abolitionists to stand their ground in the hope of convincing everyone else. Democratic procedures are not, I think, implementations of IMPARTIALITY. They are ways of taking decisions in cases of disagreement that are equally respectful of everyone's autonomy, trusting that the deliberation of all will often lead us to the right results, and giving legitimacy to that solution. But that in no way means that those who remain in the minority abandon their position. This is precisely one of the central problems of political philosophy: how can the political legitimacy of mistaken decisions be reconciled with morality? Further, for many, democratic procedures are founded precisely on the epistemic value they enjoy – when they operate in optimal conditions – for achieving morally fair results.[11]

However, Enoch himself (236 n. 18) recognizes that on non-objectivist conceptions of ethics it is harder to justify standing one's ground in cases of moral conflict, and he states this point in the following terms:

> It is sometimes suggested – though more often in the classroom than in philosophical texts – that realist metaethical views will lead to intolerance, and that this gives reason to reject them. I believe this line of thought is confused in several ways (so there's good reason why it is not common in serious philosophical texts). But I also believe that there is something right about it, something captured by the argument in the text: on non-objectivist views of morality, it is harder to justify standing one's moral ground in the face of both disagreement and conflict. But, of course, I think of this as an *advantage* of objectivist views.

In my immediate academic environment, as pointed out in footnote 6 – i.e., that of legal philosophy in Spain, Latin America and Italy – such a position is passionately defended, not only in the classroom but also in various seminars and conferences. Sometimes it is also advocated in serious philosophical texts. Ferrajoli argues, for example, that ethical cognitivism and objectivism inevitably lead to moral absolutism, and consequently to the intolerance of dissenting opinions; and he even adds: 'From this point of view, the most coherent forms

---

[11] See Carlos S. Nino, *The Constitution of Deliberative Democracy* (Yale University Press 1996), José Luis Martí, 'The Epistemic Conception of Deliberative Democracy Defended. Reasons, Rightness and Equal Political Autonomy' in S. Besson and J. L. Martí (eds) *Deliberative Democracy and Its Discontents* (Ashgate 2006) ch 2; David Etslund, *Democractic Authority: A Philosophical Framework* (Princeton University Press 2009).

of moral objectivism and cognitivism are, without a doubt, those expressed by Catholic morality.'[12]

Meanwhile, Guastini[13] accepts that no metaethical premise can logically establish conclusions of normative ethics; yet in his opinion, a liberal ethics (of tolerance) can constitute a good pragmatic reason to adopt a non-cognitivist and non-objectivist metaethics, and vice versa.

The reasons offered by Guastini in support of this thesis are the following: he plausibly argues that normative ethical views will provide some norm of conduct concerning what one's attitude to other normative ethical views should be. And he adds that liberal ethical views will assume one of the following two meta-norms:

(N1) Any other normative ethical view (different from this one) should be tolerated.

(N2) Only some normative ethical views (different from this one) should be tolerated.

while intolerant ethical views, and therefore non-liberal ones, will assume a meta-norm like the following:

(N3) No normative ethical view other than this one should be tolerated.

As can be seen, these arguments take the liberalism of tolerance and democracy to fit better with non-objectivist metaethical views; perhaps because they assume for moral preferences a postulate like IMPARTIALITY. However, I think that this is a bad argument. It is true that sometimes democratic decisions must take sides between morally indifferent preferences and, then, respecting everyone's opinion makes majority rule the salient solution. There are some clear examples of this: a few years ago in my city – Barcelona, as I already said – the city council proposed a referendum to decide whether Avinguda Diagonal, one of the main arteries of the city, which they wanted to convert into a more pedestrian-friendly avenue, should be developed into

---

[12] Luigi Ferrajoli, 'Constitucionalismo principialista y constitucionalismo garantista' (2011) Doxa. 34 Cuadernos de Filosofía del Derecho, 15–53. Although he would perhaps now be inclined to moderate that extreme position, 'La scelta come fondamento ultimo della morale' (2012) 2 Teoria Politica 177–185, and Luigi Ferrajoli and Juan Ruiz Manero, *Dos modelos de constitucionalismo. Una conversación* (Trotta 2012), often as a consequence of his dialogue with Ruiz Manero. I have dealt with this in J. J. Moreso, 'Antígona como *defeater*. Sobre el constitucionalismo garantista de Ferrajoli' (2012) 34 Doxa. 183–199 and 'Ethica more iuridico incorporata: Luigi Ferrajoli' (2013) 29 Anuario de filosofía del derecho 161–180.

[13] Riccardo Guastini, in note 6. I criticize these ideas in J. J. Moreso, 'Donde la pala se nos dobla. De nuevo sobre metaética y política' (2013) 3 *Teoria Politica* 287–299.

a *rambla* (with a wide passage for pedestrians in the middle) or as a *boulevard* (with a passage for pedestrians on each side of the road, and the roadway in the middle).[14] It is obvious that in cases like this, something like IMPARTIALITY should be imposed, and it also seems obvious that this demands – in a wide range of cases of disagreement – a decision by majority rule: the only way to equally respect everyone's preferences. It is a controversial matter how many political decisions fall into this range, but it seems obvious that some do: the ordering of priorities and the distribution of resources between health and education, for instance. Given the satisfaction of a certain threshold, the question, for instance, of whether to first finance the construction of a new school or a new health centre, may be a question of preferences that is not resolvable through moral arguments.

However, the fact that the equal consideration of all is a central element of democratic liberalism in no way implies that it is the *only* element. When we argue about including the death penalty in our system of legal sanctions, women's right to vote, universal access to education and healthcare, and also, I believe, the authorization of fox hunting, we argue about moral questions, and in such cases IMPARTIALTY does not help to settle the issue. If we accept that democracy can resolve these issues, then this is not *only* because we believe that equal consideration and respect for everyone's will is crucial, but *also* because we think that democratic procedures, including genuine deliberation that takes into account the opinions of all, increase our capacity to discover morally right answers, because democracy – as argued above – has *epistemic* value.[15] In this sense, the notion of democratic legitimacy presupposes ethical objectivism.[16] It presupposes that, in cases of moral conflict, we have no moral reasons to renounce our own position, and that views that conceive of moral judgements as mere expressions of personal preference are inadequate.

---

[14] The political circumstances of the consultation, which are no longer of any interest, led to a third proposal being imposed, which consisted in leaving the avenue as it was.

[15] Obviously there remains to be resolved the controversial question of whether, to achieve that result, it is better to previously entrench some elements, established as preconditions, such as basic rights, and subtract them from the ordinary political agenda. The vexed question of the justification of judicial review has, as will be obvious, much to do with this. Unfortunately this is not the place to say any more about this problem. But see Andrei Marmor, 'Randomized Judicial Review', in T. Bustamante, B. Gonçalves Fernandes (eds) *Democratizing Constitutional Law* (Springer 2016), ch 2, for a defence of something like IMPARTIALITY, i.e., drawing lots, for decisions on the constitutionality of laws, as a superior alternative to court decisions.

[16] See José Luis Martí, 'Democracia y subjetivismo ético', (2012) 2 *Teoria Politica* 111–136, for a perspicuous argument along these lines.

4. THE DELIBERATIVE INDISPENSABILITY OF THE NORMATIVE

So-called indispensability arguments come from philosophy of mathematics and were first developed by Quine and Putnam.[17] The following formulation of the argument (from Colyvan)[18] can be taken as a starting point:

(P1)   We ought to have ontological commitment to all and only the entities that are indispensable to our best scientific theories.

(P2)   Mathematical entities are indispensable to our best scientific theories.

(C)   We ought to have ontological commitment to mathematical entities.

Similarly, in philosophy of science, the existence of so-called theoretical entities (e.g., electrons and black holes) is accepted because the best explanation of reality offered by physics presupposes this: the existence of these entities, presupposed by our scientific theories, has to be accepted.[19] In general, an indispensability argument is an argument that guarantees the truth of a certain proposition on the basis of the indispensability of that proposition for some established purpose. If the goal, as with the previous argument, is *explanation*, then we can say that it is an explanatory indispensability argument.

In the literature, moreover, it is recognized (55) that arguments to the best explanation – such as arguing for the existence of protons from the fact that our best theories quantify over protons, and we are confident in their truth – are

---

[17] Willard van Orman Quine, 'Things and Their Place in Theories' in W. V. O. Quine, Theories and Things (Harvard University Press 1981) 1–23, Hilary Putnam, 'Philosophy of Logic', reprinted in H. Putnam, Mathematics Matter and Method: Philosophical Papers, Volume 1 (2nd edn, Cambridge University Press 1979) 323–357.

[18] Mark Colyvan, 'Indispensability Arguments in the Philosophy of Mathematics', The Stanford Encyclopedia of Philosophy (Spring 2015 Edition), E. N. Zalta (ed.), URL = http://plato.stanford.edu/archives/spr2019/entries/mathphil-indis/ accessed 14/2/2022.

[19] This is a different argument from what is known as the Moorean argument, which establishes – for instance – that the inference from 'There are natural numbers greater than 100' to 'There are natural numbers' is legitimate. Similarly, from 'Torturing babies for fun is morally wrong' we can infer 'It is a moral fact that it is wrong to torture babies for fun', and thus 'here are moral facts'. Thus we have reason to reject error theories in both mathematics and morality. As will be clear, this argument is in debt to Moore's (G. E. Moore, 'Proof an External World' (1939) 25 *Proceedings of the British Academy* 273–300) argument against scepticism about the existence of the external world. See also e.g., Kit Fine, 'The Question of Realism' (2019) 1 *Philosophers' Imprint* 1: 1–30. Enoch (117–121) uses this argument against error theories in metaethics, but not as a foundation of his defence of robust normative realism. Accordingly, its plausibility will not be analysed here.

really indispensability arguments. However, Enoch (56–67) is aware that the explanatory indispensability of normative entities is controversial: they are not part of what our best scientific theories presuppose. What he wants to show is the *deliberative* indispensability of the normative. That is to say, when I deliberate, for instance, about which school I should enrol my daughter in, I thereby involve myself in a task that presupposes that there is a right answer to that question, and that this answer does not depend on me, but rather that there is some normative truth that makes it right for me to enrol her in one school rather than another. Otherwise, what sense would there be in my deliberating? On the other hand, argues Enoch, deliberation is not optional for agents like us who confront such practical questions. Moreover, deliberating is different from *choosing* (a card from a deck, or a bottle of water in the supermarket from a row of bottles of the same brand and size): when we deliberate, we commit to our decision; we believe it to be the best decision we could take; we eliminate arbitrariness by discovering reasons for our decision.

And in this sense, for Enoch, there is room for arguments from forms of indispensability other than explanatory indispensability: among them, deliberative indispensability. With these ideas in mind, Enoch (83) sets out the following argument:

(1) If something is instrumentally indispensable to an intrinsically indispensable project, then we are (epistemically) justified (for that very reason) in believing that that thing exists.
(2) The deliberative project is intrinsically indispensable.
(3) Irreducibly normative truths are instrumentally indispensable to the deliberative project.
(4) Therefore, we are epistemically justified in believing that there are irreducibly normative truths.

In Chapter 4 Enoch combines the arguments of the two previous chapters to defend *robust moral realism*. He does not argue that the rejection of non-objectivist metaethics and the thesis of the deliberative indispensability of the normative together imply robust moral realism, but that they make it very plausible.[20]

And in Chapter 5 he rejects other positions that promise to deliver the same that robust moral realism offers, but with greater philosophical parsimony: naturalism, fictionalism, error theories and what he calls *quietism*, wherein he

---

[20] Although a sophisticated constructivism about the normative can be combined with an error theory about morality (see Richard Joyce, 'Taking Moral Skepticism Seriously' (2014) 168 *Philosophical Studies* 843–851, at 846, a possibility that Enoch notes but does not discuss (97 n. 16).

situates all those positions that consider metanormative discourse either to be unintelligible (partly) because normative practice does not need any external justification, or else to be first-order normative discourse in disguise. At the end of chapter 2 (27–38), he had already rejected, for not accounting for the objectivity of moral discourse, some constitutive forms of constructivism, and also expressivism.

With these arguments, the overall argument of the book can be summarized as follows, as elegantly put by Faraci (263):[21]

(1) Moral beliefs concern something objective.
(2) If Robust normative facts are indispensable for deliberation, we have some reason to believe in them, and thus to accept Robust Metanormative Realism.
(3) Insofar as we have reason to accept Robust Metanormative Realism, we have reason to accept Robust Metaethical Realism.
(4) Robust normative facts are indispensable for deliberation because alternatives to Robust Realism that are consistent with (1) and with normativity's role in deliberation fail.
(5) None of the metaphysical, epistemological, semantic or psychological objections to Robust Realism are significantly damaging.
(6) Therefore, we have most reason to accept Robust Realism in both metaethics and metanormative theory.

As Faraci argues, almost all philosophers nowadays accept (1). Only those metaethical views that do not account for objectivity remain excluded: eliminativist positions, caricaturized subjectivism, and crude emotivism.[22] I believe that most philosophers would also accept (2): notice that this is a conditional premise, true if its antecedent is false. And a large majority would accept (3), although some (this is part of Mackie's 1977 argument) might accept normative reasons, yet reject robust moral reasons due to the characteristics of those reasons, such as their being categorical, intrinsically linked to moti-

---

[21] David Faraci, 'Book Review: David Enoch, *Taking Morality Seriously. A Defense of Robust Realism*, (Oxford: Oxford University Press, 2011)' (2012) 46 *The Journal of Value Enquiry* 259–267, at 263.

[22] In J. J. Moreso, 'El reino de los derechos y la objetividad de la moral' (2003) 23 *Análisis filosófico* 117–150 and 'El constructivismo ético y el dilema de Eutifrón' in M. Alegre, R. Gargarella and C. Rosenkrantz, *Homenaje a Carlos S. Nino* (La Ley, 2008), 13–21, now in J. J. Moreso, *La Constitución: modelo para armar* (Marcial Pons 2009), ch 4, I try to show why these approaches are not capable of capturing the platitudes that underlie the practice of morality.

vation despite being external, and so on.²³ My doubts concern the plausibility of premises (4) and (5), as will be obvious, and I shall deal with these in the next section.

5. PARSIMONY: *ENTIA NON SUNT MULTIPLICANDA PRAETER NECESSITATEM*

Enoch (53–54) accepts a version of the principle of parsimony: classes of entities should not be multiplied unnecessarily, redundancy should be avoided: a version of Ockham's famed razor. This is a minimal version, since Enoch accepts that only those entities that are indispensable should be accepted, but not only those that are *explanatorily* indispensable, as a stronger version of the principle requires.

The question, then, is whether we need to accept normative truths that commit us to the existence of non-natural facts and properties; that is, whether normative truths (e.g., that babies should not be tortured for fun) presuppose the genuine existence of moral facts and properties among our ontological furniture.

In the literature there have been many attempts to preserve normative truths while rejecting this ontological commitment. The quasi-realist expressivism of Simon Blackburn and the distinction between properties and concepts (drawn by another expressivist, Allan Gibbard)²⁴ are two approaches that promise to deliver moral truths without any corresponding ontological commitment. On the other hand, naturalist moral realism in its various forms tries to show how moral truths are possible, while moral properties are somehow reducible to natural properties.²⁵

Nonetheless, suppose we are persuaded by Enoch's criticisms of these approaches, and that we therefore accept that there such things as *irreducible* moral truths. Does this position ontologically commit us? Must we then accept robust moral realism? In truth, I think we do not have decisive reasons to do

---

²³ See Richard Joyce, 'Metaethical Pluralism: How Both Moral Naturalism and Moral Skepticism May Be Permissible Positions' in S. Natucelli and G. Seay (eds), *Ethical Naturalism: Current Debates* (Cambridge University Press 2012) 89–109 and 'Book Review: *Taking Morality Seriously: A Defense of Robust Realism* by Enoch, David' (2013) 123 *Ethics* 365–369.

²⁴ Simon Blackburn, *Essays in Quasi-Realism* (Oxford University Press 1993), Allan Gibbard, *Thinking How to Live* (Harvard University Press 2003) 29–37.

²⁵ See Mark Schroeder, 'Realism and Reduction: The Quest of Robustness' (2005) 5 (1) *Philosophers' Imprint* 1–18. Enoch himself (109 n. 29, 270) admits his doubts concerning his objections to naturalist reductionism, and leaves open the possibility that some metaethical analogue to anomalous monism in philosophy of mind could turn out to be defensible.

so. To illustrate what I mean here, I shall discuss Enoch's objections to two different approaches: constitutive constructivism and quietism; and I shall argue that his reasons for rejecting these positions are not decisive. Meanwhile, I shall set aside his objections to error theory and fictionalism, although all these metaethical approaches overlap each other, to be sure.[26]

One of Enoch's central arguments against constitutivism is that the rational agency of moral subjects is optional, so this view does not help to ground our moral practice. However, it is not clear why rational agency is optional, while deliberation is indispensable and non-optional, which is an essential premise of Enoch's argument for deliberative indispensability. That is, for Enoch, deliberation is rationally non-optional, and he has presented, as we have seen, good arguments for this; so, it is hard to understand why, in contrast, his criticism of constitutive metaethical constructivism is that rational agency is optional, and so we need an answer for why we must be rational agents after all.[27]

While I sympathize with the plausibility of a constructivist approach in metaethics,[28] these approaches have been subjected to a repeated and detailed critique by Enoch,[29] and for that reason its detailed analysis will have to wait

---

[26] Thus, positions can be contemplated, for instance, that seek an intermediate position between platonist realism and anti-realism (John McDowell, 'Values and Secondary Qualities' in T. Honderich (ed), *Morality and Objectivity* (Routledge & Kegan Paul 1985) 110–129 or that assume a metaethical ambivalence between naturalism and scepticism (Richard Joyce, 'Metaethical Pluralism: How both Moral Naturalism and Moral Skepticism May Be Permissible Positions' in S. Natucelliand G. Seay (eds), *Ethical Naturalism: Current Debates* (Cambridge University Press 2012) 89–109.

[27] See Faraci (n 21), who criticizes this aspect specifically, and James Lenman, 'Deliberation, Schmeliberation: Enoch's Indispensability Argument' (2014) 168 *Philosophical Studies* 835–842 on the presuppositions of indispensability and, in general, Luca Ferrero, 'Constitutivism and the Inescapability of Agency' (2009) 4 *Oxford Studies in Metaethics* 303–333.

[28] See e.g., Moreso, 'El constructivismo ético...' (n 22). An approach that, as is obvious, has its origin in Kantian practical philosophy, and has in modern times been developed by authors like John Rawls ('Kantian Constructivism in Moral Theory' (1982) 77 *Journal of Philosophy* 512–572, Jürgen Habermas *Moral Consciousness and Communicative Ethics* (MIT Press 1986), Carlos S. Nino, *El constructivismo ético* (Centro de Estudios Constitucionales 1989), Christine Korsgaard, *The Sources of Normativity* (Cambridge University Press 1996), or Timothy Scanlon, *What We Owe to Each Other* (Harvard University Press 1998)). See Carla Bagnoli, 'Constructivism in Metaethics', The Stanford Encyclopedia of Philosophy (Spring 2015 Edition), Edward N. Zalta (ed.), URL = http://plato.stanford.edu/archives/spr2021/entries/constructivism-metaethics/ accessed (14/1/2022) for a perspicuous overview.

[29] David Enoch, 'Why Idealize?' (2005) 115 *Ethics* 759–787, 'Agency, Shmagency, Why Normativity Won't Come from What is Constitutive of Agency' (2006) 115 *Philosophical Review* 169–198, 'Rationality, Coherence, Convergence: A Critical

for another occasion. Here I just want to suggest that if, as a premise of the indispensability argument, it can be established that rational deliberation is non-optional, then perhaps there is also a way to consider rational agency to be non-optional, as a premise for ascertaining precisely what we should do, and derive from its constitutive elements the right moral judgements.[30] And, if that were possible, then we could account for the objectivity of morality without committing to the existence of moral facts and properties, in the robust sense postulated by Enoch.

An alternative way to defend the irreducibility of moral truths without assuming a platonist ontology has been developed in the ambit of what Enoch calls *quietism*.[31] As we know, this position holds that ontological claims are internal to their own domain, and insofar as they do not conflict with other domains – especially with the domain of empirical science – their internal validity suffices for their truth, without the need to externally postulate the existence of anything and thus commit oneself ontologically.[32] Enoch (123) argues that in this way – a position close to fictionalism – we can affirm that numbers exist, meaning only that mathematical discourse quantifies over them, given the absence of any conflict between these affirmations and the truths of empirical science. Similarly, we accept the truth of 'Sherlock Holmes lives in London', understood as a truth internal to Conan Doyle's fiction, akin to: 'In Doyle's fiction, Sherlock Holmes lives in London'. There is not just one notion of existence, but rather various notions of existence. There are ways to exist that do not have any causal implications or require the occupation of any spatiotemporal location.

Enoch's criticism (124–125) of such a view is that it does not supply us with an adequate notion of moral truth. We could imagine a process different from deliberation – counter-deliberation – that considers, for instance, causing pain to always be a reason to perform an action, and so on; and this process would

---

Comment on Michael Smith's Ethics and the A Priori' (2007) 48 *Philosophical Books* 99–108 and 'Can there be a Global, Interesting, Coherent Constructivism about Practical Reason?' (2009) 12 *Philosophical Explorations* 319–339.

[30] The possibility of this has recently been defended, with special reference to Enoch's criticisms, by Sharon Street 'What is Constructivism in Ethics and Metaethics?' (2010) 5 *Philosophy Compass* 363–384, and Michael Smith, 'A Constitutivist Theory of Reasons: Its Promise and Parts' (2013) 1 *Law, Ethics and Philosophy* 9–30.

[31] A term that is disliked by the authors to whom it is applied. Enoch (121 n. 70) humorously recounts that Thomas Nagel and Ronald Dworkin affectionately threatened to label proponents of robust moral realism as 'loudists' or 'shoutists'.

[32] Perhaps Ronald Dworkin, 'Objectivity and Truth: You'd Better Believe It', (1996) 25 *Philosophy and Public Affairs* 97–139 and *Justice for Hedgehogs* (Harvard University Press 2011) is the author who has most insisted on the impossibility of adopting that external perspective, the Archimedean point of view, in these affairs.

generate a space of internal reasons which do not conflict with the truths of science, hence we would not be able to deny their existence.

Well, recently Parfit has elaborated a set of arguments for distinguishing between various kinds of existence, where there is room for mathematical and moral truths without ontological commitment.[33]

He starts with an extremely restrictive position:

Fundamentalism: All that exists are the ultimate constituents of reality.

On this view, only subatomic particles exist, and there are no atoms, stars or chairs. As Parfit argues, this is a very implausible view. The fact that many physical objects are *composite*, in the sense that they are made of smaller elements, is consistent with the existence of those objects, which do not exist *separately* from their components.

Another view, less restrictive than the previous one, is:

Actualism: To be, or to exist, is to be actual, so there cannot be anything that is merely possible.

But then, Parfit continues, we would not be able to choose between various possible acts, nor would we have reasons to regret what we have not done, for instance. Since actualism is not plausible either, we must adopt something like:[34]

Possibilism: There are some things that are never actual but are merely possible. There are some things that might happen but never actually happen, and some things that might exist but never actually exist.

Hence Parfit denies that the expressions 'there is' and 'exist' must always be used in the same unique sense, and he adopts a pluralist view according to which there is a restricted sense of 'exist', according to which the things that exist are parts of the spatiotemporal world, while there is also another, broader sense in which there are merely possible acts and things.

The existence of possible worlds is obviously a highly controversial issue in philosophy, and I bring it up here only to show how Parfit argues that there are other candidates for existence – like numbers, propositions, logical truths and normative reasons – that do not exist in any of the previous senses.

---

[33] Derek Parfit, *On What Matters* vol 2 (Oxford University Press 2011) 464–487.
[34] Ibid., 467.

Let us start with numbers and mathematical truths. According to Parfit:[35]

> Some examples, I suggest, are mathematical truths. Nothing could be truer than the truths that 2 is greater than 1, that $2 + 2 = 4$, and that there are prime numbers greater than 100. Not even God could make these claims false. For such claims to be true, there must be a sense in which there are numbers, or in which numbers exist. But in deciding which mathematical claims are true, we don't need to answer the question whether numbers really exist in an ontological sense, though not in space or time. Similar remarks apply to some other abstract entities, such as logical truths and valid arguments. In deciding whether certain claims state such truths or arguments, we don't need to ask whether these truths or arguments exist in an ontological sense.

And this is also the kind of existence that is had by normative facts and reasons that lack ontological status:[36]

> There are some claims that are irreducibly normative in the reason-involving sense, and are in the strongest sense true. But these truths have no ontological implications. For such claims to be true, these reason-involving properties need not exist either as natural properties in the spatio-temporal world, or in some non-spatio-temporal part of reality.

This is a position that rejects naturalism, a position that is cognitivist and rationalist, but not a metaphysically committed position. It is what Parfit calls *non-metaphysical non-naturalist normative* cognitivism.

If this is an ontologically plausible view,[37] then there are irreducible normative truths without any commitment to robust realism, and without any ontological commitment. Obviously, to show this to be an ontologically plausible view, it has to be shown that moral practice produces objective judgements on which rational and reasonable agents would converge. And to do that, we would need a detailed analysis of Parfit's impressive contribution, in debate with other great contributions to the foundations of ethics: something that is beyond the purpose of the present contribution. Here it suffices to say that there are approaches, like that of Parfit, which leave room for irreducible normative truths without *robust* normative facts, and that there is room for

---

[35] Ibid., 479–480.
[36] Ibid., 486.
[37] This has been denied, for instance, by Enoch (121–133), Tristram McPherson, 'Against Quietist Normative Realism' (2011) 154 *Philosophical Studies* 223–240, Sara McGrath, 'Relax? Don't Do It! Why Realism Won't Come Cheap,' in R. Shafer-Landau (ed), *Oxford Studies in Metaethics*, Volume 9 (OUP 2014) 186–214 and David Wodak, 'Why Realists Must Reject Normative Quietism' (2017) 174 *Philosophical Studies* 2795–2817.

moral objectivity without *platonism*, just as there is room for the objectivity of mathematics without platonism.

6. CONCLUSION: OBJECTIVITY AND THE PRINCIPLE OF TOLERANCE

Enoch's important contribution, in my opinion, offers us good reasons to reject metaethical views that fail to account for the *objectivity* of moral practice. I know no rational person who holds that it is right to torture babies for fun, and this is a good reason to believe in the objective truth of the opposing claim: a truth that does not depend on our beliefs and present desires.

However, that his arguments in defence of that objectivity must be founded on robust moral realism, on the existence of non-natural facts and properties, seems more questionable to me. After all, mathematical practice and its objectivity do not seem at all threatened by the fact that philosophers of mathematics continue to debate whether the ontological foundations of that practice commit us to platonism, or whether some kind of constructivist or fictionalist approach may suffice. Similarly, in metaethics we can keep arguing about the best ontological foundations for morality, because if we guarantee the objectivity of that practice, then our debates in normative ethics can be subject to rationality. We can practice, ecumenically, what Carnap[38] – in reference to philosophy of mathematics – once called the *principle of tolerance*:

> This neutral attitude toward the various philosophical forms of language, based on the principle that everyone is free to use the language most suited to his purpose, has remained the same throughout my life. It was formulated as 'principle of tolerance' in *Logical Syntax* and I still hold it today, e.g., with respect to the contemporary controversy about a nominalist or Platonic language.

After all, whatever our metaethical position, if we are objectivists then we shall consider the moral correctness or incorrectness of, for instance, bombing territories controlled by ISIS in the Middle East, to uniquely depend on the adequacy of the reasons adduced for or against that action. And no one is in a better position than anyone else for that purpose just by the fact of ascribing to one or another of the metaethical views that guarantee the objectivity of our moral practice.

---

[38] Rudolf Carnap, 'Intellectual Autobiography', in Paul Arthur Schilpp (ed) *The Philosophy of Rudolf Carnap*, The Library of Living Philosophers, vol. 11 (Open Court 1963) 1–84, 18.

14. Virtue and objectivity in legal reasoning[1]
Amalia Amaya

1. INTRODUCTION

In the last years, legal scholars have deployed virtue theory to address a number of different problems, including, prominently, legal reasoning.[2] A virtue approach to legal reasoning places virtues, rather than rules or consequences, at the center of the theory. Despite crucial differences, both deontological and consequentialist theories of legal reasoning are principle-based, in that they understand legal reasoning as involving first and foremost the application of a number of principles (of the law, of political morality, of utility) to the particular case. They also share an orientation toward the object insofar as they focus on the analysis of the conditions under which legal decisions are justified and take properties of subjects to be largely irrelevant for the purposes of evaluating legal argument. In contrast, a virtue theory of legal reasoning is agent-centered and explains the epistemic status of legal judgments as a function of the subjective qualities of legal decision-makers.

---

[1] I am deeply thankful to Maksymilian Del Mar and the editors of this volume for valuable comments on an earlier draft.

[2] For a brief introduction to virtue jurisprudence see, Amalia Amaya, 'Law and Virtue Theory' in Mortimer Sellers and Stephan Kirste (eds), *Encyclopedia of the Philosophy of Law and Social Philosophy* (Springer 2019). Edited collections in virtue jurisprudence include Colin Farrelly and Lawrence Solum, *Virtue Jurisprudence* (Palgrave MacMillan 2008); Amalia Amaya and Hock Lai Ho, *Virtue, Law and Justice* (Hart Publishing 2012); and Amalia Amaya and Claudio Michelon, *The Faces of Virtue in Law* (Routledge 2018). For an introduction to virtue in legal reasoning, see Claudio Michelon, 'Practical Wisdom in Legal Decision-Making' in Amalia Amaya and Hock Lai Ho, ibid., 29–51 and Claudio Michelon, 'Legal Reasoning (virtues)' in Mortimer Sellers and Stephan Kirste, ibid.; and Amalia Amaya, 'Virtue and Reason in Law' in Maksymilian del Mar (ed), *New Waves in Philosophy of Law* (Palgrave MacMillan 2011) 123–145. For an edited collection that focuses on virtue in legal reasoning, see Amalia Amaya and Makysmilian Del Mar (eds), *Virtue, Emotion and Imagination in Law and Legal Reasoning* (Hart Publishing 2020).

Virtue theories of legal reasoning have been recently objected on the grounds that they introduce 'subjectivity' in legal decision-making.[3] In this chapter, I shall argue that, contrary to what the critics claim, a virtue approach to legal reasoning does not render legal reasoning subjective, it does, however, put forward a different conception of objectivity than the conception, which underwrites principle-based approaches in their different varieties, according to which objectivity results from deploying impersonal methods. Instead, a virtue theory of legal reasoning claims that subjective features of legal decision-makers are partially constitutive of the objectivity of legal judgments. More specifically, the virtuous judge, in this view, provides an objective standard for evaluating legal judgment. In contrast to the methodical conception of objectivity, which effaces the subject, this conception of objectivity is affectively loaded, contextually situated, and thoroughly embodied. Although this conception repudiates some features that are traditionally associated with objectivity, it remains, I will argue, significantly opposed to subjectivism and relativism. Hence, in advancing this conception, a virtue theory of legal reasoning articulates an alternative view of objectivity, rather than merely changing subject or abandoning the ideal all together.

The argument will proceed as follows. Section 2 examines the 'methodical' view of objectivity that is generally assumed in studies on legal reasoning – by both those who vindicate the objectivity of legal judgment and their critics. I shall suggest some reasons why this conception has been viewed as attractive and argue that it fails to provide a plausible normative standard for evaluating and assessing legal judgments. Next, in section 3, I will examine the conception of objectivity that underwrites a virtue approach to legal reasoning, which takes objectivity to be a function of personal virtue. Against this 'dialectical' view, it may be argued that it fails to provide a standard for objectively evaluating legal judgments given the prevalence of normative conflict (both among and within the virtuous). I shall examine the objection from relativism in section 4 and argue that even though it fails to undermine the objectivity of virtuous judgment, its examination is instructive as it suggests the plausibility of developing a pluralistic version of virtue jurisprudence.

2. METHODICAL OBJECTIVITY AND SUBJECT-LESS LEGAL REASONING

The ideal of objectivity in legal reasoning has been understood, in a very powerful and influential rendition of this ideal, as the aspiration to eliminate the

---

[3] See Catherine Elgin, 'Impartiality and Legal Reasoning' in Amalia Amaya and Makysmilian Del Mar, ibid., 47–59.

subjectivity of legal decision-makers, as much as this is possible, from legal judgment.[4] The objectivity of legal decisions, in this view, is a function of the success at effacing the subject from the process of legal decision-making. Legal reasoning without subjects is thus, on this approach, what objectivity in law requires. The view that objective legal reasoning is self-less legal reasoning is latent in very well-known images about how the law should operate. That judges are the mouth of the law, the depiction of the law as a perpetuum mobile, and the representation of justice as blind, all point towards the ideal of eliminating the legal subject from law's operations.[5] The assumption that objectivity involves the extirpation of the self is so deeply rooted in legal thought that it is even active in critiques of these images of the law – which are used as parts of a general critique of law's claim to objectivity. This conception of objectivity as self-effacement is at the core of judges' own views of the judicial role as well. It is also of a piece with historical conceptions of the judge as an automaton, but, more interestingly, it underwrites both formalist and activist contemporary views on the judicial function. For, again, the plea for judicial activism is oftentimes embedded in a critique of legal rationality that assumes (and subsequently repudiates) a view of objectivity as self-detachment.

In this widely shared view of legal objectivity, the quest for objectivity is a search for a method that could secure the objectivity of legal judgements, to the extent that this is possible, irrespective of the subjective qualities of the subjects who apply those methods. Once the possibility of explaining legal decision-making as the mechanical operation of deduction is thought to be unrealizable (if it ever was viewed otherwise),[6] increasingly more sophisticated conceptions of the legal method are proposed that could guarantee, when possible, de-subjectivized legal judgments. The traditional methods

---

[4] See Jaap Hage, in this volume, arguing that much of the literature on decision making can be read as dealing with the balance between 'objective' and 'subjective' approaches to law application and interpretation. Cf. Renata Grossi, 'Law, Emotion and the Objectivity Debate' (2019) 28 *Griffith Law Review* 23-36 and Douglas E. Edlin, *Common Law Judging: Subjectivity, Impartiality and the Making of the Law* (University of Michigan 2016), for arguments against the conventional understanding of objectivity in legal reasoning as opposed to subjectivity.

[5] These three images vividly represent the ideal of objectivity as 'blind sight, seeing without inference, interpretation or intelligence.' See Lorraine Daston and Peter Galison, *Objectivity* (Zone Books 2007) 17. On the, perhaps, less familiar idea of the law as a perpetuum mobile, see Carlos Pereda, *Razón e incertidumbre* (Siglo XXI 1994). This is not to say that these images can be reduced to being representations of objectivity, as they are visual devices that have a rich meaning and a complicated history. I thank Maksymilian del Mar for this point.

[6] See Fernando Atria, *La forma del derecho* (Marcial Pons 2016) (who argues, contrary to conventional wisdom, that 18th and 19th century jurists did not hold the belief that the law could be mechanically applied).

of interpretation of legal dogmatics aim at delivering legal judgments that are untainted by personal factors, as do the forms of inference discussed in rule-based approaches to legal reasoning. A similar objective drives Dworkinian approaches to legal reasoning, for Herculean adjudication is also, in an important sense, faceless adjudication, in that it relies on a method of interpretation the correct operation of which is (largely) independent of judges' personal characteristics (more on this in a moment).

The 'methodical' conception of objectivity, which locates objectivity in the impartial application of methods, is not idiosyncratic to law, but enjoys a prominent place in different knowledge domains as it is, in an important sense, a defining feature of modern conceptions of knowledge.[7] The disengagement of knowledge from subject, however, as much in law as everywhere else, is not complete. The methodical view of objectivity is more accurately viewed as incorporating a thin concept of the self, rather than as fully eliminating selfhood. Indeed, some features of the self are retained as relevant for the enterprise of seeking objective knowledge. Critically, some cognitive capacities and dispositions (most importantly, impartiality) of subjects are taken to be necessary for objectivity. For example, scientific objectivity is claimed to result from the operation of the scientific method by scientists who have the competence that is needed to deploy it properly.[8] Similarly, in law, legal methods are claimed to secure objectivity, provided that those in charge of applying those methods have the required skills and experience.[9] Dworkin allows for a thicker self as he bestows on his ideal decision-maker a number of attributes, mostly of a cognitive nature, such as acumen, intelligence, and

---

[7] Lynn Holt, *Apprehension: Reason in the Absence of Rules* (Ashgate 2002), for a critique of 'methodism', or the replacement of virtue by method, which is thought to secure objectivity as detachment. On the idea that modern conceptions of scientific knowledge locate objectivity in the scientific method thereby disengaging scientific knowledge from the character of scientists, see Steven Shapin, *A Social History of Truth: Civiliy and Science in Seventeenth-Century England* (The University of Chicago Press 1994) and *The Scientific Life: A Moral History of a Late Modern Vocation* (The University of Chicago Press 2008).

[8] See Daston and Galison (n 5) 39 (arguing that modern science retains certain personal qualifications as important for reaching objective judgments, but these qualities are viewed as matters of competence, rather than ethics).

[9] For example, Coleman and Leiter explicitly claim that the conception of modest objectivity they advocate 'involves the substantial (but not total) absence of subjectivity', for the ideal conditions for rendering judgments incorporate aspects of subjective experience. Thus, subjectivity is allowed in but only insofar as it is necessary to render judgement under ideal conditions. Jules Coleman and Brian Leiter 'Determinacy, Objectivity and Authority' (1993) 141 *University of Pennsylvania Law Review* 623 and 635.

patience, but his method of interpretation similarly excludes the relevance of personality in a more robust sense.[10]

Thus, the methodical conception of objectivity is not fully agent-independent, for some cognitive abilities are taken to be necessary to secure the objectivity of the outcomes of methods. However, other than a few selected features, which enable the impartial operation of methods, objectivity requires, in this conception, the banishing of the self. Furthermore, it is assumed that the interference of any personal quality beyond the technical and cognitive abilities required to successfully deploy the methods is not merely irrelevant for the purposes of assessing the objectivity of its outcomes but rather detrimental. Insofar as personal qualities are allowed to influence outcomes – so this conception holds – these outcomes can hardly be claimed to be objective, as they are the product of bias and idiosyncrasy.

A perspicuous defence of the methodical conception of objective legal judgement has been recently provided by Catherine Elgin. Conscious that an 'impersonal, wholly rule-based approach to legal reasoning is too impoverished to serve', she suggests that we devise 'impartial but not impersonal methods'.[11] These methods, she says, are not wholly agent-independent in that their findings are justified by inter-subjective agreement of 'qualified people' that use the method, but they are impartial in that 'it does not matter exactly who those qualify people are'.[12] This is the way, she claims, in which even though 'agents are ineliminably involved', we control for 'bias and idiosyncrasy'.[13] Despite her claim that she is advocating a 'personal' method, Elgin's view clearly illustrates the main commitments involved in the methodical view of objectivity. Technical expertise is the only subjective feature that, in addition to impartiality, is viewed as contributing to the objectivity of outcomes. Should we allow for any other personal factor to get it, bias and idiosyncrasy would issue. Furthermore, it is only because it is unavoidable – it seems – that this thin agency is allowed to play a role in the process. Given the impossibility of a 'mechanical jurisprudence' – or the complete uprooting of the self, we set for methodical objectivity – and eliminate the self as much as this is possible.

What motivates the proposal and persistent attraction of methodical views of objectivity in law? A first driving force of the methodical conception of legal objectivity is the felt need to counteract bias and arbitrariness in legal decision-making. There are, to be sure, historical reasons to be wary of unbounded models of judicial decision-making. The modern conception of

---

[10] Ronald Dworkin, *Taking Rights Seriously* (Harvard University Press 1977) 105.
[11] Elgin (n 3) 53.
[12] Ibid., 53.
[13] Ibid., 55.

the judicial function, which aspires to make judges invisible and, to the extent that this is possible, negligible for the successful application of the law, came about, in an important sense, as a reaction to the arbitrariness involved in the administration of justice of the Ancient Regime.[14] Legal methods, insofar as they provide an algorithmic procedure for legal decision-making, hold the promise of delivering legal judgements that are shielded from bias, whim and irrationality.

A second source for the appeal of the methodical conception of objectivity is scientism – i.e., the view that scientific knowledge is the only legitimate form of knowledge.[15] The history of legal theory and legal dogmatics have witnessed repeated efforts to understand law on the model of science, conceive law as a form of science, and develop approaches to legal reasoning that have the defining features of scientific forms of inference.[16] Surely, by itself, scientism does not render a methodical conception of objectivity plausible. It only does so by conjoining the (scientistic) claim that to be valuable legal knowledge should reproduce the characteristics of scientific knowledge with the further claim that scientific objectivity is a function of the scientific method. From these two assumptions it is then reasoned that the objectivity of legal judgments similarly depends on the extent to which legal reasoning is algorithmic reasoning.

A third reason which favours a methodical conception of objectivity is the traditional division between psychology and logic and, relatedly, discovery and justification.[17] These divisions allow for a neat separation between nor-

---

[14] See Atria (n 6) (for a discussion of the 'cycle of adjudication' or adjudication as a 'pendulum' that moves from one extreme to another as a reaction to the problems encountered on one of the extremes).

[15] See J. De Ridder, R. Peels and R. Woudenberg, *Scientism: Prospects and Problems* (Oxford University Press 2016).

[16] To historical forms of scientism in law, such as the 'mechanical jurisprudence' so famously criticized by Pound, one may add a similarly rich array of contemporary efforts, such as Bayesian models of legal proof or the ambition to develop all-encompassing AI models of legal decision-making. See Roscoe Pound, 'Mechanical Jurisprudence' (1908) 8 *Columbia Law Review*. That objectivity in law should be understood on the model of the natural sciences is explicitly argued by Brian Leiter 'Naturalism, Morality and Adjudication' in Brian Leiter, *Naturalizing Jurisprudence* (Oxford University Press 2007).

[17] A sharp division between epistemology and psychology is, as Haack argues, a main reason for Popper's exclusion of the knowing subject. See Susan Haack, 'Epistemology without a Knowing Subject' (1979) 33 *The Review of Metaphysics* 331 and Susan Haack, 'Personal or Impersonal Knowledge' (2019) 13 *Journal of Philosophical Investigations*, 24–25. Similarly, Kuhn also takes adherence to the distinction between discovery and justification to be a reason for the position that subjective factors are inimical to the objectivity of scientific knowledge. See Thomas S.

mative issues – as questions that pertain to the context of justification and are the proper object of logic – and empirical ones – which arise in the context of discovery and are the province of psychology. Objectivity and subjectivity are, in this picture, watertight compartments, whereas the subjectivity of decision-makers is enclosed in the empirical domain, the objectivity of legal judgments is placed in the normative one. A view of objectivity as the outcome of methods that give the right results irrespective of who uses them fits well with this picture of subjectivity and of how subjectivity and objectivity relate to each other in that it relegates subjectivity to the psychology of legal decision-making and isolates it from the logic of legal reasoning, where objectivity resides.

However, the three assumptions that apparently confer plausibility to the methodical conception of objectivity do not unproblematically obtain. First, subjectivity does not amount to arbitrariness and bias. While bias is always subjective, subjectivity is not always biased.[18] Thus, the laudable task of rendering legal judgments objective by eliminating bias and irrationality does not require that all forms of subjectivity be eliminated.

Secondly, scientism embodies an extremely reductive and impoverished view of the variety of forms of knowledge.[19] In addition, it involves a highly disputable view according to which the initially plausible claim that there should be continuity among diverse forms of knowledge translates into a justification of the imperialism of science – i.e., that the unity of knowledge should be established by fitting all forms of knowledge into the scientific mould. Moreover, even if scientific knowledge were to enjoy a place of privilege in the epistemological landscape, still this would not provide any definite support for the methodical view of legal objectivity, as the claim that objectivity enters science through the scientific method – which, as argued, is needed for scientism to provide any support to the methodical conception of legal objectivity – is also highly contested.[20]

Kuhn, 'Objectivity, Value Judgement and Theory Choice' in Thomas S. Kuhn, *The Essential Tension: Selected Studies in the Scientific Tradition and Change* (University of Chicago Press 1977) 360.

[18] See Moira Howes, 'Objectivity, Intellectual Virtue and Community' in Flavia Padovani, Alan Richardson and Jonathan Y. Tsou (eds) *Objectivity in Science*, Boston Studies in the Philosophy and History of Science (Springer 2015), 178–179 (arguing against the identification of subjectivity with bias, to the exclusion of the 'right kinds of subjective experience,' which contribute to objectivity).

[19] See De Ridder et al. (n 15).

[20] See Haack, 'Epistemology without a Knowing Subject' (n 17) (arguing against Popper's defence of an epistemology without a knowing subject and for an epistemology that involves both the subject and content of knowledge); Haack, 'Personal and Impersonal Knowledge' (n 17) (contrasting Popper's subjectless epistemology with

Last, while this is not the place to review the many ways in which the division between psychology and logic, discovery and justification, and fact and value has been the object of criticism, it seems safe to conclude that a strict division of labour between the empirical and the normative domain may no longer be viewed as sustainable.[21] Incidentally, the breakdown of these traditional dichotomies transforms the strict dichotomy between subjective/objective into a kind of outlier, a rare survivor from contemporary criticism in contemporary legal and philosophical theorizing.

Hence, the main strategies that are usually deployed to prompt adherence to the methodical conception of objectivity, and the displacement of subjectivity it carries with it, depend for their success on a number of highly questionable assumptions. There is yet another major obstacle that prevents it from delivering a viable normative standard against which to assess the objectivity of legal judgments. As is well known, methods – no matter no sophisticated – do not suffice to provide determinate guidance in a non-negligible number of cases. Criteria of interpretation are vague and ambiguous; they may be in conflict with one another; it may be unclear how they should be applied to the case at hand or whether they should be applied to the case at hand at all; there are cases in which the outcome of applying a method of interpretation yields absurd or unjust results; there are also cases in which a method delivers several outcomes, all of which are regarded as unsatisfactory; the outcomes of any method are dependent on the adequacy of the input and its correct computation; and no method of interpretation can secure its own application. Hence, indeterminacy, over-determination, underdetermination, the ever-present possibility of exceptions, misapplication and inapplicability show that methods are not sufficient to provide an objective standard against which to evaluate legal judgments.[22]

Polanyi's personal epistemology); Kuhn (n 17) (arguing that objectivity cannot enter in science through method to the exclusion of personal factors); David J. Stump, 'Pierre's Duhem Virtue Epistemology' (2006) 38 *Studies in History and Philosophy of Science*, 149 (claiming that in Duhem's account of scientific theory choice, the scientist, who has 'good sense,' is the source of objectivity).

[21] Indeed, the unfeasibility of this division of labour provides an important reason for vindicating the relevance of subjective features to the acquisition of objective knowledge. See Haack, 'Personal and Impersonal Knowledge' (n 17), 25 (arguing that Polanyi's scepticism about this distinction is an important source for his personal epistemology). See Michelon (n 2) (for an argument to the effect that the lack of a sharp distinction between discovery and justification in the legal domain opens up the possibility of viewing subjective traits of legal decision makers as contributing to the objectivity of legal judgments).

[22] Amalia Amaya, 'Virtuous Adjudication; or the Relevance of Judicial Character to Legal Interpretation' (2018) 40 *Statute Law Review* 87.

Of course, the limits of methods are no news. The acknowledgment that the practical outstrips algorithmic procedures has given rise, however, to different reactions. Some, usually associated with positivist approaches to law and adjudication, have responded by limiting the scope of objectivity: legal objectivity can only be secured in some cases that are clearly resolvable by the applicable rule. Beyond a point there are no objectively correct legal answers – there still may be objectively correct moral answers, or just no objective answers at all.[23] In contrast, others – in a Dworkinian spirit – vindicate the possibility of reaching objective legal judgments in all except a few cases that are thought to be unimportant from a practical standpoint.[24] Coherence methods, however, are, like any other method, limited in that they are also subject to the problems abovementioned.[25] The limits of methods lead others, most prominently, critical legal theorists, to question that legal objectivity is a realizable ideal or even a desirable one.[26]

Alternatively, I would argue, the acknowledgment that methods do not suffice to provide the needed guidance in a substantial number of cases does not show that objectivity should be expected of some judgments but not others, to deny its limitations, or to conclude that it should be abandoned. Instead, one might want to question whether the fact that a conception of objectivity is unattainable should not tell against that claim that it provides an appropriate standard for guiding and evaluating legal judgments. In other words, that there are different (and important) types of cases in which the methodological rules do not lead to objectively correct results does not show the limits of objectivity, but rather the inappropriateness of a conception that makes such rules the site of objectivity. Furthermore, once we free methods from the burden of furnishing a full-blown conception of objectivity, we may come to envisage that perhaps some of the alleged imperfections of methodological rules, from which the supposed limits of objectivity derive, may turn out to be features that are necessitated by the very nature of the decision-making task, as a cognitive activity that is meant to satisfactorily respond to the plurality of value as well as complex (and unexpected) configurations of facts. Thus, the suggestion is

---

[23] When legal positivism is combined with ethical subjectivism, see Matti I. Niemi 'Objective Legal Reasoning – Objectivity without Objects' in Jaakko Husa and Mark Van Hoecke (eds) *Objectivity in Law and Legal Reasoning* (Hart Publishing 2013) 69.

[24] See Ronald Dworkin, 'No Right Answer?' in P. M. S. Hacker and J. Raz (eds), *Law, Morality and Society* (Clarendon Press 1972), 75–76 and 83–84.

[25] Amalia Amaya, *The Tapestry of Reason: An Inquiry into the Nature of Coherence and its Role in Legal Argument* (Hart Publishing 2015) (for an argument to the effect that coherence methods may result in objectively justified outcomes only provided that a condition of character obtains on those who deploy those methods).

[26] For a snapshot of critical approaches to objectivity in law, see Grossi (n 4), 4–5.

that the limits of methods provide an argument not for the limits of objectivity in legal reasoning but rather for the need to articulate an alternative conception of objectivity.[27] This is what I purport to do in the next section.

3. DIALECTICAL OBJECTIVITY AND VIRTUOUS LEGAL REASONING

The quest for objectivity as a good that methods may deliver, irrespective of the properties of the agents who use them, turned out to have, as argued before, pernicious effects. It led to the transfiguration of the limits of methods into limits of objectivity, if not to the outright rejection of the ideal of objectivity. The idea that objectivity enters into legal decision-making through procedures also leads to a negative appraisal of both methods (as imperfect tools) and subjects (as threats to objectivity). Insofar as the imperfections of methods are ineliminable, so are the subjective factors, and thus objectivity is doomed to remain forever an ideal that is only partially, if at all, achievable. This detracts from its normative force – if 'ought' implies 'can' – and makes it suspect as an ideal that might help to regulate and evaluate legal argument. Alternatively, and much more positively, we could envision both methods and subjects as valuable in that they jointly contribute to establishing the objectivity of legal judgments. In this 'dialectical' conception of objectivity, objectivity is partly located in the subject; subjectivity is thus retrieved as an important constitutive factor of objectivity, rather than being opposed to objectivity.[28]

To be sure, not every subjective feature of agents stands in a positive relation to objectivity. Virtue theory, I would like to suggest, may help flesh out a dialectical conception of objectivity by furnishing criteria to tell apart the subjective factors that contribute to the objectivity of decisions from those that are detrimental to it.[29] On a virtue approach, the virtuous person provides

---

[27] See Kuhn (n 17), 366 (claiming that the fact that criteria for theory choice, on which the objectivity of scientific judgment is claimed to be analysable, does not supply the expected guidance shows the need to rethink the meaning of objectivity, rather than its limits).

[28] See Guy Axtell, 'The Dialectics of Objectivity' (2012) 6 *Journal of the Philosophy of History* 339. For a dialectical conception of objectivity about historical knowledge, see Jon A. Levisohn, 'Negotiating Historical Narratives: An Epistemology of History for History Education' (2010) 44 *Journal of Philosophy of Education* 1, and Herman Paul, 'Performing History: How Historical Scholarship is Shaped by Epistemic Virtues' (2011) 50 *History and Theory* 1. Daston and Galison's monumental work about the history of objectivity, as being tied up to the history of the scientific self, also assumes a dialectical view of objectivity. See Daston and Galison (n 5).

[29] That virtue theory and the dialectical approach support each other is argued in Axtell, ibid.

an objective standard of correctedness.[30] That is to say, virtuous judgments, i.e., the judgments that could have been taken by a virtuous decision-maker are, in this view, objective judgments.[31] The virtue standard of objectivity is agent-dependent, in that properties of agents are relevant to determining the objectivity of judgments. It is critical to note that in this approach, as in methodical objectivity, objectivity is still claimed to be a property of objects, rather than persons. More radically, other virtue approaches depart from this assumption and take objectivity to be a personal attribute.[32] In contrast, objectivity in the virtue-based approach advanced here is a theory virtue, which is partly constituted by personal virtues.[33]

This virtue-based approach to objectivity diverges from the methodical conception of objectivity in important respects. First, in the virtue approach, objectivity is not an abstract ideal but an embodied one. Despite the reference to 'the virtuous person,' since Aristotle, exemplars are taken to be not merely illustrative of the standard, but it is central for its success that it is an ideal that is incarnated in actual people.[34] Secondly, it is an ideal that is affectively loaded. Virtue, again since Aristotle, is both a matter of action and feeling.[35] Dispassionateness is not, in this view, a requirement of objectivity.[36] Rather, the engagement of the virtuous person's emotional capacities contributes,

---

[30] See Bridget Clarke, 'Virtue as Sensitivity' in Nancy Snow (ed) *The Oxford Handbook of Virtue* (Oxford University Press 2018) 9. For a thorough discussion of the virtuous person as the standard of practical reason, see Daniel G. Russell, *Practical Intelligence and the Virtues* (Oxford University Press 2009) ch. 4.

[31] A virtuous decision-maker has a large share of the traits of character that are virtues in the specific decision-making domain, where those traits are identified by its serviceability to the ends of the profession, which should involve a commitment to key human goods. See Justin Oakley and Dean Cocking, *Virtue Ethics and Professional Roles* (Cambridge University Press 2009).

[32] For a conceptualization of objectivity as a personal virtue, see Christine Swanton, *Virtue Ethics: A Pluralist View* (Oxford University Press, 2003); José Ángel Gascón, 'Pursuing Objectivity: How Virtuous Can you Get?' in Patrick Bondy and Laura Benacquista (eds) *Argumentation, Objectivity and Bias: Proceedings of the 11th International Conference of the Ontario Society for the Study of Argumentation* (2016) 1, and Howes (n 18).

[33] On the distinction between theory virtues and personal virtues, see Axtell (n 28).

[34] See Timothy Chappell, 'The Good Man is the Measure of All Things: Objectivity without World-Centredness in Aristotle's Moral Epistemology' in Christopher Gill (ed) *Virtue, Norms and Objectivity: Issues in Ancient and Modern Ethics* (Oxford University Press 2005), 45.

[35] On the emotional aspects of (Aristotelian) virtue, see Nancy Sherman, *Making Necessity a Virtue: Aristotle and Kant on Virtue* (Cambridge University Press 1997), ch. 2 and Rosalind Hursthouse, *On Virtue Ethics* (Oxford University Press 1999), ch. 5.

[36] Dispassionateness has been taken to be central to standard accounts of objectivity, see Lisa M. Heldke and Stephen H. Keller, 'Objectivity as Responsibility' (1995)

rather than detracts, from the objectivity of judgment. Lastly, objectivity is claimed to be contextually situated, rather than context transcendent.[37] Context-sensitivity is a defining characteristic of virtuous judgment. It is inimical to the nature of virtue that its deliverances should be correct for all situations, in all times, and in every circumstance.[38]

In short, on a virtue approach, self-detachment is not the mark of objectivity, rather the (virtuous) self is viewed as constitutive of objectivity. Objectivity is not the result of exiling the subject and placing objectivity in methods, not even in those that would be deployed in ideal inquiry.[39] Neither does it require that we strip agents from their personal attributes – as in views that replace ideal inquiry by an ideal inquirer by positing an agent-dependent standard of objectivity that abstracts away from personal features and circumstances.[40] Nor are personal characteristics let in but only insofar as they are necessary to ensure the competent and impartial application of methods, which are the real sites of objectivity. In the virtue approach to objectivity, the self is embraced in

---

26 *Metaphilosophy* 373. That objectivity requires absence of emotion is also a common feature of accounts of legal objectivity, see Grossi (n 4).

[37] A prominent conception of objectivity takes it to require independence from cultural, historical or personal perspectives. See Heldke and Keller, ibid., 371.

[38] This is not to say the virtue theory is particularistic in the sense of preventing rules from playing an important role in legal reasoning.

[39] As in views that take objectivity to obtain under ideal conditions – what Leiter calls 'modest objectivism'. See Brian Leiter, 'Law and Objectivity' in Jules L. Coleman, Kenneth Einar Himma and Scott J. Shapiro (eds) *The Oxford Handbook of Jurisprudence and Philosophy of Law* (Oxford University Press 2004) 971 and Coleman and Leiter (n 9).

[40] Like in approaches that tie up objectivity to ideal agents, rather than embodied ones, e.g., the 'impartial spectator.' Cf. Makymilian Del Mar, 'Common Virtue and the Perspectival Imagination: Adam Smith and Common Sense Reasoning' in Amaya and Michelon (n 2) (for an interpretation Smith's impartial spectator as the embodiment of an ordinary, rather than an ideal, observer). Arguably, Dworkin's Hercules, as discussed above, provides a prominent example of attempts to explain objectivity in terms of idealized subjects as well. Virtue theorists also feel attracted to the idea of locating objectivity in abstract ideals, such as the ideal of 'the virtuous person,' the 'spoudaios' or the 'phronimos,' which, even if they do not abstract away from human capabilities, lack the embodiment and concreteness of exemplars. See George Duke, 'The Aristotelian Spoudaios as Ethical Exemplar in Finnis' Natural Law Theory' (2013) 58 *The American Journal of Jurisprudence* 183, and Russell (n 30), ch. 4. As in ethics, in science the idea that abstract agents may provide a virtue standard for objective judgment has also been found appealing. See Milena Ivanova, 'Pierre Duhem's Good Sense as a Guide to Theory Choice' (2010) 41 *Studies in History and Philosophy of Science* 58 (arguing that 'good sense,' which is a condition of scientific knowledge, is best understood in terms of the virtues of a 'perfect,' 'ideal,' scientist, with exemplars such as Newton providing only 'traces' of the perfect scientist).

all its richness and particularity.[41] It is because of, and not despite, her embodiment, cognitive and emotional capacities as well as historical and contextual situatedness that the virtuous person perspective is claimed to be an objective one.

Despite differences, the virtue-based standard of objectivity preserves some key commitments which have been traditionally associated with objectivity (and which also figure in the methodological conception of objectivity). First, on a virtue approach, objectivity requires impartiality.[42] This is an important epistemic and moral virtue that an exemplary judge is expected to possess and exercise in the exercise of her functions.[43] It is important to note though that the conception of impartiality that a virtue standard of objectivity incorporates is not one that demands the judge to self-distance from the parties' plight but rather it requires her to reason about the case in an emotionally engaged manner. That is to say, empathy, in this approach, is not in tension with impartiality in judging.[44] It does require though a disposition to equally hear arguments in favour and against alternative views about the case, to seriously

---

[41] If virtue's deliverances, as argued by Clarke, are individualized, in the sense that 'the judgments that issue from it are formed and framed by the penumbra of images, associations, aspirations, and memories of the agent, as well as his more fully conscious commitments,' then it follows that legal judgments will not be detached from the judge's 'deepest sense of self.' (Clarke (n 30), 23. This is, admittedly, an unquiet thought, which goes to the extremes in questioning the conventional understanding that subjectivity should not play a role in adjudication. However, in this view, the inclusion of personal factors does not detract from the objectivity of judgment, although it does question the assumption that objectivity requires impersonality. That a personal point of view is not incompatible with an objective perspective is not, despite appearances, a claim alien to law. After all, the inclusion of judges' signatures in judgments is not meant to detract from their objectivity. See Makymilian Del Mar, 'Review of Douglas E. Edlin, "Common Law Judging: Subjectivity, Impartiality and the Making of Law"' (2017) 80 *The Modern Law Review* 550, and Maksymilian Del Mar, *Artefacts of Legal Inquiry: The Value of Imagination in Adjudication* (Hart Publishing, 2020), 13–14. On the possibility of objective but personal legal judgment, see Iris Van Domselaar, 'All Judges on the Couch? On Iris Murdoch and Decision-Making' in Amalia Amaya and Makysmilian Del Mar (eds), *Virtue, Emotion and Imagination in Law and Legal Reasoning* (Hart Publishing, 2020) 77.

[42] Impartiality is a central dimension in discussions of objectivity in law. See Leiter (n 39) 977 and Matthew Kramer, *Objectivity and the Rule of Law* (Cambridge University Press, 2007) 53. It is also taken to be critical to objectivity in science. Interestingly, Duham claims that in order to reach objective decisions a scientist should be an 'impartial and faithful judge.' See Ivanova (n 40) 61 and Stump (n 20) 151.

[43] Impartiality figures prominently in the list of judicial virtues. See Lawrence Solum, 'Virtue Jurisprudence: A Virtue-Centered Theory of Judging' (2003) 34 *Metaphilosophy* 178.

[44] On the claim that empathy and impartiality are not conflicting desiderata in legal decision-making, see Amy Kind, 'Empathy, Imagination and the Law' in Amalia

consider the plausibility that each may obtain and an equitable evaluation of competing claims in light of the relevant normative reasons and available evidence.

Second, and relatedly, objectivity in a virtue approach also amounts to absence of bias and arbitrariness.[45] As mentioned above, a legitimate motivation driving the methodical conception of objectivity is the elimination of bias and arbitrariness. However, to efface the self in order to isolate legal decision-making from bias and arbitrariness seems, on the face of it, an overreaction.[46] It is, of course, essential that legal decision-making should be unbiased and constrained. But it is also of fundamental importance that we let in those subjective factors that are needed for successful decision-making. The attempt to eliminate all subjectivity as a means of eliminating bias and irrationality is like throwing the baby out with the bath water. The attempt is, moreover, as argued, doomed to failure, given the limits of methods and the impossibility of disentangling knowledge from character.[47] More importantly, it is not only impossible but also undesirable: subjective features of agents are meant to contribute in many valuable ways to sound legal decision-making. While it is important that we safeguard legal decisions from bias and arbitrariness, it is equally consequential that we make sure that agents contribute to the process as needed in the best possible way. Indeed, as it turns out, the possession of virtue, moral and epistemic, is an effective way to counteract bias in argumentation.[48] Thus, subjective decision-making, in the sense of virtuous decision-making, may be relied on resulting in objective decisions, in the sense of absence of bias and arbitrariness.

Last, and more controversially, the virtuous perspective is objective in the sense that the virtuous person's response is properly connected with the

---

Amaya and Makysmilian Del Mar (eds), *Virtue, Emotion and Imagination in Law and Legal Reasoning* (Hart Publishing, 2020) 179.

[45] Freedom from bias is at the core of epistemological objectivity. See Leiter (n 39) 973. For a discussion of the relations between objectivity and bias in argument, see Anthony J. Blair, 'Mapping Objectivity and Bias in Relation to Argument' in Patrick Bondy and Laura Benacquista (eds) *Argumentation, Objectivity and Bias: Proceedings of the 11th International Conference of the Ontario Society for the Study of Argumentation* (2016) 1.

[46] The idea of the 'pendulum' in the cycle of adjudication is again to the point here. See n 14 above.

[47] As forcefully argued by Shapin (n 7).

[48] See Peter L. Samuelson and Iain C. Church, 'When Cognition Turns Vicious: Heuristics and Biases in Light of Virtue Epistemology' (2015) 28 *Philosophical Psychology* 1095, and Robert C. Roberts and Ryan West, 'Natural Epistemic Defects and Corrective Virtues' (2015) 192 *Synthese* 2557.

world.[49] The virtuous person has a sensibility to appropriately respond to the reasons that obtain in particular situations of choice.[50] The virtuous person's response is not externally validated: that is to say, there is neither the possibility (nor the need if I may say so) of any sort of validation that is external to the practice of the virtuous.[51] The virtuous response is objective insofar as it is backed up by the best possible reasons available, which issue from a refined perception of normative properties the description of which, like the description of what is 'funny' or 'creepy,' depends partially in our responses to it.[52] That is to say, the virtuous 'heightened response' to normative requirements is objective not in the sense that it involves the perception of properties that are fully independent from human subjectivity (and the presence or absence of which could be certified from a standpoint of view external to the practice), but rather because it is 'answerable' to the world, where such answerability is enabled, instead of precluded, by the exercise of subjective sensibilities. Thus, the virtuous judgement is 'at once robustly subjective and robustly objective'.[53] Furthermore, its objectivity is in part the result of it being shaped by the refined subjective capacities that are characteristic of the virtuous person.

Thus far I have argued that, in contrast to the methodical conception of objectivity, which suppresses the self by offloading judgment into impersonal methods, a virtue theory embeds a dialectical conception of objectivity, which takes subjectivity (of the proper kind) to be a contributor, rather than a threat, to objectivity. Now, it could be argued that I have not succeeded after all in carving out a space for the objective that is subjectively infused. The virtue approach to objectivity may have the resources to counteract subjectivism (in the sense of bias, partiality, and irrationality); it might even be the case that it evades anti-realism (and that it secures some sort of connection with a relatively mind-independent reality), still it fails to avoid another -ism with which objectivity is usually contrasted, namely, relativism. The next section

---

[49] This is the metaphysical sense of objectivity. See Leiter (n 39) 970. There are positions about how virtue theory is related to metaphysical objectivity. It is also highly controversial how the Aristotelian view – which is still dominant in virtue theory – should be interpreted. Here, I endorse the view according to which virtue theory embraces metaphysical objectivity in a way that, however, does not reject, but rather requires, the intervention of human subjectivity. This view has, to my knowledge, been most forcefully articulated by Clarke's discussion of the sensitivity model of virtue. See Clarke (n 30).

[50] John McDowell, 'Virtue and Reason' in Roger Crisp and Michael Slote (eds), *Virtue Ethics* (Oxford University Press 1997) 143.

[51] See McDowell, ibid., 60 and Clarke (n 30), para. 6.

[52] See Clarke (n 30), para. 10.

[53] Ibid., para. 12.

examines the prospects of showing that virtuous judgement does not succumb to the relativist charge.

4. OBJECTIVE PLURALISM AND VIRTUOUS JUDGMENT

The claim that the virtuous legal decision-maker provides an objective standard for legal reasoning may be objected to on the grounds that this standard seems to license incompatible courses of action, thereby failing to provide determinate guidance as to which decision is right in the particular case.[54] Two main kind of cases should be distinguished here: cases in which there is disagreement among the virtuous legal decision-makers and cases in which the virtuous decision-maker feels ambivalence. In cases of disagreement, different responses seem to be correct from the perspective of different *phronimi*. In cases of ambivalence, different normative perspectives result on different responses, all of which seem correct to the virtuous legal decision-maker. Thus, experiences of intra and inter conflict show that a virtuous standard for legal reasoning could, at most, certify that a decision is correct *relative* to a perspective, but it sheds serious doubts over whether it can deliver objective judgements.

The import of the objection from relativism is aggravated by the high diversity (cultural and otherwise) that obtains in contemporary societies.[55] The vast differences that there are in ideological, religious, and political commitments and, more generally, the great diversity of cultures that coexist in modern communities make disagreement pervasive in public deliberation and legal decision-making. Diverse communities may identify different character traits as virtues or conceptualize the same virtues differently. Ambivalence is also more likely to be present as decision-makers belong simultaneously to different communities, which may result in conflicting visions as to what it is that virtue requires in the particular cases.[56] These two phenomena are not, moreover, independent, as ambivalence may result from the experience of

---

[54] See James Wallace, 'Virtue, Reason and Principle' in James Wallace, *Normativity and the Will: Selected Essays in Moral Psychology and Practical Reason* (Oxford University Press 2006), 258.

[55] See Bridget Clarke, 'Virtue and Disagreement' (2010) 13 *Ethical Theory and Moral Practice* 283.

[56] See Amelie Rorty, 'The Ethics of Collaborative Ambivalence' (2014) 18 *The Journal of Ethics* 402. See also Susan Feldman, 'Objectivity, Pluralism and Relativism: A Critique of MacIntyre's Theory of Virtue' (1986) XXIV *The Southern Journal of Philosophy* (315) 307 (arguing that individuals may experience 'double vision,' because of the existence of conflicting traditions informing individual lives).

moral disagreement, when one party comes to appreciate that the other party's positions may be correct, not in light of the other party's commitments, but from her own perspective.[57]

A first step in the direction of meeting the objection of relativism is to limit its reach by emphasizing the extent to which the virtues, in an Aristotelian view, are anchored to basic features of human nature.[58] This grounding of the virtues on human nature restricts the variation that there might be among which traits of character are virtues and how they may be specified in different communities.[59] For example, which decisions are required by mercy would vary across communities, as there are different ways of filling in the concept of mercy. Radical moral disagreement, however, in which one party takes mercy to be a virtue, whereas another party endorses ruthlessness as a virtue is excluded.[60] Arguably, this view on the nature of the virtues also prevents deep disagreement involving a communication breakdown from arising, for disagreeing parties would, despite differences, be advancing competing specifications of the same virtues.[61] The claim that virtues are grounded in human nature plausibly restricts the scope of disagreement among the virtuous legal decision-makers. Similarly, it would also reduce the extent and degree to which the virtuous judge may experience ambivalence on account of her affiliation to different communities. Nevertheless, even if it decreases the potential impact of the relativist charge, it still allows for extensive conflict among and within virtuous legal decision-makers. Insofar as this is so, exemplary decision-makers fail to provide a standard that can be relied on to identify an objectively correct answer. At best – the critic may argue – grounding virtues in human nature downsizes rather than meets the objection from relativism.[62]

One could address frontally the charge from relativism by denying the possibility of conflict among or within the virtuous. There cannot be a genuine disagreement among virtuous legal decision-makers: when two seemingly virtuous people disagree all that signals is that there is a character flaw in

---

[57] This is the phenomenon of 'collaborative ambivalence,' as described in Rorty, ibid.

[58] See Christopher W. Gowans, 'Virtue Ethics and Moral Relativism' in S. D. Hales (ed) *A Companion to Relativism* (Blackwell 2011) 391, for a discussion of naturalistic responses to this objection.

[59] See Martha Nussbaum, 'Non-Aristotelian Virtues: An Aristotelian Approach' (1988) XIII *Midwest Studies in Philosophy* 32.

[60] See Gowans (n 58) 403.

[61] Nussbaum (n 59) 36.

[62] See Gowans (n 58) (arguing that this strategy concedes a lot to the moral relativist).

one of the disagreeing parties.⁶³ Similarly, the experience of ambivalence in a purportedly virtuous legal decision-maker indicates that he is a continent agent, rather than a virtuous one.⁶⁴ This response, although effective, burdens virtue theory with a monolithic view of virtue – in which virtue is unified and univocal – which does not seem to be required by any plausible interpretation of what the unity of virtuous persons may entail.⁶⁵ In addition, it depicts the virtuous person as one who does not waver and knows immediately what needs to be done, which does not sit well with the phenomenology of virtue and underscores the relevance of effort (a 'perpetual' one, in Murdoch's words) that virtue requires.⁶⁶ In addition, the denial that disagreement and ambivalence may have a place within a virtue theory deprives the virtuous person of the goods that experiences of conflict, as important opportunities for moral development, may deliver.⁶⁷ Finally, this move disposes of the problem by diminishing the importance of conflict in the legal (and, more generally, practical) domain, thereby rendering virtue theory irrelevant to address some of the central challenges facing legal decision-makers in contemporary societies.

A more promising way to meet the objection from relativism is to embrace conflict, both inter-personal and intra-personal, as an important element of practical life – including the life of the virtuous people – but deny that this should render a virtuous standard for legal reasoning relativistic. A virtue theory of legal reasoning should provide guidance as to how to address nor-

---

⁶³ For a discussion of this view, see Clarke (n 55) and Christine Swanton, 'Virtue Ethics and the Problem of Moral Disagreement' (2010) 38 *Philosophical Topics* 157.

⁶⁴ For a discussion of this position, see Susan Stark, 'Virtue and Emotion' (2001) 35 *Noûs* 440, Kristján Kristjánsson, 'The Trouble with Ambivalent Emotions' (2010) 85 *Philosophy* 485, and David Carr, 'Virtue, Mixed Emotions and Moral Ambivalence' (2009) 84 *Philosophy* 31.

⁶⁵ For a critique of a monolithic conception of virtue, see Kristjánsson, ibid., 500. For an argument in support of a view of the unity of virtuous persons that makes room for ambivalence, see Carr, ibid.

⁶⁶ See Iris Murdoch, *Metaphysics as a Guide to Morals* (Penguin 1992) 268. On the idea that effort is a critical component on the phenomenology of virtue, see Julia Annas, 'The Phenomenology of Virtue' (2008) 7 *Phenomenology and the Cognitive Sciences* 21. In contrast, a portrait of the virtuous person as someone who immediately sees into the right is put forward by intuitionist interpretations of McDowell's model of virtue. See Wallace (n 54), 254. For a critique of this interpretation, see Clarke (n 30) para. 5 and Clarke (n 55). The construction of the sensibility that virtue consists in as one that requires effort is critical for avoiding a depiction of the virtuous person as a 'passive' agent, who is merely 'confronted, as it were, by the world's moral fabric' rather than actively engaged in construing the best solution to the case at stake. On the potential passivity of a model that explains the contribution of subjectivity to legal argument in terms of 'response,' or 'sensitivity,' see Del Mar (n 41), 549.

⁶⁷ I take up this point later.

mative conflict and, more precisely, how to reach outcomes that have a claim to objectivity in the face of such conflict. Critically, however, conflict management in cases of both disagreement and ambivalence need not deliver one single outcome in all cases for objectivity to be preserved. More than one legal outcome, in this view, could be the result of virtuous legal decision-making, but this does not detract from their objectivity.[68] Cases in which different virtuous legal decision-makers would take discordant decisions and cases in which a virtuous legal decision-maker is ambivalent between incompatible courses of action do not suggest that relativism is inherent to a virtue approach to legal decision-making, but rather the plausibility of a virtue jurisprudence that is committed to objective pluralism.

Objective pluralism is the view that there may be more than one course of action that is correct in an objective sense.[69] A central commitment of this view is that values are heterogenous, plural and irreducible.[70] The impossibility of establishing a hierarchy among values or reducing them to one single value, does not impede deliberation, but opens up the possibility that different courses of action, which may be differently responsive to the diverse values involved, may turn out to be objectively justified. This, however, does not amount to relativism.[71] The objectivist pluralist claim is not that different solutions could be justified relative to different perspectives but rather that different solutions are justified when considered from a single perspective. The plurality of justified outcomes is, in this view, a corollary of the nature of values, not the result of the existence of incommensurable moral perspectives or the denial of the possibility of providing justifications that are not indexed to specific moral practices or traditions.

Critically, the proposal to wed virtue jurisprudence to objective pluralism does not amount to an ad hoc strategy to salvage the virtue account of legal reasoning from the charge of relativism, as objective pluralism is not a foreign element to contemporary virtue theory. Indeed, even though objective pluralism has been more explicitly developed in 20th century philosophy, most

---

[68] See Solum (n 43) (arguing that a virtue-centred account of judging allows for the possibility that two inconsistent outcomes in the same case could be legally correct).

[69] See Agustín Vicente and Agustín Arrieta, 'Moral Ambivalence, Relativism and Pluralism' (2016) 31 *Acta Analytica* 209–210.

[70] See Dag E. Thorsen, 'Value Pluralism and Normative Reasoning' unpublished manuscript (2004) 6.

[71] On the differences between pluralism and relativism, see J. D. G. Evans, 'Cultural Realism: The Ancient Philosophical Background' in D. Archard (ed) *Philosophy and Pluralism* (Oxford University Press 2009) 47–48; Thorsen, ibid., 20–25; and Carla Yumatle, 'Pluralism' in M. Gibbons (ed) *The Encyclopedia of Political Thought* (Wiley and Sons 2015) 2–4.

prominently by Isaiah Berlin, its origins can be traced back to Aristotle.[72] More importantly, a core commitment of contemporary virtue ethics – in its neo-Aristotelian version – is the existence of plural irreducible values.[73] In this view, deliberation is a complex endeavour that cannot be simplified by any procedure that could allow us to identify as correct the course of action that best maximizes a single value. Neither can it be facilitated by the operation of rules that could impose a lexical order among the conflicting values involved. This, however, as objective pluralism has it, does not preclude deliberation about the values at stake and reaching results that are objective in the sense of being backed by the best reasons available. Thus, objective pluralism is in consonance with the virtue ethics perspective on the nature of values and deliberation.

The suggestion, in a nutshell, is that a pluralistic virtue approach to legal reasoning provides a framework wherein the objectivity of virtuous judgment may be vindicated in the face of normative conflict.[74] There may be cases in which virtuous judges may disagree or feel ambivalent about which decision ought to be taken. Normative conflict is not, on this approach, to be avoided, but a natural consequence of the complexity of the practical domain and the nature of values. Furthermore, from a virtue perspective, normative conflict is a valuable tool for the development and refinement of one's practical outlook.[75] When virtuously faced, ambivalence and disagreement trigger, rather than impede, deliberation.[76] They provide opportunities to broaden and deepen one's understanding of the values involved and how they relate to each other and thereby perfect virtue.[77] This virtuous deliberation shall lead to the identifi-

---

[72] On the Aristotelian origins of objective pluralism, Joshua Cherniss and Henry Hardy, 'Isaiah Berlin' in E. Zalta (ed) *The Stanford Encyclopedia of Philosophy* (Fall 2020 edition) https://plato.stanford.edu/archives/fall2020/entries/berlin/ accessed 27 June 2022; Evans (n 71) 48 and Martha Nussbaum, 'The Discernment of Perception: An Aristotelian Conception of Private and Public Rationality' (1986) 1 *Proceedings of the Boston Area Colloquium in Ancient Philosophy* 151.

[73] See Nussbaum, ibid.

[74] It is important to notice that this version of pluralistic ethics is distinct from Swanton's pluralistic virtue ethics. See Swanton (n 32).

[75] See Carr (n 64) (arguing that intra-personal conflict fosters the development of virtue). On the claim that inter-personal conflict provides opportunities for perfecting virtue, see Clarke (n 55) 287–289.

[76] See Cristiano L. Guarana and Morela Hernandez, 'Identified Ambivalence: When Cognitive Conflicts Can Help Individuals Overcome Cognitive Traps' (2016) 101 *Journal of Applied Psychology* 1013 (for an argument to the effect that ambivalence, when properly identified, triggers deliberation).

[77] The practice of including dissenting judgments as well as the fact that judges often signal their own doubts have been claimed to provide important resources for future developments in the law. See Del Mar, *Review of D. E. Edlin Common Law*

cation of a right answer, if there is one.[78] But, given the nature of values, there is no assurance that this should be the case. Insofar as these answers, however, could result from a virtuous deliberation and thus be responsive to the different reasons that obtain in the specific case, the lack of uniqueness does not translate into a loss of objectivity.

5. CONCLUSIONS

In this chapter I have argued that a virtue theory of legal reasoning does not abandon the ideal of objectivity in legal judgment but it does put forward a conception of objectivity other than the methodical conception according to which objectivity amounts to the deployment of methods that suppress, to the extent that this is possible, the subjectivity of legal decision-makers. Instead, a virtue approach to legal reasoning accords to subjectivity an indispensable role in reaching judgments that have a claim to objectivity. This approach, I have argued, embeds a dialectical conception of objectivity, which situates objectivity partially in subjects. More specifically, the virtue theory of legal reasoning takes the virtuous decision-maker to provide an objective standard for evaluating and assessing legal judgment. This standard, unlike the methodical one, is affectively loaded, embodied, and contextually situated. Thus, a virtue theory departs from conventional views on objectivity in that it refuses to equate objectivity with impersonality. Nevertheless, it retains the idea, which is central in standard discussions of objectivity in legal reasoning, that objective legal judgments are impartial, unbiased, and anchored to relatively mind-independent facts.

I have then defended the virtuous legal decision-maker as an objective standard for legal reasoning against the charge of relativism. Virtuous legal decision-makers may disagree or feel ambivalent among different courses of action, and thereby the virtuous person standard may fail to pick up one answer as objectively correct. Cultural variation aggravates this problem by making it more likely that this standard licenses a diversity of answers, which could only be assessed as correct relative to a given perspective. Even after controlling for variation in the specification of the virtues that an exemplary legal decision-maker should possess, through grounding them in human nature, virtue standards fail to adjudicate among several competing courses of action and identify one as objectively correct.

Judging (n 41) 551. See Del Mar, *Artefacts of Legal Inquiry* (n 41) (for a thorough development of this argument). Thus, these practices in legal judgment point towards the relevance of intra and inter-personal conflict to further reflection about law's values.

[78] See McDowell (n 50) 144, n 5.

I have responded to this objection by claiming that a pluralist virtue standard allows for normative conflict (both inter- and intra-personal) in a way that does not detract from its objectivity. That is to say, objective pluralism, rather than relativism, best accounts for the plurality of responses which, in some situations, may be validated by the virtuous judge as a standard for legal reasoning. A virtue standard for assessing and evaluating legal judgment would lead to the identification of a right answer, if there is one, but result in more than one objectively correct outcome otherwise. Although a virtue theory allows us to expand the possibility of reaching objective judgments to cases that would not be governed by methods – and which would therefore fall, on a methodical account, beyond the domain of objectivity – it does not lead to a determinate answer in all cases. The source of the indeterminacy, however, is neither the purported limits of the theory, nor the plurality of incommensurable normative frameworks, but rather it is traceable to the nature of values as plural and irreducible. Hence, that the theory admits of indeterminacy does not show that it succumbs to relativism but rather that it gives as determinate a guidance as the matter of the practical affords.

An important implication as to the scope and aims of a theory of legal reasoning follows from endorsing the shift from the methodical conception of objectivity to the dialectical one that virtue jurisprudence suggests. As argued, from a dialectical perspective, the quest for objectivity in legal reasoning is to be advanced not by insulating the legal decision-maker from the decisions, but rather by ensuring that he contributes to the process of decision-making in a way that enhances the possibilities that it may result in objective outcomes (whether plural or unique). Legal reasoning without subjects is thus not only unachievable but also undesirable for the purposes of reaching objective judgments. Objectivity, in this view, is not endangered but rather achieved when subjectivity – of the proper kind – is factored in. This makes, I would argue, character a central concept in a theory of legal reasoning. Questions about which traits of character are virtues in the context of legal decision-making, how to best conceptualize them and, critically, how to cultivate them become the proper concern of a theory of legal reasoning. Objectivity, in short, is earned by perfecting character, rather than by the incessant pursuit of subject-less argument.

Index

actualism 268
Adler, M. 100–101
Alexy, R. 63, 120
anti-realism 217
Aristotle 19–21, 290
autonomous reasoning
    balancing normative arguments 224–7
    bindingness 225, 229–32
    consent by reasonable person criteria 228–9
    example 225–6, 230–31
    generally 223
    limitations of 223, 225
    substantive definitive validity, and 229–32

Bamberger, K. 197
Bambrough, R. 17–18
Barczentewicz, M. 99
beliefs
    belief-based model of 'bullshit' 51–4
    intentional theory of meaning, and 155
Bentham, J. 88
Berlin, I. 289–90
bias, freedom from 7–10, 12–13, 19, 21–2, 32, 119–20, 284
Biber, D. 174
Bix, B. 148
Blackburn, S. 234, 245–7, 251, 265
Brandom, R. 136–43
'bullshit,' interpretation of
    activity-centred model 50–51, 57, 66
    belief-based model 51–4
    generally 48–50, 57
    indifference to truth model 50–51, 57, 66
    intentions, role of 54–7
    misrepresentation, as 50–51
    morality, role of 55–7
    output-centred model 51–4
    pragmatic legal cognitivism 64–9

caricaturized subjectivism 256–7, 264
Carnap, R. 270
causal chain theory 150
Church of the Holy Trinity v. United States 103
'city' analogy (Leiter) 93–4, 97
'consideration,' common law concept
    diachronic corpus analysis 180–84
    historical development 179–80
core-dependant homonym approach to objectivity 19–22
correctness, objectivity of 63–4, 68, 86, 137–9, 217–18, 221–3, 227–8, 242, 270

Daston, L. 1, 4, 7, 33
de Waal, C. 55
development of objectivity 1–2, 33, 46
dialectical objectivity 280–86
domain objectivity 242–3
Dworkin, R.
    chain novel model of law 134–5
    constructivist theory of law 44, 123–4
    facts-value distinction, on 240–41, 244–5
    fundamental pragmatism of 249
    Hart's theory of law, and 25, 102, 127, 133–5, 144
    independence and impartiality in law 274–5
    indeterminacy of law, on 133–5
    judicial discretion, limitations of 135–6, 141–2
    law as an activity, on 142
    legal positivism, on 115–16

morality and law
    Blackburn's moral theory, on 245–7
    law *vs.* philosophical approaches 247–9
    legal reasoning, moral objectivity in 235–7, 239–49
    metaethical arguments, on 233–4, 239–40, 247–8
    relationship between 235–7
    theory of responsibility 246–7
dynamic rules 36

Elgin, C. 275
emotivism 107, 112, 117, 264
empirical methods
    art, compared with 7
    role of objectivity in 1–4, 9–13
        negative objectivity criteria 12–14
Enoch, D.
    moral realism, on
        caricaturized subjectivism 256–7
        constitutive constructivism, criticism of 266–7
        impartiality argument 254–61
        interpersonal conflicts 257–8, 260–61
        non-objectivist conceptions of ethics, and 259–60
        normative truths, deliberate indispensability 254, 263–5
        ontological commitment, absence of 265–70
        overview 253–4
        parsimony principle, and 265–70
        quietism, criticism of 267
        review of 257–61
epistemic objectivity 91–3, 217–18, 242
equality in law
    a priori and *a posteriori*, distinction between 83–4
existence, theories of 267–9
experts
    realist theory of meaning, role in 152

recognition of facts by 39–40
external theory of meaning 149–55

facts
    collective recognition of 39–40, 46
    facts-value distinction 87–94, 240–41, 244–5
    intersubjectivity of 39–40, 45–6
    law and facts, links between 77
    legal constructivism, and 44–6
    objective facts 37–9
    rule application, and 36–7, 43–4
    rule-based facts 39–43, 46
    social facts 39–40, 45–6
fair trial, as basis for rule of law 59–61
family resemblances approach to objectivity 17–19
Faraci, D. 264
Ferrajoli, L. 259–60
Finnis, J. 90–93, 244
Fish, S. 155–60
Forst, R. 59–61
Frankfurt, H.G. 48–57, 66
Fuller, L. 59
functionalism 151–2
fundamentalism 268

Galison, P. 1, 4, 7, 33
Gardner, J. 100–101
general theory of norms (*see* pure theory of law)
Gibbard, A. 265
Goldsworthy, J. 99
Green, M. 147–8
Greenberg, M. 200
Guastini, R. 260

Halliday, M. 169, 186–7
Hart, H.L.A. 40, 86
    concept of law, on
        abstract norms theory, Dworkin's views on 127, 133–5, 144
        facts-value distinction 87–8
        interdeterminancy of norms, on 131–3, 135
        internal and external dimensions 129, 131

legal objectivity, on 109, 133, 142–4
legislation and precedent, roles of 131–3
obligations, role of 127–9
officials, role of 99–101, 103–4, 141–2
primary and secondary rules, need for both 97–102
rule of recognition 99, 107, 109, 130–33
rules, role of 129–30
validity and efficacy 98–9, 109
Weber's theory, comparison with 89–90, 95–7, 102–4
Hershovitz, S. 148
Himma, K.E. 99
human dignity
moral right to justification 60–61
Human Rights Act 1998
compatibility requirements 207–9, 213
Hume, D. 105–6, 119
facts-values distinction 240–41
value subjectivism, and 107
values, sceptical analysis of 110–115

ideal epistemic circumstances 38–9
ideal-types concept 91–3
impartiality
methodological concept of legal objectivity, and 274–6, 291
moral realism, in 254–61
virtuous objectivity, in 283–4
imputation
anomalies, definition of 82–3
causality, relationship with 73–4, 80–82
cognition of norms, and 75–6
concept development 71–2
conformity in law, and 84
definition 74
equality rule, role of 83–5
is/ought, and 73–4, 76–7, 81–2, 108–9
limitations of 82–3
ontological analysis, role of 76–81

perception of lawyers, relevance of 74–5
peripheral imputation 73–4
primary and secondary norms 81–2
pure theory of law, and 73–5
scientific objectivity, and 71–2, 74–5, 83–5
supervenience, interpretation as 77–83
indispensability argument
deliberate indispensability of normative truths 254, 263–5
overview 262–3
intentionalist theory of meaning
legal texts, objectivity in 155–60
interpretative canons
complexity of 193
legal norms, interaction with 205–14
modifying effect of application on legislation/constitutional powers
compatibility requirements 207–9, 213
determinants of legal content, changes to 212–13
epistemic canons 198–9
equitable override, power of 202–3
generally 197–8
institutional divisions, and 200
intrinsicality of legal content 209–13
judicial declarations of invalidity 201–2
legal validity, and 201–3, 207
meta-semantic holism 212–13
moral impact theory of law, and 200
non-positivist approach 199–200
positivist approach 199
regulative canons 201–3
supervenience, and 205–14
US constitutional avoidance doctrine 199
types of 195–7
uses of
criticism of 195–7
justifications for 193–4

is/ought
  imputation, and 73–4, 76–7, 81–2, 108–9
  legal rules, and 108–9
  values, sceptical analysis of 110–115

James, W. 63

Kelsen, H. 71–9, 83–4, 108, 121
knowledge
  see also legal cognitivism
  domain objectivity, and 242–3
  legal knowledge
    identification of 112–13
    object of 112
    recognition of 115
    scope of 115–16
  objectivity of knowledge 32–4
    common understandings as basis for 114–15
    general approach 106
    projectivism, and 106
  reliability of
    scepticism, and 105
  subject, disengagement from 274–5
  subjectivity of knowledge 33–4
    general approach 106–7
Kramer, M. 99
Kripke, S. 148, 150

Lacey, N. 89–90
language
  causal chain theory 150
  legal language
    functions of 168–9
    historical influences on 169
    textual context, role of 171–2
  linguistic deference 152
  linguistic studies 169
    'consideration,' common law of 179–84
    electronic methods 173–4
    functional linguistics 170
    metafunctions 170–71, 186–7
    ordinary meanings 175–7
    specialised terms and meanings 177–8
    uses of 172–3, 178, 184–5

natural language (*see* natural language)
philosophy of language 147–8
semantic externalism 149–55
semantic objectivity 167–9
social function of 168–70
systemic functionalist approach 169–70
law, generally
  see also rule of law
  distinction from morality 47, 86, 109–10
  equality in law
    importance of 84–5
    a priori and *a posteriori*, distinction between 83–4
  fair trial, role and importance of 59–60
  idea of law, and 84
  norms (*see* legal norms)
  objectivity about law *vs.* objectivity of law 46–7
  obligations, role of 127
  philosophy of law
    meaning of law 147–8
    philosophy of language, influences of 147–8
    rule-following 148–9
  positive law as social phenomenon 47
  precedent, drawbacks of 131–2
  principles, role of 116
  pure theory of law (*see* pure theory of law)
  purpose of 120
  role of objectivity in 3–4, 34, 46–7
    normatism, and 71–2
  society, role in 120
Lee, T. 175–7
legal cognitivism
  cognitive assumptions, and 61–3, 66–9
  criticism of 58, 63
  legal interpretation, objectivity in 121–4
  legal scepticism, and 58
  moral basis for 61–4
  normative fallacy, and 64
  normative standing basis for 61–2

pragmatic legal cognitivism 61–4
  aims and intentions 65
  assertions *vs.* assumptions 67–9
  'bullshit,' perception as 64–9
  principle claim 64–5
legal constructivism
  constitutive constructivism, criticism of 266–7
  Dworkin's constructivist theory of law 44, 123–4
  objectivity, implications for 44–6
  principles of 44, 256
legal interpretation
  bias, freedom from
  complexity of 193
  'consideration,' common law of
    diachronic corpus analysis 180–84
    historical background 179–80
  corpus linguistics studies
    'consideration,' common law of 179–84
    electronic methods 173–4
    ordinary meanings 175–7
    specialised terms and meanings 177–8
    uses of 172–3, 178, 184–5
  interpretive canons, role of (*see* interpretative canons)
  legal dogmatics, scientific interpretation of 108
  meaning of law, and 147–8
  meaning, theories of
    arguments and disagreements, role of 164–5
    communication, role of 156
    criticism of 153–5, 158–9, 163–5
    empirical enquiry, role of 157–8
    external/realist theory 152–54
    intentionalist theory 155–60
    ordinary or plain meanings 164–5
    'reasonable author' 157
    rule of law, and 153
  objective interpretation
    best constructive interpretations 123–4
    features of 121–4
    impartiality 12–13, 123, 254–61
  objectivity in legal texts (*see* legal texts, objectivity in)
  philosophy of language, role of 147–8
  rule-following 148–9, 162–3
  semantic objectivity 167–9
  textual context 171–2
  Wittgenstein on 146–9, 154–5, 161–6
legal norms
  abstract norms 127
    Hart and Dworkin on 127, 131–5, 144
    rule of recognition, and 99, 107, 109, 130, 132–3
  authority and responsibility, symmetry of 141
  autonomy *vs.* objective validity of law (*see* autonomous reasoning)
  communication, relevance of 140
  correctness 139
  epistemic objectivity 217–18, 242
  external objectivity 216, 218–19
  indeterminacy of norms 131–3
  interpretative canons interaction with 205–14
  moral autonomy, challenges of 227–9
  normative judgments
    normative statements and arguments, distinction from 219
    objective validity of 222–4, 228–9
  normative justification 216–18
    autonomous reasoning, and 223–7
    bindingness 225, 229–32
    consent by reasonable person criteria 228–9
    example structure 225–6, 230–31
    individual autonomy, and 227–9
    levels of argument, relevance of 219

moral autonomy, and 227–8
  reasonable convergence
    229–32
  substantive definitive validity
    229–32
normative propositions 218–19
normative statements and arguments
  balancing 224–7
  bindingness 225, 229–32
  descriptive statements 222–3
  justifications for 216–18
  normative assertions/
    judgments, distinction
    from 219
  normative propositions,
    compared with 218–19
  objective validity 216–17,
    220–24
  purpose of 223
  types of normative speech
    219–21
normative statuses of performances
  137–8
objectivity in, theories of
  Brandom on 136–43
  Dworkin on 127, 133–5, 142–4
  Hart on 127, 131–5, 141–4
obligations and rules, role of
  127–30
ontological objectivity 217
regulist theory 136–7
semantic objectivity 218–19
social institution of norms theory
  136–43
substantive definitive validity
  229–32
legal positivism
  ethical subjectivism, and 110
  facts and values distinction 87–94
  Hart and Weber on 87–94
  interpretative canons, benefits of
    199
  law and facts, links between 77
  law and morality
    differences between 86,
      109–10
    legal reasoning, role in 235–6
  objectivity, and 107–10
  reparability thesis of 109

Scandinavian legal realism 112–13,
  116
social thesis of 107
validity of legal propositions, basis
  for 235
value subjectivism, and 116
legal realism
  interpretative canons, criticism of
    196
  Scandinavian legal realism 112–13,
    116
legal reasoning
  approaches, generally
    comparison of 271
    limitations of 280
  autonomous reasoning
    balancing normative arguments
      224–7
    example 225–6, 230–31
    generally 223
    individual autonomy 227–9
    limitations of 223, 225
  autonomy vs. objective validity
    of law (see autonomous
    reasoning)
  dialectical objectivity 280–86
  methodological objectivity
    impartiality and independence
      274–6, 291
    limitations of 277–80
    metaphysical conceptions,
      compared with 238–45
    moral objectivity, and 238–43,
      250–51
    overview 273–6
    psychology-logic division, and
      276–8
    scientism, and 276–7
    virtuous objectivity, differences
      from 281–2, 285–6, 291
  moral objectivity, and
    importance of 237–8
    internal vs. external morality
      statements 245
    lawyers, interpretation by
      243–52
    logical objectivity 238–9
    metaethics, role of 233–5,
      239–40, 247–8, 256, 270

metaphysical *vs.*
    methodological
    conceptions of 238–45,
    250–51
non-positivist basis for 235–7
positivist basis for 235
rationality, role of 250–51
relational aspects 247
moral realism
    caricaturized subjectivism
        256–7
    democratic liberalism, and
        260–61
    impartiality argument 254–61
    interpersonal conflicts 257–8,
        260–61
    non-objectivist conceptions of
        ethics, and 259–60
    normative truths, deliberate
        indispensability 254,
        263–5
    ontological commitment,
        absence of 265–70
    overview 253–4
    parsimony principle, and
        265–70
    review of 257–61
morality role in
    generally 235–6
    projectivism 245, 247
    queerness argument 246–7
    rationality, and 249–51
    scepticism, and 236–7
normative arguments
    autonomous reasoning, and
        224–7
    bindingness 225, 229–32
    justifications for 216–18,
        224–7
    objectivity 216–17, 221–4
objectivity in
    best constructive interpretations
        123–4
    characteristics of 119–24
    freedom from bias, and 119–20
    human fallibility 124
    objective *vs.* subjective
        application of law 34,
        46
    priority, role of 122

statutes and precedents,
    interpretation of 121–4
Scandinavian legal realism 112–13,
    116
self-effacement concept of
    objectivity 273–6
truth, role in 119
virtue theory of
    bias and arbitrariness, freedom
        from 284
    characteristics of 280–85
    conflict management, and
        286–91
    criticism of 271
    dialectical concept 280–86
    impartiality requirement
        283–384
    methodological approach,
        differences from 281–2,
        285–6, 291
    objective pluralism 286–92
    overview 271
    relativism, objection of 286–9
    self, role of 282–3
legal sources (*see* sources of law)
legal texts, objectivity in
    arguments and disagreements, role
        of 164–5
    external/realist theory of meaning
        150–54
    intentionalist theory of meaning
        155–60
    ordinary or plain meanings 164–5
legislation
    interpretation of
        modifying effect of
            interpretative canons
            (*see* interpretative
            canons)
        objectivity in 121–4
    limitations of 131–2
Leiter, B. 91–4, 97
linguistics
    concordances 172–3
    corpus linguistics
        'consideration,' interpretation of
            179–84
        definition 173–4
        'emolument,' interpretation of
            185

history of 172
'no-vehicles-in-the-park' rule
    175–7
ordinary meanings,
    interpretation of 175–7
representativeness in 174
specialised terms and meanings,
    interpretation of 177–8
uses of 172–3, 178, 184–5
grammar and lexis, distinction
    between 173
linguistic shifts and standardisation
    183
metafunctions 170–71, 186–7
role of, generally 169
text, meaning of 170–71
textual context 171–2
Llewellyn, K. 196
Locke, J. 15, 106
lying 50, 55–6, 66

MacCormick, N. 89
Mackie, J.L. 246–7, 264
Manor, R. 68
Marmor, A. 238
Mattila, H. 168–9
meaning of objectivity
bias, freedom from 7–10, 12–13,
    19–22, 32, 119–20
core-dependant homonym approach
    19–22
determinacy criterion 13–14
family resemblances approach
    17–19
generally 4–5
impartiality criterion 12–13
invariance, and 15–16
metaphors, role of 15–16
mind-independence criterion 12,
    31, 38–9
negative definitions 12–14
normative definitions 6–11
objectivity by design 13–14
polysemy, responses to 14–19
reductive definitions 14–16
subjectivity, compared with 7–10,
    33–4, 46
trust, role of 9–11, 21–2
truth, and 8, 14–15
meaning, theories of

causal chain theory 150
communication, role of 156
criticism of 153–5, 158–9
empirical enquiry, role of 157–8
external/realist theory 150–54
intentionalist theory 155–60
ordinary or plain meanings 164–5
'reasonable author' 157
rule-following 148–9, 162–3
metaethics
morality, and 233–5, 239–40,
    247–8, 256, 270
scepticism of 234
tolerance, and 270
metaphors 15–16
methodological objectivity 273–6
impartiality and independence
    274–6, 291
limitations of 277–80
overview 273–6
psychology-logic division, and
    276–8
scientism, and 276–7
virtuous objectivity, differences
    from 81–282, 285–6, 291
mind-independence
meaning of objectivity, and 12, 31,
    38–9
misrepresentation, forms of 50–51
Moore, M. S. 150–51
moral impact theory of law 200
morality
'bullshit,' role in 55–7
cultural variations in 114–15
individual autonomy, and 227–9
law, and
    autonomous reasoning 227–9
    connection between 115–16
    distinction from 47, 86, 109–10
    facts-values distinction 240–41
    human feelings, relevance of
        112, 117
    objectivity, importance of
        235–8
legal cognitivism, and 61–4
legal reasoning, and
    autonomous reasoning 227–9
    importance of objectivity in
        237–8

legal *vs.* philosophical
    perceptions 243–51
metaphysical *vs.*
    methodological
    conceptions of morality
    238–45, 250–51
normative ethical views,
    justification for 259–60
pervasiveness 234
role in, generally 235–6
social source of objectivity
    249–50
metaethical arguments 233–5,
    239–40, 247–8, 256, 270
moral knowledge, objectivity of
    113–14
moral realism, and
    Enoch on, review of 257–61
    impartiality argument 254–61
    irreducible moral truths 265–6
    non-natural facts, acceptance
        of 265
    normative truths, deliberate
        indispensability 254,
        263–5
moral right to justification 60–61
non-objectivist conceptions of
    ethics, justifications for
    259–60
objectivity, and 113–15, 227–9
realist theory of meaning, and
    151–2
supervenience, and 233–4
truth, and 240–41
virtues and vices, interpretation of
    110–115
Mouritsen, S. 175–7

Nagel, T. 14–15, 120
natural language
    characteristics of 35
    facts, role of 35–7
    mind-dependency, and 38–9
    propositions, role of 35–6
    rules, role of 36–7
    states of affairs 35–6, 39
    terms, role of 36
naturalism 112–14, 117, 269
Neumann, U. 61
'no-vehicles-in-the-park' rule 175–7

normatism 71–2
Nozick, R. 15–16

objective entities 37
objective facts 37–9
objective knowledge 32–4
objective pluralism 286–92
objectivisation 119
objectivism 106
obligations
    characteristics of 129
    Hart on 127–31
    rules, relationship between 128–30
ontological objectivity 217

Parfit, D. 268–70
parsimony principle 265–70
Patterson, D. 164
Plato 19–20
positive law
    interpretative canons, interaction
        with 199, 205–14
    pure theory of law 71–4
    social phenomenon, as 47
Posner, R.A. 196
possibilism 268
Postema, G. 237
precedent
    interpretation, objectivity in 121–4
    limitations of 131–2
projectivism 106, 245, 247
pure theory of law
    bridging principles 76–7
    equality rule in 83–5
    idea of law, and 84
    imputation, role of 73–5
    limitations of 83
    a priori and *a posteriori,* distinction
        between 83–4
    scientific objectivity 71–2, 74–5
    supervenience, and 77–83
Putnam, H. 149, 262

queerness argument, legal reasoning
    246–7
quietism 267
Quine, W. 262

Rawls, J. 15, 119

Raz, J. 99, 201, 233–4, 236–7, 242–4
realism
   see also legal realism; moral realism
   anti-realism 217
   realist theory of meaning 150–54
   robust realism, acceptance of 264–6, 269–70
   Scandinavian legal realism 112–13, 116
reasonableness
   moral autonomy, and 228–9
recognition of facts 39–40, 46
right to justification
   rule of law, and 60–61
Ross, A, 112–13, 116
Ross, S. 197
rule of law
   formal conception of 58–9
      fair trial basis of 59–61
   right to justification, and 60–61
   semantic externalism, and 153
   substantive conception of 59
rules
   characteristics of 36
   competence-conferring rules 40–42
   counts as rules 36, 41
   dynamic rules 36
   efficacy of 41
   facts, correspondence with 36–7, 43–4
   indeterminacy of law, and 131–3
   legal rules, definition 108
   obligations, relationship with 128–30
   recognition of 41–3
   rule-based facts 39–43, 46
   rule-based rules 41–3
   rule-following, role in legal interpretation 148–9, 162–3
   social rules 39–41
   types of 36

Scalia, A. 103
Scandinavian legal realism 112–13, 116
scepticism
   criticism of approaches to 115–17
   legal cognitivism, and 58
   morality and legal reasoning, on 236–7
   reliability of knowledge, and 105
   values, sceptical analysis of 110–115
scientific objectivity 32, 71–2, 74–5, 83–5, 274
scientism 276–7
self-effacement concept of objectivity 273
semantic externalism 149–55
semantic objectivity 218–19
Simmons, N. 100
social institution of norms theory 136–43
social rules 39–41
Solum, L. 196
sources of law
   interpretation, objectivity in 121–4
states of affairs 35–6, 39
strong conception of objectivity
   basis for 108
   definition 139
   forms of objectivity 216–18
   judicial discretion, and 142–4
   legal positivism, and 108–10
   rules of recognition, and 109
   values, sceptical analysis of 110–115
subjectivism 107
   caricaturized subjectivism 256–7, 264
   ethical subjectivism 110
   moral realism, and 256–7
   value subjectivism 110, 116
subjectivity
   freedom from bias, and 284
   knowledge, of 33–4, 106–7
   objectivity compared with 7–10, 33–4, 46
   subjectivity of statements 216–17
Sunstein, C. 196–7
supervenience
   compatibility requirements 207–9, 213
   definition 78, 204–5
   internal relations 205–6
   interpretative canons, modifying effect on legislation/ constitutional powers 205–14
   legal positivism, and 77
   moral objectivity, and 233–4

pure theory of law/imputation,
      interpretation in 77–83

tolerance, principle of 270
trust, role of
    meaning of objectivity 9–11, 21–2
truth
    see also legal cognitivism
    belief-based model of 'bullshit'
        51–4
    indifference to truth model of
        'bullshit' 50–51, 66
    indispensability argument
        deliberate indispensability of
            normative truths 254,
            263–5
        overview 262–3
    irreducible moral truths, acceptance
        of 265–6
    legal reasoning, role in 119
        mathematical truths 269
    meaning of objectivity 8, 14–15
    misrepresentation, and 50–51
    moral truths, irreducibility of 267–8
    morality, and 240–41
    theories of truth in law 61

values
    see also morality
    'city' analogy (Leiter) 93–4
    cultural values 92
    epistemic values *vs.* moral values
        91–3, 242
    facts-value distinction 87–94,
        240–41, 244–5
    human society, of 106–7
    objectivity of 106
    sceptical analysis of 110–115
    self-evidence of 244
    'unity of value' concept 244–5
    value subjectivism 110, 116

virtues and vices 110–115
virtue theory of legal reasoning
    bias and arbitrariness, freedom from
        284
    characteristics of 280–85
    conflict management, and 286–91
    criticism of 272
    dialectical objectivity 280–86
    impartiality requirement 283–4
    methodological approach,
        differences from 281–2,
        285–6, 291
    objective pluralism 286–92
    overview 271
    relativism, objection of 286–9
    self, role of 282–3
virtues and vices 110–115

weak conception of objectivity
    basis for 117–20
    definition 139
    features of objective legal
        interpretation 120–24
    impartiality in 12–13
    judicial discretion, and 142–4
    legal interpretation, role of 118–19
    objective validity of norms 216
Weber, M.
    concept of law, on
        facts-value distinction 88–94
        Hart's theory, comparison with
            89–90, 95–7, 102–4
        ideal-types concept 91–3
        social science, and 87, 94–7,
            104
Wedgwood, R. 258
Wittgenstein, L. 17–19
    criticism of 148–9, 160–65
    theories of meaning, on 148–9,
        154–5, 161–6
    words and intentions, on 159–60